Betty Crocker

ANNUAL RECIPES

2·0·0·8

General Mills

Director, Book and Online Publishing: Kim Walter

Manager, Cookbook Publishing: Lois Tlusty

Recipe Development and Testing: Betty Crocker Kitchens

Photography and Food Styling: General Mills Photo Studio

Editor: Sharon Sanders

Book Designer: Tracey J. Hambleton

ISBN-10: 1–59486–752–6

ISBN-13: 978–1–59486–752–1

2   4   6   8   10   9   7   5   3   1   hardcover

Cover Image: Chocolate Malt Ice Cream Cake (page 336)

For more great ideas, visit www.bettycrocker.com

CONTENTS

Turkey-Biscuit Pot Pie (page 148)

Introduction

Welcome to the expanded 2008 edition of *Betty Crocker Annual Recipes*. We've gathered more than 300 recipes from the past year of *Betty Crocker* magazine to share with you. We've bound them into a beautiful, hardcover volume—with gorgeous color photographs of all the dishes—that will sit proudly on your cookbook shelf. As always, the recipes are thoroughly tested for ultimate ease of preparation, outstanding taste and reliability.

As you've come to expect, we have delectable preparations suited for all times of the day and all courses of a meal. Start your morning with Basil Breakfast Strata and close the evening with Spiced Dessert Coffee. Lunch on Chicken Kabob Caesar Salad, Beef and Provolone Focaccia Sandwiches or Italian Tuna Toss. For supper, gather everyone around the table to share Flank Steak with Smoky Honey Mustard Sauce, Grilled Corn with Chili-Lime Spread and Quick Peach Cobbler. It's all here for you. But this volume is more than just a collection of recipes. We want this cookbook to help you integrate your cooking with your lifestyle to make it seamless. Our "Inspired Entertaining: Menus for Special Times" is a comprehensive resource for party planning throughout the upcoming year. And by turning to "Seasonal Selections: Cooking with the Calendar," you'll know exactly which recipes to select if you want to make the most of seasonally available ingredients.

We've addressed special concerns as well. Look for the "Quick" label to find recipes that are ready to cook or bake in 20 minutes or less or can be prepared in 30 minutes or less. Recipes with "Low Fat" labels show you which dishes have 10 grams of fat or less per serving (3 grams or less in the sides and desserts), making it simple to stick to your healthy eating plan without sacrificing flavor.

Appearing throughout the recipe chapters are mini-primers on selected "In Season" ingredients that will educate you about best cooking techniques and applications. Included are Pears, Cherries, Limes, Artichokes, Cranberries, Strawberries and Turkey.

We've saved the best until last. This year, we've got three big desserts chapters that are practically a book unto themselves. You and your kids will have fun baking all of our novelty cakes and cupcakes like Pull-Apart Turtle Cupcakes, Bug Cupcakes, Frog Cupcakes, Treasure Chest Cake, Groovy Jeans Cake, Happy Birthday Cell Phone Cake and May Day Baskets. With our tutorial on "Make & Bake Cake Basics," you'll soon be serving elegant pastries like Cream-Filled Butter Pecan Birthday Cake, Deep Dark Mocha Torte and Raspberry-Laced Vanilla Cake.

Of course, the compendium wouldn't be complete without dozens more recipes for classic pies, cheesecakes, tarts, cookies, brownies, fruit crisps and ice cream creations.

By now, we hope that you're as excited as we are by this spectacular cookbook. Thank you for welcoming us back into your kitchen this year!

Betty Crocker

Inspired Entertaining

MENUS FOR SPECIAL TIMES

Without birthdays, holidays, graduations, sporting events and other occasions for sharing good times, life would just pass in a blur. With the help of the twelve seasonal menus that follow, we hope you cook up some delightful memories for yourself, your family, friends and neighbors.

New Year's Day Open House

Layered Shrimp Spread (page 101)

Wild Mushroom-Stuffed Pork Roast (page 154)

Mixed Greens with Cranberry Vinaigrette (page 70)

Red Velvet Torte (page 290)

Italian Fruit Punch (page 25)

Coffee and Tea

Coffee-Table Tailgate

Parmesan Cheese Chex® Mix (page 42)

Three-Cheese Logs (page 50)

Slow Cooker Italian Shredded Beef Hoagies (page 95)

Assorted Soft Drinks and Beers

Romantic Repast

Mango-Pepper Salsa Crostini (page 81)

Spring Onion Soup with Garlic Croutons (page 73)

Lemon-Thyme Chicken Breasts (page 130)

Asparagus with Tomatoes (page 171)

Coeur à la Crème (page 342)

Sparkling Wine

Festive Spring Brunch

Basil Breakfast Strata (page 18)
Salmon and Asparagus Salad (page 117)
Strawberry-Rhubarb Angel Torte (page 277)
Peachy Mimosas (page 27)

School's Out

Barbecue Pork Bites (page 152)
Italian Pesto Pizza (page 78)
Cheesy Chicken Quesadillas (page 125)
Tortellini, Broccoli and Bacon Salad (page 59)
Mud Slide Ice Cream Cake (page 334)

Summer Celebration!

Minted Watermelon Basket (page 54)
Picnic Pasta Salad (page 52)
Hamburger Steaks with Grilled Onions (page 165)
Grilled Corn with Chili-Lime Spread (page 170)
S'mores Cupcakes (page 191)
Chilled Beverages

Dining Beneath the Stars

Prosciutto-Pesto Napoleons (page 85)
Shrimp Kabobs with Fresh Herbs (page 112)
Strawberry-Melon-Spinach Salad (page 53)
Piña Colada Tart (page 329)
Assorted Wines

Finger-Foods Fest

Cheese Tray with Olive Rosemary Skewers (page 35)
Black Bean and Corn Wonton Cups (page 46)
Tortellini Kabobs (page 49)
Genoa Salami Stacks (page 28)
Bread and Spreads Platter (page 34)
Profiteroles (page 337)
Cherry Mini-Cakes (page 188)
Chocolate-Almond Cheesecake Bites (page 331)
Assorted Beverages

Spooky Halloween Happening

Zippy Dill Vegetable Dip (page 29)
Slow Cooker Beef and Bean Chili (page 74)
Halloween Brownies (page 214)
Scary Cat Cookies (page 232)
Giant Witch Cookies (page 233)
Cider

Harvest at Home

Honey-Dijon Brined Turkey Breast (page 146)
Green Beans with Browned Butter (page 181)
Mixed Greens with Cranberry Vinaigrette (page 70)
Apple, Pear and Cranberry Pie (page 298)
Sparkling Cider or Wine

A-Caroling Supper

Pepper Jack Cheese Ball (page 38)
Old-Fashioned Oven Beef Stew (page 167)
Broccoli with Roasted Red Peppers and Hazelnuts
  (page 179)
Peppermint Shortbread Bites (page 235)
Dark Chocolate Hazelnut Truffles (page 344)
Hot Cocoa, Coffee, Hot Tea

Noshing on New Year's Eve

Antipasto Picks (page 44)
Tortellini Kabobs (page 49)
Crab Bites (page 105)
Three-Cheese Logs (page 50)
Amaretto Cheese-Filled Apricots (page 45)
Tiny Lemon Gem Tarts (page 328)
Sparkling Wine

Fall

Winter

Anytime

Breads and Breakfasts

Baked Goods and Good Morning Fare

Lemon-Currant Cream Scones (page 8)

Basil Breakfast Strata (page 18)

Citrus Macadamia Nut Bread

Prep Time: 15 min Start to Finish: 2 hr 25 min

2½ cups Gold Medal® all-purpose flour
1 cup granulated sugar
1 cup orange juice
½ cup vegetable oil
1 tablespoon grated lemon peel
1 tablespoon grated lime peel
2 teaspoons baking powder
½ teaspoon salt
2 eggs, beaten
½ cup coarsely chopped macadamia nuts
   Powdered sugar, if desired

1. Heat oven to 350°F. Grease bottom only of 9 × 5-inch loaf pan with shortening. In large bowl, mix all ingredients except nuts and powdered sugar with spoon until moistened. Stir in nuts. Pour into pan.

2. Bake 50 to 60 minutes or until toothpick inserted in center comes out clean.

3. Cool bread in pan 10 minutes. Loosen sides of bread from pan; remove from pan to wire rack. Cool completely, about 1 hour. Sprinkle with powdered sugar before slicing.

1 loaf (16 slices)
1 Slice: Calories 220 (Calories from Fat 90); Total Fat 10g (Saturated 1.5g; Trans 0g); Cholesterol 25mg; Sodium 150mg; Total Carbohydrate 30g (Dietary Fiber 0g; Sugars 14g); Protein 3g
% Daily Value: Vitamin A 0%; Vitamin C 6%; Calcium 4%; Iron 6%
Exchanges: 1 Starch, 1 Other Carbohydrate, 2 Fat
Carbohydrate Choices: 2

KITCHEN TIPS

✿ The loaf can be baked in advance and frozen. For easier slicing, try cutting the loaf when it is only partially thawed.

✿ Wrap loaf in plastic wrap, and finish thawing at room temperature.

Chocolate Chip Pumpkin Bread

Prep Time: 15 min Start to Finish: 3 hr 10 min

4 cups Gold Medal all-purpose flour
2 teaspoons baking soda
1 teaspoon salt
1 teaspoon ground cinnamon
$\frac{1}{2}$ teaspoon ground nutmeg
2 cups sugar
$\frac{3}{4}$ cup butter or margarine, softened
4 eggs
$\frac{1}{2}$ cup water
1 can (15 ounces) pumpkin (not pumpkin pie mix)
1 cup plus 2 tablespoons miniature semisweet chocolate chips
2 tablespoons chopped pecans
2 teaspoons sugar

1. Heat oven to 350°F. Grease bottom only of two 8 × 4-inch loaf pans with shortening; lightly flour (or spray bottoms of pans with cooking spray; do not flour).

2. In medium bowl, stir flour, baking soda, salt, cinnamon and nutmeg until mixed; set aside.

3. In large bowl, beat 2 cups sugar and the butter with electric mixer on medium speed 1 to 2 minutes or until creamy. Add eggs, one at a time, beating well after each addition. Beat in water and pumpkin on low speed. Add flour mixture; beat on low speed about 1 minute or until moistened. Stir in 1 cup of the chocolate chips. Spread evenly in pans. Sprinkle tops with remaining 2 tablespoons chocolate chips, the pecans and 2 teaspoons sugar.

4. Bake 1 hour 5 minutes to 1 hour 15 minutes or until toothpick inserted in center come out clean. Cool in pans 10 minutes; remove from pans to cooling rack. Cool completely, about 1$\frac{1}{2}$ hours.

2 loaves (16 slices each)
1 Slice: Calories 200 (Calories from Fat 70); Total Fat 7g (Saturated 3.5g; Trans 0g); Cholesterol 40mg; Sodium 190mg; Total Carbohydrate 30g (Dietary Fiber 1g; Sugars 16g); Protein 3g
% Daily Value: Vitamin A 45%; Vitamin C 0%; Calcium 0%; Iron 6%
Exchanges: 1 Starch, 1 Other Carbohydrate, 1 Fat
Carbohydrate Choices: 2

KITCHEN TIPS

✿ To ensure that your loaf has a gently rounded top and no "lipping" at the edges, grease or spray only the bottom of the pan.
✿ It's okay if the top of your loaf has a large, lengthwise crack; this is common in quick breads.

Ginger-Carrot-Nut Bread

Prep Time: 15 min Start to Finish: 3 hr 25 min

2 eggs
¾ cup packed brown sugar
⅓ cup vegetable oil
½ cup milk
1 teaspoon vanilla
2 cups Gold Medal all-purpose flour
2 teaspoons baking powder
1 teaspoon ground ginger
½ teaspoon salt
1 cup shredded carrots (about 2 medium)
½ cup chopped nuts

1. Heat oven to 350°F. Grease bottom only of 8 × 4-inch loaf pan with shortening; lightly flour (or spray bottom of pan with cooking spray; do not flour).

2. In large bowl, beat eggs and brown sugar with electric mixer on medium speed until creamy. Beat in oil, milk and vanilla. Beat in flour, baking powder, ginger and salt until smooth. Stir in carrots and nuts. Spread in pan.

3. Bake 50 to 60 minutes or until toothpick inserted in center comes out clean. Cool in pan 10 minutes; remove from pan to cooling rack. Cool completely, about 2 hours.

1 loaf (16 slices)
1 Slice: Calories 180 (Calories from Fat 70); Total Fat 8g (Saturated 1g; Trans 0g); Cholesterol 25mg; Sodium 150mg; Total Carbohydrate 24g (Dietary Fiber 1g; Sugars 11g); Protein 3g
% Daily Value: Vitamin A 25%; Vitamin C 0%; Calcium 6%; Iron 6%
Exchanges: 1 Starch, ½ Other Carbohydrate, 1½ Fat
Carbohydrate Choices: 1½

KITCHEN TIPS

✿ Serve slices of this fragrant loaf with whipped cream cheese.
✿ The reason only the bottom of the pan is greased is to keep the loaf from sinking around the edges.

Almond-Tres Leches Muffins

Prep Time: 20 min Start to Finish: 50 min

$1/2$ cup butter or margarine, softened

$2/3$ cup sugar

$1/2$ teaspoon almond extract

2 eggs

2 cups Gold Medal all-purpose flour

2 teaspoons baking powder

$1/3$ cup (from 14-ounce can) sweetened condensed milk (not evaporated)

$1/3$ cup whipping cream

$1/3$ cup milk

$3/4$ cup sliced almonds

Additional sweetened condensed milk ($1/4$ cup)

1. Heat oven to 400°F. Grease 12 regular-size muffin cups with shortening or line with paper baking cups.

2. In large bowl, beat butter and sugar with electric mixer on medium speed until smooth. Beat in almond extract and eggs. With spoon, stir in flour, baking powder, $1/3$ cup condensed milk, the whipping cream, milk and $1/2$ cup of the almonds just until moistened. Divide batter evenly among muffin cups ($3/4$ full). Sprinkle remaining $1/4$ cup almonds evenly over batter in cups.

3. Bake 15 to 20 minutes or until light golden brown. Remove muffins from pan to cooling rack. Cool 10 minutes. Drizzle 1 teaspoon additional sweetened condensed milk over top of each muffin. Serve warm.

12 muffins

1 Muffin: Calories 310 (Calories from Fat 140); Total Fat 15g (Saturated 8g; Trans 0.5g); Cholesterol 70mg; Sodium 170mg; Total Carbohydrate 37g (Dietary Fiber 1g; Sugars 20g); Protein 6g
% Daily Value: Vitamin A 8%; Vitamin C 0%; Calcium 10%; Iron 8%
Exchanges: $1 1/2$ Starch, 1 Other Carbohydrate, 3 Fat
Carbohydrate Choices: $2 1/2$

KITCHEN TIPS

✿ Depending on the type of muffin pan you use, you may get 15 muffins.
✿ To avoid soggy muffins, take them out of the pan immediately after removing them from the oven.

Honey-Bran Muffins

Prep Time: 15 min Start to Finish: 35 min

¼ cup wheat bran
3 tablespoons boiling water
¼ cup milk
¼ cup honey
3 tablespoons vegetable oil
1 egg
1½ cups Gold Medal all-purpose flour
1½ teaspoons baking powder
½ teaspoon ground cinnamon
¼ teaspoon salt
   Granulated sugar, if desired

1. Heat oven to 400°F. Place paper baking cups in each of 6 regular-size muffin cups; spray paper baking cups with cooking spray.

2. In small bowl, mix wheat bran and boiling water; set aside.

3. In medium bowl, beat milk, honey, oil and egg with spoon until well mixed. Stir in bran mixture, flour, baking powder, cinnamon and salt just until flour is moistened. Divide batter evenly among muffin cups. Sprinkle with granulated sugar.

4. Bake 15 to 20 minutes or until golden brown and tops spring back when touched lightly in center. Immediately remove from pan to cooling rack.

6 muffins
1 Muffin: Calories 250 (Calories from Fat 70); Total Fat 8g (Saturated 1.5g; Trans 0g); Cholesterol 35mg; Sodium 240mg; Total Carbohydrate 38g (Dietary Fiber 2g; Sugars 12g); Protein 5g
% Daily Value: Vitamin A 0%; Vitamin C 0%; Calcium 10%; Iron 10%
Exchanges: 1½ Starch, 1 Other Carbohydrate, 1½ Fat
Carbohydrate Choices: 2½

KITCHEN TIPS

❁ Oat bran or wheat germ can be used instead of the wheat bran.
❁ Try serving these yummy muffins with honey butter. To make, simply combine 3 tablespoons softened butter with 1 tablespoon honey.

Pumpkin-Cranberry Muffins

Prep Time: 15 min Start to Finish: 40 min

2 cups Gold Medal all-purpose flour
¾ cup sugar
3 teaspoons baking powder
1 teaspoon ground cinnamon
½ teaspoon ground ginger
¼ teaspoon salt
1 cup canned pumpkin (not pumpkin pie mix)
½ cup vegetable oil
2 eggs
1 cup sweetened dried cranberries
½ cup chopped pecans
  Coarse sugar, if desired

1. Heat oven to 400°F. Grease 12 regular-size muffin cups with shortening or line with paper baking cups.

2. In large bowl, mix flour, sugar, baking powder, cinnamon, ginger and salt. Stir in pumpkin, oil, eggs, cranberries and pecans just until moistened. Divide batter evenly among muffin cups. Sprinkle coarse sugar evenly over batter in each cup.

3. Bake 20 to 25 minutes or until toothpick inserted in center comes out clean. Remove muffins from pan to cooling rack. Serve warm.

12 muffins
1 Muffin: Calories 300 (Calories from Fat 120); Total Fat 14g (Saturated 2g; Trans 0g); Cholesterol 35mg; Sodium 180mg; Total Carbohydrate 40g (Dietary Fiber 2g; Sugars 21g); Protein 4g
% Daily Value: Vitamin A 60%; Vitamin C 0%; Calcium 8%; Iron 10%
Exchanges: 1½ Starch, 1 Other Carbohydrate, 2½ Fat
Carbohydrate Choices: 2½

KITCHEN TIPS

❀ Instead of cranberries, try making these muffins with dried cherries.

❀ Take care not to overmix the batter. Overmixing can result in tough muffins with peaked tops and tunnels inside.

Lemon-Currant Cream Scones

Prep Time: 20 min Start to Finish: 50 min

2 cups Gold Medal all-purpose flour
$^1/_4$ cup granulated sugar
3 teaspoons baking powder
$^1/_2$ teaspoon salt
$^1/_2$ cup dried currants
1 teaspoon grated lemon peel
$1^1/_3$ cups whipping cream
1 cup powdered sugar
2 to 3 tablespoons lemon juice
Additional grated lemon peel, if desired

1. Heat oven to 400°F. Lightly grease cookie sheet with shortening or spray with cooking spray.

2. In large bowl, mix flour, granulated sugar, baking powder and salt with fork. Mix in currants and 1 teaspoon lemon peel. Add whipping cream all at once; stir just until dry ingredients are moistened.

3. On floured surface, gently knead dough 6 or 7 times or until smooth. Pat dough $^3/_4$ inch thick. Cut with 2-inch round cutter. Place 2 inches apart on cookie sheet.

4. Bake 12 to 15 minutes or until light golden brown. Cool 15 minutes. Meanwhile, in small bowl, stir powdered sugar and enough lemon juice until smooth and thin enough to drizzle. Drizzle over scones. Top with additional lemon peel. Serve warm.

15 scones
1 Scone: Calories 180 (Calories from Fat 60); Total Fat 7g (Saturated 4g; Trans 0g); Cholesterol 25mg; Sodium 180mg; Total Carbohydrate 29g (Dietary Fiber 0g; Sugars 15g); Protein 2g
% Daily Value: Vitamin A 4%; Vitamin C 0%; Calcium 8%; Iron 6%
Exchanges: 1 Starch, 1 Other Carbohydrate, 1 Fat
Carbohydrate Choices: 2

KITCHEN TIPS

❂ Feel free to mix the dry ingredients ahead of time and store in a resealable plastic food-storage bag.

❂ If your family isn't big on currants, leave them out and stir in $^1/_2$ cup of dried blueberries instead.

Maple-Nut Scones

Prep Time: 20 min Start to Finish: 40 min

Topping

3 tablespoons Gold Medal all-purpose flour

2 tablespoons granulated sugar

2 tablespoons finely chopped nuts, toasted*

2 tablespoons firm butter or margarine

Scones

2 cups Gold Medal all-purpose flour

2 tablespoons packed brown sugar

2 teaspoons baking powder

$\frac{1}{4}$ teaspoon salt

$\frac{1}{2}$ cup firm butter or margarine

$\frac{1}{2}$ cup coarsely chopped nuts, toasted

$\frac{1}{3}$ cup pure maple syrup or maple-flavored syrup

1 egg

About 2 tablespoons milk

Additional milk

1. Heat oven to 400°F (375°F for dark or nonstick cookie sheet). In small bowl, mix 3 tablespoons flour, the granulated sugar and 2 tablespoons nuts. Cut in 2 tablespoons butter, using pastry blender or fork, until crumbly; set aside.

2. In large bowl, mix 2 cups flour, the brown sugar, baking powder and salt. Cut in $\frac{1}{2}$ cup butter, using pastry blender (or pulling 2 table knives through ingredients in opposite directions), until mixture looks like fine crumbs. Stir in $\frac{1}{2}$ cup nuts. Stir in maple syrup, egg and just enough of the 2 tablespoons milk so dough leaves sides of bowl and starts to form a ball.

3. Place dough on lightly floured surface; gently roll in flour to coat. Knead lightly 10 times. Pat or roll into 8-inch circle on ungreased cookie sheet. Brush with additional milk. Sprinkle with topping. Cut into 8 wedges, but do not separate.

4. Bake 15 to 18 minutes or until golden brown. Immediately remove from cookie sheet; carefully separate wedges. Serve warm.

8 scones

1 Scone: Calories 390 (Calories from Fat 200); Total Fat 22g (Saturated 8g; Trans 1g); Cholesterol 65mg; Sodium 300mg; Total Carbohydrate 43g (Dietary Fiber 2g; Sugars 15g); Protein 5g
% Daily Value: Vitamin A 10%; Vitamin C 0%; Calcium 10%; Iron 10%
Exchanges: 2 Starch, 1 Other Carbohydrate, 4 Fat
Carbohydrate Choices: 3

KITCHEN TIPS

✿ Serve these tender scones warm with a dollop of honey butter or a drizzle of maple syrup.

✿ Both pure maple syrup and maple-flavored syrup work in this recipe; use whichever you prefer.

✿ To toast nuts, bake uncovered in ungreased shallow pan in 350°F oven 6 to 10 minutes, stirring occasionally, until golden brown.

Orange Scone Wedges with Cream Cheese Filling

Prep Time: 25 min Start to Finish: 40 min

Filling

6	ounces cream cheese, softened
1/4	cup granulated sugar
1	tablespoon grated orange peel

Scones

1³/₄	cups Gold Medal all-purpose flour
3	tablespoons granulated sugar
2	teaspoons baking powder
1/4	teaspoon salt
6	tablespoons firm butter or margarine
1	tablespoon grated orange peel
1/4	cup whipping cream
1	egg
1	egg, beaten
2	tablespoons coarse white sugar

1. Heat oven to 400°F. In small bowl, beat all filling ingredients with electric mixer on medium speed until smooth; set aside.

2. In large bowl, mix flour, 3 tablespoons sugar, the baking powder and salt. Cut in butter, using pastry blender (or pulling 2 table knives through ingredients in opposite directions), until mixture looks like fine crumbs. Stir in 1 tablespoon orange peel, whipping cream and 1 egg.

3. Place dough on lightly floured surface; gently roll in flour to coat. Knead lightly 10 times. Divide dough in half. Pat or roll each half into 9-inch round, about 1/4 inch thick. Spread filling over half of each round.

4. Fold each dough round in half over filling. With sharp knife, cut each half-round into 6 wedges. On ungreased cookie sheet, place wedges 1 inch apart. Brush tops with beaten egg; sprinkle with coarse sugar.

5. Bake 10 to 15 minutes or until light golden brown. Immediately remove from cookie sheet to cooling rack. Serve warm.

12 scones

1 Scone: Calories 250 (Calories from Fat 130); Total Fat 15g (Saturated 9g; Trans 0.5g); Cholesterol 75mg; Sodium 240mg; Total Carbohydrate 24g (Dietary Fiber 0g; Sugars 10g); Protein 5g
% Daily Value: Vitamin A 10%; Vitamin C 0%; Calcium 8%; Iron 8%
Exchanges: 1 Starch, 1/2 Other Carbohydrate, 3 Fat
Carbohydrate Choices: 1 1/2

KITCHEN TIPS

✿ Coarse sugar is also called decorating sugar and has larger granules than regular sugar.

✿ These rich scones filled with orange-flavored cream cheese need no extra butter or jam.

Orange Scone Wedges with Cream Cheese Filling

Chocolate Streusel Coffee Cake

Prep Time: 20 min Start to Finish: 1 hr 35 min

Coffee Cake

1½ cups Gold Medal all-purpose flour
¾ cup granulated sugar
1 teaspoon ground cinnamon
¾ teaspoon baking powder
¼ teaspoon baking soda
½ teaspoon salt
½ cup firm butter or margarine, cut into pieces
⅔ cup buttermilk
1 egg
1 teaspoon vanilla

Streusel

¼ cup Gold Medal all-purpose flour
¼ cup packed brown sugar
1 tablespoon baking cocoa
2 tablespoons butter or margarine, softened
¼ cup miniature semisweet chocolate chips

1. Heat oven to 350°F (325°F for dark or nonstick pan). Grease bottom only of 8-inch square pan with shortening or spray bottom with cooking spray.

2. In large bowl, stir 1½ cups flour, the granulated sugar, cinnamon, baking powder, baking soda and salt until mixed. Cut in butter, using pastry blender (or pulling 2 table knives through ingredients in opposite directions), until mixture is crumbly. Add buttermilk, egg and vanilla. Beat with electric mixer on medium speed 1 minute. Spread in pan.

3. In small bowl, mix all streusel ingredients except chocolate chips with fork until mixture is crumbly. Sprinkle over batter. Sprinkle with chocolate chips.

4. Bake 35 to 45 minutes or until toothpick inserted in center comes out clean. Cool 30 minutes. Serve warm.

9 servings
1 Serving: Calories 340 (Calories from Fat 140); Total Fat 15g (Saturated 8g; Trans 1g); Cholesterol 60mg; Sodium 320mg; Total Carbohydrate 46g (Dietary Fiber 1g; Sugars 26g); Protein 4g
% Daily Value: Vitamin A 10%; Vitamin C 0%; Calcium 6%; Iron 10%
Exchanges: 1 Starch, 2 Other Carbohydrate, 3 Fat
Carbohydrate Choices: 3

KITCHEN TIPS

✿ If you like the taste combination of chocolate and orange, add 2 teaspoons grated orange peel to the cake batter.
✿ Store leftover buttermilk in the freezer for up to 3 months. Before using, thaw and shake well.

Cinnamon Streusel Coffee Cake

Prep Time: 10 min Start to Finish: 35 min

Streusel Topping

- 1/3 cup Original Bisquick® mix
- 1/3 cup packed brown sugar
- 1/2 teaspoon ground cinnamon
- 2 tablespoons firm butter or margarine

Coffee Cake

- 2 cups Original Bisquick mix
- 2/3 cup milk or water
- 2 tablespoons granulated sugar
- 1 egg

1. Heat oven to 375°F. Grease bottom and side of 9-inch round pan with shortening or cooking spray. In small bowl, mix 1/3 cup Bisquick mix, the brown sugar and cinnamon. Cut in butter, using fork or pastry blender, until mixture is crumbly; set aside.

2. In medium bowl, stir all coffee cake ingredients until blended. Spread in pan. Sprinkle with topping.

3. Bake 18 to 22 minutes or until golden brown. Serve warm or cool.

6 servings
1 Serving: Calories 310 (Calories from Fat 110); Total Fat 12g (Saturated 4.5g; Trans 1.5g); Cholesterol 50mg; Sodium 720mg; Total Carbohydrate 46g (Dietary Fiber 0g; Sugars 21g); Protein 5g % Daily Value: Vitamin A 4%; Vitamin C 0%; Calcium 15%; Iron 10% Exchanges: 1 1/2 Starch, 1 1/2 Other Carbohydrate, 2 Fat Carbohydrate Choices: 3

KITCHEN TIPS

✿ To serve 12, either make two coffee cakes or cut one into smaller slices.

Chai-Spiced Tea Cakes

Prep Time: 15 min Start to Finish: 2 hr 10 min

- ½ cup boiling water
- 4 tea bags black tea
- ¾ cup water
- 1 box Betty Crocker® SuperMoist® yellow cake mix
- ⅓ cup vegetable oil
- 3 eggs
- 2 teaspoons sugar
- ½ teaspoon ground cardamom
- ½ teaspoon ground cinnamon
- ¼ teaspoon ground cloves
- ¼ teaspoon ground nutmeg
- ½ cup Betty Crocker Rich & Creamy® creamy white frosting (from 1-pound container)

1. Heat oven to 350°F. Grease bottoms and sides of two 8- or 9-inch round cake pans with shortening or cooking spray.

2. In 2-cup measuring cup, pour boiling water over tea bags. Let steep 3 to 4 minutes. Discard tea bags. Add ¾ cup water to tea to make 1¼ cups.

3. In large bowl, beat cake mix, tea, oil and eggs with electric mixer on low speed 30 seconds. Beat on medium speed 2 minutes, scraping bowl occasionally. Divide batter between pans. In small bowl, mix sugar, cardamom, cinnamon, cloves and nutmeg; sprinkle over each cake. Pull knife through batter in swirl design.

4. Bake 8-inch pans 33 to 38 minutes, 9-inch pans 28 to 33 minutes, or until toothpick inserted in center comes out clean. Cool 15 minutes. Run knife around sides of pans to loosen cakes. On serving plate, place each cake, bottom side down; gently brush off excess crumbs. Cool completely, about 1 hour.

5. In small microwavable bowl, microwave frosting on High 10 to 15 seconds or until thin enough to drizzle. Place in small resealable plastic food-storage bag; cut off tiny corner of bag. Drizzle frosting over cakes. Store loosely covered at room temperature.

16 servings
1 Serving: Calories 230 (Calories from Fat 90); Total Fat 10g (Saturated 2.5g; Trans 1g); Cholesterol 40mg; Sodium 240mg; Total Carbohydrate 32g (Dietary Fiber 0g; Sugars 20g); Protein 2g
% Daily Value: Vitamin A 0%; Vitamin C 0%; Calcium 6%; Iron 4%
Exchanges: 1 Starch, 1 Other Carbohydrate, 2 Fat
Carbohydrate Choices: 2

KITCHEN TIPS

- Use 4 teaspoons loose tea instead of the tea bags; strain and discard tea leaves from brewed tea.
- Serve with sliced cantaloupe or a bunch of grapes for a luxurious between-meal snack.

Low Fat

Fresh Herb-Topped Rolls

Prep Time: 15 min Start to Finish: 1 hr 30 min

- 1 tablespoon cornmeal
- 1 loaf (1 pound) frozen honey-wheat or white bread dough, thawed as directed on package
- 36 fresh Italian (flat-leaf) parsley leaves
- 1 egg
- 1 tablespoon water

1. Heat oven to 375°F. Grease cookie sheet with shortening or cooking spray; sprinkle with cornmeal. Divide thawed dough into 12 equal portions.

2. Shape each portion of dough into a ball. Place rolls on cookie sheet. Spray sheet of plastic wrap with cooking spray; place sprayed side down over rolls. Cover with towel. Let rise in warm place 45 to 60 minutes or until doubled in size.

3. Meanwhile, place rinsed parsley leaves on paper towels; pat dry. With kitchen scissors, cut stems from leaves.

4. In custard cup, beat egg and water with fork. Brush mixture over top of each roll. Dip parsley leaves into egg mixture; place 3 leaves on top of each roll. Brush remaining egg mixture over parsley-topped rolls.

5. Bake 15 to 20 minutes or until golden brown. Immediately remove from cookie sheet. Serve warm.

12 rolls
1 Roll: Calories 110 (Calories from Fat 15); Total Fat 1.5g (Saturated 0g; Trans 0g); Cholesterol 20mg; Sodium 260mg; Total Carbohydrate 20g (Dietary Fiber 0g; Sugars 2g); Protein 4g
% Daily Value: Vitamin A 4%; Vitamin C 0%; Calcium 6%; Iron 8%
Exchanges: 1½ Starch
Carbohydrate Choices: 1

KITCHEN TIPS

✿ Any fresh flat-leaf herb, such as dill weed, sage or marjoram, can be substituted for the Italian parsley.
✿ Place the parsley leaves close together on the rolls; they'll shrink during baking, increasing the space between them.

Cheesy Texas Toast

Prep Time: 10 min Start to Finish: 10 min

¼ cup butter or margarine, softened

4 slices thick-cut white bread, about 1 inch thick

½ teaspoon seasoned salt

¼ cup grated Parmesan cheese (1 ounce)

8 servings
1 Serving: Calories 130 (Calories from Fat 70); Total Fat 7g (Saturated 4.5g; Trans 0.5g); Cholesterol 20mg; Sodium 340mg; Total Carbohydrate 13g (Dietary Fiber 0g; Sugars 1g); Protein 3g
% Daily Value: Vitamin A 4%; Vitamin C 0%; Calcium 8%; Iron 6%
Exchanges: 1 Starch, 1 Fat
Carbohydrate Choices: 1

1. Set oven control to broil. Spread butter on both sides of bread slices. Sprinkle both sides with seasoned salt. Sprinkle tops of bread with half of the cheese. Place on rack in broiler pan.

2. Broil with tops 4 to 6 inches from heat 2 minutes. Turn bread, sprinkle with remaining cheese.

3. Cut each slice diagonally in half. Serve warm or cool.

KITCHEN TIPS

✹ Mix ½ teaspoon garlic salt into 2 tablespoons of olive oil and drizzle over bread before broiling.

✹ Rich, nutty Asiago cheese is a great-tasting alternative to the Parmesan cheese.

Sausage-Cranberry Strata

Prep Time: 30 min Start to Finish: 5 hr 45 min

1½   pounds bulk pork sausage

10   English muffins, diced (about 12 cups)

4   medium green onions, sliced (¼ cup)

1   cup sweetened dried cranberries

8   eggs

1½   cups milk

1   cup sour cream

½   teaspoon salt

¼   teaspoon pepper

3   cups shredded Monterey Jack cheese (12 ounces)

1. Spray 13 × 9-inch (3-quart) glass baking dish with cooking spray. In 12-inch skillet, cook sausage over medium heat 8 to 10 minutes, stirring occasionally, until no longer pink; drain.

2. Spread half of the diced muffins in dish; top with half of the sausage, half of the onions and half of the cranberries. Repeat layers with remaining muffins, sausage, onions and cranberries.

3. In large bowl, beat eggs, milk, sour cream, salt and pepper with wire whisk until well blended; pour over mixture in dish. Sprinkle cheese over top. Spray sheet of foil with cooking spray; place sprayed side down over pan. Cover; refrigerate at least 4 hours but no longer than 24 hours.

4. Heat oven to 325°F. Bake covered 30 minutes. Uncover; bake 30 to 40 minutes longer or until top is golden brown and knife inserted in center comes out clean. Cut into squares.

12 servings
1 Serving: Calories 440 (Calories from Fat 220); Total Fat 25g (Saturated 12g; Trans 0g); Cholesterol 205mg; Sodium 730mg; Total Carbohydrate 33g (Dietary Fiber 2g; Sugars 16g); Protein 22g
% Daily Value: Vitamin A 15%; Vitamin C 0%; Calcium 35%; Iron 15%
Exchanges: 1 Starch, 1 Other Carbohydrate, 2½ Medium-Fat Meat, 2½ Fat
Carbohydrate Choices: 2

KITCHEN TIPS

⚙ Use 12 cups cubed bread in place of the English muffins.
⚙ Try hot and spicy sausage for a flavor kick.

Cranberry Cornbread

Prep Time: 15 min Start to Finish: 45 min

- 1¼ cups Gold Medal all-purpose flour
- ¾ cup cornmeal
- ⅓ cup sugar
- 2 teaspoons baking powder
- ½ teaspoon salt
- 2 eggs
- ¾ cup milk
- ¼ cup vegetable oil
- 1 cup chopped fresh or frozen cranberries
- 2 tablespoons sugar

1. Heat oven to 400°F. Grease bottom and sides of 8-inch square pan with shortening or spray with cooking spray.

2. In large bowl, stir flour, cornmeal, ⅓ cup sugar, baking powder and salt until mixed. Add eggs, milk and oil; beat with spoon until mixed.

3. In small bowl, toss cranberries and 2 tablespoons sugar until coated. Fold into batter. Spread in pan.

4. Bake 25 to 30 minutes or until toothpick inserted in center comes out clean. Serve warm.

9 servings
1 Serving: Calories 230 (Calories from Fat 70); Total Fat 8g (Saturated 1.5g; Trans 0g); Cholesterol 50mg; Sodium 260mg; Total Carbohydrate 35g (Dietary Fiber 2g; Sugars 12g); Protein 5g
% Daily Value: Vitamin A 2%; Vitamin C 0%; Calcium 10%; Iron 8%
Exchanges: 1 Starch, 1 Other Carbohydrate, 2 Fat
Carbohydrate Choices: 2

KITCHEN TIPS

⊕ If you have fresh cranberries left over, place them on a cookie sheet and freeze. Once frozen, put them in a freezer bag and store in the freezer.

⊕ This recipe uses two ingredients indigenous to North America: cranberries and corn.

Basil Breakfast Strata

Prep Time: 15 min Start to Finish: 9 hr

- 6 eggs
- 3½ cups milk
- 1 teaspoon salt
- ½ teaspoon pepper
- 8 cups 1-inch cubes French bread
- 2 cups shredded mozzarella cheese (8 ounces)
- ¼ cup basil pesto
- ½ cup grated Parmesan cheese (2 ounces)

1. Spray 13 × 9-inch (3-quart) glass baking dish with cooking spray. In large bowl, beat eggs with wire whisk until foamy. Beat in milk until blended; beat in salt and pepper. Set aside.

2. Place bread cubes in baking dish. Sprinkle with mozzarella cheese. Pour egg mixture over top, pressing lightly to moisten bread. Using spoon, swirl pesto through mixture. Sprinkle Parmesan cheese over top. Cover with plastic wrap; refrigerate at least 8 hours but no longer than 24 hours.

3. Heat oven to 350°F. Remove plastic wrap; bake uncovered 40 to 45 minutes or until strata is puffed and knife inserted in center comes out clean. Let stand 5 minutes before serving. Cut into squares.

12 servings
1 Serving: Calories 240 (Calories from Fat 110); Total Fat 13g (Saturated 6g; Trans 0g); Cholesterol 125mg; Sodium 600mg; Total Carbohydrate 16g (Dietary Fiber 0g; Sugars 4g); Protein 15g
% Daily Value: Vitamin A 8%; Vitamin C 0%; Calcium 30%; Iron 6%
Exchanges: 1 Starch, 1½ Medium-Fat Meat, 1 Fat
Carbohydrate Choices: 1

KITCHEN TIPS

⊕ Place Basil Breakfast Strata and the Kielbasa Kabobs (page 162) in the oven together; they each bake for the same amount of time.

Basil Breakfast Strata

Cranberry Cornbread

Betty Crocker
IN SEASON

Pears

Truly a fruit worth waiting for, pears require patience. Picked unripe, pears slowly soften and become sweeter as they ripen. A favorite fall and winter fruit (but available year-round), pears are enjoyed for their juicy, sweet flavor and tender texture.

Anjou

Anjou pears come in a variety of autumnal colors, from light green to yellow-green to fiery red. Anjou pears, with their squat shape, are firm and have a mealy texture. They are juicy with a sweet-spicy flavor. These pears do not change color upon ripening. Eat fresh, and use in salads and desserts.

Asian

Asian pears have a less traditional pear shape and more of an apple shape. This Asian variety is firm and juicy with an apple-pear flavor. These pears, also known as Chinese pears and apple pears, have a crunchy texture. Eat fresh, use in salads or bake.

Bartlett

Bartlett pears are the most common pear, with smooth green skins that turn buttery yellow when ripe. Bartletts can also be red, then do not change color with ripening. When ripe, Bartlett pears have a juicy, sweet flavor and perfumy aroma. Terrific for eating fresh and using in salads and desserts.

Bosc

Bosc pears have a slender shape with a longer top and long, thin stem. They have a mottled tan-gold color that remains from picking to ripening. Bosc pears have a subtle nutty flavor and buttery texture. Use for baking and poaching as well as for eating fresh.

Health Highlights

▶ A medium pear (about the size of an adult fist), at only a slim 100 calories each and low on the glycemic index, is a good source of dietary fiber, providing 16 percent of the recommended daily allowance. Fiber helps sustain blood sugar levels and helps with gastrointestinal regularity. Pectin, a type of fiber, seems to help lower blood cholesterol levels. Diets high in fiber may also reduce the risk of heart disease and some types of cancer.

▶ Pears are a good source of vitamin C. This antioxidant promotes healing, boosts the immune system and reduces free radical damage.

▶ Potassium, an important mineral in heart health and nerve and muscle function, can be easily released during exercise. Choose a pear to reload potassium levels.

Comice

Comice pears are short and squat with a greenish yellow color and red blush when ripe. Their sweet, juicy flesh and buttery texture make them best for eating fresh.

Forelle

Forelle pears are small with a bell shape. Green before ripening, these pears turn a golden yellow with a red blush when ripe. Sweet and quite juicy, Forelle pears are great eaten fresh and used in salads and desserts.

Seckel

Seckel pears are petite red or red and green pears. Sometimes even small enough to be bite-size, these tiny pears pack a super-sweet flavor that makes them terrific for snacking or using in appetizers and desserts.

CHOOSE

▶ Look for firm or hard unripe pears with no bruises or cuts and with stems that are in place.

▶ Pears are one of a handful of fruits that are actually better if ripened after picking. Because they are delicate, it's better to ripen pears at home rather than purchasing them ripe.

STORE/RIPEN

▶ Store hard, unripe pears in a paper bag or covered fruit bowl at room temperature. Check daily for ripeness.

▶ You can also refrigerate unripe pears until you are ready to ripen them; then keep at room temperature.

▶ You cannot test ripeness by color because some varieties will not change color after picking.

▶ To check for ripeness, gently press the stem end of the pear with your thumb.

▶ To keep ripe pears longer, refrigerate them three to five days after ripening.

PREPARE

▶ If eating whole, simply wash pears.

▶ Wash, peel and cut pears for salads and desserts and when serving them sliced. Use a small, sharp knife or vegetable peeler to remove the thin skin.

▶ To halve pears, cut in half lengthwise and remove the core with a small knife.

▶ If you want to poach or stuff whole pears, use a melon baller to remove the core from the bottom of the pear, leaving the pear intact.

▶ Brush sliced pears that will not be immediately eaten with a little lemon juice to prevent browning.

▶ A medium pear will give you about 1 cup of slices.

Recipes to try using pears:

Sour Cream–Pear Fold-Over Pie, page 300

Peachy Pear-Coconut Crumble, page 313

Apple, Pear and Cranberry Pie, page 298

Beverages and Appetizers

Exceptional Sips and Nibbles

Italian Fruit Punch (page 25)

...chy Cream Cheese-Jalapeño Spread (page 39)

Spiced Dessert Coffee

Prep Time: 5 min Start to Finish: 15 min

6	cups water
³⁄₄	cup strong ground coffee (such as French roast)
1¹⁄₂	teaspoons ground cinnamon
8	whole cloves
¹⁄₄	cup packed brown sugar
¹⁄₂	cup whipped cream topping in aerosol can, if desired

1. Pour water into 10-cup coffeemaker. In filter basket, mix remaining ingredients except whipped cream. Brew coffee.

2. Pour coffee into mugs. Top with whipped cream.

8 servings (³⁄₄ cup each)
1 Serving: Calories 30 (Calories from Fat 0); Total Fat 0g (Saturated 0g; Trans 0g); Cholesterol 0mg; Sodium 5mg; Total Carbohydrate 7g (Dietary Fiber 0g; Sugars 7g); Protein 0g
% Daily Value: Vitamin A 0%; Vitamin C 0%; Calcium 0%; Iron 0%
Exchanges: ¹⁄₂ Other Carbohydrate
Carbohydrate Choices: ¹⁄₂

KITCHEN TIPS

⚙ Serve coffee in pottery mugs with cinnamon sticks as stirrers for a fun presentation.

⚙ Grate a sprinkling of fresh nutmeg on top of the whipped cream garnish.

— Low Fat —

Italian Fruit Punch

Prep Time: 15 min Start to Finish: 10 hr

Ice Ring

1   can (12 ounces) frozen lemonade concentrate, thawed

4   cans water

2   cups (about 12 large) frozen strawberries

2   lemons, cut into 1/4-inch slices, slices cut in half

Fresh mint leaves, if desired

Punch

1   can (12 ounces) frozen lemonade concentrate, thawed

1   can (12 ounces) frozen limeade concentrate, thawed

3   cups cold water

4   cups lemon-lime soda pop, chilled

1   bottle (1 liter) sparkling water, chilled

1. In pitcher, mix 1 can lemonade concentrate and 4 cans water. Pour 2 cups of the lemonade into 12-cup fluted tube cake pan. Freeze in coldest section of freezer about 45 minutes or until thin coating of ice forms on surface. Crack ice crust with small, sharp knife to expose liquid underneath. Working quickly, place strawberries, lemon slices and mint leaves in liquid, making sure each piece is partially submerged. Return pan to freezer about 1 hour or until lemonade is frozen solid. Remove from freezer and add remaining lemonade. Freeze at least 8 hours or overnight.

2. In 2-quart pitcher, mix 1 can lemonade concentrate, the limeade concentrate and 3 cups water. Refrigerate until ready to use.

3. Just before serving, pour limeade mixture, soda pop and sparkling water into punch bowl. Dip pan with ice ring very quickly into warm water, then turn upside down to unmold ice ring. Float ring in punch bowl.

28 servings (1/2 cup each)
1 Serving: Calories 90 (Calories from Fat 0); Total Fat 0g (Saturated 0g; Trans 0g); Cholesterol 0mg; Sodium 15mg; Total Carbohydrate 23g (Dietary Fiber 0g; Sugars 20g); Protein 0g
% Daily Value: Vitamin A 0%; Vitamin C 30%; Calcium 0%; Iron 0%
Exchanges: 1 1/2 Other Carbohydrate
Carbohydrate Choices: 1 1/2

KITCHEN TIPS

✿ The ice ring can be unmolded in advance. Place in a plastic bag and keep in the freezer until ready to use.

Peachy Mimosas

Special Raspberry Punch

Special Raspberry Punch

Prep Time: 25 min Start to Finish: 2 hr 25 min

- 4 boxes (10 ounces each) frozen raspberries, thawed, undrained
- 1 can (6 ounces) frozen lemonade concentrate, thawed
- 1 bottle (2 liters) ginger ale, chilled

1. In 4-quart Dutch oven, cook raspberries over medium heat 10 minutes, stirring frequently; cool slightly. Push through strainer with large spoon to remove seeds. Refrigerate raspberry juice at least 2 hours.

2. In punch bowl or large pitcher, mix raspberry juice and lemonade concentrate. Stir in ginger ale. Serve immediately over ice.

24 servings (1/2 cup each)
1 Serving: Calories 100 (Calories from Fat 0); Total Fat 0g (Saturated 0g; Trans 0g); Cholesterol 0mg; Sodium 10mg; Total Carbohydrate 25g (Dietary Fiber 2g; Sugars 22g); Protein 0g
% Daily Value: Vitamin A 0%; Vitamin C 15%; Calcium 0%; Iron 2%
Exchanges: 1/2 Fruit, 1 Other Carbohydrate
Carbohydrate Choices: 1 1/2

KITCHEN TIPS

✿ Use frozen strawberries and limeade concentrate in place of the raspberries and lemonade. There's no need to strain the cooked strawberries.

Peachy Mimosas

Prep Time: 5 min Start to Finish: 5 min

- 2 cups orange juice, chilled
- 2 cups peach nectar, chilled
- 1 bottle (1 liter) regular or nonalcoholic dry champagne or sparking wine, chilled

1. In 1 1/2-quart pitcher, mix orange juice and peach nectar.

2. Pour champagne into glasses until half full. Fill glasses with juice mixture.

12 servings (2/3 cup each)
1 Serving: Calories 100 (Calories from Fat 0); Total Fat 0g (Saturated 0g; Trans 0g); Cholesterol 0mg; Sodium 10mg; Total Carbohydrate 11g (Dietary Fiber 0g; Sugars 9g); Protein 0g
% Daily Value: Vitamin A 4%; Vitamin C 30%; Calcium 0%; Iron 2%
Exchanges: 1/2 Fruit, 1 Fat
Carbohydrate Choices: 1

KITCHEN TIPS

✿ Dip the rim of each champagne glass into water and then into sugar to frost.

Genoa Salami Stacks

Prep Time: 20 min Start to Finish: 25 min

24   slices ($\frac{1}{4}$ to $\frac{1}{2}$ inch thick) French baguette bread (from 10-ounce loaf)

$1\frac{1}{2}$ cups finely shredded lettuce

$\frac{1}{4}$ cup creamy Caesar dressing

6   thin slices (about $\frac{1}{2}$ ounce each) provolone cheese, cut into fourths

24   thin slices Genoa salami (4 ounces), folded in half twice

4   roma (plum) tomatoes, thinly sliced

$\frac{3}{4}$ teaspoon garlic-pepper blend

$\frac{1}{3}$ cup shredded fresh basil leaves or chopped fresh parsley

1. Heat oven to 375°F. Place bread slices in ungreased 15 × 10 × 1-inch pan. Bake 5 to 7 minutes or until crisp; cool.

2. In small bowl, mix lettuce and dressing. Top each bread slice with lettuce mixture. Layer cheese, salami and tomatoes on bread. Sprinkle with garlic-pepper blend and basil.

24 appetizers
1 Appetizer: Calories 60 (Calories from Fat 40); Total Fat 4g (Saturated 1.5g; Trans 0g); Cholesterol 5mg; Sodium 180mg; Total Carbohydrate 4g (Dietary Fiber 0g; Sugars 0g); Protein 3g
% Daily Value: Vitamin A 2%; Vitamin C 2%; Calcium 4%; Iron 0%
Exchanges: $\frac{1}{2}$ Starch, $\frac{1}{2}$ Fat
Carbohydrate Choices: 0

KITCHEN TIPS

❂ Lightly drizzle olive oil over the toasted bread instead of using Caesar dressing.
❂ Tuck fresh sprigs of oregano and basil among the salami stacks, and garnish with cherry tomatoes and olives.

Zippy Dill Vegetable Dip

Prep Time: 20 min Start to Finish: 20 min

½ package (0.7-ounce size) dill dip mix (about 4 teaspoons)

1 container (8 ounces) sour cream

2 tablespoons finely sliced chives

1 tablespoon lemon juice

1 cup ready-to-eat baby-cut carrots

2 cups broccoli florets

½ pint (1 cup) cherry or grape tomatoes

1 medium cucumber, cut into ¼-inch slices (2 cups)

1. In medium bowl, mix dip mix (dry), sour cream, chives and lemon juice.

2. On serving platter, arrange carrots, broccoli, tomatoes and cucumber slices. Serve with dip.

8 servings (2 tablespoons dip and 8 vegetable pieces each)
1 Serving: Calories 80 (Calories from Fat 45); Total Fat 5g (Saturated 2.5g; Trans 0g); Cholesterol 10mg; Sodium 220mg; Total Carbohydrate 6g (Dietary Fiber 2g; Sugars 3g); Protein 2g
% Daily Value: Vitamin A 50%; Vitamin C 40%; Calcium 6%; Iron 0%
Exchanges: 1 Vegetable, 1 Fat
Carbohydrate Choices: ½

KITCHEN TIPS

✿ To slice chives easily and quickly, snip with kitchen scissors.

✿ Add fresh pea pods, orange and yellow bell pepper strips and jicama sticks to the vegetable assortment to create variety and crunch.

Cherry-Cheese Mold

Prep Time: 30 min Start to Finish: 1 hr 30 min

1 package (8 ounces) cream cheese, softened

4 ounces Muenster cheese, shredded (1 cup)

4 ounces white Cheddar cheese, shredded (1 cup)

2 tablespoons finely chopped onion

2 tablespoons cherry-flavored liqueur

1 cup pitted fresh or frozen (thawed and drained) dark sweet cherries

¾ cup honey-roasted sliced almonds

3 packages (2.82 ounces each) mini-toasts (96 toasts)

1. In food processor, place cheeses, onion and liqueur. Cover; process until smooth and well mixed; spoon into large bowl. Chop ¾ cup of the cherries. Reserve remaining ¼ cup cherries and 2 tablespoons of the almonds. Stir chopped cherries and remaining almonds into cheese mixture until well mixed and mixture is pink.

2. Line 3-cup bowl or heart-shaped mold with double layer of cheesecloth. Spoon cheese mixture into mold. Cover; refrigerate at least 1 hour but no longer than 24 hours.

3. Unmold cheese mixture onto serving plate. Cut reserved cherries in half. Garnish top of cheese mold with halved cherries and reserved almonds. Serve with mini-toasts.

24 servings (2 tablespoons spread and 4 mini-toasts each)
1 Serving: Calories 140 (Calories from Fat 80); Total Fat 9g (Saturated 4g; Trans 0g); Cholesterol 20mg; Sodium 160mg; Total Carbohydrate 11g (Dietary Fiber 1g; Sugars 2g); Protein 5g
% Daily Value: Vitamin A 4%; Vitamin C 0%; Calcium 8%; Iron 6%
Exchanges: ½ Starch, ½ High-Fat Meat, 1 Fat
Carbohydrate Choices: 1

KITCHEN TIPS

❂ You can use an assortment of small crackers instead of the mini-toasts.

❂ The honey-roasted sliced almonds, often used in salads, are found in packages in the produce department.

Cherry-Cheese Mold

Cherries

Cherries are one of the sweetest fruits of summer. Even though they have a relatively short season, their intense flavor and color make for a strong showing in summer desserts, salads, main dishes and even appetizers.

Lambert

Lambert cherries are dark red and slightly smaller than Bing cherries. They have a noticeable heart shape and rich, sweet flavor. Lambert cherries are available in May and June.

Bing

One of the most popular varieties, Bing cherries have a deep red-purple to almost black color and are firm and juicy. They have a sweet, intense flavor that makes them so popular. Look for Bing cherries in May and June.

Rainier

Rainier cherries are easily recognized by their shiny yellow and pink-blushed skin. The fruit of this cherry is white and the juice colorless. They have a delicate, sweet flavor. Peak season is May through the first part of July.

Blink, and cherry season can pass you by. Unlike many fruits that are available year-round, fresh cherries are but a brief, seasonal delight. Enjoy their sweet or tart splendor and the prized nutrition inside.

CHOOSE

Select cherries that are plump, shiny and firm with green stems. Avoid cherries with soft or bruised spots, cracks or cuts. Cherries without stems deteriorate faster because of the broken skin.

STORE

Cherries are completely ripe when shipped, so they are very perishable. Refrigerate unwashed cherries immediately. They'll keep for up to a week.

PREPARE

Wash cherries thoroughly. Many people's favorite way to enjoy cherries is *au naturel*—straight off the tree. But putting them in salads and desserts, on ice cream and yogurt or even on cereal are terrific ways to use cherries. If you're not eating them off the stem, you'll need to pit them. Use a sharp paring knife to cut open each cherry and remove the pit or use a cherry pitter, which removes the pit, or stone, and leaves the cherry whole. One pound of cherries will yield about 2½ cups of pitted cherries.

Freezing cherries: Remove the stems, wash and pat dry. Pit the cherries, if desired. Place on a cookie sheet and freeze until firm, then transfer cherries to freezer containers or plastic freezer bags. Frozen unpitted whole cherries are a terrific frozen treat on a hot summer day—just watch out for the pits!

To cook cherries for a sauce or topping: Cook for just a few minutes so the cherries retain their texture and color. Cook about 3 minutes or until cherries are softened and thoroughly heated.

Nutrition Highlights

▶ Vitamin C
▶ Phytonutrients
▶ Fiber
▶ Beta-carotene
(tart cherries only)

Health Highlights

▶ **Phytonutrients:** Phytonutrients are the healthful plant pigments that give cherries and other fruits and vegetables their brilliant color. They can provide health benefits above and beyond the vitamins and minerals naturally found in produce. In fact, the combination of phytonutrients, fiber and vitamins found in fruits such as cherries helps to pack a powerful punch against some illnesses such as cancer and heart disease. Specifically, the anthocyanins in cherries seem to have an anti-inflammatory action that may reduce the risk of disease.

▶ **Antioxidants:** Several of the nutrients in cherries, including beta-carotene and vitamin C, act as antioxidants, potentially protecting cells in the body from damage. In fact, cherries make the top-10 list of fruits with antioxidant power.

Bread and Spreads Platter

Prep Time: 20 min Start to Finish: 20 min

    2   containers (8 ounces each) chives-and-onion
        cream cheese spread
    ¼   cup roasted red bell peppers, diced and
        drained (from 7-ounce jar)
    ¼   cup chopped pimiento-stuffed green olives
    2   tablespoons refrigerated basil pesto (from
        7-ounce container)
        Leaf lettuce leaves
    1   loaf (20 inch) baguette French bread
        (12 ounces), cut into ¼-inch slices

1. Among 3 small bowls, divide cream cheese. Stir bell
peppers into cream cheese in 1 bowl. Stir olives into
cream cheese in another bowl. Stir pesto into cream
cheese in third bowl.

2. Line serving platter with lettuce leaves. Mound 3
spreads on lettuce leaves. Surround with bread
slices.

18 servings (2 teaspoons of each spread and 3 bread slices each)
1 Serving: Calories 140 (Calories from Fat 80); Total Fat 9g (Saturated
5g; Trans 0g); Cholesterol 25mg; Sodium 330mg; Total Carbohydrate
11g (Dietary Fiber 0g; Sugars 1g); Protein 4g
% Daily Value: Vitamin A 10%; Vitamin C 8%; Calcium 4%; Iron 6%
Exchanges: ½ Starch, ½ High-Fat Meat, 1 Fat
Carbohydrate Choices: 1

KITCHEN TIPS

✿ Radicchio, a ruby-red salad green, makes colorful "bowls"
for these tasty spreads. Or, use Bibb or leaf lettuce leaves.

✿ Make little paper flags identifying the three spreads. Attach
them to toothpicks and place in the spreads.

Cheese Tray with Olive Rosemary Skewers

Prep Time: 45 min Start to Finish: 45 min

1 round (7 ounces) Gouda or Edam cheese

48 to 96 assorted large pitted or stuffed olives (such as Kalamata and large pimiento-stuffed green olives), drained

24 sprigs rosemary, each 4 inches long

1½ pounds assorted cheeses (such as Colby-Monterey Jack, dill Havarti, sharp Cheddar and Monterey Jack)

Assorted crackers

24 servings (¹⁄₂₄ of ingredients and 2 crackers each)
1 Serving: Calories 200 (Calories from Fat 140); Total Fat 15g (Saturated 8g; Trans 1g); Cholesterol 40mg; Sodium 400mg; Total Carbohydrate 6g (Dietary Fiber 0g; Sugars 1g); Protein 9g
% Daily Value: Vitamin A 8%; Vitamin C 0%; Calcium 25%; Iron 4%
Exchanges: ½ Starch, 1 High-Fat Meat, 1½ Fat
Carbohydrate Choices: ½

KITCHEN TIPS

✿ Use thick rosemary sprigs for the skewers so they won't break. You also can use 3- to 4-inch party picks.

1. Remove paper and wax from cheese round. On center of 12- to 14-inch platter, place cheese round. Thread 2 to 4 olives on each rosemary sprig. Insert sprigs into cheese round.

2. Cut assorted cheeses into slices and shapes, such as triangles, squares, cubes and sticks; arrange around cheese round. Serve with crackers.

Sugar 'n Spice Dip

Prep Time: 15 min Start to Finish: 15 min

1	tablespoon packed brown sugar or honey
$\frac{1}{4}$	teaspoon ground cinnamon
	Dash ground nutmeg
2	containers (6 ounces each) Yoplait® Thick & Creamy vanilla yogurt
$2\frac{1}{2}$	cups cubed honeydew melon ($\frac{1}{2}$ melon)
$1\frac{3}{4}$	cups red raspberries (8 ounces)

1. In small bowl, mix brown sugar, cinnamon and nutmeg. Stir in yogurt.

2. Spoon yogurt mixture into small serving bowl. Sprinkle with additional ground cinnamon. Serve with melon and raspberries.

10 servings (2 tablespoons dip, 3 cubes melon and 5 raspberries each)
1 Serving: Calories 70 (Calories from Fat 5); Total Fat 0.5g (Saturated 0g; Trans 0g); Cholesterol 0mg; Sodium 30mg; Total Carbohydrate 13g (Dietary Fiber 2g; Sugars 10g); Protein 2g
% Daily Value: Vitamin A 4%; Vitamin C 25%; Calcium 6%; Iron 0%
Exchanges: $\frac{1}{2}$ Fruit, $\frac{1}{2}$ Other Carbohydrate
Carbohydrate Choices: 1

KITCHEN TIPS

✪ To save time, purchase pre-cut fruit, available in the produce department. You will usually find several varieties of melon and pineapple.

✪ Ground nutmeg loses its flavor quickly. If you don't use nutmeg often, purchase whole nutmeg and grate your own with a fine grater.

Sugar 'n Spice Dip

Pepper Jack Cheese Ball

Prep Time: 15 min Start to Finish: 15 min

1½ cups shredded pepper Jack cheese
(6 ounces)

1 cup shredded sharp Cheddar cheese
(4 ounces)

2 packages (3 ounces each) cream cheese,
softened

1 tablespoon lime juice

½ teaspoon onion powder

¼ cup sliced ripe olives

¼ cup chopped fresh cilantro

¾ cup nacho-flavored tortilla chips, crushed
Assorted crackers or tortilla chips

18 servings (2 tablespoons cheese ball and 4 crackers each)
1 Serving: Calories 190 (Calories from Fat 120); Total Fat 13g
(Saturated 6g; Trans 1.5g); Cholesterol 25mg; Sodium 310mg; Total
Carbohydrate 12g (Dietary Fiber 0g; Sugars 1g); Protein 6g
% Daily Value: Vitamin A 6%; Vitamin C 0%; Calcium 10%; Iron 4%
Exchanges: 1 Starch, ½ High-Fat Meat, 1½ Fat
Carbohydrate Choices: 1

KITCHEN TIPS

❁ If you make the cheese ball ahead and refrigerate it, let it
stand at room temperature about 15 minutes before
serving. It will be much easier to spread.

❁ If you prefer, you could use chopped olives instead of
sliced.

1. In food processor, place cheeses, lime juice and
onion powder. Cover; process until well mixed.
Spoon into medium bowl. Stir in olives and cilantro.

2. Place crushed tortilla chips on waxed paper. Spoon
cheese mixture onto chips. Roll to coat cheese ball
with chips. Serve with crackers.

Peachy Cream Cheese-Jalapeño Spread

Prep Time: 15 min Start to Finish: 15 min

- ¼ cup peach or apricot preserves
- ½ red jalapeño chili, seeded and finely chopped
- ½ green jalapeño chili, seeded and finely chopped
- 1 package (8 ounces) cream cheese, cut in half
  Assorted crackers and/or cocktail pumpernickel or rye bread

1. In small bowl, mix preserves and chilies. On small serving plate, place blocks of cream cheese. Spoon preserves mixture over cheese.

2. Serve with crackers or cocktail bread.

8 servings (2 tablespoons spread and 3 crackers each)
1 Serving: Calories 190 (Calories from Fat 120); Total Fat 13g (Saturated 7g; Trans 1.5g); Cholesterol 30mg; Sodium 190mg; Total Carbohydrate 15g (Dietary Fiber 0g; Sugars 6g); Protein 3g
% Daily Value: Vitamin A 8%; Vitamin C 2%; Calcium 2%; Iron 4%
Exchanges: ½ Starch, ½ Other Carbohydrate, 2½ Fat
Carbohydrate Choices: 1

KITCHEN TIPS

✪ You could use one whole red or one whole green jalapeño chili, but the combination of the red and green is very attractive.

✪ The remaining chilies will keep in the refrigerator for several days. Dice a little into taco meat or almost any casserole to add a bit of flavor and heat.

Bacon-Tomato Dip

Prep Time: 15 min Start to Finish: 15 min

1 container (8 ounces) reduced-fat sour cream

¼ cup reduced-fat mayonnaise or salad dressing

2 tablespoons cooked real bacon pieces (from 2.8-ounce package)

1 medium tomato, seeded and diced (¾ cup)

2 medium green onions, sliced (2 tablespoons)

Assorted fresh vegetables (bell pepper strips, broccoli, cauliflowerets, cucumber slices, radishes)

1. In medium bowl, mix sour cream and mayonnaise. Stir in bacon, tomato and onions.

2. Serve with vegetables for dipping.

12 servings (2 tablespoons dip and 3 vegetable pieces each)
1 Serving: Calories 60 (Calories from Fat 40); Total Fat 4.5g (Saturated 2g; Trans 0g); Cholesterol 10mg; Sodium 75mg; Total Carbohydrate 4g (Dietary Fiber 1g; Sugars 2g); Protein 2g
% Daily Value: Vitamin A 30%; Vitamin C 30%; Calcium 4%; Iron 0%
Exchanges: 1 Vegetable, 1 Fat
Carbohydrate Choices: 0

KITCHEN TIPS

✿ Packages of cooked real bacon pieces are found near the salad dressings in the grocery store. If you prefer, you can cook and crumble bacon yourself.

✿ To seed the tomato, cut it in half and squeeze gently over the sink to remove seeds and juice. You can use your fingers to help remove the seeds.

Pesto-Pepperoni Roll-Ups

Prep Time: 15 min Start to Finish: 15 min

½ cup refrigerated basil pesto (from 7-ounce container)

4 pesto-flavored or plain flour tortillas (8 to 10 inch)

1 package (3.5 ounces) sliced pepperoni

2 roma (plum) tomatoes, seeded and chopped

¼ cup chopped yellow or orange bell pepper

¼ cup chopped ripe olives, drained

½ cup shredded mozzarella cheese (2 ounces)

1. Spread 2 tablespoons pesto evenly over each tortilla. Arrange 12 pepperoni slices on pesto on each tortilla. Sprinkle tomatoes, bell pepper, olives and cheese evenly over pepperoni to within ½ inch of edges of tortillas.

2. Roll up tortillas tightly. Cut each roll into 8 slices.

32 slices
1 Slice: Calories 60 (Calories from Fat 35); Total Fat 4g (Saturated 1g; Trans 0g); Cholesterol 5mg; Sodium 130mg; Total Carbohydrate 4g (Dietary Fiber 0g; Sugars 0g); Protein 2g
% Daily Value: Vitamin A 0%; Vitamin C 4%; Calcium 4%; Iron 2%
Exchanges: ½ Starch, ½ Fat
Carbohydrate Choices: 0

KITCHEN TIPS

✪ If you like extra-spicy food, choose the spicy variety of pepperoni for these appetizers.

✪ Toss the leftover pesto with hot cooked pasta for a delicious side dish at another meal.

Pizza Dip

Prep Time: 15 min Start to Finish: 15 min

1 package (8 ounces) cream cheese, softened
1/2 cup pizza sauce
2 cloves garlic, finely chopped
1/2 cup chopped pepperoni
1 can (2 1/4 ounces) sliced ripe olives, drained
1/3 cup finely diced red bell pepper
5 medium green onions, sliced (1/3 cup)
1/2 cup shredded mozzarella cheese (2 ounces)
1/4 cup thinly sliced fresh basil leaves
  Colored tortilla chips

1. Set oven control to broil. On 12- to 13-inch round ovenproof serving plate, spread cream cheese in thin layer. In small bowl, mix pizza sauce and garlic; spread over cream cheese. Top with pepperoni, olives, bell pepper and onions. Sprinkle with mozzarella cheese.

2. Broil with top 4 inches from heat 1 to 2 minutes or until mozzarella cheese is melted. Sprinkle with basil. Serve immediately with tortilla chips.

20 servings (2 tablespoons dip and 6 chips each)
1 Serving: Calories 130 (Calories from Fat 80); Total Fat 9g (Saturated 3.5g; Trans 0g); Cholesterol 15mg; Sodium 220mg; Total Carbohydrate 8g (Dietary Fiber 0g; Sugars 0g); Protein 3g
% Daily Value: Vitamin A 6%; Vitamin C 4%; Calcium 4%; Iron 4%
Exchanges: 1/2 Starch, 1/2 High-Fat Meat, 1 Fat
Carbohydrate Choices: 1/2

KITCHEN TIPS

✿ For fun dippers, cut individual-size baked pizza crusts into small wedges.
✿ Toss the extra pizza sauce with cooked cheese-filled tortellini for a quick lunch.

Parmesan Cheese Chex® Mix

Prep Time: 15 min Start to Finish: 15 min

1 bag (3.5 ounces) PopSecret® HomeStyle microwave popcorn (from 10.5-ounce box)
3 cups Corn Chex® cereal
3 cups Rice Chex® cereal
3 cups Wheat Chex® cereal
4 cups cheese-flavored crackers
3 tablespoons butter or margarine, melted
2/3 cup grated Parmesan cheese

1. Microwave popcorn as directed on bag.

2. In large resealable plastic food-storage bag, mix cereals, crackers and popcorn. Drizzle with butter; seal bag. Shake until evenly coated.

3. Add cheese; seal bag. Shake until evenly coated.

42 servings (1/2 cup each)
1 Serving: Calories 80 (Calories from Fat 30); Total Fat 3.5g (Saturated 1.5g; Trans 0.5g); Cholesterol 0mg; Sodium 170mg; Total Carbohydrate 10g (Dietary Fiber 0g; Sugars 0g); Protein 2g
% Daily Value: Vitamin A 2%; Vitamin C 2%; Calcium 4%; Iron 15%
Exchanges: 1/2 Starch, 1/2 Fat
Carbohydrate Choices: 1/2

KITCHEN TIPS

✿ This is a good snack for kids to take in the car. Seal small portions in snack-size resealable plastic bags to have ready for those trips to the pool or grocery store.
✿ Choose from the wide variety of cheese crackers available; square white or yellow Cheddar cheese crackers, fish-shaped crackers and cheese-flavored twists are just a few.

Pizza Dip

Parmesan Cheese Chex® Mix

Antipasto Picks

Prep Time: 30 min Start to Finish: 1 hr 30 min

1/3 cup extra-virgin olive oil

1/4 cup red wine vinegar

1 teaspoon grated lemon peel

1 clove garlic, sliced

1 teaspoon Italian seasoning

1/2 teaspoon crushed red pepper flakes

1/2 pound mozzarella cheese, cut into 3/4-inch cubes

1 jar (4.5 ounces) Green Giant® whole mushrooms, drained

4 slices (3 1/4 ounces) prosciutto (from deli)

8 thin slices hard salami, cut in half

1/2 cup medium pitted ripe olives, drained

1 jar (6 to 7 ounces) marinated artichoke hearts, drained

28 bamboo skewers or toothpicks (4 inch)

1. In medium bowl, mix oil, vinegar, lemon peel, garlic, Italian seasoning and red pepper flakes. Stir in cheese and mushrooms. Cover; refrigerate at least 1 hour but no longer than 24 hours.

2. Cut prosciutto slices lengthwise into 1-inch strips, cut strips into about 3-inch pieces. Drain mushroom mixture.

3. Pleat prosciutto pieces and salami half-slices. Spear prosciutto or salami with skewers; add assortment of mushrooms, olives and/or artichokes to skewers. Add cheese cube to end of each skewer. (Each skewer should have 6 pieces.)

14 servings (2 picks each)
1 Serving: Calories 150 (Calories from Fat 100); Total Fat 12g (Saturated 3.5g; Trans 0g); Cholesterol 15mg; Sodium 360mg; Total Carbohydrate 3g (Dietary Fiber 1g; Sugars 0g); Protein 8g
% Daily Value: Vitamin A 4%; Vitamin C 2%; Calcium 15%; Iron 4%
Exchanges: 1 High-Fat Meat, 1 Fat
Carbohydrate Choices: 0

KITCHEN TIPS

✿ Antipasto bars in Italy offer a wide selection of mushrooms, grilled vegetables, cured meats and cheeses. This antipasto appetizer offers variety, as well.

✿ If you have a preference, you could use all prosciutto or all salami for these appetizers.

Amaretto Cheese-Filled Apricots

Prep Time: 20 min Start to Finish: 1 hr 20 min

4 ounces cream cheese (half of 8-ounce package), softened

$1/3$ cup slivered almonds, toasted and chopped

$1/4$ cup chopped dried cherries or sweetened dried cranberries

2 tablespoons amaretto liqueur

30 soft whole dried apricots

1. In small bowl, mix cream cheese, $1/4$ cup of the almonds, the cherries and amaretto with spoon. Spoon into small resealable plastic food-storage bag. Cut $1/2$ inch off 1 corner of bag.

2. With fingers, open apricots along one side so they resemble partially open clamshells. Pipe about 1 teaspoon cheese mixture into each apricot.

3. Finely chop remaining almonds. Dip cheese edge of apricots into almonds. Refrigerate 1 hour to chill before serving.

30 Apricots
1 Apricot: Calories 45 (Calories from Fat 20); Total Fat 2g (Saturated 1g; Trans 0g); Cholesterol 0mg; Sodium 10mg; Total Carbohydrate 6g (Dietary Fiber 0g; Sugars 5g); Protein 0g
% Daily Value: Vitamin A 6%; Vitamin C 0%; Calcium 0%; Iron 0%
Exchanges: $1/2$ Fruit, $1/2$ Fat
Carbohydrate Choices: $1/2$

KITCHEN TIPS

❀ These filled apricots would be a beautiful addition to a cheese and fruit platter.

❀ Golden apricots have a jewel-like appearance. Used in this appetizer, they would be lovely served at a wedding shower tea.

❀ To toast nuts, bake uncovered in ungreased shallow pan in 350°F oven 6 to 10 minutes, stirring occasionally, until light brown.

Black Bean and Corn Wonton Cups

Prep Time: 30 min Start to Finish: 30 min

36 wonton skins

²/₃ cup Old El Paso® Thick'n Chunky salsa

¼ cup chopped fresh cilantro

½ teaspoon ground cumin

½ teaspoon chili powder

1 can (15.25 ounces) Green Giant Niblets® whole kernel corn, drained

1 can (15 ounces) Progresso® black beans, rinsed, drained

¼ cup plus 2 tablespoons sour cream
Cilantro sprigs, if desired

1. Heat oven to 350°F. Gently fit 1 wonton skin into each of 36 small muffin cups, 1³/₄ × 1 inch, pressing against bottom and side. Bake 8 to 10 minutes or until light golden brown. Remove from pan; cool on wire rack 5 minutes.

2. Meanwhile, in medium bowl, mix remaining ingredients except sour cream and cilantro sprigs. Just before serving, spoon bean mixture into wonton cups. Top each with ½ teaspoon sour cream. Garnish each with cilantro sprig.

36 cups
1 Cup: Calories 50 (Calories from Fat 5); Total Fat 1g (Saturated 0g; Trans 0g); Cholesterol 0mg; Sodium 105mg; Total Carbohydrate 10g (Dietary Fiber 0g; Sugars 0g); Protein 2g
% Daily Value: Vitamin A 0%; Vitamin C 0%; Calcium 0%; Iron 4%
Exchanges: ½ Other Carbohydrate, ½ Very Lean Meat
Carbohydrate Choices: ½

KITCHEN TIPS

❀ Look for the wonton skins in the produce section of the grocery store.

❀ The wonton cups can be baked a day ahead. Wrap loosely and store at room temperature.

Low Fat

Party Potatoes

Prep Time: 15 min Start to Finish: 1 hr 50 min

12   small new potatoes (about 1¹⁄₂ pounds)

¹⁄₂   cup sour cream

      Dill weed sprigs or chopped fresh chives

1. In 3-quart saucepan, heat 1 inch water to boiling. Add potatoes. Cover; heat to boiling. Reduce heat. Simmer 20 to 25 minutes or until tender; drain. Cool 30 minutes to 1 hour.

2. Cut potatoes in half; place cut sides up on serving tray. (Cut thin slice from bottom of each potato half, if necessary, to help stand upright.) Top each potato half with 1 teaspoon sour cream and dill weed sprig. Cover; refrigerate until serving.

24 servings
1 Serving: Calories 30 (Calories from Fat 10); Total Fat 1g (Saturated 0.5g; Trans 0g); Cholesterol 0mg; Sodium 0mg; Total Carbohydrate 5g (Dietary Fiber 0g; Sugars 0g); Protein 0g
% Daily Value: Vitamin A 0%; Vitamin C 2%; Calcium 0%; Iron 2%
Exchanges: ¹⁄₂ Starch
Carbohydrate Choices: ¹⁄₂

KITCHEN TIPS

❂ New potatoes are young potatoes and can have red, yellow or brown skin. Because the skin is very thin and tender, new potatoes don't need to be peeled.

❂ For a spark of color, sprinkle a little finely diced red bell pepper or red onion over the potatoes.

Tortellini Kabobs

Tortellini Kabobs

Prep Time: 15 min Start to Finish: 1 hr 30 min

25 uncooked refrigerated or dried cheese-filled spinach tortellini

$^1\!/_2$ cup reduced-fat Italian dressing

12 small whole mushrooms

12 small cherry tomatoes

12 bamboo skewers (6 inch) or rosemary sprigs
    Lettuce leaves, if desired

1. Cook and drain tortellini as directed on package. Cool 15 minutes.

2. Place dressing in shallow dish. Stir in tortellini, mushrooms and tomatoes. Cover; refrigerate 1 to 2 hours, stirring once to coat.

3. Drain tortellini mixture. On each skewer, thread tortellini, mushrooms and tomatoes alternately. (For rosemary sprigs, use your fingers to remove all but the top leaves; thread ingredients from the bottom.) Serve on bed of lettuce leaves.

12 kabobs
1 Kabob: Calories 35 (Calories from Fat 10); Total Fat 1g (Saturated 0g; Trans 0g); Cholesterol 0mg; Sodium 95mg; Total Carbohydrate 5g (Dietary Fiber 0g; Sugars 0g); Protein 2g
% Daily Value: Vitamin A 2%; Vitamin C 2%; Calcium 0%; Iron 0%
Exchanges: $^1\!/_2$ Starch
Carbohydrate Choices: $^1\!/_2$

KITCHEN TIPS

❂ For a change of flavor, use one of the balsamic vinaigrettes available in the salad dressing aisle instead of the Italian dressing.

❂ Marinated pitted olives can be used in place of some of the mushrooms. Many large grocery stores offer olive bars with a wide variety of olives.

Three-Cheese Logs

Prep Time: 15 min Start to Finish: 2 hr 15 min

1 package (8 ounces) cream cheese, softened

1 tablespoon Worcestershire sauce

1 teaspoon ground mustard

2 cups shredded sharp Cheddar cheese (8 ounces)

$^1/_2$ cup crumbled Stilton cheese

$^1/_2$ cup roasted red bell peppers, chopped and drained (from 7-ounce jar)

$^1/_4$ cup chopped fresh chives

$^1/_2$ cup finely chopped walnuts or pecans

1 large apple, sliced

Assorted crackers

1. In large bowl, stir cream cheese, Worcestershire sauce and mustard until blended. Stir in Cheddar and Stilton cheeses, bell peppers and chives.

2. Divide cheese mixture in half. Shape each half into a log. Roll logs in walnuts. Wrap each log separately in plastic wrap or waxed paper. Refrigerate about 2 hours or until firm.

3. Place cheese logs on serving platter. Serve with apple slices and crackers.

20 servings (2 tablespoons spread, 1 apple slice and 1 cracker each)
1 Serving: Calories 150 (Calories from Fat 110); Total Fat 12g (Saturated 6g; Trans 0.5g); Cholesterol 25mg; Sodium 190mg; Total Carbohydrate 5g (Dietary Fiber 0g; Sugars 2g); Protein 5g % Daily Value: Vitamin A 10%; Vitamin C 15%; Calcium 10%; Iron 2 Exchanges: $^1/_2$ Starch, $^1/_2$ High-Fat Meat, $1^1/_2$ Fat Carbohydrate Choices: $^1/_2$

KITCHEN TIPS

✿ Stilton is a pungent English blue cheese. Another blue cheese, such as Gorgonzola or American blue cheese, could be substituted.

✿ Chives lose their flavor when dried, so try to use fresh chives.

Salads
Salads

and Soups
and Soup

Smaller Dishes for Lunch or Supper

Steak and Potato Salad (page 68)

Spring Onion Soup with Garlic Croutons (page 73)

Picnic Pasta Salad

Prep Time: 20 min Start to Finish: 2 hr 20 min

- 1 package (16 ounces) farfalle (bow-tie) pasta
- 1 can (8 ounces) tomato sauce
- 1 cup Italian dressing
- 1 tablespoon chopped fresh or 1 teaspoon dried basil leaves
- 1 tablespoon chopped fresh or 1 teaspoon dried oregano leaves
- 1 cup sliced fresh mushrooms (3 ounces)
- 5 roma (plum) tomatoes, coarsely chopped (1½ cups)
- 1 large cucumber, coarsely chopped (1½ cups)
- 1 medium red onion, chopped (1½ cups)
- 1 can (2¼ ounces) sliced ripe olives, drained

1. Cook and drain pasta as directed on package. Rinse with cold water; drain.

2. In large bowl, mix tomato sauce, dressing, basil and oregano. Add pasta and remaining ingredients; toss.

Cover and refrigerate at least 2 hours until chilled but no longer than 48 hours.

26 servings (½ cup each)
1 Serving: Calories 120 (Calories from Fat 40); Total Fat 4.5g (Saturated 0g; Trans 0g); Cholesterol 0mg; Sodium 220mg; Total Carbohydrate 17g (Dietary Fiber 2g; Sugars 2g); Protein 3g
% Daily Value: Vitamin A 2%; Vitamin C 4%; Calcium 2%; Iron 6%
Exchanges: 1 Starch, 1 Fat
Carbohydrate Choices: 1

KITCHEN TIPS

- Use cooked and drained tricolor tortellini for this salad recipe.
- Omit mushrooms and use roasted red bell pepper slices instead.

Quick & Low Fat

Strawberry-Melon-Spinach Salad

Prep Time: 10 min Start to Finish: 10 min

Orange-Honey Dressing

- 1/4 cup orange juice
- 1/4 cup honey
- 2 tablespoons vegetable oil
- 2 teaspoons Dijon mustard

Salad

- 12 cups bite-size pieces spinach
- 2 cups sliced strawberries
- 2 cups cubed cantaloupe
- 6 medium green onions, sliced (6 tablespoons)

1. In tightly covered container, shake all dressing ingredients.

2. In very large bowl, toss all salad ingredients with dressing.

16 servings (1 cup each)
1 Serving: Calories 60 (Calories from Fat 15); Total Fat 2g (Saturated 0g; Trans 0g); Cholesterol 0mg; Sodium 35mg; Total Carbohydrate 9g (Dietary Fiber 1g; Sugars 8g); Protein 1g
% Daily Value: Vitamin A 60%; Vitamin C 45%; Calcium 4%; Iron 4%
Exchanges: 1/2 Other Carbohydrate, 1 Vegetable, 1/2 Fat
Carbohydrate Choices: 1/2

KITCHEN TIPS

✿ Try a variety of fruits for this recipe. Blackberries, raspberries, honeydew melon and grapes add extra color and flavor.

Minted Watermelon Basket

Prep Time: 1 hr Start to Finish: 1 hr 15 min

1 whole watermelon, about 17 inches long
1 cup green grapes
3 cups cantaloupe balls
$\frac{1}{4}$ cup finely chopped fresh mint leaves
2 tablespoons lemon juice
$\frac{1}{4}$ cup sugar
1 cup fresh strawberries
Additional fresh mint leaves

1. Using long sharp knife, cut a thin slice from end of watermelon, being careful not to cut into flesh of watermelon. Stand watermelon on cut end. Using a washable marker, mark handle at top of basket by drawing 2 parallel lines that are $2\frac{1}{2}$ inches apart, starting at top of watermelon and drawing lines about 6 inches down each side.

2. Using a sharp knife, cut out a wedge-shaped piece of watermelon from each side, leaving the handle intact. Using a large spoon, gently scoop out watermelon flesh, leaving about 4 inches of flesh at bottom of watermelon.

3. With a small knife or garnishing tool, make "V" or scallop cuts about 2 inches apart on cut sides and handle of watermelon basket.

4. Cut watermelon into 1-inch chunks or use melon ball tool to make balls of watermelon. Measure 3 cups watermelon and place in large bowl. Refrigerate remaining watermelon for another use.

5. Add grapes and cantaloupe to watermelon in bowl. Gently mix in $\frac{1}{4}$ cup mint, the lemon juice and sugar. Refrigerate fruit mixture and watermelon basket separately until ready to use. Just before serving, fill watermelon basket with fruit mixture. Garnish with strawberries and additional mint leaves.

16 servings ($\frac{1}{2}$ cup each)
1 Serving: Calories 45 (Calories from Fat 0); Total Fat 0g (Saturated 0g; Trans 0g); Cholesterol 0mg; Sodium 5mg; Total Carbohydrate 10g (Dietary Fiber 0g; Sugars 9g); Protein 0g
% Daily Value: Vitamin A 25%; Vitamin C 35%; Calcium 0%; Iron 0%
Exchanges: $\frac{1}{2}$ Fruit
Carbohydrate Choices: $\frac{1}{2}$

KITCHEN TIPS

⚜ Place fragile fruits, such as kiwifruit, raspberries and strawberries, near the top of the basket because they crush easily.

⚜ The fruits can be prepared ahead and refrigerated in separate containers. Use any fruit combination you like. Clean fragile fruits the day of serving.

Mixed Greens Salad with Warm Walnut Dressing

Prep Time: 15 min Start to Finish: 15 min

6	cups mixed field greens (about 5 ounces)
6	tablespoons olive or vegetable oil
1/2	cup walnut halves
3	tablespoons red wine vinegar
1/4	teaspoon salt

4 servings
1 Serving: Calories 290 (Calories from Fat 260); Total Fat 29g (Saturated 3.5g; Trans 0g); Cholesterol 0mg; Sodium 170mg; Total Carbohydrate 5g (Dietary Fiber 2g; Sugars 1g); Protein 3g
% Daily Value: Vitamin A 80%; Vitamin C 20%; Calcium 6%; Iron 8%
Exchanges: 1 Vegetable, 6 Fat
Carbohydrate Choices: 1/2

KITCHEN TIPS

❂ For a gourmet flair, try using balsamic or raspberry-flavored vinegar.

1. Divide field greens among 4 salad plates.

2. Place 1 tablespoon of the oil in medium microwavable bowl. Add walnut halves; stir to coat. Microwave uncovered on High 2 minutes 30 seconds to 3 minutes, stirring every 30 seconds, until walnuts are fragrant.

3. Stir in remaining 5 tablespoons oil and the vinegar. Microwave uncovered on High about 30 seconds or until dressing is warm but not boiling. Add salt; stir until dressing is well mixed. Pour over salads. Serve immediately.

Spanish Olive Salad

Prep Time: 15 min Start to Finish: 15 min

About 1$\frac{1}{2}$ heads red leaf lettuce, torn into bite-size pieces (8 cups tightly packed)

2 large oranges, peeled, sliced

$\frac{1}{3}$ cup assorted marinated olives, pitted

$\frac{1}{2}$ small red onion, thinly sliced into rings (about $\frac{1}{2}$ cup)

$\frac{1}{2}$ cup balsamic vinaigrette dressing

1. Divide lettuce among 8 salad plates. Top with orange slices, olives and onion rings.

2. Just before serving, drizzle dressing over salads.

8 servings
1 Serving: Calories 100 (Calories from Fat 70); Total Fat 8g (Saturated 1g; Trans 0g); Cholesterol 0mg; Sodium 250mg; Total Carbohydrate 7g (Dietary Fiber 2g; Sugars 4g); Protein 0g
% Daily Value: Vitamin A 45%; Vitamin C 45%; Calcium 4%; Iron 2%
Exchanges: 1 Vegetable, 1$\frac{1}{2}$ Fat
Carbohydrate Choices: $\frac{1}{2}$

KITCHEN TIPS

✿ Use blood oranges from Spain, if available, for an authentic and beautiful salad.

Italian Chicken Salad

Prep Time: 10 min Start to Finish: 10 min

4 cups cut-up cooked chicken

2 bags (10 ounces each) ready-to-eat Italian-blend salad greens

2 cans (14 ounces each) artichoke hearts, drained, chopped

2 cans (4$\frac{1}{4}$ ounces each) chopped ripe olives

$\frac{1}{2}$ cup zesty Italian dressing

1. In very large (9-quart) bowl, mix all ingredients except dressing.

2. Toss salad with dressing until coated.

24 servings ($\frac{3}{4}$ cup each)
1 Serving: Calories 100 (Calories from Fat 45); Total Fat 5g (Saturated 1g; Trans 0g); Cholesterol 20mg; Sodium 230mg; Total Carbohydrate 5g (Dietary Fiber 2g; Sugars 1g); Protein 8g
% Daily Value: Vitamin A 30%; Vitamin C 15%; Calcium 4%; Iron 6%
Exchanges: 1 Vegetable, 1 Lean Meat, $\frac{1}{2}$ Fat
Carbohydrate Choices: $\frac{1}{2}$

KITCHEN TIPS

✿ Use a balsamic vinaigrette dressing instead of the zesty Italian.

Italian Chicken Salad

Spanish Olive Salad

Tortellini, Broccoli and Bacon Salad

Taos Tumble Salad

Tortellini, Broccoli and Bacon Salad

Prep Time: 25 min Start to Finish: 1 hr 25 min

- 2 bags (19 ounces each) frozen cheese-filled tortellini
- 4 cups broccoli florets
- 2 cups cherry tomatoes, each cut in half
- 2 tablespoons chopped fresh chives
- 1 cup reduced-fat coleslaw dressing
- 1 pound bacon, crisply cooked, crumbled
- 1/4 cup sunflower nuts

1. Cook and drain tortellini as directed on package. Rinse with cold water; drain.

2. In large (4-quart) bowl, mix tortellini, broccoli, tomatoes, chives and dressing. Cover and refrigerate at least 1 hour to blend flavors.

3. Just before serving, stir in bacon. Sprinkle with nuts.

24 servings (about 1/2 cup each)
1 Serving: Calories 160 (Calories from Fat 80); Total Fat 9g (Saturated 2.5g; Trans 0g); Cholesterol 45mg; Sodium 340mg; Total Carbohydrate 14g (Dietary Fiber 1g; Sugars 5g); Protein 6g
% Daily Value: Vitamin A 8%; Vitamin C 25%; Calcium 4%; Iron 6%
Exchanges: 1 Starch, 1/2 High-Fat Meat, 1 Fat
Carbohydrate Choices: 1

KITCHEN TIPS

✿ Omit the chives from the recipe. Just before serving, garnish the top of the salad with thinly sliced rings of red onion.

Quick

Taos Tumble Salad

Prep Time: 5 min Start to Finish: 5 min

- 2/3 cup Caesar dressing
- 1 teaspoon ground cumin
- 2 bags (10 ounces each) classic romaine lettuce salad or hearts of romaine lettuce
- 1 pint (2 cups) grape tomatoes or cherry tomatoes
- 1 cup shredded Cheddar cheese (4 ounces)
- 2 cups coarsely broken lime-flavored or regular tortilla chips

1. In small bowl, mix dressing and cumin. In large bowl, toss remaining ingredients with dressing mixture.

2. Sprinkle with additional cheese and chips if desired. Serve immediately.

8 servings
1 Serving: Calories 290 (Calories from Fat 190); Total Fat 21g (Saturated 5g; Trans 0g); Cholesterol 15mg; Sodium 430mg; Total Carbohydrate 17g (Dietary Fiber 3g; Sugars 3g); Protein 6g
% Daily Value: Vitamin A 90%; Vitamin C 40%; Calcium 10%; Iron 10%
Exchanges: 1 Starch, 1 Vegetable, 4 Fat
Carbohydrate Choices: 1

KITCHEN TIPS

✿ Try using shredded taco-flavored Cheddar cheese.

Limes

In the late 1700s, British sailors were issued a daily ration of lime juice to ward off scurvy on long sea voyages—hence the nickname "limey." The vitamin C–rich juice was served with a ration of rum (officers watched to make sure the sailors consumed both). Today, limes are still associated with a number of alcoholic beverages, from margaritas to mojitos, but their refreshing, tart flavor also provides zing to pies and preserves, as well as fish and poultry marinades. Although there are several varieties of limes, the two most commonly available in the United States are Persian limes and Key limes.

Persian Limes

Chances are when you think of limes, Persian limes come to mind. These oval-shaped, smooth-skinned bright green fruits are the most common variety found at grocery stores.

Shop: Look for brightly colored fruit that feels heavy for its size. Persian limes should feel hard when squeezed. A few brown spots won't diminish the flavor, but avoid limes with hard, shriveled skins.

Store: Whole limes can be stored in a plastic bag in the refrigerator for up to 10 days. Once limes are sliced, they will keep in the fridge for up to 5 days.

Use: Use lime wedges as garnish. Squeeze the juice over fish. Lime juice can also be used to make beverages, pies and frozen desserts.

By the Numbers:

Sure, you can purchase lime juice, but you can't beat the real deal in terms of taste. Here are some measurements:

▶ **1 medium lime** = 1 to 2 tablespoons juice

▶ **1 medium lime** = 1 to 2 teaspoons grated peel

Key (Mexican) Limes

Key limes are small—think golf ball-size—round in shape and yellow-green in color. They have more seeds, are less acidic and are more sour tasting than Persian limes.

CHOOSE

▶ Select smooth, firm fruit that is heavy for its size.

STORE/RIPEN

▶ Store Key limes in a plastic bag in the refrigerator for up to a week.

PREPARE

▶ Without a doubt, Key limes are most often used to make Key Lime Pie, but they can also be used similarly to Persian limes (see left).

FOR A LUSCIOUS RECIPE USING LIMES, TURN TO

No-Bake Lime Chiffon Pie, page 310

Chicken Kabob Caesar Salad

Prep Time: 20 min Start to Finish: 20 min

- 1 pound boneless skinless chicken breasts, cut into 1-inch pieces
- 8 medium green onions, cut into 4-inch pieces
- 1 large red bell pepper, cut into wedges
- ¾ cup Caesar dressing
- 1 bag (10 ounces) ready-to-eat romaine lettuce
- ½ cup croutons
- ¼ cup shredded Parmesan cheese

1. Heat gas or charcoal grill. On each of four 10-inch metal skewers, thread chicken, onions and bell pepper alternately, leaving ¼-inch space between each piece. Brush with ¼ cup of the dressing.

2. Place kabobs on grill. Cover grill; cook over medium heat 10 to 12 minutes or until chicken is no longer pink in center.

3. Arrange kabobs on lettuce; top with croutons and cheese. Serve with remaining ½ cup dressing.

4 servings
1 Serving: Calories 450 (Calories from Fat 280); Total Fat 31g (Saturated 6g; Trans 0g); Cholesterol 75mg; Sodium 670mg; Total Carbohydrate 11g (Dietary Fiber 3g; Sugars 5g); Protein 30g
% Daily Value: Vitamin A 120%; Vitamin C 170%; Calcium 15%; Iron 15%
Exchanges: ½ Other Carbohydrate, 1 Vegetable, 4 Very Lean Meat, 6 Fat
Carbohydrate Choices: 1

Black Bean Chili Salad

Prep Time: 10 min Start to Finish: 10 min

Chili Vinaigrette Dressing

- $1/4$ cup red wine vinegar
- 2 tablespoons vegetable oil
- $1/2$ teaspoon chili powder
- $1/4$ teaspoon ground cumin
- 1 small clove garlic, finely chopped

Salad

- 1 cup Green Giant Niblets frozen whole kernel corn (from 1-pound bag), rinsed to thaw, drained
- 1 cup diced jicama
- 1 medium tomato, seeded and chopped ($3/4$ cup)
- 2 medium green onions, sliced (2 tablespoons)
- 2 cans (15 ounces each) black beans, rinsed, drained

1. In large glass or plastic bowl, mix all dressing ingredients.

2. Stir in all salad ingredients.

4 servings
1 Serving: Calories 390 (Calories from Fat 70); Total Fat 8g (Saturated 1.5g; Trans 0g); Cholesterol 0mg; Sodium 10mg; Total Carbohydrate 62g (Dietary Fiber 15g; Sugars 8g); Protein 18g
% Daily Value: Vitamin A 10%; Vitamin C 25%; Calcium 15%; Iron 30%
Exchanges: $3^{1}/_{2}$ Starch, $1/2$ Other Carbohydrate, 1 Very Lean Meat, 1 Fat
Carbohydrate Choices: 4

KITCHEN TIPS

❊ What's jicama? Sometimes referred to as the "Mexican potato," this sweet and nutty root vegetable can be enjoyed raw or cooked.

Neptune Pasta Salad

Prep Time: 25 min Start to Finish: 25 min

- 1 box Betty Crocker Suddenly Salad® Caesar pasta salad mix
- 1/4 cup cold water
- 3 tablespoons vegetable oil
- 1 package (8 ounces) refrigerated flake-style imitation crabmeat
- 1 1/2 cups broccoli florets

1. Fill 3-quart or larger saucepan two-thirds full of water. Heat to boiling. Add contents of Pasta pouch to boiling water. Gently boil about 12 minutes, stirring occasionally, until pasta is tender; drain. Rinse with cold water until chilled; drain.

2. In large bowl, mix Seasoning mix, water and oil. Stir in pasta mixture, imitation crabmeat and broccoli. Toss with Croutons and Parmesan Topping just before serving.

4 servings
1 Serving: Calories 350 (Calories from Fat 110); Total Fat 12g (Saturated 1.5g; Trans 0g); Cholesterol 15mg; Sodium 1220mg; Total Carbohydrate 43g (Dietary Fiber 2g; Sugars 5g); Protein 16g
% Daily Value: Vitamin A 6%; Vitamin C 50%; Calcium 4%; Iron 10%
Exchanges: 2 Starch, 1/2 Other Carbohydrate, 1 Vegetable, 1 Very Lean Meat, 2 Fat
Carbohydrate Choices: 3

KITCHEN TIPS

✿ Add 1 cup cherry tomato halves for a burst of color and vine-ripe flavor!

Dijon Chicken and Pasta Salad

Prep Time: 25 min Start to Finish: 25 min

- 1 box Betty Crocker Suddenly Salad classic pasta salad mix
- 3 tablespoons cold water
- 2 tablespoons vegetable oil
- 2 tablespoons Dijon mustard
- 1 cup cubed cooked chicken

1. Fill 3-quart or larger saucepan two-thirds full of water. Heat to boiling. Add contents of Pasta pouch to boiling water. Gently boil about 12 minutes, stirring occasionally, until pasta is tender; drain. Rinse with cold water until chilled; drain.

2. In large bowl, mix Seasoning mix, water, oil and mustard. Stir in pasta mixture and chicken. Toss with Topping before serving.

4 servings
1 Serving: Calories 320 (Calories from Fat 100); Total Fat 11g (Saturated 1.5g; Trans 0g); Cholesterol 30mg; Sodium 1080mg; Total Carbohydrate 38g (Dietary Fiber 2g; Sugars 5g); Protein 16g
% Daily Value: Vitamin A 0%; Vitamin C 0%; Calcium 4%; Iron 15%
Exchanges: 2 Starch, 1/2 Other Carbohydrate, 1 1/2 Lean Meat, 1 Fat
Carbohydrate Choices: 2 1/2

KITCHEN TIPS

✿ One cup of frozen cooked (thawed) imitation crabmeat chunks instead of chicken turns this into a seafood delight.

Dijon Chicken and Pasta Salad

Neptune Pasta Salad

Easy Club Salad

Prep Time: 15 min Start to Finish: 15 min

6	cups bite-size pieces lettuce
1½	cups cut-up cooked chicken
1	medium tomato, cut into eighths
⅓	cup Thousand Island dressing
⅓	cup Betty Crocker Bac-Os® bacon flavor bits or chips
	Hard-cooked egg slices, if desired

1. In large bowl, toss all ingredients except egg slices.

2. Garnish salad with egg slices.

4 servings
1 Serving: Calories 210 (Calories from Fat 110); Total Fat 12g
(Saturated 2.5g; Trans 0g); Cholesterol 50mg; Sodium 370mg; Total
Carbohydrate 6g (Dietary Fiber 2g; Sugars 4g); Protein 19g
% Daily Value: Vitamin A 10%; Vitamin C 10%; Calcium 6%; Iron 8%
Exchanges: 1 Vegetable, 2½ Lean Meat, 1 Fat
Carbohydrate Choices: ½

KITCHEN TIPS

❀ In a hurry? Just use two 6-ounce cans of chunk chicken, drained, instead of the cooked chicken.

Quick

Antipasto Dinner Salad

Prep Time: 15 min Start to Finish: 15 min

2 pints (4 cups) deli vinaigrette-style pasta salad with vegetables

$1/2$ pound Cheddar cheese, cut into $1/2$-inch cubes ($1^1/2$ cups)

$1/2$ pound hard salami, cut into $1/2$-inch pieces ($1^1/2$ cups)

2 hard-cooked eggs, cut into wedges

1 medium tomato, cut into wedges

$1/2$ cup pitted ripe olives, drained

1. In large bowl, mix pasta salad, cheese and salami.

2. Garnish salad with eggs, tomato and olives.

4 servings
1 Serving: Calories 670 (Calories from Fat 430); Total Fat 48g (Saturated 21g; Trans 1g); Cholesterol 210mg; Sodium 2000mg; Total Carbohydrate 24g (Dietary Fiber 4g; Sugars 7g); Protein 35g
% Daily Value: Vitamin A 35%; Vitamin C 60%; Calcium 35%; Iron 20%
Exchanges: 1 Starch, $1/2$ Other Carbohydrate, 1 Vegetable, 4 High-Fat Meat, 3 Fat
Carbohydrate Choices: $1^1/2$

KITCHEN TIPS

✿ If the deli vinaigrette-style pasta salad with vegetables is not available, cook your favorite pasta and toss it with balsamic vinaigrette or Italian dressing and 2 cups assorted cut-up fresh vegetables.

Steak and Potato Salad

Prep Time: 30 min Start to Finish: 30 min

¾ pound small red potatoes, cut in half

⅔ cup honey Dijon dressing

1 boneless beef top sirloin steak, ¾ inch thick (about ¾ pound)

¼ teaspoon salt

¼ teaspoon coarsely ground pepper

4 cups bite-size pieces romaine lettuce

2 medium tomatoes, cut into thin wedges

½ cup thinly sliced red onion

1. Heat gas or charcoal grill. In 2- or 2½-quart saucepan, place potatoes; add enough water to cover potatoes. Heat to boiling; reduce heat to medium. Cook uncovered 5 to 8 minutes or just until potatoes are tender.

2. Drain potatoes; place in medium bowl. Add 2 tablespoons of the dressing; toss to coat. Place potatoes in grill basket (grill "wok") if desired. Brush beef with 1 tablespoon of the dressing; sprinkle with salt and pepper.

3. Place beef and grill basket on grill. Cover grill; cook over medium heat 8 to 15 minutes, turning once, until beef is desired doneness and potatoes are golden brown. Cut beef into thin slices.

4. Divide lettuce, tomatoes and onion among 4 plates. Top with beef and potatoes; drizzle with remaining dressing. Sprinkle with additional pepper if desired.

4 servings
1 Serving: Calories 340 (Calories from Fat 150); Total Fat 17g (Saturated 3g; Trans 0g); Cholesterol 50mg; Sodium 430mg; Total Carbohydrate 25g (Dietary Fiber 4g; Sugars 8g); Protein 22g
% Daily Value: Vitamin A 80%; Vitamin C 25%; Calcium 6%; Iron 20%
Exchanges: 1 Starch, ½ Other Carbohydrate, 1 Vegetable, 2½ Lean Meat, 1½ Fat
Carbohydrate Choices: 1½

Steak and Potato Salad

Asian Steak Salad

Prep Time: 25 min Start to Finish: 25 min

- ¼ cup citrus vinaigrette
- ¼ cup teriyaki marinade and sauce (from 10-ounce bottle)
- 1 pound cut-up beef for stir-fry
- 1 package (3 ounces) Oriental-flavor ramen noodle soup mix
- 1 bag (10 ounces) romaine and leaf lettuce mix
- 1 cup fresh snow (Chinese) pea pods, strings removed
- ½ cup julienne-cut carrots (from 10-ounce bag)
- 1 can (11 ounces) mandarin orange segments, drained

1. In small bowl, mix citrus vinaigrette and teriyaki marinade; set aside.

2. Spray 12-inch skillet with cooking spray; heat over medium-high heat. Place beef in skillet; sprinkle with 1 teaspoon seasoning from soup mix. (Discard remaining seasoning packet.) Cook beef 4 to 6 minutes, stirring occasionally, until brown. Stir in 1 tablespoon of the vinaigrette mixture.

3. Into large bowl, break block of noodles into small pieces. Add lettuce, pea pods, carrots and orange segments. Add remaining vinaigrette mixture; toss until well coated. Divide mixture among 6 plates; top with beef.

6 servings
1 Serving: Calories 200 (Calories from Fat 80); Total Fat 8g (Saturated 1.5g; Trans 0g); Cholesterol 45mg; Sodium 770mg; Total Carbohydrate 11g (Dietary Fiber 2g; Sugars 7g); Protein 20g
% Daily Value: Vitamin A 90%; Vitamin C 25%; Calcium 4%; Iron 15%
Exchanges: ½ Other Carbohydrate, 1 Vegetable, 2½ Lean Meat
Carbohydrate Choices: 1

Mixed Greens with Cranberry Vinaigrette

Prep Time: 20 min Start to Finish: 20 min

Vinaigrette
- ⅓ cup vegetable oil
- ¼ cup frozen (thawed) cranberry juice concentrate
- 1 teaspoon Dijon mustard
- ¼ teaspoon salt
- ½ cup sweetened dried cranberries

Salad
- 2 bags (5 ounces each) mixed spring greens
- 1 small bunch watercress, torn into pieces
- 2 tart red apples, thinly sliced, slices cut in half
- 1 avocado, pitted, peeled and sliced

1. In small bowl, beat all vinaigrette ingredients except cranberries with wire whisk until smooth. Stir in cranberries.

2. In serving bowl, toss all salad ingredients with vinaigrette just before serving.

12 servings (1⅓ cups each)
1 Serving: Calories 130 (Calories from Fat 80); Total Fat 8g (Saturated 1g; Trans 0g); Cholesterol 0mg; Sodium 70mg; Total Carbohydrate 12g (Dietary Fiber 2g; Sugars 9g); Protein 0g
% Daily Value: Vitamin A 25%; Vitamin C 15%; Calcium 0%; Iron 2%
Exchanges: ½ Other Carbohydrate, 1 Vegetable, 1½ Fat
Carbohydrate Choices: 1

KITCHEN TIPS

- ❂ Watercress has small, crisp, dark green leaves and a peppery flavor. It is sold in small bunches in the produce section of the supermarket.
- ❂ Use any type of mixed greens for this salad; try baby greens, spring mix or Italian mix.

Mixed Greens with Cranberry Vinaigrette

Asian Steak Salad

Quick & Low-Fat

Italian Tuna Toss

Prep Time: 15 min Start to Finish: 15 min

1 bag (10 ounces) mixed salad greens

1 bag (12 ounces) cauliflowerets (about 2¼ cups)

1 medium cucumber, sliced (1½ cups)

2 cans (6 ounces each) tuna in water, drained

1 jar (2 ounces) sliced pimientos, drained (¼ cup)

⅓ cup Italian dressing

¼ cup Betty Crocker Bac-Os bacon flavor bits or chips

1. In large bowl, toss all ingredients except dressing and bacon bits.

2. Toss salad with dressing and bacon bits.

6 servings
1 Serving: Calories 160 (Calories from Fat 60); Total Fat 7g (Saturated 0.5g; Trans 0g); Cholesterol 15mg; Sodium 230mg; Total Carbohydrate 8g (Dietary Fiber 3g; Sugars 4g); Protein 16g
% Daily Value: Vitamin A 50%; Vitamin C 70%; Calcium 6%; Iron 10%
Exchanges: 1 Vegetable, 2 Very Lean Meat, 1 Fat
Carbohydrate Choices: ½

KITCHEN TIPS

❂ This salad is also delicious made with ¼ pound diced salami (about ¾ cup) instead of the tuna.

Spring Onion Soup with Garlic Croutons

Prep Time: 30 min Start to Finish: 45 min

Croutons

- 3 tablespoons butter or margarine
- 1 cup $^3/_4$-inch cubes day-old French bread (crusts removed)
- 1 teaspoon garlic powder

Soup

- 3 tablespoons butter or margarine
- 1 medium white onion, finely chopped ($^1/_2$ cup)
- 4 cups water
- 2 tablespoons chicken soup base (from 8-ounce jar)
- 16 medium green onions, sliced (1 cup)
- $^1/_2$ teaspoon pepper
- 4 tablespoons shredded Parmesan cheese

1. Heat oven to 375°F. In 15 × 10 × 1-inch pan or cookie sheet with sides, melt 3 tablespoons butter in oven. Add bread cubes and garlic powder to butter; toss well to combine. Bake about 10 minutes, stirring occasionally, until bread cubes are crisp and brown.

2. Meanwhile, in 2-quart saucepan, melt 3 tablespoons butter over medium heat. Add white onion; cook over medium heat 5 to 7 minutes, stirring occasionally, until onion is translucent. Stir in water, soup base, green onions and pepper. Heat to boiling; reduce heat. Simmer uncovered 10 minutes. Stir before serving.

3. Top each serving with $^1/_4$ cup croutons and 1 tablespoon cheese.

4 servings (1 cup each)
1 Serving: Calories 240 (Calories from Fat 180); Total Fat 20g (Saturated 12g; Trans 1g); Cholesterol 50mg; Sodium 1560mg; Total Carbohydrate 10g (Dietary Fiber 1g; Sugars 3g); Protein 5g
% Daily Value: Vitamin A 15%; Vitamin C 6%; Calcium 15%; Iron 6%
Exchanges: $^1/_2$ Starch, $^1/_2$ Medium-Fat Meat, 3$^1/_2$ Fat
Carbohydrate Choices: $^1/_2$

KITCHEN TIPS

✿ The soup can be prepared up to a day ahead through step 2 and refrigerated for advance party preparation.

Slow Cooker Beef and Bean Chili

Prep Time: 25 min Start to Finish: 8 hr 25 min

1 tablespoon olive or vegetable oil

1 large onion, coarsely chopped (1 cup)

2 teaspoons finely chopped garlic

2 tablespoons chili powder

1 tablespoon ground cumin

1 teaspoon salt

1/8 teaspoon pepper

2 pounds beef stew meat

2 cans (15 ounces each) Progresso® black beans, rinsed, drained

2 cans (14.5 ounces each) diced tomatoes with green chilies, undrained

1/2 cup water

1. In 12-inch skillet, heat oil over medium-high heat. Add onion and garlic; cook 4 to 5 minutes, stirring frequently, until onion is softened.

2. Stir in chili powder, cumin, salt, pepper and beef. Cook 6 to 8 minutes, stirring occasionally, until beef is lightly browned.

3. In 3- to 4-quart slow cooker, place beef mixture. Stir in beans, tomatoes and water.

4. Cover; cook on Low heat setting 8 to 10 hours. Stir well before serving.

5 servings (1 1/2 cups each)
1 Serving: Calories 630 (Calories from Fat 230); Total Fat 26g (Saturated 9g; Trans 1g); Cholesterol 105mg; Sodium 810mg; Total Carbohydrate 51g (Dietary Fiber 13g; Sugars 10g); Protein 49g
% Daily Value: Vitamin A 20%; Vitamin C 15%; Calcium 20%; Iron 60%
Exchanges: 2 Starch, 1 Other Carbohydrate, 1 Vegetable, 6 Lean Meat, 1 1/2 Fat
Carbohydrate Choices: 3 1/2

KITCHEN TIPS

❂ If you're not a fan of black beans, kidney beans are a great substitute.
❂ Packages of stew meat can have pieces of different sizes. Cut any large pieces into smaller same-size pieces so that everything cooks in the same amount of time.

Beef Fajita Salad

Prep Time: 30 min Start to Finish: 30 min

1½ cups Old El Paso Thick'n Chunky salsa
¼ cup olive or vegetable oil
2 teaspoons chili powder
1 teaspoon ground cumin
1 teaspoon garlic salt
1 beef sirloin steak, about 1 inch thick
2 medium bell peppers, sliced
1 medium onion, sliced
9 cups bite-size pieces romaine lettuce
Guacamole and sour cream, if desired

1. Heat gas or charcoal grill. In small bowl, mix salsa and oil; set aside.

2. In another small bowl, mix chili powder, cumin and garlic salt. Sprinkle mixture over both sides of beef. Place bell peppers and onion in grill basket (grill "wok").

3. Place beef and grill basket on grill. Cover grill; cook over medium heat about 5 minutes for medium-rare or about 7 minutes for medium; turn beef. Shake grill basket or stir vegetables. Cover grill; cook 5 to 7 minutes longer or until desired beef doneness.

4. In large bowl, toss lettuce, grilled pepper and onion and half of the salsa mixture. Cut beef diagonally into ½-inch slices; place on salad. Serve with remaining salsa mixture. Top with guacamole and sour cream, if desired.

6 servings
1 Serving: Calories 240 (Calories from Fat 110); Total Fat 12g (Saturated 2g; Trans 0g); Cholesterol 45 mg; Sodium 660 mg; Total Carbohydrate 14g (Dietary Fiber 3g; Sugars 6 g); Protein 19g
% Daily Value: Vitamin A 130%; Vitamin C 80%; Calcium 4%; Iron 15%
Exchanges: ½ Other Carbohydrate, 1 Vegetable, 2½ Lean Meat, 1 Fat
Carbohydrate Choices: 1

Turkey-Spaetzle Soup

Prep Time: 25 min Start to Finish: 35 min

- 2 tablespoons vegetable oil
- 1 large onion, finely chopped (½ cup)
- 1 medium carrot, finely chopped (½ cup)
- 1 medium stalk celery, finely chopped (½ cup)
- 1 clove garlic, finely chopped
- ¼ cup Gold Medal all-purpose flour
- 2 teaspoons dried thyme leaves
- ¼ teaspoon pepper
- 2 cups diced cooked turkey
- 1 can (49½ ounces) chicken broth (6 cups)
- 1 bag (12 ounces) frozen spaetzle
  Chopped fresh parsley, if desired

1. In 4-quart saucepan, heat oil over medium-high heat. Add onion, carrot, celery and garlic; cook about 2 minutes, stirring frequently, until crisp-tender.

2. Gradually stir in flour, thyme and pepper; cook about 1 minute, stirring constantly. Stir in turkey and broth; heat to boiling.

3. Stir in frozen spaetzle. Cook 2 to 3 minutes, stirring occasionally, until spaetzle are tender. Sprinkle with parsley.

6 servings (1⅓ cups each)
1 Serving: Calories 240 (Calories from Fat 90); Total Fat 10g (Saturated 2.5g; Trans 0g); Cholesterol 70mg; Sodium 1180mg; Total Carbohydrate 17g (Dietary Fiber 2g; Sugars 2g); Protein 21g
% Daily Value: Vitamin A 30%; Vitamin C 2%; Calcium 4%; Iron 15%
Exchanges: 1 Starch, 2½ Lean Meat, ½ Fat
Carbohydrate Choices: 1

KITCHEN TIPS

✿ If you prefer, substitute 3 cups frozen egg noodles (from a 16-ounce bag) for the spaetzle.

✿ Spaetzle are tiny egg noodles that are firm enough to use in soup. They have a rich, eggy flavor.

Pizzas, Sandwiches and Burgers

Fun Forkless Foods

Slow Cooker Italian Shredded Beef Hoagies (page 95)

Italian Pesto Pizza (page 78)

Italian Pesto Pizza

Prep Time: 25 min Start to Finish: 25 min

$\frac{1}{2}$ cup basil pesto

1 package (14 ounces) prebaked original Italian pizza crust or other 12-inch ready-to-serve pizza crust

2 cups shredded mozzarella cheese (8 ounces)

3 large roma (plum) tomatoes, cut into $\frac{1}{4}$-inch slices

$\frac{1}{2}$ cup whole basil leaves

$\frac{1}{4}$ cup shredded Parmesan cheese

1. Heat gas or charcoal grill. Brush pesto over pizza crust. Sprinkle 1 cup of the mozzarella cheese over pesto. Arrange tomato slices and basil leaves on cheese. Sprinkle with remaining 1 cup mozzarella cheese and the Parmesan cheese.

2. Place pizza on grill. Cover grill; cook over medium heat 6 to 8 minutes or until crust is crisp and cheese is melted. (If crust browns too quickly, place a piece of foil between crust and grill.)

4 servings

1 Serving: Calories 640 (Calories from Fat 320); Total Fat 36g (Saturated 14g; Trans 0.5g); Cholesterol 50mg; Sodium 1160mg; Total Carbohydrate 50g (Dietary Fiber 3g; Sugars 2g); Protein 31g
% Daily Value: Vitamin A 25%; Vitamin C 6%; Calcium 60%; Iron 20%
Exchanges: 3 Starch, 1 Vegetable, 3 Medium-Fat Meat, 4 Fat
Carbohydrate Choices: 3

KITCHEN TIPS

✿ If you have lots of fresh basil, make your own pesto. Place 2 cups firmly packed basil leaves, $\frac{3}{4}$ cup grated Parmesan cheese, $\frac{1}{4}$ cup pine nuts, $\frac{1}{2}$ cup olive oil and 3 cloves garlic in a blender or food processor. Cover and blend on medium speed about 3 minutes or until smooth.

Brie Quesadilla with Mango Guacamole

Prep Time: 35 min Start to Finish: 35 min

Guacamole

1 medium avocado, pitted, peeled and quartered

$^1/_2$ small jalapeño chili, seeded, finely chopped

1 small clove garlic, finely chopped

2 tablespoons lime juice

$^1/_4$ cup chopped fresh cilantro

$^1/_8$ teaspoon salt

$^1/_2$ medium mango, pitted, peeled and diced

Quesadillas

6 (8-inch) Old El Paso flour tortillas for burritos (from 11.5-ounce package)

1 round (6 to 7 ounces) Brie cheese, cut into $^1/_8$-inch strips (not wedges)

$^1/_4$ pound thinly sliced cooked ham (from deli)

1 tablespoon vegetable oil

1. In food processor, place all guacamole ingredients except mango. Cover; process with 3 or 4 on/off turns until coarsely chopped. Place in small bowl; stir in mango. Set aside.

2. Top half of each tortilla with cheese and ham. Fold tortilla over and press down. Brush tops with oil.

3. Heat 12-inch skillet over medium-high heat. Place 3 quesadillas, oil sides down, in skillet. Brush tops with half of remaining oil. Cook 2 to 3 minutes, turning once, until both sides are golden brown and cheese is melted. Repeat with remaining quesadillas and oil. Cut each into 4 wedges. Serve with guacamole.

24 servings (1 wedge and 1 tablespoon guacamole each)
1 Serving: Calories 80 (Calories from Fat 45); Total Fat 5g (Saturated 2g; Trans 0g); Cholesterol 10mg; Sodium 190mg; Total Carbohydrate 7g (Dietary Fiber 0g; Sugars 0g); Protein 3g
% Daily Value: Vitamin A 0%; Vitamin C 4%; Calcium 4%; Iron 2%
Exchanges: $^1/_2$ Starch, 1 Fat
Carbohydrate Choices: $^1/_2$

KITCHEN TIPS

✿ If you prefer, you can mash the guacamole ingredients with a fork instead of using a food processor.

✿ The quesadillas can be assembled, wrapped and refrigerated several hours before cooking.

Mango-Pepper Salsa Crostini

Grilled Artichoke Bruschetta

Grilled Artichoke Bruschetta

Prep Time: 20 min Start to Finish: 20 min

8 slices (4 × 3 × ¹/₂ inch) Italian or French bread
1 tablespoon extra-virgin olive oil
1 jar (7.5 ounces) marinated artichoke hearts, well drained, chopped
1 jar (2 ounces) diced pimientos, well drained
¹/₃ cup chopped pitted Kalamata olives
¹/₂ cup chives-and-onion cream cheese (from 8-ounce container)

1. Heat gas or charcoal grill. Brush 1 side of bread slices with oil. On ungreased cookie sheet, place bread, oil sides down. In medium bowl, mix remaining ingredients. Spread artichoke mixture over bread slices.

2. Place slices, oil sides down, on grill (remove from cookie sheet). Cover grill; cook over low heat 4 to 5 minutes or until bottoms are golden brown and topping is hot. Cut slices in half.

16 bruschetta
1 Bruschetta: Calories 70 (Calories from Fat 35); Total Fat 4g
(Saturated 1.5g; Trans 0g); Cholesterol 5mg; Sodium 180mg; Total
Carbohydrate 7g (Dietary Fiber 1g; Sugars 0g); Protein 2g
% Daily Value: Vitamin A 4%; Vitamin C 4%; Calcium 2%; Iron 4%
Exchanges: ¹/₂ Starch, 1 Fat
Carbohydrate Choices: ¹/₂

KITCHEN TIPS

✿ If you can't find pitted olives, lay the flat side of a chef's knife over each olive on a work surface; press firmly on knife with the heel of your hand to loosen the pit.

✿ Assemble the bruschetta several hours ahead of time. Cover and refrigerate them until you are ready to grill.

✿ To broil, set oven to broil. Brush 1 side of bread slices with oil. Place slices, oil sides up, on rack in broiler pan. Broil with tops 6 inches from heat about 2 minutes or until golden brown. Remove from oven. Turn bread slices over; spread with artichoke mixture. Broil 6 to 8 minutes or until topping is hot.

Mango-Pepper Salsa Crostini

Prep Time: 30 min Start to Finish: 1 hr 30 min

¹/₂ medium mango, pitted, peeled and diced (¹/₂ cup)
1 medium green onion, thinly sliced (1 tablespoon)
¹/₄ cup diced red bell pepper
2 tablespoons chopped fresh cilantro
¹/₄ jalapeño chili, seeded, finely chopped
2 tablespoons lime juice
1 container (8 ounces) pineapple cream cheese spread
32 thin slices baguette French bread

1. In medium glass or plastic bowl, mix all ingredients except cream cheese and bread. Cover; refrigerate 1 hour to blend flavors.

2. Spread cream cheese on baguette slices. Spoon about 1 teaspoon salsa over cream cheese, using slotted spoon.

32 crostini
1 Crostini: Calories 50 (Calories from Fat 20); Total Fat 2.5g
(Saturated 1.5g; Trans 0g); Cholesterol 5mg; Sodium 110mg; Total
Carbohydrate 6g (Dietary Fiber 0g; Sugars 0g); Protein 1g
% Daily Value: Vitamin A 2%; Vitamin C 6%; Calcium 0%; Iron 2%
Exchanges: ¹/₂ Starch, ¹/₂ Fat
Carbohydrate Choices: ¹/₂

KITCHEN TIPS

✿ Fruit salsas are very popular. You can use a purchased fruit salsa instead of making your own.

✿ Peel and dice the remaining mango and spoon it over ice cream for a mango sundae.

Mediterranean Bread Crisps

Prep Time: 15 min Start to Finish: 15 min

3 tablespoons butter or margarine, softened

3 tablespoons crumbled feta cheese

12 thin slices French bread

3 tablespoons chopped Greek olives

Fresh oregano leaves, if desired

6 servings (2 crisps each)
1 Serving: Calories 130 (Calories from Fat 70); Total Fat 8g (Saturated 4.5g; Trans 0.5g); Cholesterol 20mg; Sodium 270mg; Total Carbohydrate 12g (Dietary Fiber 0g; Sugars 0g); Protein 3g
% Daily Value: Vitamin A 4%; Vitamin C 0%; Calcium 4%; Iron 4%
Exchanges: ½ Starch, ½ High-Fat Meat, 1 Fat
Carbohydrate Choices: 1

1. Heat gas or charcoal grill. In small bowl, mix butter and cheese; set aside.

2. Place bread on grill. Cover grill; cook over medium heat 3 to 5 minutes or until lightly toasted.

3. Spread cheese mixture over toasted sides of bread. Sprinkle with olives. Place bread, olive sides up, on grill. Cover; cook 3 to 5 minutes or until cheese is melted. Garnish with oregano leaves.

KITCHEN TIPS

❈ To bake the crisps in the oven, place the bread slices on an ungreased cookie sheet, top as directed and bake at 400°F for 10 minutes or until crisp.

❈ If you prefer, you can substitute ripe olives or green olives for the Greek olives.

Basil-Turkey Mini Focaccia Sandwiches

Prep Time: 20 min Start to Finish: 1 hr 5 min

Focaccia

- 1 can (13.8 ounces) Pillsbury refrigerated pizza crust
- 1 tablespoon olive or vegetable oil
- $1/2$ teaspoon garlic powder
- $1/2$ teaspoon Italian seasoning
- $1/4$ cup shredded Parmesan cheese (1 ounce)

Filling

- 1 container (6.5 ounces) herb-and-garlic spreadable cheese, softened
- 2 medium roma (plum) tomatoes, thinly sliced
- 1 package (1 ounce) fresh basil leaves, stems removed
- $1/2$ pound thinly sliced smoked turkey (from deli)

1. Heat oven to 400°F. Grease large cookie sheet with shortening or cooking spray. Unroll pizza crust dough; press into 12 × 8-inch rectangle on cookie sheet. With end of handle of wooden spoon, press indentations in top, about 1 inch apart. Brush dough with oil. Sprinkle with garlic powder, Italian seasoning and Parmesan cheese.

2. Bake 10 to 13 minutes or until golden brown. Cool 30 minutes; cut in half horizontally.

3. Spread cut side of bottom of focaccia with spreadable cheese. Top with single layer of tomatoes and basil. Layer turkey evenly over basil. Place top of focaccia, cut side down, over turkey; press down. Pierce through all layers with toothpicks, placing them every $1^{1}/_{2}$ inches over focaccia. With long serrated knife, cut between toothpicks into squares.

40 mini-sandwiches
1 Sandwich: Calories 50 (Calories from Fat 25); Total Fat 2.5g (Saturated 1.5g; Trans 0g); Cholesterol 10mg; Sodium 160mg; Total Carbohydrate 5g (Dietary Fiber 0g; Sugars 0g); Protein 0g
% Daily Value: Vitamin A 2%; Vitamin C 0%; Calcium 0%; Iron 2%
Exchanges: $1/2$ Starch, $1/2$ Fat
Carbohydrate Choices: $1/2$

KITCHEN TIPS

❀ Use purchased focaccia bread, if you prefer. Most purchased focaccia breads are round, so the number of mini sandwiches will vary.

❀ You can use fresh spinach leaves instead of the fresh basil.

Corned Beef and Swiss Mini Slices

Prep Time: 30 min Start to Finish: 30 min

1 loaf (20-inch) baguette French bread (12 ounces), cut horizontally in half

½ cup Thousand Island dressing

3 roma (plum) tomatoes, thinly sliced

½ pound thinly sliced corned beef

8 slices (1 ounce each) Swiss cheese, cut into 2-inch strips

1. Heat gas or charcoal grill for indirect-heat cooking as directed by manufacturer. Cut 1 (18 × 10-inch) sheet of heavy-duty foil. Spread cut sides of baguette with dressing. Layer both halves evenly with tomatoes, corned beef and cheese. Place bread halves on foil.

2. Place bread halves (on foil) on grill for indirect cooking. Cover grill; cook over low heat about 10 minutes or until cheese is melted. Cut into 1½-inch slices.

24 slices

1 Slice: Calories 120 (Calories from Fat 60); Total Fat 7g (Saturated 2.5g; Trans 0g); Cholesterol 20mg; Sodium 260mg; Total Carbohydrate 8g (Dietary Fiber 0g; Sugars 0g); Protein 6g
% Daily Value: Vitamin A 2%; Vitamin C 0%; Calcium 10%; Iron 4%
Exchanges: ½ Starch, ½ Medium-Fat Meat, 1 Fat
Carbohydrate Choices: ½

KITCHEN TIPS

✿ For classic Reuben sandwich flavor, set out small bowls of sauerkraut and baby dill pickles to accompany the mini slices.

✿ If your grill has hot spots, move the sandwiches occasionally as they cook.

Prosciutto-Pesto Napoleons

Prep Time: 25 min Start to Finish: 1 hr 25 min

1 sheet frozen puff pastry (from 17.3-ounce box)

1 egg, beaten

1 tablespoon sesame seed

1/4 cup refrigerated basil pesto (from 7-ounce container)

1 cup roasted red bell peppers (from 7-ounce jar), drained, cut into thin strips and drained on paper towels

1/4 pound thinly sliced prosciutto, cut crosswise into strips

1. Thaw pastry at room temperature 30 minutes. Heat oven to 400°F. Unfold pastry; brush top with beaten egg. Sprinkle with sesame seed. Cut pastry into thirds along fold lines. Cut each strip crosswise into 8 rectangles, each 3 × 1¼ inches. On ungreased cookie sheets, place rectangles 2 inches apart.

2. Bake about 15 minutes or until puffed and golden brown. Remove from cookie sheets to wire rack. Cool completely, about 15 minutes.

3. Cut each rectangle in half horizontally. Spread 1/2 teaspoon pesto on cut side of bottom of each rectangle. Top with bell peppers and prosciutto strips. Place tops of rectangles over prosciutto.

24 Napoleons
1 Napoleon: Calories 80 (Calories from Fat 50); Total Fat 5g (Saturated 1.5g; Trans 0g); Cholesterol 20mg; Sodium 105mg; Total Carbohydrate 5g (Dietary Fiber 0g; Sugars 0g); Protein 2g
% Daily Value: Vitamin A 6%; Vitamin C 8%; Calcium 0%; Iron 4%
Exchanges: 1/2 Starch, 1 Fat
Carbohydrate Choices: 1/2

KITCHEN TIPS

✿ Classic dessert napoleons consist of layers of puff pastry filled with custard and fruit. You'll enjoy this impressive savory version.

✿ Puff pastry is very easy to work with. Just thaw it and cut it to shape. All of the work is done for you.

Party Ribbon Sandwiches

Prep Time: 35 min Start to Finish: 4 hr 35 min

Shrimp Salad Sandwich Filling

1	cup frozen cooked deveined peeled salad shrimp, thawed
1	tablespoon finely chopped fresh parsley
1	teaspoon lemon juice
1/4	teaspoon pepper
1/2	teaspoon dried dill weed
1/4	cup mayonnaise or salad dressing

Curried Turkey Sandwich Filling

1	cup chopped smoked cooked turkey
1/4	teaspoon pepper
1/2	teaspoon curry powder
1/3	cup mayonnaise or salad dressing
1/4	cup finely chopped celery

Cream Cheese and Olive Sandwich Filling

1	package (3 ounces) cream cheese, softened
1	cup shredded Mexican cheese blend
1/4	cup mayonnaise or salad dressing
1/4	cup sliced Spanish olives

Bread

8	slices white bread, crusts removed
8	slices whole wheat bread, crusts removed

1. Place all shrimp filling ingredients in food processor. Cover; process 3 to 5 seconds or until mixture is creamy. Remove from food processor; set aside.

2. Place all turkey filling ingredients except celery in food processor. Cover; process 3 to 5 seconds or until mixture is creamy. Stir in celery. Remove from food processor; set aside.

3. Place all cheese and olive filling ingredients except olives in food processor. Cover; process 3 to 5 seconds or until mixture is creamy. Stir in olives.

4. To assemble ribbon sandwiches, place one slice white bread on cutting board. Spread 5 tablespoons cheese and olive filling over white bread. Top with 1 slice wheat bread; spread with 1/4 cup turkey filling. Top with 1 slice white bread; spread with 1/4 cup shrimp filling. Top with 1 slice wheat bread. Repeat process 3 more times to make a total of 4 sandwich stacks. Wrap each in plastic wrap; refrigerate at least 4 hours but no longer than 24 hours.

5. Just before serving, cut each sandwich stack in half lengthwise and then crosswise into 4 slices.

32 sandwiches
1 Sandwich: Calories 110 (Calories from Fat 60); Total Fat 7g (Saturated 2g; Trans 0g); Cholesterol 20mg; Sodium 220mg; Total Carbohydrate 7g (Dietary Fiber 0g; Sugars 1g); Protein 4g
% Daily Value: Vitamin A 2%; Vitamin C 0%; Calcium 4%; Iron 4%
Exchanges: 1/2 Starch, 1/2 Lean Meat, 1 Fat
Carbohydrate Choices: 1/2

KITCHEN TIPS

❁ Garnish platters of Party Ribbon Sandwiches with edible flowers.

Caesar Focaccia Subs

Prep Time: 25 min Start to Finish: 25 min

3 round Italian focaccia breads (about 10 inches in diameter)

1 cup Caesar dressing

12 to 20 romaine lettuce leaves

12 ounces thinly sliced smoked turkey

12 ounces thinly sliced salami

12 ounces sliced smoked provolone cheese

24 servings
1 Serving: Calories 310 (Calories from Fat 160); Total Fat 18g (Saturated 5g; Trans 0g); Cholesterol 30mg; Sodium 810mg; Total Carbohydrate 24g (Dietary Fiber 1g; Sugars 0g); Protein 13g
% Daily Value: Vitamin A 10%; Vitamin C 2%; Calcium 10%; Iron 10%
Exchanges: 1½ Starch, 1 High-Fat Meat, 2 Fat
Carbohydrate Choices: 1½

KITCHEN TIPS

❂ Try preparing subs with specialty focaccia bread, such as sun-dried tomato or spinach-Parmesan.

1. Cut each bread horizontally in half. Drizzle dressing evenly over cut sides of bottom and top halves of bread.

2. Layer lettuce, turkey, salami and cheese on bottom halves. Top with top halves. Secure loaves with toothpicks or small skewers. Cut each loaf into 8 wedges.

Ranch Chicken Fillet Sandwiches

Prep Time: 35 min Start to Finish: 1 hr 35 min

¼ cup ranch dressing

1 tablespoon chopped fresh chives

4 boneless skinless chicken breasts (about 1¼ pounds)

4 slices Canadian-style bacon

4 whole-grain sandwich buns, split

¼ cup ranch dressing

2 tablespoons mayonnaise or salad dressing

2 tablespoons chopped fresh parsley

1 medium cucumber, thinly sliced

1 very large tomato, sliced

1. In shallow glass or plastic dish, mix ¼ cup dressing and the chives. Add chicken; turn to coat. Cover; refrigerate 1 to 2 hours, turning chicken occasionally.

2. Heat gas or charcoal grill. Place chicken on grill. Cover grill; cook over medium heat 15 to 20 minutes, turning once or twice, until juice of chicken is clear when center of thickest part is cut (170°F). Add bacon to grill for last 2 to 3 minutes of cooking time to heat. If desired, add buns, cut sides down, for last 4 minutes of cooking time until toasted.

3. In small bowl, mix ¼ cup dressing, the mayonnaise and parsley; spread on cut sides of buns. Layer bacon, chicken, cucumber and tomato in each bun.

4 sandwiches
1 Sandwich: Calories 530 (Calories from Fat 260); Total Fat 29g (Saturated 5g; Trans 0g); Cholesterol 110mg; Sodium 910mg; Total Carbohydrate 26g (Dietary Fiber 4g; Sugars 8g); Protein 42g
% Daily Value: Vitamin A 15%; Vitamin C 10%; Calcium 8%; Iron 20%
Exchanges: 1½ Starch, 5½ Very Lean Meat, 5 Fat
Carbohydrate Choices: 2

Slow Cooker Chicken Caesar Sandwiches

Prep Time: 20 min Start to Finish: 6 hr 55 min

2 pounds boneless skinless chicken thighs

1 package (1.2 ounces) Caesar dressing mix

1 can (10¾ ounces) condensed cream of chicken soup

⅓ cup shredded Parmesan cheese

¼ cup chopped fresh parsley

½ teaspoon coarsely ground pepper

2 cups shredded romaine lettuce

12 "dollar" buns (about 2½ inch)

1. In 3- to 4-quart slow cooker, place chicken. Cover; cook on Low heat setting 6 to 7 hours.

2. Remove chicken from cooker, using slotted spoon; place on cutting board. Discard liquid in cooker. Use 2 forks to pull chicken into shreds. In cooker, mix dressing mix, (dry) soup, cheese, parsley and pepper; gently fold in chicken. Increase heat setting to High. Cover; cook 30 to 35 minutes or until mixture is hot.

3. To serve, spoon ¼ cup chicken mixture onto lettuce in each bun. Chicken mixture will hold on Low heat setting up to 2 hours; stir occasionally.

12 sandwiches
1 Sandwich: Calories 250 (Calories from Fat 100); Total Fat 11g (Saturated 3.5g; Trans 0g); Cholesterol 50mg; Sodium 620mg; Total Carbohydrate 19g (Dietary Fiber 1g; Sugars 3g); Protein 21g
% Daily Value: Vitamin A 15%; Vitamin C 4%; Calcium 10%; Iron 15%
Exchanges: 1 Starch, 2½ Lean Meat, ½ Fat
Carbohydrate Choices: 1

KITCHEN TIPS

✿ Boneless skinless turkey thighs work great in this recipe, too. Just use the same amount of turkey as chicken.

Turkey-Cucumber-Dill Sandwiches

Prep Time: 15 min Start to Finish: 15 min

1/4 cup mayonnaise or salad dressing

1 tablespoon dried dill weed

8 slices multigrain bread

1/2 pound sliced cooked turkey (from deli)

4 slices (1 ounce each) dill Havarti or Muenster cheese

16 thin slices cucumber

4 lettuce leaves

1. In small bowl, mix mayonnaise and dill weed. Spread on 1 side of each bread slice.

2. Top 4 bread slices with turkey, cheese, cucumber and lettuce. Top with remaining bread.

4 sandwiches

1 Sandwich: Calories 420 (Calories from Fat 230); Total Fat 25g (Saturated 9g; Trans 0.5g); Cholesterol 65mg; Sodium 1240mg; Total Carbohydrate 28g (Dietary Fiber 4g; Sugars 8g); Protein 21g
% Daily Value: Vitamin A 10%; Vitamin C 2%; Calcium 25%; Iron 15%
Exchanges: 2 Starch, 2 Lean Meat, 3 1/2 Fat
Carbohydrate Choices: 2

KITCHEN TIPS

✿ Add carrot and celery sticks with your favorite dip for an easy summer meal. Serve ice cream and fresh berries for dessert.

Italian Country Sandwich

Prep Time: 10 min Start to Finish: 10 min

1 uncut loaf (1 pound) Italian peasant-style rustic bread or ciabatta bread

1/3 cup rosemary-flavored or plain olive oil

1/4 pound thinly sliced hard salami

1/4 pound sliced provolone cheese

1/4 pound thinly sliced prosciutto

1 small red onion, thinly sliced

1. Cut bread loaf horizontally in half. Drizzle oil over cut sides of bread.

2. Layer salami, cheese, prosciutto and onion on bottom of bread; add top of bread. Cut loaf into 4 pieces.

4 servings

1 Serving: Calories 740 (Calories from Fat 380); Total Fat 42g (Saturated 13g; Trans 1g); Cholesterol 60mg; Sodium 1860mg; Total Carbohydrate 60g (Dietary Fiber 3g; Sugars 3g); Protein 30g
% Daily Value: Vitamin A 4%; Vitamin C 0%; Calcium 30%; Iron 25%
Exchanges: 4 Starch, 2 1/2 High-Fat Meat, 4 Fat
Carbohydrate Choices: 4

KITCHEN TIPS

✿ If rosemary olive oil is not available, you can make your own. In a small saucepan, warm 1 cup olive oil with 1 or 2 sprigs of washed and dried fresh rosemary for 8 to 10 minutes. Cool; discard rosemary. Pour oil into a jar with a tight-fitting lid. Store in refrigerator up to 2 weeks.

Italian Country Sandwich

Turkey-Cucumber-Dill Sandwiches

Beef and Provolone Focaccia Sandwiches

Prep Time: 10 min Start to Finish: 10 min

1 round loaf (12 ounces) focaccia bread (9 inch)

¼ cup basil pesto

8 ounces thinly sliced cooked roast beef (from deli)

1 medium tomato, thinly sliced

8 slices (¾ ounce each) provolone cheese

2 or 3 romaine leaves

1. Cut focaccia horizontally in half to make 2 layers. Spread pesto over cut sides.

2. Layer beef, tomato, cheese and romaine between layers. Cut filled focaccia into 6 wedges. Serve immediately or wrap each wedge in plastic wrap. Refrigerate until serving or up to 24 hours.

6 sandwiches
1 Sandwich: Calories 420 (Calories from Fat 220); Total Fat 24g (Saturated 9g; Trans 0g); Cholesterol 50mg; Sodium 830mg; Total Carbohydrate 29g (Dietary Fiber 2g; Sugars 1g); Protein 21g
% Daily Value: Vitamin A 15%; Vitamin C 6%; Calcium 25%; Iron 20%
Exchanges: 2 Starch, 2 Lean Meat, 3½ Fat
Carbohydrate Choices: 2

KITCHEN TIPS

❁ If you've never had focaccia, you're in for a treat. It's a wonderful round loaf of Italian bread that has been seasoned with olive oil, salt and sometimes spices. It's available fresh at many bakeries and often can be found packaged in the deli or bakery area of large grocery stores.

Pita Beef Pockets

Prep Time: 15 min Start to Finish: 15 min

1/3 cup horseradish mustard

2 pita breads (6 inch), cut in half to form pockets

1/2 pound thinly sliced cooked roast beef (from deli)

1 small tomato, thinly sliced

4 slices (1 ounce each) provolone cheese
Baby spinach leaves or lettuce leaves

1. Spread mustard on inside of pita pocket halves.

2. Fill pockets with beef, tomato, cheese and spinach.

4 sandwiches
1 Sandwich: Calories 340 (Calories from Fat 160); Total Fat 17g (Saturated 8g; Trans 0.5g); Cholesterol 60mg; Sodium 690mg; Total Carbohydrate 20g (Dietary Fiber 2g; Sugars 2g); Protein 25g
% Daily Value: Vitamin A 30%; Vitamin C 10%; Calcium 25%; Iron 20%
Exchanges: 1 1/2 Starch, 3 Lean Meat, 1 1/2 Fat
Carbohydrate Choices: 1

KITCHEN TIPS

✿ If you don't have horseradish mustard, stir together 1/4 cup country-style Dijon mustard and 2 tablespoons horseradish, or use creamy Dijon mustard.

Grilled Turkey Panini Sandwiches

Slow Cooker Italian Shredded Beef Hoagies

Grilled Turkey Panini Sandwiches

Prep Time: 45 min Start to Finish: 45 min

- ¾ cup mayonnaise
- ¼ cup basil pesto
- 16 slices crusty Italian bread
- ¼ cup butter or margarine, softened
- 8 slices cooked turkey (¾ pound)
- 1 can (14 ounces) artichoke hearts, drained, chopped
- 3 medium roma (plum) tomatoes, sliced
- 8 slices (1 ounce each) Fontina or provolone cheese

1. In small bowl, mix mayonnaise and pesto.

2. Spread 1 side of each bread slice with butter. Turn bread slices butter sides down; spread other sides with 1 tablespoon pesto mixture each. Top 8 bread slices with turkey, artichokes, tomatoes and cheese. Top with remaining bread slices, butter sides up.

3. In sandwich grill or 12-inch skillet, cook sandwiches over medium heat 3 to 4 minutes, turning once, until bread is toasted and cheese is melted.

8 sandwiches
1 Sandwich: Calories 570 (Calories from Fat 360); Total Fat 39g (Saturated 14g; Trans 1g); Cholesterol 95mg; Sodium 860mg; Total Carbohydrate 28g (Dietary Fiber 4g; Sugars 2g); Protein 26g
% Daily Value: Vitamin A 15%; Vitamin C 6%; Calcium 25%; Iron 15%
Exchanges: 2 Starch, 3 Lean Meat, 5½ Fat
Carbohydrate Choices: 2

KITCHEN TIPS

✿ No need to use artichoke hearts if someone doesn't like them. The sandwiches have plenty of filling without them.

✿ Fontina cheese has a mild, nutty flavor and melts easily, making it perfect for sandwiches.

Slow Cooker Italian Shredded Beef Hoagies

Prep Time: 15 min Start to Finish: 8 hr 15 min

- 1 beef boneless arm roast, trimmed of fat (2 pounds)
- 2 medium onions, sliced
- 1 can (14.5 ounces) Italian-seasoned diced tomatoes, undrained
- ¼ cup tomato paste
- 8 hoagie buns, toasted if desired
- 2 cups shredded mozzarella cheese (8 ounces)

1. If beef roast comes in netting or is tied, remove netting or strings. In 4- to 5-quart slow cooker, place onions. Place beef on onions. In small bowl, mix diced tomatoes and tomato paste; pour over beef.

2. Cover; cook on Low heat setting 8 to 10 hours.

3. Remove beef from cooker; place on cutting board. Use 2 forks to pull beef into shreds. Return beef to cooker. Spoon about ½ cup beef mixture onto each bun. Top each with ¼ cup cheese.

8 sandwiches
1 Sandwich: Calories 540 (Calories from Fat 150); Total Fat 16g (Saturated 7g; Trans 1g); Cholesterol 65mg; Sodium 890mg; Total Carbohydrate 56g (Dietary Fiber 4g; Sugars 11g); Protein 43g
% Daily Value: Vitamin A 6%; Vitamin C 6%; Calcium 30%; Iron 30%
Exchanges: 3 Starch, ½ Other Carbohydrate, 1 Vegetable, 4½ Lean Meat
Carbohydrate Choices: 4

KITCHEN TIPS

✿ Spoon the beef over hot pasta instead of buns and top with grated cheese for an Italian-style supper.

Slow Cooker Barbecue Beef Sandwiches

Prep Time: 20 min Start to Finish: 7 hr 50 min

- 1 beef boneless chuck roast (3 pounds)
- 1 cup barbecue sauce
- ½ cup apricot or peach preserves
- ⅓ cup chopped green bell pepper
- 1 tablespoon Dijon mustard
- 2 teaspoons packed brown sugar
- 1 small onion, sliced
- 12 kaiser rolls or burger buns, split

1. Trim excess fat from beef. Cut beef into 4 pieces; place in 4- to 5-quart slow cooker.

2. In medium bowl, mix remaining ingredients except buns; pour over beef.

3. Cover; cook on Low heat setting 7 to 8 hours or until beef is tender.

4. Remove beef from slow cooker; place on cutting board. Cut into thin slices; return to cooker. Cover; cook on Low heat setting 20 to 30 minutes longer or until beef is hot. Fill buns with beef mixture.

12 sandwiches

1 Sandwich: Calories 430 (Calories from Fat 140); Total Fat 16g (Saturated 5g; Trans 1g); Cholesterol 65mg; Sodium 570mg; Total Carbohydrate 45g (Dietary Fiber 2g; Sugars 14g); Protein 26g
% Daily Value: Vitamin A 0%; Vitamin C 4%; Calcium 6%; Iron 25%
Exchanges: 1½ Starch, 1½ Other Carbohydrate, 3 Lean Meat, 1½ Fat
Carbohydrate Choices: 3

KITCHEN TIPS

✿ For a delicious kick, serve these flavorful sandwiches with horseradish sauce.

✿ These meaty sandwiches can be served *au jus*. Pour the juices left in the slow cooker into small bowls and serve with the sandwiches for dipping. This makes each bite extra delicious!

Summer Ham and Egg Salad Sandwiches

Prep Time: 20 min Start to Finish: 20 min

$1/2$ cup chopped fully cooked ham

$1/2$ cup chopped broccoli florets

$1/2$ cup chopped celery

$1/2$ cup mayonnaise or salad dressing

1 tablespoon chopped fresh chives

2 teaspoons chopped fresh or $3/4$ teaspoon dried marjoram leaves

$1/4$ teaspoon onion salt

3 hard-cooked eggs, chopped
   Lettuce leaves

8 slices herb or whole wheat bread

1. In medium bowl, mix all ingredients except lettuce and bread.

2. Place lettuce leaf on 4 of the bread slices. Spoon egg mixture onto lettuce. Top with remaining bread.

4 sandwiches
1 Sandwich: Calories 440 (Calories from Fat 260); Total Fat 29g (Saturated 5g; Trans 0g); Cholesterol 180mg; Sodium 840mg; Total Carbohydrate 29g (Dietary Fiber 4g; Sugars 8g); Protein 15g
% Daily Value: Vitamin A 10%; Vitamin C 20%; Calcium 8%; Iron 15%
Exchanges: 2 Starch, $1^{1}/2$ Medium-Fat Meat, 4 Fat
Carbohydrate Choices: 2

KITCHEN TIPS

✿ Need a foolproof way to hard-cook eggs? It's easy. Just place eggs in saucepan, and add cold water to cover eggs by 1 inch. Cover; heat to boiling. Remove from heat; let stand covered 15 minutes. Drain. Immediately cool in cold water. Tap egg to crack the shell, roll between hands to loosen, then peel.

Baby Burgers

Prep Time: 30 min   Start to Finish: 30 min

1	pound lean (at least 80%) ground beef
2	teaspoons dried minced onion
1	teaspoon parsley flakes
$^3/_4$	teaspoon seasoned salt
4	slices (1 ounce each) American cheese, cut into quarters
8	slices white bread, toasted, crusts trimmed, cut into quarters
16	thin slices roma (plum) tomatoes (2 small), if desired
16	thin hamburger-style dill pickle slices, if desired
	Ketchup, if desired
	Mustard, if desired

1. Heat gas or charcoal grill. In medium bowl, mix beef, onion, parsley and seasoned salt. Divide into 16 portions. Shape each portion into a ball and flatten to $^1/_2$-inch-thick patty, about $1^1/_2$ inches in diameter. On each of 4 (12-inch) metal skewers, thread 4 patties horizontally, leaving space between each.

2. Place patties on grill. Cover grill; cook over medium heat 8 to 10 minutes, turning once, until patties are no longer pink in center (160°).

3. Top each burger with cheese piece. Place each burger on toast square. Top with tomato slice and another toast square. Place pickle slice on top; spear with toothpick to hold layers together. Serve with ketchup and mustard for dipping.

16 appetizer burgers
1 Burger: Calories 110 (Calories from Fat 50); Total Fat 6g (Saturated 2.5g; Trans 0g); Cholesterol 25mg; Sodium 270mg; Total Carbohydrate 7g (Dietary Fiber 0g; Sugars 0g); Protein 8g
% Daily Value: Vitamin A 0%; Vitamin C 0%; Calcium 6%; Iron 6%
Exchanges: $^1/_2$ Starch, 1 Medium-Fat Meat
Carbohydrate Choices: $^1/_2$

KITCHEN TIPS

❂ These cute little burgers can be mixed and shaped ahead of time. Just cover and refrigerate them until you are ready to grill.

❂ Some plum tomatoes are quite large. Select smaller tomatoes for this recipe so they are about the same size as the burgers.

❂ Note: To broil patties, set oven control to broil. Thread patties on skewers as directed. Place patties on rack in broiler pan. Broil with tops 6 inches from heat 8 to 10 minutes, turning once, until no longer pink in center.

Shellfish and Fish

Catch of the Day—Your Way

Easy Paella (page 111)

Planked Salmon Platter (page 115)

Shrimp-Salsa Nachos

Prep Time: 30 min Start to Finish: 30 min

1 medium tomato, seeded and finely chopped (¾ cup)

2 medium green onions, thinly sliced (2 tablespoons)

2 tablespoons chopped fresh cilantro

2 tablespoons seafood cocktail sauce

½ teaspoon red pepper sauce

30 scoop-shaped tortilla chips

⅔ cup finely shredded Mexican cheese blend (5 ounces)

30 small cooked peeled deveined shrimp, thawed if frozen, tail shells removed

1. In small bowl, mix tomato, onions, cilantro, cocktail sauce and pepper sauce. Set aside.

2. On 2 microwavable plates, divide tortilla chips. Spoon about 1 teaspoon cheese into each chip.

Microwave 1 plate at a time uncovered on High about 30 seconds or until cheese is melted. Repeat with second plate.

3. Just before serving, top each nacho with 1 rounded teaspoon tomato salsa and 1 shrimp.

30 nachos
1 Nacho: Calories 35 (Calories from Fat 15); Total Fat 2g (Saturated 1g; Trans 0g); Cholesterol 10mg; Sodium 65mg; Total Carbohydrate 2g (Dietary Fiber 0g; Sugars 0g); Protein 2g
% Daily Value: Vitamin A 2%; Vitamin C 0%; Calcium 4%; Iron 0%
Exchanges: ½ Very Lean Meat, ½ Fat
Carbohydrate Choices: 0

KITCHEN TIPS

❂ Fill the little tortilla cups just before you serve them so they don't get soggy.

❂ Small salad shrimp are a good size for this appetizer.

Quick & Low Fat

Layered Shrimp Spread

Prep Time: 15 min Start to Finish: 15 min

1 container (8 ounces) pineapple cream cheese spread

$\frac{1}{2}$ cup peach or apricot preserves

2 tablespoons seafood cocktail sauce

1 bag (4 ounces) frozen cooked salad shrimp, thawed, drained

2 medium green onions, thinly sliced (2 tablespoons)

$\frac{1}{4}$ cup coconut chips

   Assorted crackers

1. On 10- to 12-inch serving plate, spread cream cheese to within 1 inch of edge of plate. In small bowl, mix preserves and cocktail sauce. Spread over cream cheese.

2. Top evenly with shrimp. Sprinkle with onions and coconut. Serve with crackers.

16 servings (2 tablespoons spread and 3 crackers each)
1 Serving: Calories 150 (Calories from Fat 80); Total Fat 8g (Saturated 4g; Trans 1g); Cholesterol 25mg; Sodium 240mg; Total Carbohydrate 15g (Dietary Fiber 0g; Sugars 7g); Protein 4g
% Daily Value: Vitamin A 4%; Vitamin C 2%; Calcium 0%; Iron 4%
Exchanges: $\frac{1}{2}$ Starch, $\frac{1}{2}$ Other Carbohydrate, $\frac{1}{2}$ Very Lean Meat, $1\frac{1}{2}$ Fat
Carbohydrate Choices: 1

KITCHEN TIPS

✿ This recipe updates a favorite classic shrimp spread with fruit flavors for a little sweetness.

✿ Coconut chips are larger than flaked or shredded coconut. They can usually be found in the baking aisle. Flaked coconut could be substituted.

Pesto-Salmon Roulades

Prep Time: 15 min Start to Finish: 15 min

- 1 package (6 ounces) smoked salmon lox
- 1/3 cup refrigerated basil pesto (from 7-ounce container)
- 1/2 cup drained roasted red bell peppers (from 7-ounce jar), cut into thin strips
- 28 roasted-garlic bagel chips (from 5.5-ounce bag)

1. Cut each salmon piece in half lengthwise so that it is about 3/4 inch wide. Spread each with about 1/2 teaspoon of the pesto; top with roasted bell pepper strip. Carefully roll up.

2. Place each roulade on bagel chip. Serve immediately.

28 roulades
1 Roulade: Calories 30 (Calories from Fat 20); Total Fat 2g (Saturated 0g; Trans 0g); Cholesterol 0mg; Sodium 80mg; Total Carbohydrate 1g (Dietary Fiber 0g; Sugars 0g); Protein 2g
% Daily Value: Vitamin A 4%; Vitamin C 8%; Calcium 0%; Iron 0%
Exchanges: 1/2 Lean Meat
Carbohydrate Choices: 0

KITCHEN TIPS

❋ Salmon lox is sliced very thinly, so handle the slices carefully to avoid tearing them.

Salmon-Pimiento Appetizers

Prep Time: 15 min Start to Finish: 15 min

- 1 package (4.5 ounces) smoked salmon (hot-smoked), skin removed, flaked
- 1/3 cup pimiento cheese spread (from 5-ounce jar)
- 2 teaspoons mayonnaise or salad dressing
- 2 medium green onions, thinly sliced (2 tablespoons)
- 1/8 teaspoon pepper
- 16 slices cocktail pumpernickel bread
- 16 thin slices seedless cucumber
- 2 tablespoons tiny dill weed sprigs

1. In medium bowl, mix salmon, cheese spread, mayonnaise, onions and pepper. Spread evenly on bread slices.

2. Cut cucumber slices in half almost to edge and twist; place on salmon mixture. Garnish with dill weed sprigs.

16 appetizers
1 Appetizer: Calories 45 (Calories from Fat 20); Total Fat 2g (Saturated 1g; Trans 0g); Cholesterol 5mg; Sodium 150mg; Total Carbohydrate 4g (Dietary Fiber 0g; Sugars 0g); Protein 3g
% Daily Value: Vitamin A 0%; Vitamin C 0%; Calcium 0%; Iron 0%
Exchanges: 1/2 Starch, 1/2 Fat
Carbohydrate Choices: 0

KITCHEN TIPS

❋ Salmon can be hot-smoked or cold-smoked. Cold-smoked salmon (lox) is usually sliced very thinly and doesn't flake.
❋ You could substitute a 6-ounce can of boneless skinless salmon, drained, for the smoked salmon.

Pesto-Salmon Roulades

Salmon-Pimiento Appetizers

Mini Crab Points

Prep Time: 15 min Start to Finish: 15 min

$\frac{1}{4}$ cup mayonnaise or salad dressing

1   small clove garlic, finely chopped

1   can (6 ounces) crabmeat, well drained, flaked

$\frac{1}{4}$ cup finely chopped celery

2   tablespoons diced red bell pepper

2   medium green onions, thinly sliced (2 tablespoons)

$\frac{1}{4}$ teaspoon seafood seasoning (from 6-ounce container)

4   slices whole wheat bread, toasted

Chopped fresh parsley

16 servings

1 Serving: Calories 50 (Calories from Fat 30); Total Fat 3g (Saturated 0.5g; Trans 0g); Cholesterol 10mg; Sodium 100mg; Total Carbohydrate 4g (Dietary Fiber 0g; Sugars 0g); Protein 3g
% Daily Value: Vitamin A 2%; Vitamin C 6%; Calcium 0%; Iron 2%
Exchanges: $\frac{1}{2}$ Starch, $\frac{1}{2}$ Fat
Carbohydrate Choices: 0

KITCHEN TIPS

✺ These garlicky crab appetizers are similar to crab or lobster rolls, popular sandwiches served on the eastern seaboard.

✺ If you have leafy tips handy after chopping the celery, you could use them instead of the parsley to garnish the appetizers.

1. In medium bowl, mix mayonnaise and garlic. Stir in crabmeat, celery, bell pepper, onions and seafood seasoning.

2. Top toasted bread with crab mixture. Cut diagonally into quarters. Sprinkle with parsley.

Quick

Crab Bites

Prep Time: 15 min Start to Finish: 40 min

- ³/₄ cup mayonnaise or salad dressing
- ³/₄ cup grated Parmesan cheese
- ¹/₂ teaspoon finely chopped garlic
- 8 medium green onions, finely chopped (¹/₂ cup)
- 1 can (14 ounces) artichoke hearts, drained, sliced
- 1 pouch (6 ounces) ready-to-eat crabmeat, flaked
- 3 packages (2.1 ounces each) frozen baked mini fillo dough shells (15 shells each), thawed

1. Heat oven to 375°F. Line cookie sheet with foil or cooking parchment paper.

2. In large bowl, mix all ingredients except fillo shells with spoon about 2 minutes or until well blended.

3. Place fillo shells on cookie sheet. Fill each shell with about 1 tablespoon crab mixture. Bake 20 to 25 minutes or until shells are puffed and golden brown. Serve warm.

45 appetizers
1 Appetizer: Calories 50 (Calories from Fat 30); Total Fat 3.5g (Saturated 0.5g; Trans 0g); Cholesterol 5mg; Sodium 85mg; Total Carbohydrate 3g (Dietary Fiber 0g; Sugars 0g); Protein 2g
% Daily Value: Vitamin A 0%; Vitamin C 0%; Calcium 2%; Iron 0%
Exchanges: ¹/₂ Very Lean Meat, ¹/₂ Fat
Carbohydrate Choices: 0

KITCHEN TIPS

❂ Garnish each crab bite with half of a cherry tomato to add color.

❂ Mini fillo dough shells can be found in the frozen pastry section of most large grocery stores.

Betty Crocker
IN SEASON

Artichokes

Celebrate in style with amazing artichokes. Elegant and unique, artichokes are a native Mediterranean vegetable. The part of the artichoke plant that we eat is the flower bud. This delectable vegetable is not quick to fix but is slowly savored, one leaf at a time. It's prized for its delicately flavored "heart," which sits at the base of the artichoke hidden by the fuzzy choke.

Choose: Artichokes should be plump, compact and heavy for their size. They should have fresh green leaves. Depending on the variety, the shape may be like a globe or more of a cone. Almost all artichokes eaten in the United States are grown in California and they are available year-round. Baby artichokes are tiny versions of the traditional globe artichokes and are completely edible because they have no fuzzy chokes. Four medium globe artichokes will weigh about 1 pound.

Store: Store unwashed artichokes in the refrigerator up to 4 days.

Prepare: Wash artichokes under cold water. Pull off any small or discolored lower leaves. Remove the stem by cutting it even with the base of the artichoke, using a stainless-steel knife to prevent the artichoke from discoloring. If you like, trim off the top quarter of the artichoke and the tips of the leaves. To prevent discoloring, dip it in cold water mixed with a small amount of lemon juice (1 tablespoon lemon juice to 1 quart water).

To Stuff (if desired)

Prepare as directed above. Sharply rap or hit the base of the artichoke on a countertop. Gently spread the leaves and pull out the central cone. Using a spoon, scrape out any remaining purple leaves and fuzz. Stuff the center and between the leaves with a favorite bread or rice stuffing mixture. Boil, steam or microwave as directed below.

To Cook

BOIL By heating 6 quarts water and 2 tablespoons lemon juice to boiling in 8-quart Dutch oven or large pot. Place 4 medium artichokes in boiling water; boil uncovered 20 to 30 minutes, rotating occasionally, until the leaves pull out easily and the bottoms are tender when pierced with a knife.

STEAM By placing steamer basket in 4-quart Dutch oven with $1/2$ inch water; add 4 medium artichokes to basket. Cover tightly and heat to boiling; reduce heat to low. Steam 20 to 25 minutes or until bottoms are tender when pierced with a knife.

MICROWAVE By placing 2 medium artichokes in 8 × 4-inch microwavable loaf dish; add $1/4$ cup water. Cover with plastic wrap, folding back one edge $1/4$ inch to release steam. Microwave on High 9 to 11 minutes or until bottoms are tender when pierced with a knife.

Nutrition Highlights

▶ Vitamin C   ▶ Fiber   ▶ Folate

Artichokes are a unique vegetable, not only in appearance but also in origin. Their tiered leaves are actually an unopened flower bud from a pant that is a member of the thistle family. Within each bud is a bouquet of wonderful nutrients, each of which is a grand addition to any diet. Note: Canned artichoke hearts are not as rich in nutrients as fresh whole (cooked) artichokes. When canned, they can contain significantly higher amounts of sodium. The same holds true for marinated hearts. Check and compare product labels to find the one that is lowest in sodium.

Health Highlights

▶ **Antioxidants:** Artichokes make the list of the top 20 foods with the most antioxidants. According to the U.S. Department of Agriculture, artichokes rank number seven overall and number three in the vegetable category. Antioxidants help protect cells in the body from damage.

▶ **Healthy cells:** Both folate and vitamin C are important in the creation of healthy new cells in the body.

▶ **Fiber:** One serving of artichoke (half of an artichoke) contains 3 grams of fiber, which is 10 percent of daily adult recommendation.

The Art of Eating Artichokes

So how do you eat an artichoke?
It looks like a daunting task, but once you've bitten, you'll be smitten!

► Artichokes can be enjoyed hot or chilled. If you like, cook them ahead and store covered in the refrigerator for up to a week.

► To eat whole, pull off the outer leaves one at a time. Dip the fleshy end into sauce, then pull the leaf through your teeth to remove the fleshy part. Discard leaves as you eat them.

► The leaves can be removed and used as an edible base for appetizers. Try spreading a flavored soft cheese or hummus on the leaves.

► Remove the central cone by pulling it out. Using a spoon, scrape out any remaining purple leaves and fuzz.

► The bottom, known as the heart, is edible. Cut it into pieces, and serve with sauce if desired.

► Just remember: The parts of the artichoke you eat are the tender, fleshy part of the leaf and the heart or bottom.

Make It Quick

For convenience, artichoke hearts are also available in cans and jars or frozen. Canned artichoke hearts come in brine, so they need to be drained. They can be rinsed to reduce their high sodium content. Marinated artichoke hearts, sold in jars, are preserved in flavored oil or vinaigrette marinade. Because of the difference in oil and flavor, do not substitute canned artichoke hearts for marinated artichoke hearts in jars. Frozen artichoke hearts have no added ingredients. Simply follow the package directions when cooking them. They are perfect anytime you want to enjoy all the elegance of artichokes without the time and effort.

Banderillas

Prep Time: 25 min Start to Finish: 25 min

4 asparagus spears, each cut into 6 (1-inch) pieces

1/2 cup water

24 frilled toothpicks or cocktail-size skewers

24 cooked peeled deveined tiny shrimp (about 90 count per pound), tails removed

24 small pieces (1 × 1/2 inch each) fully cooked smoked ham

24 pitted green Spanish olives

1/4 cup olive or vegetable oil

4 cloves garlic, sliced

1/4 cup finely chopped fresh parsley

1/4 cup finely chopped dill pickle

1. In 1-quart microwavable bowl, place asparagus and add water. Cover with plastic wrap, folding back one edge 1/4 inch to vent steam. Microwave on High about 2 minutes or until asparagus is just tender and can be pierced with a fork; drain. Immediately rinse with cold water; drain.

2. On each toothpick, skewer 1 shrimp, 1 asparagus piece, 1 ham piece and 1 olive.

3. In small microwavable bowl, place 1 tablespoon of the oil and the garlic. Microwave uncovered on High 30 to 60 seconds or until garlic is softened. In food processor or blender, place parsley, cooked garlic in oil, pickle and remaining 3 tablespoons oil; cover and process about 1 minute or until mixture is smooth. Serve banderillas with sauce.

24 appetizers
1 Appetizer: Calories 40 (Calories from Fat 30); Total Fat 3.5g (Saturated 0.5g; Trans 0g); Cholesterol 10mg; Sodium 140mg; Total Carbohydrate 0g (Dietary Fiber 0g; Sugars 0g); Protein 2g
% Daily Value: Vitamin A 2%; Vitamin C 0%; Calcium 0%; Iron 0%
Exchanges: 1 Fat
Carbohydrate Choices: 0

KITCHEN TIPS

⊛ Banderillas, named for their similarity to the colorful ornamental darts used in the bullring, are a familiar form of tapas in northern Spain.

⊛ The trick to eating banderillas is to put everything on the toothpick in your mouth at the same time so that the flavors blend. Use just a dab of sauce to add zest.

Basil- and Crabmeat-Topped Cucumbers

Prep Time: 40 min Start to Finish: 40 min

1 medium English cucumber

1 package (3 ounces) cream cheese, softened

2 tablespoons mayonnaise or salad dressing

¼ cup chopped fresh basil leaves

2 tablespoons finely chopped red onion

2 teaspoons grated lemon peel

1 cup frozen cooked crabmeat, thawed, flaked

2 tablespoons capers, if desired

Small basil leaves or chopped fresh basil, if desired

1. Score cucumber lengthwise with tines of fork if desired. Cut into 36 (¼-inch) slices.

2. In small bowl, beat cream cheese with electric mixer on low speed until creamy. Beat in mayonnaise until well blended. Stir in chopped basil, onion, lemon peel and crabmeat.

3. Spread or pipe about 1 teaspoon crabmeat mixture on each cucumber slice. Sprinkle with capers. Garnish with basil leaves.

36 appetizers

1 Appetizer: Calories 19 (Calories from Fat 15); Total Fat 1.5g (Saturated 0.5g; Trans 0g); Cholesterol 5mg; Sodium 20mg; Total Carbohydrate 0g (Dietary Fiber 0g; Sugars 0g); Protein 1g
% Daily Value: Vitamin A 0%; Vitamin C 0%; Calcium 0%; Iron 0%
Exchanges: Free
Carbohydrate Choices: 0

KITCHEN TIPS

❁ English cucumbers, also called hothouse cucumbers, have very small seeds and thin skins that don't require peeling, so they work well for this appetizer.

❁ If you can't find frozen crabmeat, use a 6-ounce can of crabmeat, well drained.

Low Fat

Easy Paella

Prep Time: 35 min Start to Finish: 1 hr 30 min

³/₄ pound uncooked large shrimp, peeled and deveined

³/₄ pound sea scallops, each cut in half

2 tablespoons olive or vegetable oil

Generous pinch plus 1 teaspoon saffron threads

6 cloves garlic, finely chopped

5 medium onions, chopped (2¹/₂ cups)

2 cans (14.5 ounces each) diced tomatoes with garlic and onion, undrained

1 can (14 ounces) artichoke hearts, drained, coarsely chopped

³/₄ pound smoked turkey sausage, cut into ¹/₄-inch slices, slices cut in half

2 cups uncooked basmati rice

4 cups chicken broth

1 teaspoon paprika

Chopped fresh parsley, if desired

1. Heat oven to 375°F. Spray two 11 × 7-inch glass baking dishes with cooking spray. In medium bowl, toss shrimp and scallops with 1 tablespoon of the oil and generous pinch of the saffron threads; cover and refrigerate.

2. In 4-quart Dutch oven, heat remaining 1 tablespoon oil over medium heat. Cook garlic and onions in oil about 5 minutes, stirring frequently, until onions are crisp-tender. Stir in tomatoes, artichokes and sausage. Cook 2 minutes, stirring frequently. Stir in rice. Spread half of rice mixture evenly in each baking dish.

3. In 2-quart saucepan, heat broth, paprika and 1 teaspoon saffron threads to boiling. Pour 2 cups broth mixture evenly over rice mixture in each baking dish.

4. Cover with foil. Bake 35 minutes. Place shrimp and scallops on rice mixture in each dish. Cover and bake 15 to 20 minutes or until shrimp are pink and scallops are white and opaque. Sprinkle with parsley.

8 servings
1 Serving: Calories 400 (Calories from Fat 80); Total Fat 9g (Saturated 2g; Trans 0g); Cholesterol 75mg; Sodium 1300mg; Total Carbohydrate 55g (Dietary Fiber 5g; Sugars 6g); Protein 25g
% Daily Value: Vitamin A 10%; Vitamin C 15%; Calcium 10%; Iron 30%
Exchanges: 3 Starch, ¹/₂ Other Carbohydrate, 1 Vegetable, 2 Lean Meat
Carbohydrate Choices: 3¹/₂

KITCHEN TIPS

✿ Paella originated in Valencia, Spain, and is named for the special shallow, wide pan used in the traditional preparation.

Shrimp Kabobs with Fresh Herbs

Prep Time: 35 min Start to Finish: 55 min

Marinade

12	sprigs rosemary (6 inches long)
1/4	cup fresh lemon juice
3	tablespoons olive or vegetable oil
1/2	teaspoon salt
1/2	teaspoon pepper

Kabobs

24	fresh large basil leaves
24	uncooked peeled deveined large shrimp (1 1/2 pounds)
12	small pattypan squash, cut in half
24	cherry tomatoes
24	large cloves garlic

1. Strip leaves from rosemary sprigs, leaving 1 inch of leaves at top; set aside. Measure 1 tablespoon rosemary leaves; chop. In small bowl, mix chopped rosemary leaves and remaining marinade ingredients.

2. Wrap basil leaf around each shrimp. For each kabob, thread shrimp, squash half, tomato and garlic clove alternately on stem of rosemary sprig, leaving 1/4-inch space between each piece. (Start threading at stem end, pulling through to leaves at top.) Repeat each layer.

3. In ungreased 13 × 9-inch (3-quart) glass baking dish, place kabobs. Pour marinade over kabobs. Cover and refrigerate 20 minutes. Heat gas or charcoal grill. Remove kabobs from marinade; reserve marinade. Place kabobs on grill. Cover grill; cook over medium heat about 12 minutes, turning and brushing with marinade 2 or 3 times, until shrimp are pink. Discard any remaining marinade.

6 servings

1 Serving: Calories 170 (Calories from Fat 45); Total Fat 5g (Saturated 1g; Trans 0g); Cholesterol 160mg; Sodium 290mg; Total Carbohydrate 12g (Dietary Fiber 3g; Sugars 4g); Protein 20g
% Daily Value: Vitamin A 20%; Vitamin C 30%; Calcium 10%; Iron 20%
Exchanges: 1/2 Other Carbohydrate, 1 Vegetable, 2 1/2 Very Lean Meat, 1/2 Fat
Carbohydrate Choices: 1

Spicy Grilled Shrimp

Prep Time: 20 min Start to Finish: 45 min

20 bamboo skewers (6 inch)
 1 cup canned coconut milk (not cream of coconut)
 2 teaspoons curry powder
 2 teaspoons cornstarch
 1 teaspoon honey
 ¼ teaspoon salt
60 uncooked peeled deveined medium shrimp (about 2 pounds), thawed if frozen, tail shells removed
 ¼ cup olive or vegetable oil
 1 teaspoon red pepper sauce

1. Soak skewers in water at least 30 minutes before using to prevent burning. Meanwhile, heat gas or charcoal grill. In small microwavable bowl, mix coconut milk, curry powder, cornstarch, honey and salt. Microwave uncovered on High about 2 minutes, stirring every 30 seconds, until mixture bubbles and thickens; set aside.

2. In large bowl, place shrimp. Drizzle with oil and pepper sauce; toss to coat. Thread 3 shrimp on each skewer, leaving space between each.

3. Place kabobs on grill. Cover grill; cook over medium heat 4 to 6 minutes or until shrimp are pink. Serve with coconut-curry sauce.

20 servings (1 kabob and about 2 teaspoons sauce each)
1 Serving: Calories 80 (Calories from Fat 45); Total Fat 5g (Saturated 2.5g; Trans 0g); Cholesterol 65mg; Sodium 110mg; Total Carbohydrate 2g (Dietary Fiber 0g; Sugars 0g); Protein 7g
% Daily Value: Vitamin A 0%; Vitamin C 0%; Calcium 0%; Iron 6%
Exchanges: 1 Very Lean Meat, 1 Fat
Carbohydrate Choices: 0

KITCHEN TIPS

❀ To serve these spicy shrimp as a main dish, thread on 8 to 10 (12-inch) skewers. Serve with yellow rice and asparagus.
❀ Arrange the kabobs on a platter and garnish with sprigs of fresh herbs for a pretty presentation.

Planked Salmon Platter

Planked Salmon Platter

Prep Time: 50 min Start to Finish: 1 hr 50 min

Salmon

- 1   untreated cedar plank, 12 × 6 inches
- 1   salmon fillet, about 1 inch thick (1 pound)
- 2   tablespoons mayonnaise or salad dressing
- 2   teaspoons Dijon mustard
- 1   teaspoon grated lemon peel

Accompaniments

- ½   cup sour cream
- 1   teaspoon chopped fresh or ½ teaspoon dried dill weed
- 1   jar (3½ ounces) small capers, drained
- ¼   cup spicy brown mustard
- 2   hard-cooked eggs, finely chopped
- 1   cup thinly sliced cucumber
- 32   slices cocktail rye bread

1. Soak cedar plank in water 1 to 2 hours.

2. Heat gas or charcoal grill for indirect-heat cooking as directed by manufacturer. Place salmon, skin side down, on plank. In small bowl, mix mayonnaise, mustard and lemon peel. Brush generously over salmon.

3. Place plank with salmon on grill for indirect cooking. Cover grill; cook over medium heat 25 to 30 minutes or until salmon flakes easily with fork.

4. Remove salmon from plank to platter, using large spatula, or leave salmon on plank and place on large wood cutting board or platter.

5. In small bowl, mix sour cream and dill weed. Place remaining accompaniments except bread in individual small bowls. Place sour cream mixture and remaining accompaniments around salmon. Serve salmon and accompaniments with bread.

16 servings (2 tablespoons salmon, 2 bread slices and ¹⁄₁₆ of accompaniments each)
1 Serving: Calories 120 (Calories from Fat 50); Total Fat 6g (Saturated 2g; Trans 0g); Cholesterol 50mg; Sodium 270mg; Total Carbohydrate 8g (Dietary Fiber 0g; Sugars 1g); Protein 8g
% Daily Value: Vitamin A 2%; Vitamin C 0%; Calcium 2%; Iron 4%
Exchanges: ½ Starch, 1 Very Lean Meat, 1 Fat
Carbohydrate Choices: ½

KITCHEN TIPS

- Cedar planks can be purchased at home improvement stores. A 6-inch-wide, 6-foot-long untreated plank will give you 6 (1-foot) reusable planks for grilling.
- Experiment by serving with different breads. Cocktail bread, for instance, is also sold in pumpernickel flavor.
- To broil salmon, set oven control to broil. Place salmon, skin side down, on rack in broiler pan. (Do not use cedar plank.) Broil with top 6 inches from heat about 15 minutes or until salmon flakes easily with fork.

Spicy Grilled Shrimp Platter

Prep Time: 20 min Start to Finish: 1 hr 20 min

4	cups water
2	tablespoons kosher (coarse) salt
2	tablespoons sugar
1	tablespoon crushed red pepper flakes
3	cloves garlic, sliced
1	teaspoon paprika
30	uncooked peeled deveined shrimp (1¼ pounds of 26–30 count size), thawed if frozen, tail shells removed
⅓	cup seafood cocktail sauce
⅓	cup refrigerated honey mustard dressing
⅓	cup spicy hot peanut sauce (from 7-ounce bottle)

1. In 2-quart saucepan, heat 1 cup of the water to boiling. Add salt, sugar, red pepper flakes, garlic and paprika; stir to dissolve salt.

2. Remove from heat. Add remaining 3 cups cold water. Place shrimp in large resealable plastic food-storage bag. Pour brine mixture over shrimp. Seal bag, pushing out air. Place bag in dish or plastic container. Refrigerate 1 hour.

3. Heat gas or charcoal grill. Remove shrimp from brine mixture; discard brine. On each of 6 (12-inch) metal skewers, thread shrimp, leaving ¼-inch space between each.

4. Place shrimp on grill. Cover grill; cook over medium heat 5 to 6 minutes, turning once, until shrimp are pink.

5. In 3 separate small bowls, place cocktail sauce, dressing and peanut sauce. Arrange bowls on platter; add shrimp to platter.

10 servings (3 shrimp and ½ tablespoon of each sauce each)
1 Serving: Calories 100 (Calories from Fat 45); Total Fat 5g (Saturated 1g; Trans 0g); Cholesterol 80mg; Sodium 440mg; Total Carbohydrate 4g (Dietary Fiber 0g; Sugars 3g); Protein 10g
% Daily Value: Vitamin A 4%; Vitamin C 2%; Calcium 2%; Iron 8%
Exchanges: 1½ Very Lean Meat, 1 Fat
Carbohydrate Choices: 0

KITCHEN TIPS

✿ To broil shrimp, set oven control to broil. Place shrimp on rack in broiler pan. Broil with tops 6 inches from heat 6 to 8 minutes, turning once, until shrimp are pink.

✿ For an attractive presentation, garnish the platter with grilled fresh lemon wedges and fresh herbs.

✿ If using bamboo skewers, soak them in water at least 30 minutes before using so they won't burn and char during grilling.

Salmon and Asparagus Salad

Prep Time: 30 min Start to Finish: 30 min

Dressing

- 1/3 cup maple-flavored syrup
- 2 tablespoons Dijon mustard
- 2 tablespoons olive or vegetable oil

Salad

- 1 salmon fillet, 1/2 inch thick (about 1 pound)
- 1 pound asparagus spears
- 4 cups fresh baby salad greens
- 1 cup shredded carrots
- 2 hard-cooked eggs, cut into 8 wedges

1. Heat gas or charcoal grill. In small bowl, mix all dressing ingredients with wire whisk.

2. Cut salmon into 4 pieces. Brush salmon with 1 tablespoon dressing. Toss asparagus with 1 tablespoon dressing. Place asparagus in grill basket. Place salmon, skin side down, on grill. Add grill basket. Cover grill; cook over medium heat, asparagus 7 to 10 minutes and salmon 10 to 15 minutes, shaking grill basket or turning asparagus, until salmon flakes easily with fork and asparagus is crisp-tender.

3. Slide pancake turner between salmon and skin to remove each piece from skin. Divide salad greens, carrots and eggs among 4 plates. Top each with salmon and asparagus. Serve with remaining dressing.

4 servings
1 Serving: Calories 390 (Calories from Fat 150); Total Fat 17g (Saturated 3.5g; Trans 0g); Cholesterol 180mg; Sodium 360mg; Total Carbohydrate 28g (Dietary Fiber 4g; Sugars 14g); Protein 32g
% Daily Value: Vitamin A 140%; Vitamin C 30%; Calcium 8%; Iron 15%
Exchanges: 1 Other Carbohydrate, 2 Vegetable, 4 Lean Meat, 1 Fat
Carbohydrate Choices: 2

Dilled Salmon and Vegetable Packet

Prep Time: 40 min Start to Finish: 40 min

1 salmon fillet, $1/2$ to $3/4$ inch thick (about $1^1/4$ pounds)

2 tablespoons olive or vegetable oil

2 teaspoons chopped fresh or $1/2$ teaspoon dried dill weed

2 teaspoons chopped fresh parsley

1 teaspoon garlic salt

2 medium tomatoes, seeded and coarsely chopped ($1^1/2$ cups)

1 medium yellow summer squash, sliced ($1^1/2$ cups)

1 cup fresh snap pea pods, strings removed

1. Heat gas or charcoal grill. Cut salmon fillet into 4 serving pieces.

2. In small bowl, mix oil, dill weed, parsley and garlic salt. In heavy-duty foil bag, place salmon, tomatoes, squash and pea pods. Brush oil mixture over salmon and vegetables. Double-fold open end of bag.

3. Place bag on grill. Cover grill; cook over medium heat 15 to 20 minutes or until salmon flakes easily with fork. Place bag on serving plate; unfold.

4 servings
1 Serving: Calories 290 (Calories from Fat 140); Total Fat 15g (Saturated 3.5g; Trans 0g); Cholesterol 95mg; Sodium 330mg; Total Carbohydrate 6g (Dietary Fiber 2g; Sugars 3g); Protein 32g
% Daily Value: Vitamin A 20%; Vitamin C 20%; Calcium 4%; Iron 10%
Exchanges: $1^1/2$ Vegetable, 4 Lean Meat, $1/2$ Fat
Carbohydrate Choices: $1/2$

KITCHEN TIPS

✿ For variety, try making this packet using halibut, tuna or swordfish instead of the salmon.

Citrus Salmon

Prep Time: 15 min Start to Finish: 40 min

1 salmon fillet (3 pounds)

$1/2$ teaspoon salt

$1/4$ cup finely chopped fresh parsley

$1/4$ cup finely chopped fresh tarragon leaves

$1/4$ cup grated lemon peel

$1/2$ cup orange juice

2 tablespoons white balsamic vinegar

1 tablespoon olive or vegetable oil

1. Heat oven to 375°F. Spray 13 × 9-inch (3-quart) glass baking dish with cooking spray. Pat salmon dry with paper towel. Place salmon, skin side down, in dish. Sprinkle with salt.

2. In small bowl, mix parsley, tarragon and lemon peel. Press mixture evenly on salmon.

3. In same bowl, mix orange juice, vinegar and oil; set aside.

4. Bake 10 minutes. Pour juice mixture over salmon; bake 10 to 15 minutes longer or until salmon flakes easily with fork. Serve salmon with orange sauce from pan.

8 servings
1 Serving: Calories 230 (Calories from Fat 90); Total Fat 10g (Saturated 2.5g; Trans 0g); Cholesterol 95mg; Sodium 240mg; Total Carbohydrate 3g (Dietary Fiber 0g; Sugars 2g); Protein 31g
% Daily Value: Vitamin A 15%; Vitamin C 15%; Calcium 4%; Iron 8%
Exchanges: 4 Lean Meat
Carbohydrate Choices: 0

KITCHEN TIPS

✿ White balsamic vinegar is made from Italian Trebbiano grapes. It has a smooth, pungent, sweet flavor.

✿ Salmon skin can be easily removed after cooking; slide a knife between the skin and flesh to separate.

Citrus Salmon

Dilled Salmon and Vegetable Packet

Creamy Seafood Lasagna

Prep Time: 20 min Start to Finish: 1 hr 20 min

 9 uncooked lasagna noodles
¼ cup butter or margarine
 1 medium onion, finely chopped (½ cup)
 2 cloves garlic, finely chopped
¼ cup Gold Medal all-purpose flour
 2 cups half-and-half
 1 cup chicken broth
⅓ cup dry sherry or chicken broth
½ teaspoon salt
¼ teaspoon pepper
 1 egg, slightly beaten
½ cup grated Parmesan cheese
 1 container (15 ounces) ricotta cheese
¼ cup chopped fresh parsley
 2 packages (8 ounces each) frozen salad-style imitation crabmeat, thawed, drained and chopped
 2 packages (4 ounces each) frozen cooked salad shrimp, thawed, drained
 3 cups shredded mozzarella cheese (12 ounces)
 1 tablespoon chopped fresh parsley, if desired

1. Heat oven to 350°F. Cook noodles as directed on package.

2. Meanwhile, in 3-quart saucepan, melt butter over medium heat. Add onion and garlic; cook 2 to 3 minutes, stirring occasionally, until onion is crisp-tender. Stir in flour; cook and stir until bubbly. Gradually stir in half-and-half, broth, sherry, salt and pepper. Heat to boiling, stirring constantly. Boil and stir 1 minute. Remove from heat and set aside.

3. In medium bowl, mix egg, Parmesan cheese, ricotta cheese and ¼ cup parsley; set aside.

4. Drain noodles. In ungreased 13 × 9-inch (3-quart) glass baking dish, spread ¾ cup of the sauce. Top with 3 noodles. Spread half of the crabmeat and half of the shrimp over noodles; spread with ¾ cup of the sauce. Sprinkle with 1 cup of the mozzarella cheese; top with 3 noodles. Spread ricotta mixture over noodles; spread with ¾ cup of the sauce. Sprinkle with 1 cup of the mozzarella cheese; top with 3 noodles. Spread with remaining crabmeat, shrimp and sauce. Sprinkle with remaining 1 cup mozzarella cheese.

5. Bake 40 to 45 minutes or until cheese is light golden brown. Let stand 15 minutes before cutting. Sprinkle with 1 tablespoon parsley.

8 servings

1 Serving: Calories 560 (Calories from Fat 260); Total Fat 29g (Saturated 18g; Trans 1g); Cholesterol 180mg; Sodium 1380mg; Total Carbohydrate 34g (Dietary Fiber 2g; Sugars 5g); Protein 41g
% Daily Value: Vitamin A 25%; Vitamin C 4%; Calcium 60%; Iron 15%
Exchanges: 2 Starch, 5 Very Lean Meat, 5 Fat
Carbohydrate Choices: 2

KITCHEN TIPS

✪ Make it extra special by using refrigerated or frozen (thawed) real crabmeat in place of the imitation.

✪ Can't find ricotta cheese? Use dry-curd cottage cheese instead.

Low Fat

Surf and Turf Kabobs

Prep Time: 20 min Start to Finish: 50 min

¾ pound boneless beef sirloin steak (¾ inch thick), trimmed of fat

12 uncooked peeled deveined medium or large shrimp, thawed if frozen, tail shells removed

½ cup teriyaki marinade and sauce (from 10-ounce bottle)

¼ teaspoon coarsely ground pepper

12 bamboo skewers (4 to 6 inch)

1. Cut beef into 24 (¾-inch) pieces. In medium bowl, mix beef, shrimp and teriyaki sauce. Sprinkle with pepper. Cover; refrigerate 30 minutes, stirring frequently. Meanwhile, soak skewers in water at least 30 minutes before using to prevent burning.

2. Spray grill rack with cooking spray. Heat gas or charcoal grill. On each skewer, thread 1 beef piece, 1 shrimp and another beef piece, leaving space between each piece; reserve marinade.

3. Place kabobs on grill. Cover grill; cook over medium heat 5 to 6 minutes, turning once and brushing with marinade once or twice, until shrimp are pink. Discard any remaining marinade.

12 kabobs

1 Kabob: Calories 50 (Calories from Fat 10); Total Fat 1g (Saturated 0g; Trans 0g); Cholesterol 25mg; Sodium 480mg; Total Carbohydrate 2g (Dietary Fiber 0g; Sugars 1g); Protein 8g
% Daily Value: Vitamin A 0%; Vitamin C 0%; Calcium 0%; Iron 6%
Exchanges: 1 Lean Meat
Carbohydrate Choices: 0

KITCHEN TIPS

❂ To broil kabobs, set oven control to broil. Spray broiler pan rack with cooking spray. Place kabobs on rack in broiler pan. Broil kabobs with tops 4 to 6 inches from heat 5 to 6 minutes, turning once and basting with marinade once or twice, until shrimp are pink.

❂ Assemble these kabobs several hours ahead; cover and refrigerate them until you are ready to grill.

❂ These flavorful kabobs would be delicious served with a spicy peanut sauce.

Mediterranean Tuna Steaks

Prep Time: 35 min Start to Finish: 35 min

  1 medium tomato, chopped (³⁄₄ cup)
 ¹⁄₄ cup crumbled feta cheese (1 ounce)
  2 tablespoons chopped Kalamata or ripe olives
  3 tablespoons chopped fresh basil or oregano leaves
 ¹⁄₄ cup olive or vegetable oil
 ¹⁄₂ teaspoon garlic salt
 ¹⁄₄ teaspoon pepper
  4 tuna steaks, 1 inch thick (about 2 pounds)

1. In medium bowl, gently toss tomato, cheese, olives and 1 tablespoon of the basil. Cover; refrigerate until serving.

2. Spray grill rack with cooking spray. Heat gas or charcoal grill. In small bowl, mix remaining 2 tablespoons basil, the oil, garlic salt and pepper. Brush mixture over tuna.

3. Place tuna on grill. Cover grill; cook over medium-high heat 5 minutes. Turn carefully; brush with any remaining oil mixture. Cover; cook 10 to 15 minutes longer or until tuna flakes easily with fork and is slightly pink in center. Serve topped with tomato mixture.

4 servings
1 Serving: Calories 430 (Calories from Fat 250); Total Fat 27g (Saturated 6g; Trans 0g); Cholesterol 140mg; Sodium 360mg; Total Carbohydrate 2g (Dietary Fiber 0g; Sugars 1g); Protein 45g
% Daily Value: Vitamin A 10%; Vitamin C 6%; Calcium 6%; Iron 10%
Exchanges: 6¹⁄₂ Very Lean Meat, 4¹⁄₂ Fat
Carbohydrate Choices: 0

Chicken and Turkey Dishes

Chicken and Turkey

Plates Worth Crowing About

Herb-Scented Roast Turkey with Cornbread Stuffing (page 142)

Cheesy Chicken Quesadillas (page 125)

Asian Chicken Salad Lettuce Cups

Prep Time: 15 min Start to Finish: 15 min

2 cups finely chopped cooked chicken

4 medium green onions, diagonally sliced ($\frac{1}{4}$ cup)

1 can (8 ounces) sliced water chestnuts, drained and finely chopped

$\frac{1}{2}$ cup spicy peanut sauce (from 7-ounce bottle)

1 tablespoon chopped fresh mint leaves

$\frac{1}{4}$ teaspoon crushed red pepper flakes

24 small (about 3 inch) Bibb lettuce leaves (about 1$\frac{1}{2}$ heads), breaking larger leaves into smaller size

$\frac{1}{2}$ cup chopped roasted salted peanuts

1. In medium bowl, mix all ingredients except lettuce and peanuts.

2. Spoon about 2 tablespoons chicken mixture onto each lettuce leaf. Sprinkle with peanuts.

24 servings
1 Serving: Calories 60 (Calories from Fat 35); Total Fat 3.5g (Saturated 0.5g; Trans 0g); Cholesterol 10mg; Sodium 35mg; Total Carbohydrate 2g (Dietary Fiber 0g; Sugars 0g); Protein 5g
% Daily Value: Vitamin A 4%; Vitamin C 2%; Calcium 0%; Iron 0%
Exchanges: $\frac{1}{2}$ Lean Meat, $\frac{1}{2}$ Fat
Carbohydrate Choices: 0

KITCHEN TIPS

✿ Increase the crushed red pepper flakes to $\frac{1}{2}$ teaspoon if you like spicy-hot food.

✿ If you have leftover fresh mint leaves, drop a few in a pitcher of iced tea for a refreshing summer drink.

Quick & Low Fat

Cheesy Chicken Quesadillas

Prep Time: 25 min Start to Finish: 25 min

- 1 cup chopped cooked chicken
- ¼ cup ranch dressing
- 2 teaspoons chili powder
- ½ teaspoon grated lime peel
- 4 flour tortillas (8 to 10 inch)
- 1 cup shredded Mexican cheese blend (4 ounces)
- 2 medium green onions, thinly sliced (2 tablespoons)
- 1 tablespoon vegetable oil
  Sour cream, if desired

1. Heat gas or charcoal grill. In medium bowl, mix chicken, dressing, chili powder and lime peel. Spread chicken mixture over half of each tortilla; sprinkle with cheese and onions. Fold tortilla over and press down. Brush tops with half of the oil.

2. Place quesadillas, oil sides down, on grill. Brush tops with remaining oil. Cover grill; cook over medium-low heat 4 to 6 minutes, turning once, until both sides are golden brown and cheese is melted. Cut each into 8 wedges. Serve with sour cream.

32 servings (1 wedge each)
1 Serving: Calories 50 (Calories from Fat 30); Total Fat 3g (Saturated 1g; Trans 0g); Cholesterol 10mg; Sodium 70mg; Total Carbohydrate 3g (Dietary Fiber 0g; Sugars 0g); Protein 3g
% Daily Value: Vitamin A 0%; Vitamin C 0%; Calcium 4%; Iron 0%
Exchanges: ½ Starch, ½ Fat
Carbohydrate Choices: 0

KITCHEN TIPS

- To cook in skillet, heat 12-inch skillet over medium-high heat. Place quesadilla, oil side down, in skillet. Brush top with oil. Cook 2 to 3 minutes, turning once, until both sides are golden brown and cheese is melted. Repeat with remaining quesadillas.
- Purchase a cooked chicken breast at the deli, and remove the skin and bones. This will yield about 1 cup of cooked chicken.
- If you purchase refrigerated or frozen cooked chicken, cut up any of the larger pieces of chicken.

Super Chicken Nachos

Prep Time: 10 min Start to Finish: 15 min

6 ounces tortilla chips

$\frac{1}{2}$ cup chopped ripe avocado

$\frac{1}{2}$ teaspoon ground cumin

1 large tomato, seeded and chopped (1 cup)

1 cup shredded cooked chicken

1 cup shredded Monterey Jack cheese (4 ounces)

Salsa and sour cream, if desired

6 servings
1 Serving: Calories 280 (Calories from Fat 150); Total Fat 16g (Saturated 5g; Trans 0g); Cholesterol 35mg; Sodium 290mg; Total Carbohydrate 20g (Dietary Fiber 2g; Sugars 1g); Protein 14g
% Daily Value: Vitamin A 10%; Vitamin C 4%; Calcium 15%; Iron 10%
Exchanges: 1 Starch, $\frac{1}{2}$ Other Carbohydrate, $1\frac{1}{2}$ Medium-Fat Meat, $1\frac{1}{2}$ Fat
Carbohydrate Choices: 1

KITCHEN TIPS

✿ For spicy nachos, use pepper Jack cheese.

✿ If you have leftover avocado, mix it with a little lemon or lime juice to keep it from turning brown. Plan to use it within a day in a salad or on grilled burgers.

1. Heat oven to 400°F. Line cookie sheet with foil. Place tortilla chips on cookie sheet. In small bowl, mix avocado, cumin and tomato; spoon over chips. Top with chicken and cheese.

2. Bake 3 to 5 minutes or until cheese is melted. Serve with salsa and sour cream.

Fettuccine with Chicken and Vegetables

Prep Time: 25 min Start to Finish: 25 min

- 1 package (9 ounces) refrigerated fettuccine
- 2 cups small fresh broccoli florets
- 1/3 cup Italian dressing
- 1 pound uncooked chicken breast strips for stir-fry
- 1 medium red onion, cut into thin wedges
- 1/4 teaspoon garlic-pepper blend
- 1/2 cup roasted red bell peppers (from 7-ounce jar), drained and sliced

  Shredded Parmesan cheese, if desired

1. Cook and drain fettuccine and broccoli as directed on fettuccine package. Toss with 2 tablespoons of the dressing. Cover to keep warm.

2. Meanwhile, spray 12-inch skillet with cooking spray; heat over medium-high heat. Add chicken and onion to skillet; sprinkle with garlic-pepper blend. Cook 4 to 6 minutes, stirring occasionally, until chicken is no longer pink in center.

3. Stir bell peppers and remaining dressing into chicken mixture. Cook 2 to 3 minutes, stirring occasionally, until warm. Serve chicken mixture over fettuccine and broccoli. Serve with cheese.

4 servings
1 Serving: Calories 420 (Calories from Fat 120); Total Fat 13g (Saturated 1.5g; Trans 0g); Cholesterol 70mg; Sodium 380mg; Total Carbohydrate 42g (Dietary Fiber 4g; Sugars 6g); Protein 34g
% Daily Value: Vitamin A 25%; Vitamin C 60%; Calcium 6%; Iron 15%
Exchanges: 2 Starch, 1/2 Other Carbohydrate, 1 Vegetable, 3 1/2 Very Lean Meat, 2 Fat
Carbohydrate Choices: 3

Southwest Chicken and Couscous

Prep Time: 25 min Start to Finish: 25 min

 1 cup frozen bell pepper and onion stir-fry (from 1-pound bag)
 1 can (15 ounces) black beans with cumin and chili spices, undrained
 ½ cup Old El Paso Thick'n Chunky salsa
 1 package (9 ounces) frozen cooked Southwest-seasoned chicken breast strips
 ½ cup Green Giant Niblets frozen whole kernel corn (from 1-pound bag)
 2 cups water
 1½ cups uncooked couscous
 ¼ cup chopped fresh cilantro

1. Spray 12-inch skillet with cooking spray; heat over medium-high heat. Cook stir-fry vegetables in skillet 2 to 3 minutes, stirring frequently, until crisp-tender.

2. Stir in beans, salsa, frozen chicken and corn. Heat to boiling; reduce heat to low. Cover; simmer about 5 minutes, stirring occasionally, until chicken is thoroughly heated.

3. Meanwhile, heat water to boiling. Stir in couscous; remove from heat. Cover; let stand 5 minutes. Fluff with fork. Spoon couscous onto serving plates. Top with chicken mixture. Sprinkle with cilantro.

4 servings
1 Serving: Calories 470 (Calories from Fat 35); Total Fat 4g (Saturated 1g; Trans 0g); Cholesterol 40mg; Sodium 1080mg; Total Carbohydrate 79g (Dietary Fiber 11g; Sugars 5g); Protein 30g
% Daily Value: Vitamin A 20%; Vitamin C 15%; Calcium 10%; Iron 20%
Exchanges: 5 Starch, 2 Very Lean Meat
Carbohydrate Choices: 5

Tuscan Rosemary Chicken and White Beans

Prep Time: 30 min Start to Finish: 30 min

- ¹/₃ cup Italian dressing
- 4 boneless skinless chicken breasts (about 1¹/₄ pounds)
- ¹/₄ cup water
- 2 medium carrots, sliced (1 cup)
- 2 medium stalks celery, sliced (1 cup)
- ¹/₄ cup coarsely chopped sun-dried tomatoes in oil, drained
- 1 teaspoon dried rosemary leaves, crushed
- 1 can (19 ounces) Progresso cannellini beans, rinsed and drained

1. In 12-inch skillet, heat dressing over medium-high heat. Cook chicken in dressing 2 to 3 minutes on each side or until lightly browned.

2. Reduce heat to medium-low. Add water, carrots, celery, tomatoes and rosemary to skillet. Cover; simmer about 10 minutes or until juice of chicken is clear when center of thickest part is cut (170°F) and carrots are crisp-tender.

3. Stir in beans. Cover; cook 5 to 6 minutes or until beans are thoroughly heated.

4 servings
1 Serving: Calories 450 (Calories from Fat 130); Total Fat 14g (Saturated 2g; Trans 0g); Cholesterol 90mg; Sodium 320mg; Total Carbohydrate 36g (Dietary Fiber 9g; Sugars 5g); Protein 43g
% Daily Value: Vitamin A 80%; Vitamin C 8%; Calcium 15%; Iron 30%
Exchanges: 2¹/₂ Starch, 5 Very Lean Meat, 2 Fat
Carbohydrate Choices: 2¹/₂

Buffalo Chicken Kabobs

Prep Time: 40 min Start to Finish: 40 min

  1 pound boneless skinless chicken breasts, cut into 24 cubes
 24 refrigerated new potato wedges (from 1 pound 4 ounce bag)
 24 pieces (about 1 inch) celery
  2 tablespoons olive or vegetable oil
  1 teaspoon red pepper sauce
 1/2 teaspoon black and red pepper blend
 1/2 teaspoon seasoned salt
  6 cups torn romaine lettuce
 1/2 cup shredded carrot
 1/2 cup blue cheese dressing

1. Heat gas or charcoal grill. On each of eight 8- to 10-inch metal skewers, thread chicken, potatoes and celery alternately, leaving 1/4-inch space between each piece. Mix oil and pepper sauce; brush over chicken and vegetables. Sprinkle with pepper blend and seasoned salt.

2. Place kabobs on grill. Cover grill; cook over medium heat 15 to 20 minutes, turning occasionally, until chicken is no longer pink in center and potatoes are tender.

3. On 4 individual serving plates, arrange lettuce and carrot. Top each with 2 kabobs. Serve with dressing.

4 servings
1 Serving: Calories 390 (Calories from Fat 210); Total Fat 24g (Saturated 3g; Trans 0g); Cholesterol 75mg; Sodium 600mg; Total Carbohydrate 15g (Dietary Fiber 4g; Sugars 6g); Protein 28g
% Daily Value: Vitamin A 130%; Vitamin C 20%; Calcium 8%; Iron 10%
Exchanges: 1/2 Starch, 1 Vegetable, 3 1/2 Very Lean Meat, 4 1/2 Fat
Carbohydrate Choices: 1

Low Fat

Lemon-Thyme Chicken Breasts

Prep Time: 35 min Start to Finish: 35 min

  1 tablespoon freshly grated lemon peel
  4 teaspoons chopped fresh thyme leaves
  2 teaspoons garlic salt
 1/2 teaspoon pepper
  4 boneless skinless chicken breasts (about 1 1/4 pounds)

1. Spray grill rack with cooking spray. Heat gas or charcoal grill. In small bowl, mix all ingredients except chicken. Sprinkle mixture over chicken.

2. Place chicken on grill. Cover grill; cook over medium heat 15 to 20 minutes, turning once, until juice of chicken is clear when center of thickest part is cut (170°F). Garnish with additional fresh thyme if desired.

4 servings
1 Serving: Calories 170 (Calories from Fat 40); Total Fat 4.5g (Saturated 1.5g; Trans 0g); Cholesterol 85mg; Sodium 560mg; Total Carbohydrate 1g (Dietary Fiber 0g; Sugars 0g); Protein 31g
% Daily Value: Vitamin A 0%; Vitamin C 4%; Calcium 2%; Iron 8%
Exchanges: 4 1/2 Very Lean Meat, 1/2 Fat
Carbohydrate Choices: 0

KITCHEN TIPS

✿ Serve with a salad of mixed greens and sliced strawberries, crusty herb bread and tall glasses of iced tea.

Buffalo Chicken Kabobs

Lemon-Thyme Chicken Breasts

Grilled Seasoned Chicken Drummies

Grilled Mexican Citrus Chicken

Low Fat

Grilled Seasoned Chicken Drummies

Prep Time: 20 min Start to Finish: 35 min

1	container (16 ounces) plain yogurt
2	tablespoons curry powder
1	tablespoon paprika
1	teaspoon garlic salt
20 to 24	chicken drummettes (about 2 pounds)
$\frac{1}{4}$	cup shredded peeled cucumber
1	clove garlic, finely chopped
$\frac{1}{2}$	teaspoon salt
$\frac{1}{2}$	teaspoon lemon juice
2	tablespoons chopped fresh mint leaves

1. Heat gas or charcoal grill. In large bowl, mix $\frac{1}{2}$ cup of the yogurt, the curry powder, paprika and garlic salt. Add chicken, stirring to coat all surfaces. Let stand 15 minutes.

2. Meanwhile, in small bowl, mix remaining yogurt and remaining ingredients.

3. Place chicken on grill. Cover grill; cook over medium heat 8 to 12 minutes, turning once or twice, until juice of chicken is clear when thickest part is cut to bone (180°F). Serve with yogurt dip. Sprinkle dip with additional chopped fresh mint leaves if desired.

20 to 24 appetizers (1 drummette and 1 tablespoon dip each)
1 Serving: Calories 60 (Calories from Fat 25); Total Fat 3g (Saturated 1g; Trans 0g); Cholesterol 20mg; Sodium 140mg; Total Carbohydrate 2g (Dietary Fiber 0g; Sugars 1g); Protein 7g
% Daily Value: Vitamin A 4%; Vitamin C 0%; Calcium 6%; Iron 4%
Exchanges: 1 Medium-Fat Meat
Carbohydrate Choices: 0

KITCHEN TIPS

❁ The chicken can be marinated the day before in the refrigerator. The dip can also be made ahead and refrigerated.

❁ Chicken drummettes, or drummies, are the meaty portions of the chicken wings. You can purchase them in packages. If you prefer, buy chicken wings and separate each one into 2 pieces.

Grilled Mexican Citrus Chicken

Prep Time: 1 hr 15 min Start to Finish: 4 hr 15 min

$\frac{1}{2}$	cup orange juice
$\frac{1}{2}$	cup lime juice
$\frac{1}{2}$	cup olive or vegetable oil
$\frac{1}{4}$	cup chopped fresh cilantro
$\frac{1}{4}$	cup chopped onion
4	teaspoons chili powder
2	teaspoons ground cumin
1	teaspoon salt
$\frac{1}{2}$	teaspoon red pepper sauce
2	cut-up whole chickens (3 to $3\frac{1}{2}$ pounds each)

1. In large shallow glass dish or 2-gallon resealable plastic food-storage bag, mix all ingredients except chicken. Add chicken; turn to coat with marinade. Cover dish or seal bag and refrigerate, turning chicken occasionally, at least 3 hours but no longer than 24 hours.

2. Heat gas or charcoal grill. Remove chicken from marinade; reserve marinade. Place chicken, skin sides up, on grill. Cover grill; cook over medium heat 15 to 20 minutes.

3. Turn chicken. Cover grill; cook 20 to 40 minutes longer, turning and brushing 2 to 3 times with marinade, until juice of chicken is clear when thickest piece is cut to bone (170°F for breasts; 180°F for thighs and legs). Discard any remaining marinade.

8 servings
1 Serving: Calories 380 (Calories from Fat 210); Total Fat 23g (Saturated 4.5g; Trans 0g); Cholesterol 115mg; Sodium 420mg; Total Carbohydrate 4g (Dietary Fiber 0g; Sugars 2g); Protein 37g
% Daily Value: Vitamin A 10%; Vitamin C 10%; Calcium 4%; Iron 10%
Exchanges: $5\frac{1}{2}$ Lean Meat, $1\frac{1}{2}$ Fat
Carbohydrate Choices: 0

KITCHEN TIPS

❁ To reduce grilling time, use 8 boneless skinless chicken breasts; grill them for 15 to 20 minutes, turning once.

Maple and Mustard-Glazed Chicken

Prep Time: 1 hr 5 min Start to Finish: 1 hr 5 min

$^3/_4$ cup maple-flavored syrup

$^1/_2$ cup Dijon mustard

  2 tablespoons chopped fresh chives

  1 cut-up whole chicken (3 to 3$^1/_2$ pounds)

  1 teaspoon seasoned salt

$^1/_4$ teaspoon coarse pepper

1. Heat gas or charcoal grill. In 1-quart saucepan, mix maple syrup, mustard and chives.

2. Sprinkle both sides of chicken pieces with seasoned salt and pepper. Place chicken, skin sides up, on grill. Cover grill; cook over medium heat 15 minutes; turn chicken. Cover; cook 20 to 40 minutes longer, turning occasionally and brushing 2 or 3 times with mustard mixture, until juice of chicken is clear when thickest piece is cut to bone (170°F for breasts; 180°F for thighs and legs).

3. Heat remaining mustard mixture to boiling; boil 1 minute. Serve sauce with chicken.

4 servings

1 Serving: Calories 560 (Calories from Fat 200); Total Fat 22g (Saturated 6g; Trans 0.5g); Cholesterol 130mg; Sodium 1280mg; Total Carbohydrate 50g (Dietary Fiber 0g; Sugars 23g); Protein 41g
% Daily Value: Vitamin A 10%; Vitamin C 2%; Calcium 4%; Iron 15%
Exchanges: 3$^1/_2$ Other Carbohydrate, 6 Lean Meat, 1 Fat
Carbohydrate Choices: 3

KITCHEN TIPS

✪ Coleslaw, baked beans, buttermilk biscuits and strawberry shortcake are perfect accompaniments to this tasty chicken. Don't forget the lemonade!

Turkey Cutlets with Snap Peas and Carrots

Prep Time: 20 min Start to Finish: 40 min

1 pound uncooked turkey breast cutlets, about ¼ inch thick

½ cup honey-Dijon dressing

1 cup baby-cut carrots, cut lengthwise in half

¼ cup water

2 cups fresh snap pea pods, strings removed

1. Place turkey in shallow glass or plastic dish. Pour dressing over turkey; turn turkey to coat evenly. Cover dish; let stand 20 minutes at room temperature.

2. Spray 12-inch skillet with cooking spray; heat over medium heat. Drain dressing from turkey; pat turkey dry. Cook turkey in skillet 3 to 5 minutes, turning once, until brown.

3. Add carrots and water. Top turkey and carrots with pea pods. Cover; cook 7 to 9 minutes or until carrots are tender and turkey is no longer pink in center.

4 servings

1 Serving: Calories 240 (Calories from Fat 100); Total Fat 11g (Saturated 2g; Trans 0g); Cholesterol 75mg; Sodium 260mg; Total Carbohydrate 8g (Dietary Fiber 2g; Sugars 5g); Protein 27g
% Daily Value: Vitamin A 80%; Vitamin C 15%; Calcium 4%; Iron 10%
Exchanges: 1 Vegetable, 3½ Very Lean Meat, 2 Fat
Carbohydrate Choices: ½

KITCHEN TIPS

❂ Serve this dish with a side salad of sliced tomatoes and cucumbers, and sourdough bread.

Turkey-Green Chili Enchiladas

Turkey-Green Chili Enchiladas

Prep Time: 20 min Start to Finish: 1 hr 5 min

Sauce

- 2 tablespoons vegetable oil
- 1 large onion, finely chopped (1 cup)
- 2 cloves garlic, finely chopped
- 1 cup chicken broth
- 2 tablespoons semisweet chocolate chips
- 1 tablespoon ground ancho chilies
- 1 teaspoon ground cumin
- $\frac{1}{2}$ teaspoon salt
- 1 can (28 ounces) fire-roasted crushed tomatoes, undrained

Enchiladas

- 2 cups shredded cooked turkey
- 1 cup sour cream
- $1\frac{1}{2}$ cups shredded Cheddar cheese (6 ounces)
- 2 cans (4.5 ounces each) Old El Paso chopped green chilies, undrained
- 1 package (11.5 ounces) Old El Paso flour tortillas for burritos (8 tortillas)
- 1 cup shredded Monterey Jack cheese (4 ounces)

1. Heat oven to 350°F. Lightly spray 13 × 9-inch (3-quart) glass baking dish with cooking spray.

2. In 12-inch skillet, heat oil over medium-high heat. Add onion and garlic, cook about 1 minute, stirring frequently, until onion is tender. Stir in remaining sauce ingredients. Heat to boiling. Reduce heat to low, cook uncovered 15 minutes, stirring occasionally.

3. In medium bowl, mix all enchilada ingredients except tortillas and Monterey Jack cheese. Spread about $\frac{1}{2}$ cup turkey mixture over each tortilla; top with 2 tablespoons sauce. Roll up tortillas; arrange seam sides down in baking dish. Pour remaining sauce over tortillas. Top with Monterey Jack cheese.

4. Spray sheet of foil with cooking spray; place sprayed side down over baking dish. Bake 30 to 45 minutes or until thoroughly heated.

8 servings

1 Serving: Calories 470 (Calories from Fat 250); Total Fat 27g (Saturated 13g; Trans 0.5g); Cholesterol 85mg; Sodium 1520mg; Total Carbohydrate 33g (Dietary Fiber 2g; Sugars 8g); Protein 24g
% Daily Value: Vitamin A 30%; Vitamin C 10%; Calcium 35%; Iron 20%
Exchanges: 1$\frac{1}{2}$ Starch, $\frac{1}{2}$ Other Carbohydrate, 3 Lean Meat, 3$\frac{1}{2}$ Fat
Carbohydrate Choices: 2

KITCHEN TIPS

- The foil used to cover the baking dish is sprayed with cooking spray to keep the cheese from sticking.
- Chocolate chips add depth to the flavor of the sauce.

Betty Crocker
MAKES IT EASY

Ultimate Turkey Guide

TIPS AND TECHNIQUES TO HELP YOU PREPARE THE PERFECT TURKEY

Selecting Your Turkey

Ready-to-cook whole turkeys can range in size from 8 to 24 pounds. How much should you buy? Allow about 1 pound of uncooked whole turkey per person. That makes enough for a feast, as well as leftovers. Choose a turkey that is plump and meaty with smooth, cream-colored skin.

There's no difference in quality between fresh and frozen turkeys. Keep fresh whole turkeys refrigerated and cook them within 1 to 2 days of buying. Store frozen whole turkeys in your freezer at 0°F for up to 6 months.

Thawing Your Turkey

There are three safe ways to thaw a frozen turkey. Thawing at room temperature is not recommended because it promotes bacterial growth.

1. Gradual Thaw in Refrigerator (Preferred Method)
Refrigerate frozen turkey (in original packaging) on a tray to collect liquids. Allow 24 hours per 5 pounds of whole turkey. Follow the timetable below.

APPROXIMATE WEIGHT (POUNDS)	THAWING TIME (IN REFRIGERATOR)	
8 to 12	1 to 2 days	Once thawed, the turkey can be refrigerated up to 2 days before roasting.
12 to 16	2 to 3 days	
16 to 20	3 to 4 days	
20 to 24	4 to 5 days	

2. Gradual Thaw in Cold Water
To thaw a turkey more quickly, use this method. Leave the turkey in its original packaging, free from tears or holes. Put in a sink or clean large container filled with cold water that you change often. Allow 30 minutes per pound for whole turkeys. An 8- to 12-pound turkey will thaw in about 5 hours.

3. Quick Thaw in Microwave
To thaw a turkey even faster, follow the microwave manufacturer's directions.

Preparing Your Turkey

Stuff the turkey just before cooking. This will prevent bacteria from contaminating the stuffing. Never prestuff a turkey and refrigerate or freeze it for later roasting.

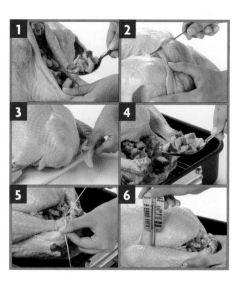

1. Turn turkey breast down for easier filling of neck cavity. Fill neck cavity lightly with stuffing.
2. Fasten neck skin to back of turkey with skewer.
3. Turn turkey breast side up. Fold wings across back of turkey so tips are touching.
4. Fill body cavity lightly with stuffing.
5. Tuck legs under band of skin at tail (if present), or tie together with heavy string, then tie to tail if desired.
6. Insert ovenproof thermometer so tip is in thickest part of inside thigh and does not touch bone.

Roasting Your Turkey

For golden brown skin and moist, tender meat, roast your turkey at 325°F according to the Roasting Turkey Timetable below. For an equally tender and delicious turkey, you can roast at 450°F according to the timetable for high-heat roasting below.

1. Place turkey with breast side up on a rack in a shallow roasting pan. Brush with melted butter, margarine or oil. If using an oven-proof meat thermometer, place it so the tip is in the thickest part of the inside thigh and does not touch bone.

2. When two-thirds through the roasting time, cut the band of skin at the tail, or remove the tie or skewer holding the legs together to allow inside of thighs to cook through.

3. Begin checking turkey for doneness about 1 hour before end of recommended roasting time. Turkey is done when thermometer reads 180°F and legs move easily when lifted or twisted. Thermometer placed in center of stuffing will read 165°F. If the turkey is golden brown but is not done, place a tent of foil loosely over the turkey.

4. When the turkey is done, transfer it with breast side up to a carving board and let stand loosely covered with foil for 15 to 20 minutes.

Roasting Turkey Timetable

Follow this timetable for regular roasting or high-heat roasting. For prestuffed turkeys, follow package directions—do not use this timetable.

READY-TO-COOK WEIGHT (pounds)	APPROXIMATE ROASTING TIME AT 325°F (hours)	HIGH-HEAT ROASTING TIME AT 450°F (hours)
WHOLE TURKEY (STUFFED)		
8 to 12	3 to $3\frac{1}{2}$	Not recommended
12 to 14	$3\frac{1}{2}$ to 4	
14 to 18	4 to $4\frac{1}{4}$	
18 to 20	$4\frac{1}{4}$ to $4\frac{3}{4}$	
20 to 24	$4\frac{3}{4}$ to $5\frac{1}{4}$	
WHOLE TURKEY (NOT STUFFED)		
8 to 12	$2\frac{3}{4}$ to 3	45 minutes to $1\frac{1}{4}$
12 to 14	3 to $3\frac{3}{4}$	
14 to 18	$3\frac{3}{4}$ to $4\frac{1}{4}$	$1\frac{1}{2}$ to $1\frac{3}{4}$
18 to 20	$4\frac{1}{4}$ to $4\frac{1}{2}$	
20 to 24	$4\frac{1}{2}$ to 5	$2\frac{3}{4}$ to $3\frac{1}{4}$
TURKEY BREAST (BONE-IN)		
2 to 4	$1\frac{1}{2}$ to 2	Not recommended
3 to 5	$1\frac{1}{2}$ to $2\frac{1}{2}$	
5 to 7	2 to $2\frac{1}{2}$	

Carving Your Turkey

Place the turkey with breast side up and with its legs to your right if you're right-handed. Remove skewers or ties. Remove stuffing from the bird before carving and put it in a separate serving dish or container.

1. While gently pulling the legs away from the body, cut through the joint between leg and body. Separate the drumstick and thigh by cutting down through the connecting joint. Serve the drumsticks and thighs whole or carve them. To carve, slice meat from drumstick at an angle and slice thigh parallel to the bone.

2. Make a deep horizontal cut into the breast just above the wing.

3. Insert fork into the top of the breast. Starting halfway up the breast, carve thin slices down to the horizontal cut, working from outer edge of bird to the center. Repeat steps on the other side of the turkey.

Cut through the joint between leg and body.

Make a horizontal cut in the breast above the wing.

Carve thin slices down the horizontal cut.

Herb-Scented Roast Turkey with Cornbread Stuffing

Prep Time: 30 min Start to Finish: 5 hr 30 min

1 tablespoon chopped fresh or 2 teaspoons dried rosemary leaves, crumbled

1 tablespoon chopped fresh or 2 teaspoons dried sage leaves, crumbled

1 teaspoon salt

1/4 teaspoon pepper

2 cloves garlic, finely chopped

1 whole turkey (12 pounds), thawed if frozen Cornbread Stuffing (page 186)

1/4 cup butter or margarine, melted Foolproof Gravy (page 145) Fresh herb sprigs, if desired

1. Heat oven to 325°F. In small bowl, mix rosemary, sage, salt, pepper and garlic; rub into turkey skin.

2. Make Cornbread Stuffing. Turn turkey breast side down. Fill neck cavity lightly with stuffing; fasten neck skin to back of turkey with skewer.

3. Turn turkey breast side up. Fold wings across back of turkey so tips are touching. Fill body cavity lightly with stuffing (do not pack stuffing because it will expand during roasting). Tuck legs under band of skin at tail (if present), or tie together with heavy string.

4. On rack in shallow roasting pan, place turkey, breast side up. Brush with melted butter. Do not add water. Insert ovenproof meat thermometer so tip is in thickest part of inside thigh and does not touch bone.

5. Roast uncovered 4 to 5 hours, brushing with pan juices every 30 minutes and loosely covering with foil when turkey begins to turn golden. Turkey is done when thermometer reads 180°F and legs move easily when lifted or twisted. Thermometer placed in center of stuffing should read 165°F when done.

6. Place turkey on warm platter; cover with foil to keep warm. Let stand 15 to 20 minutes for easiest carving. While turkey is standing, make Foolproof Gravy. Garnish turkey with herb sprigs. Cover and refrigerate any remaining turkey and stuffing separately.

12 servings
1 Serving: Calories 830 (Calories from Fat 450); Total Fat 50g (Saturated 19g; Trans 2g); Cholesterol 235mg; Sodium 1440mg; Total Carbohydrate 43g (Dietary Fiber 4g; Sugars 13g); Protein 51g
% Daily Value: Vitamin A 20%; Vitamin C 0%; Calcium 10%; Iron 20% Exchanges: 2 Starch, 1 Other Carbohydrate, 6 1/2 Lean Meat, 6 Fat Carbohydrate Choices: 3

KITCHEN TIPS

❀ Be sure to let the turkey stand for about 20 minutes before carving. You'll be rewarded with evenly cooked, moist and juicy turkey meat.

❀ A 12-pound turkey should serve 12 hungry people and still give you enough leftovers for sandwiches the next day.

Cherry-Glazed Turkey with Dried Cherry-Apple Stuffing

Prep Time: 30 min Start to Finish: 5 hr 25 min

2 tablespoons chopped fresh sage leaves
1 teaspoon salt
1/2 teaspoon pepper
1 whole turkey (12 pounds), thawed if frozen
  Dried Cherry-Apple Stuffing (page 183)
1/2 cup cherry preserves or jam
1/4 cup ruby port or chicken broth

1. Heat oven to 325°F. Grease 13 × 9-inch (3-quart) glass baking dish with shortening or cooking spray. In small bowl, mix sage, salt and pepper; rub into turkey skin.

2. Make Dried Cherry-Apple Stuffing. Turn turkey breast side down. Fill neck cavity lightly with 1 cup of the stuffing (do not pack stuffing because it will expand during roasting). Fasten neck skin of turkey to back with skewer.

3. Turn turkey breast side up. Fold wings across back of turkey so tips are touching. Fill body cavity lightly with 3 cups of the stuffing (do not pack stuffing because it will expand during roasting). Place remaining stuffing in baking dish. Cover with foil; refrigerate until ready to bake. Tuck legs under band of skin at tail (if present), or tie together with heavy string.

4. On rack in shallow roasting pan, place turkey, breast side up. Insert ovenproof meat thermometer so tip is in thickest part of inside thigh and does not touch bone.

5. Cover turkey loosely with foil or roaster cover; roast 3 hours. Meanwhile, in small bowl, mix preserves and port; set aside.

6. Uncover turkey; place stuffing in baking dish in oven. Roast 45 minutes to 1 hour 30 minutes longer, brushing turkey with glaze frequently, until thermometer reads 180°F and legs move easily when lifted or twisted. Remove stuffing from oven after 40 to 50 minutes of baking time or when thoroughly heated (165°F).

7. Place turkey on warm platter; cover with foil to keep warm. Let stand 15 to 20 minutes for easiest carving. Cover and refrigerate any remaining turkey and stuffing separately.

12 servings
1 Serving: Calories 780 (Calories from Fat 340); Total Fat 38g (Saturated 12g; Trans 1.5g); Cholesterol 165mg; Sodium 1210mg; Total Carbohydrate 57g (Dietary Fiber 4g; Sugars 20g); Protein 51g
% Daily Value: Vitamin A 20%; Vitamin C 2%; Calcium 10%; Iron 25%
Exchanges: 2 Starch, 2 Other Carbohydrate, 6 1/2 Lean Meat, 3 1/2 Fat
Carbohydrate Choices: 4

KITCHEN TIPS

☺ Use fresh herbs, cherries and plums to decorate the platter.
☺ Cherry preserves and ruby port give a rich, deep mahogany color and slightly sweet flavor to the turkey. Substitute cherry juice for the port if desired.

Betty Crocker
MAKES IT EASY

Great Gravy

Whisk up your smoothest and best-tasting gravy ever with these terrific tips!

Smooth Secrets

▶ Keep it lump-free by using a wire whisk and rapidly beating the drippings while adding the flour.

▶ Measure accurately. (Too little fat can make the gravy lumpy; too much fat can make the gravy greasy.)

▶ Be sure the mixture remains at a full boil for 1 minute so that the gravy doesn't have a starchy flavor.

▶ If you don't have enough drippings, you can use water from cooking potatoes, wine or tomato juice.

▶ If you have plenty of pan drippings, you can double or triple the recipe.

▶ For thinner gravy, decrease meat drippings and flour to 1 tablespoon each.

Making Gravy

Return drippings to the roasting pan, then stir in flour.

Stir in the turkey juices. Heat to boiling, stirring constantly. Cook over low heat, stirring constantly and scraping up brown bits, until mixture is smooth and bubbly.

Gravy RX

WHAT IF MY GRAVY IS:	QUICK FIXES
Greasy	Put a slice of fresh bread on top of the gravy for a few seconds to absorb the fat; remove bread before it breaks into pieces.
Lumpy	Pour into food processor and process until smooth, or press gravy through a strainer; return to saucepan and heat.
Too Thin	Dissolve 1 tablespoon flour in 2 tablespoons water; stir into gravy with fork or wire whisk. Boil and stir 1 minute.
Too Pale	Stir in browning sauce, soy sauce or Worcestershire sauce (start with 1 teaspoon).
Too Salty	Add a peeled raw potato, cut into eighths. Cook and stir 5 to 10 minutes; then remove potato pieces.

Foolproof Gravy

Prep Time: 10 min Start to Finish: 15 min

$^1/_2$ cup turkey drippings (fat and juices from roasted turkey)*

$^1/_2$ cup Gold Medal all-purpose flour

3 cups liquid (juices from roasted turkey or chicken broth)

Browning sauce, if desired

$^1/_2$ teaspoon salt

$^1/_4$ teaspoon pepper

3 cups; 12 servings ($^1/_4$ cup each)

*If necessary, add chicken broth to turkey drippings to equal $^1/_2$ cup.

1 Serving: Calories 70 (Calories from Fat 60); Total Fat 6g (Saturated 2g; Trans 0g); Cholesterol 5mg; Sodium 150mg; Total Carbohydrate 3g (Dietary Fiber 0g; Sugars 0g); Protein 0g
% Daily Value: Vitamin A 0%; Vitamin C 0%; Calcium 0%; Iron 0%
Exchanges: 1$^1/_2$ Fat
Carbohydrate Choices: 0

KITCHEN TIPS

⚙ For added flavor, use vegetable cooking water or vegetable broth as part of the 3 cups of liquid.

⚙ The trick to smooth, creamy gravy is to use a wire whisk when adding the flour to the drippings. Beat the drippings rapidly with the whisk while adding the flour and you won't get lumps.

1. Pour drippings from roasting pan into bowl, leaving brown particles in pan. Return $^1/_2$ cup drippings to roasting pan. (Measure accurately because too little fat makes gravy lumpy.)

2. Stir in flour with wire whisk. (Measure accurately so gravy is not greasy.) Cook over medium heat, stirring constantly, until mixture is smooth and bubbly. Remove from heat.

3. Stir in liquid. Heat to boiling, stirring constantly. Boil and stir 1 minute. Stir in a few drops of browning sauce. Stir in salt and pepper. Strain if desired.

Honey-Dijon Brined Turkey Breast

Prep Time: 15 min Start to Finish: 14 hr 25 min

11 cups cold water

1 cup honey

½ cup Dijon mustard

⅓ cup salt

1 whole bone-in turkey breast (5 to 6 pounds), thawed if frozen

3 tablespoons olive or vegetable oil

1 teaspoon dried marjoram leaves

1 teaspoon ground mustard

1 teaspoon garlic-pepper blend

1. In 6-quart container or stockpot, stir water, honey, Dijon mustard and salt until honey and salt are dissolved. Add turkey breast to brine mixture. Cover; refrigerate at least 12 hours but no longer than 24 hours.

2. Heat gas or charcoal grill for indirect cooking as directed by manufacturer. Remove turkey from brine mixture; rinse thoroughly under cool running water and pat dry. Discard brine.

3. In small bowl, mix remaining ingredients; brush over turkey. Insert ovenproof meat thermometer into turkey so tip is in thickest part of breast and does not touch bone.

4. Place turkey on unheated side of 2-burner gas grill or over drip pan on charcoal grill. (If using one-burner gas grill, cook over low heat.) Cover grill; cook over medium heat 1 hour.

5. Rotate turkey ½ turn; cook covered 45 to 60 minutes longer or until thermometer reads 170°F.

6. Remove turkey from grill. Cover with foil; let stand 5 to 10 minutes before slicing.

8 servings
1 Serving: Calories 400 (Calories from Fat 160); Total Fat 18g (Saturated 5g; Trans 0g); Cholesterol 145mg; Sodium 460mg; Total Carbohydrate 5g (Dietary Fiber 0g; Sugars 4g); Protein 54g
% Daily Value: Vitamin A 4%; Vitamin C 0%; Calcium 2%; Iron 10%
Exchanges: 7½ Lean Meat
Carbohydrate Choices: ½

KITCHEN TIPS

✿ The brine mixture adds salt and flavor to the turkey, so try to buy a turkey that hasn't been injected with saline solution. An injected turkey will work in this recipe, but it will taste a little saltier.

✿ Brining a turkey keeps the meat very moist during cooking.

Low Fat

Plum-Glazed Turkey Tenderloins

Prep Time: 40 min Start to Finish: 1 hr 10 min

1   cup plum jam
¼   cup dry sherry or chicken broth
2   tablespoons olive or vegetable oil
2   teaspoons chopped fresh rosemary leaves
1½ teaspoons garlic salt
¼   teaspoon pepper
1   medium onion, finely chopped (½ cup)
2   pounds turkey breast tenderloins (about 6 tenderloins)

1. In small bowl, mix all ingredients except turkey. In shallow glass dish, place turkey. Pour half of the plum mixture over turkey; turn turkey to coat. Cover dish; refrigerate 30 minutes, turning once. Reserve remaining half of plum mixture to serve with turkey.

2. Heat gas or charcoal grill for indirect-heat cooking. Remove turkey from marinade; reserve marinade for basting.

3. Place turkey on grill for indirect cooking. Cover grill; cook over medium-high heat 25 to 30 minutes, turning and brushing occasionally with reserved marinade, until juice of turkey is clear when center of thickest part is cut (170°F). Discard any remaining marinade. Heat reserved plum mixture. Serve with sliced turkey.

6 servings
1 Serving: Calories 350 (Calories from Fat 50); Total Fat 6g (Saturated 1g; Trans 0g); Cholesterol 100mg; Sodium 330mg; Total Carbohydrate 39g (Dietary Fiber 1g; Sugars 27g); Protein 36g
% Daily Value: Vitamin A 0%; Vitamin C 6%; Calcium 4%; Iron 10%
Exchanges: ½ Starch, 2 Other Carbohydrate, 5 Very Lean Meat, ½ Fat
Carbohydrate Choices: 2½

Turkey-Biscuit Pot Pie

Prep Time: 25 min Start to Finish: 55 min

Filling

2½ cups ready-to-eat baby-cut carrots (12 ounces)

2 cups cut-up fresh broccoli

3 tablespoons butter or margarine

1 medium onion, finely chopped (½ cup)

3 tablespoons Gold Medal all-purpose flour

2 cups chicken or turkey broth

1 tablespoon chopped fresh or 1 teaspoon dried sage leaves

2 cups cubed cooked turkey

Biscuits

4 slices bacon

1 cup Original Bisquick mix

½ cup milk

½ cup shredded Cheddar cheese (2 ounces)

1. Heat oven to 400°F. In 2-quart saucepan, heat 1 cup water to boiling. Add carrots and broccoli; cook about 4 minutes or until carrots and broccoli are crisp-tender. Drain.

2. Meanwhile, in 3-quart saucepan, melt butter over medium heat. Add onion; cook about 2 minutes, stirring occasionally, until tender. Beat in flour with wire whisk. Gradually beat in broth and sage. Reduce heat to medium-low; cook about 5 minutes, stirring occasionally, until sauce thickens.

3. Stir carrots, broccoli and turkey into sauce. Spoon turkey mixture into ungreased 2-quart casserole.

4. Place bacon on microwavable plate; cover with microwavable paper towel. Microwave on High 4 to 6 minutes or until crisp. Crumble bacon; place in medium bowl. Add remaining biscuit ingredients; stir just until blended. Spoon biscuit batter around edge of turkey mixture.

5. Bake uncovered 25 to 30 minutes or until biscuit crust is golden brown.

6 servings (1 cup each)
1 Serving: Calories 360 (Calories from Fat 170); Total Fat 18g (Saturated 8g; Trans 1g); Cholesterol 75mg; Sodium 940mg; Total Carbohydrate 25g (Dietary Fiber 3g; Sugars 6g); Protein 23g
% Daily Value: Vitamin A 130%; Vitamin C 25%; Calcium 15%; Iron 10%
Exchanges: 1 Starch, ½ Other Carbohydrate, 1 Vegetable, 2½ Lean Meat, 2 Fat
Carbohydrate Choices: 1½

KITCHEN TIPS

✿ You can find fresh sage in small bunches year-round in the produce section of supermarkets.

✿ An easy biscuit topping made with Bisquick mix tops this family-friendly pot pie.

Pork and Beef Dishes

Savory . . . Succulent . . . Substantial

Beef Tenderloin with Red Wine Sauce (page 161)

Seven-Layer Rigatoni (page 153)

Empanadillas

Prep Time: 40 min Start to Finish: 1 hr 5 min

 8 ounces bulk spicy pork sausage
 1 medium onion, finely chopped (½ cup)
 1 teaspoon finely chopped garlic
 ¼ cup raisins, finely chopped
 ¼ cup pitted green olives, finely chopped
 1 teaspoon ground cumin
 1 package (17.3 ounces) frozen puff pastry, thawed
 1 egg
 1 teaspoon water
    Fresh cilantro, if desired

1. Heat oven to 400°F. Line large cookie sheet with foil or cooking parchment paper; lightly spray with cooking spray.

2. In 10-inch skillet, cook sausage, onion and garlic over medium-high heat 5 to 7 minutes, stirring occasionally, until sausage is no longer pink. Stir in raisins, olives and cumin; remove from heat.

3. On lightly floured surface, roll 1 sheet of pastry into 12 × 9-inch rectangle, trimming edges if necessary. Cut into twelve 3-inch squares.

4. Place 1 tablespoon sausage mixture on each pastry square. In small bowl, beat egg and water with fork until well blended. Brush egg mixture on edges of pastry squares. Fold pastry over filling to make triangles; press edges with fork to seal. Place on cookie sheet. Repeat with remaining pastry and sausage mixture. Brush tops of triangles with egg mixture.

5. Bake 20 to 25 minutes or until golden brown. Serve warm. Garnish with cilantro.

24 appetizers
1 Appetizer: Calories 140 (Calories from Fat 90); Total Fat 10g (Saturated 3.5g; Trans 1g); Cholesterol 35mg; Sodium 110mg; Total Carbohydrate 11g (Dietary Fiber 0g; Sugars 1g); Protein 3g
% Daily Value: Vitamin A 0%; Vitamin C 0%; Calcium 0%; Iron 6%
Exchanges: ½ Starch, 2 Fat
Carbohydrate Choices: 1

KITCHEN TIPS

❂ For a less spicy version, substitute ground beef or ground turkey for the sausage.
❂ Empanadillas are great appetizers because they can be prepared and kept frozen until baking time. Freeze on a cookie sheet, then store in a plastic bag.

Grilled Taco Nachos

Prep Time: 35 min Start to Finish: 35 min

2 pounds bulk pork sausage

10 cups tortilla chips

2 cans (4.5 ounces each) Old El Paso chopped green chilies, drained

4 teaspoons Old El Paso taco seasoning mix (from 1.25-ounce package)

4 roma (plum) tomatoes, chopped (1⅓ cups)

4 medium green onions, sliced (¼ cup)

4 cups finely shredded Colby-Monterey Jack cheese blend (1 pound)

Old El Paso Thick'n Chunky salsa, if desired

1. Heat gas or charcoal grill. Cut 2 (30 × 18-inch) sheets of heavy-duty foil; spray with cooking spray. In 12-inch skillet, cook sausage over medium-high heat 5 to 7 minutes, stirring occasionally, until no longer pink; drain.

2. Spread tortilla chips on centers of foil sheets. In large bowl, mix sausage, chilies and seasoning mix; spoon over tortilla chips. Top with tomatoes and onions. Sprinkle with cheese.

3. Wrap foil securely around tortilla chips. Place foil packets, seam sides up, on grill. Cover grill; cook over medium heat 8 to 10 minutes or until cheese is melted. Serve with salsa.

8 servings
1 Serving: Calories 580 (Calories from Fat 370); Total Fat 41g (Saturated 17g; Trans 0.5g); Cholesterol 100mg; Sodium 1170mg; Total Carbohydrate 25g (Dietary Fiber 1g; Sugars 2g); Protein 27g
% Daily Value: Vitamin A 20%; Vitamin C 10%; Calcium 45%; Iron 15%
Exchanges: 1½ Starch, 3 High-Fat Meat, 3½ Fat
Carbohydrate Choices: 1½

KITCHEN TIPS

☼ Taco nachos can be prepared in the oven. Bake foil packets in 350°F oven 15 to 20 minutes or until cheese is melted.

Barbecue Pork Bites

Prep Time: 35 min Start to Finish: 50 min

- 1 pork tenderloin (³⁄₄ to 1 pound)
- 1 tablespoon chili powder
- 1 teaspoon ground cumin
- 1 teaspoon packed brown sugar
- ¹⁄₄ teaspoon garlic powder
- ¹⁄₈ teaspoon ground red pepper (cayenne)
- ¹⁄₂ cup mayonnaise or salad dressing
- ¹⁄₂ teaspoon ground mustard
- 1 medium green onion, finely chopped (1 tablespoon)

1. Cut pork into 32 (1-inch) pieces; place in medium bowl. In small bowl, mix chili powder, cumin, brown sugar, garlic powder and red pepper. Reserve 2 teaspoons spice mixture; sprinkle remaining mixture over pork pieces; stir to coat completely. Let stand 15 minutes.

2. In small bowl, mix mayonnaise, mustard, reserved 2 teaspoons spice mixture and the onion; set aside.

3. Heat gas or charcoal grill. Spray grill basket (grill "wok") with cooking spray. Spoon pork into basket.

4. Place basket on grill. Cover grill; cook over medium heat 10 to 12 minutes, shaking basket or stirring pork once or twice until pork is no longer pink in center. Serve with toothpicks and mayonnaise mixture for dipping.

8 servings (4 pork pieces and 1 tablespoon dip each)
1 Serving: Calories 160 (Calories from Fat 110); Total Fat 13g (Saturated 2g; Trans 0g); Cholesterol 30mg; Sodium 105mg; Total Carbohydrate 2g (Dietary Fiber 0g; Sugars 1g); Protein 10g
% Daily Value: Vitamin A 6%; Vitamin C 0%; Calcium 0%; Iron 6%
Exchanges: 1¹⁄₂ Lean Meat, 1¹⁄₂ Fat
Carbohydrate Choices: 0

KITCHEN TIPS

- To broil pork, set oven control to broil. Spray rack of broiler pan with cooking spray. Place pork on rack. Broil with tops 6 inches from heat about 10 minutes, turning once, until no longer pink in center.
- This amount of pork fits nicely in most grill baskets, but you could also thread the pieces on skewers to cook them.
- If you're using bamboo skewers, soak them in water for 30 minutes before using. Turn the skewers once during cooking.

Seven-Layer Rigatoni

Prep Time: 25 min Start to Finish: 1 hr 5 min

3 cups uncooked rigatoni pasta (9 ounces)

1 pound bulk Italian pork sausage

1 can (28 ounces) crushed tomatoes, undrained

3 tablespoons chopped fresh or 3 teaspoons dried basil leaves

3 cloves garlic, finely chopped

1 package (8 ounces) sliced fresh mushrooms (3 cups)

1 jar (7 ounces) roasted red bell peppers, drained and chopped

1 cup shredded Parmesan cheese (4 ounces)

2½ cups shredded mozzarella cheese (10 ounces)

1. Heat oven to 375°F. Spray 13 × 9-inch (3-quart) glass baking dish with cooking spray. Cook and drain pasta as directed on package.

2. Meanwhile, in 10-inch skillet, cook sausage over medium heat 8 to 10 minutes, stirring occasionally, until no longer pink; drain. In small bowl, mix tomato, basil and garlic.

3. In baking dish, layer half each of the pasta, sausage, mushrooms, roasted peppers, Parmesan cheese, tomato mixture and mozzarella cheese. Repeat layers.

4. Bake 35 to 40 minutes or until hot and cheese is golden brown.

8 servings
1 Serving: Calories 410 (Calories from Fat 170); Total Fat 19g (Saturated 9g; Trans 0g); Cholesterol 50mg; Sodium 870mg; Total Carbohydrate 33g (Dietary Fiber 3g; Sugars 6g); Protein 26g
% Daily Value: Vitamin A 35%; Vitamin C 40%; Calcium 45%; Iron 15%
Exchanges: 2 Starch, 3 Medium-Fat Meat, ½ Fat
Carbohydrate Choices: 2

KITCHEN TIPS

✿ Look in the produce department for jars of chopped garlic packed in water to keep on hand for dishes that call for garlic.

✿ Slash the fat in this family-favorite casserole to 14 grams per serving by using ¾ pound of Italian-seasoned ground turkey instead of the pork sausage.

Wild Mushroom-Stuffed Pork Roast

Prep Time: 25 min Start to Finish: 1 hr 30 min

- 1 package (1 ounce) dried porcini mushrooms
- 1 boneless pork loin roast (3 pounds)
- 1 tablespoon butter or margarine
- 1 medium onion, finely chopped ($\frac{1}{2}$ cup)
- 1 package (8 ounces) fresh baby portabella mushrooms, finely chopped
- $\frac{1}{2}$ cup herb-seasoned stuffing crumbs (do not use stuffing cubes)
- 2 tablespoons olive or vegetable oil
- $\frac{1}{2}$ teaspoon salt
- $\frac{1}{4}$ teaspoon pepper
  Fresh sage leaves, if desired

1. Heat oven to 375°F. In small bowl, place dried porcini mushrooms. Cover mushrooms with hot water; let stand 10 minutes.

2. Meanwhile, cut pork roast horizontally to $\frac{1}{2}$ inch from one long side without cutting all the way through (pork will open like a book); set aside. In 10-inch skillet, melt butter over medium-high heat. Add onion; cook and stir about 1 minute or until tender.

3. Drain porcini mushrooms well; chop. Add porcini and portabella mushrooms to butter in skillet; cook about 4 minutes, stirring occasionally, until mushrooms are tender. Stir in stuffing crumbs.

4. Spoon mushroom mixture into opening in pork; close pork over stuffing and secure with string. Place stuffed pork in shallow roasting pan. Brush with oil; sprinkle with salt and pepper. Insert ovenproof meat thermometer so tip is in center of thickest part of pork.

5. Roast uncovered 45 to 55 minutes or until thermometer reads 150°F. Remove pork from pan; cover with foil and let stand 10 minutes until thermometer reads 160°F. Remove strings from pork before carving. Garnish with sage.

8 servings
1 Serving: Calories 350 (Calories from Fat 170); Total Fat 18g (Saturated 6g; Trans 0g); Cholesterol 115mg; Sodium 290mg; Total Carbohydrate 8g (Dietary Fiber 1g; Sugars 2g); Protein 40g
% Daily Value: Vitamin A 0%; Vitamin C 0%; Calcium 0%; Iron 10%
Exchanges: 1 Vegetable, $5\frac{1}{2}$ Lean Meat, $\frac{1}{2}$ Fat
Carbohydrate Choices: $\frac{1}{2}$

KITCHEN TIPS

- Porcini mushrooms are wild mushrooms with a pale brown color and pungent, woodsy flavor.
- One ounce of dried mushrooms makes about $\frac{1}{2}$ cup chopped rehydrated mushrooms.

Creamy Bow Ties with Ham and Vegetables

Prep Time: 30 min Start to Finish: 30 min

2 cups uncooked farfalle (bow-tie) pasta (4 ounces)

$^1/_2$ cup chive-and-onion cream cheese spread (from 8-ounce container)

$^3/_4$ cup half-and-half

1 cup baby-cut carrots, cut lengthwise in half if large

8 ounces asparagus, cut into $1^1/_2$-inch pieces

$1^1/_2$ cups cooked ham strips (1 × $^1/_4$ inch)

$^1/_4$ teaspoon dried marjoram leaves

1. Cook and drain pasta as directed on package.

2. Meanwhile, in 12-inch nonstick skillet, mix cream cheese spread and half-and-half. Cook over medium heat 2 to 3 minutes, stirring constantly, until melted and smooth.

3. Stir in carrots. Cook 4 minutes, stirring occasionally. Stir in asparagus. Cover; cook 4 to 5 minutes, stirring occasionally, until vegetables are crisp-tender.

4. Stir in ham, pasta and marjoram. Cook, stirring occasionally, just until thoroughly heated.

4 servings

1 Serving: Calories 510 (Calories from Fat 180); Total Fat 20g (Saturated 10g; Trans 0g); Cholesterol 75mg; Sodium 1250mg; Total Carbohydrate 57g (Dietary Fiber 5g; Sugars 6g); Protein 25g
% Daily Value: Vitamin A 90%; Vitamin C 15%; Calcium 10%; Iron 20%
Exchanges: 3 Starch, $^1/_2$ Other Carbohydrate, 1 Vegetable, 2 Lean Meat, $2^1/_2$ Fat
Carbohydrate Choices: 4

KITCHEN TIPS

✿ To reduce calories to 460 and fat to 12 grams per serving, use low-fat cream cheese with chives and onion, and if it is available in your area, use fat-free half-and-half.

Honey BBQ Pork Packets

Southwestern Pork Chops

Honey BBQ Pork Packets

Prep Time: 1 hr Start to Finish: 1 hr

$1/2$ cup barbecue sauce

$1/4$ cup honey

2 teaspoons ground cumin

4 boneless pork rib or loin chops

2 large ears corn, each cut into 6 pieces

1 cup ready-to-eat baby-cut carrots, cut lengthwise in half

2 cups refrigerated cooked new potato wedges (from 20-ounce bag)

2 medium green onions, sliced (2 tablespoons)

1. Heat gas or charcoal grill. Cut 4 (18 × 12-inch) sheets of heavy-duty foil; spray with cooking spray. In small bowl, mix barbecue sauce, honey and cumin. Place 1 pork chop, 3 pieces of corn, $1/4$ cup carrots, $1/2$ cup potato wedges and $1/2$ tablespoon green onions on center of each foil sheet. Spoon 3 table-spoons sauce mixture over pork and vegetables on each sheet.

2. Bring up 2 sides of foil so edges meet. Seal edges, making tight $1/2$-inch fold; fold again, allowing space for heat circulation and expansion. Fold other sides to seal.

3. Place packets on grill. Cover grill; cook over medium-low heat 15 to 20 minutes, rotating packets $1/2$ turn after 10 minutes, until pork is no longer pink and meat thermometer inserted in center reads 160°F. To serve, cut large X across top of each packet; carefully fold back to allow steam to escape.

4 servings
1 Serving: Calories 470 (Calories from Fat 110); Total Fat 12g (Saturated 4g; Trans 0g); Cholesterol 85mg; Sodium 480mg; Total Carbohydrate 57g (Dietary Fiber 6g; Sugars 31g); Protein 35g
% Daily Value: Vitamin A 80%; Vitamin C 8%; Calcium 4%; Iron 15%
Exchanges: 2 Starch, 2 Other Carbohydrate, 4 Lean Meat
Carbohydrate Choices: 4

Low Fat

Southwestern Pork Chops

Prep Time: 20 min Start to Finish: 1 hr 20 min

1 tablespoon chili powder

1 teaspoon ground cumin

$1/4$ teaspoon ground red pepper (cayenne)

$1/4$ teaspoon salt

1 large clove garlic, finely chopped

8 pork loin or rib chops, about $1/2$ inch thick (about 2 pounds)

1. In small bowl, mix all ingredients except pork; rub evenly on both sides of pork. Cover; refrigerate 1 hour to blend flavors.

2. Heat gas or charcoal grill. Place pork on grill. Cover grill; cook over medium heat 8 to 10 minutes, turning frequently, until no longer pink in center.

8 servings
1 Serving: Calories 130 (Calories from Fat 60); Total Fat 6g (Saturated 2g; Trans 0g); Cholesterol 50mg; Sodium 115mg; Total Carbohydrate 0g (Dietary Fiber 0g; Sugars 0g); Protein 18g
% Daily Value: Vitamin A 6%; Vitamin C 0%; Calcium 0%; Iron 6%
Exchanges: $2^{1}/2$ Lean Meat
Carbohydrate Choices: 0

KITCHEN TIPS

✿ To keep food from sticking and to make cleanup a breeze, brush the grill rack with vegetable oil or spritz with cooking spray before heating the grill.

Glazed Peppered Steaks

Prep Time: 20 min Start to Finish: 20 min

$1/2$ cup orange marmalade

$1/4$ cup white balsamic vinegar

  2 teaspoons coarse ground black pepper

$1/2$ teaspoon salt

  4 boneless beef top loin steaks (New York, Kansas City or strip steaks), about $3/4$ inch thick (6 to 8 ounces each)

Grated orange peel, if desired

1. Set oven control to broil. In small bowl, mix marmalade and vinegar. Rub pepper and salt on both sides of each beef steak; place on rack in broiler pan.

2. Broil with tops of steaks 4 to 6 inches from heat 8 to 12 minutes, turning once and brushing with marmalade mixture during last 2 minutes of broiling. Garnish with orange peel.

4 servings
1 Serving: Calories 380 (Calories from Fat 100); Total Fat 12g (Saturated 4.5g; Trans 0.5g); Cholesterol 75mg; Sodium 360mg; Total Carbohydrate 29g (Dietary Fiber 0g; Sugars 20g); Protein 39g
% Daily Value: Vitamin A 0%; Vitamin C 4%; Calcium 2%; Iron 20%
Exchanges: 2 Other Carbohydrate, 5 Lean Meat
Carbohydrate Choices: 2

KITCHEN TIPS

✿ Sweet glazes can burn quickly on the broiler, so it's important to brush the steaks with the glaze only during the last few minutes of broiling.

✿ To grill steaks, heat gas or charcoal grill. Make glaze. Rub pepper and salt on both sides of each steak. Place steaks on grill. Cover grill; cook 8 to 12 minutes, turning once or twice and brushing with marmalade glaze during last 2 minutes of cooking.

Flank Steak with Smoky Honey Mustard Sauce

Prep Time: 30 min Start to Finish: 30 min

$1/4$ cup honey mustard dressing

  1 tablespoon frozen (thawed) orange juice concentrate

  1 tablespoon water

  1 small clove garlic, finely chopped

  1 chipotle chili in adobo sauce (from 7-ounce can), finely chopped

  1 beef flank steak (about $1^1/2$ pounds)

  6 flour tortillas (8 to 10 inch)

1. Heat gas or charcoal grill. In small bowl, mix all ingredients except beef and tortillas; reserve 2 tablespoons sauce.

2. Make cuts about $1/2$ inch apart and $1/8$ inch deep in diamond pattern in both sides of beef. Brush reserved sauce on both sides of beef.

3. Place beef on grill. Cover grill; cook over medium heat 17 to 20 minutes, turning once, until desired doneness. Cut beef across grain into thin slices. Serve with remaining sauce and tortillas.

6 servings
1 Serving: Calories 350 (Calories from Fat 130); Total Fat 14g (Saturated 4g; Trans 1g); Cholesterol 50mg; Sodium 330mg; Total Carbohydrate 27g (Dietary Fiber 1g; Sugars 2g); Protein 30g
% Daily Value: Vitamin A 0%; Vitamin C 4%; Calcium 6%; Iron 20%
Exchanges: $1^1/2$ Starch, $1/2$ Other Carbohydrate, $3^1/2$ Lean Meat, $1/2$ Fat
Carbohydrate Choices: 2

KITCHEN TIPS

✿ Flank steak is known to be a less tender cut and should be very thinly sliced across the grain for serving. It is typically used for fajitas or London broil.

Glazed Peppered Steaks

Flank Steak with Smoky Honey Mustard Sauce

Easy Bacon Cheeseburger Lasagna

Prep Time: 30 min Start to Finish: 3 hr 55 min

1½ pounds lean (at least 80%) ground beef
2 medium onions, chopped (1 cup)
¼ teaspoon salt
⅛ teaspoon pepper
1 can (28 ounces) chunky tomato sauce
1 cup water
1 egg
1 container (15 ounces) ricotta cheese
1 cup shredded Swiss cheese (4 ounces)
¼ cup chopped fresh parsley
8 slices bacon, crisply cooked, crumbled (½ cup)
12 uncooked lasagna noodles
2 cups shredded Cheddar cheese (8 ounces)

1. Spray 13 × 9-inch (3-quart) glass baking dish with cooking spray. In 12-inch skillet, cook beef, onions, salt and pepper over medium-high heat 5 to 7 minutes, stirring occasionally, until beef is brown; drain. Stir in tomato sauce and water. Heat to boiling; reduce heat to medium-low. Simmer uncovered 10 minutes.

2. In medium bowl, beat egg with fork. Stir in ricotta cheese, Swiss cheese, parsley and ¼ cup of the bacon.

3. Spread about 1 cup of the beef mixture in baking dish. Top with 4 uncooked noodles. Spread half of the ricotta mixture, 2 cups beef mixture and ¾ cup of the Cheddar cheese over noodles. Repeat layers once, starting with 4 noodles. Top with remaining noodles, beef mixture, Cheddar cheese and bacon. Spray 15-inch sheet of foil with cooking spray. Cover lasagna with foil, sprayed side down. Refrigerate at least 2 hours but no longer than 24 hours.

4. Heat oven to 350°F. Bake covered 45 minutes. Uncover and bake about 30 minutes longer or until bubbly and golden brown. Cover and let stand 10 minutes before cutting.

8 servings
1 Serving: Calories 600 (Calories from Fat 290); Total Fat 32g (Saturated 16g; Trans 1g); Cholesterol 145mg; Sodium 1140mg; Total Carbohydrate 37g (Dietary Fiber 4g; Sugars 7g); Protein 41g
% Daily Value: Vitamin A 25%; Vitamin C 10%; Calcium 45%; Iron 25%
Exchanges: 2 Starch, ½ Other Carbohydrate, 5 Medium-Fat Meat, 1 Fat
Carbohydrate Choices: 2½

KITCHEN TIPS

❁ Try substituting Italian sausage for the ground beef.
❁ To reduce the fat in this recipe to 15 grams and the calories to 460 per serving, substitute ground turkey for the beef and use reduced-fat cheeses and 4 slices bacon.

Beef Tenderloin with Red Wine Sauce

Prep Time: 20 min Start to Finish: 1 hr 35 min

Beef

1	beef tenderloin roast (3 pounds)
¹⁄₂	teaspoon salt
¹⁄₂	teaspoon freshly cracked black pepper

Sauce

6	tablespoons butter or margarine
¹⁄₂	cup finely chopped shallots (3 medium)
1	cup dry red wine or dry Marsala wine
1	cup beef broth
¹⁄₂	teaspoon pepper

1. Heat oven to 400°F. If necessary, trim fat from beef. Turn small end of beef under about 6 inches. Tie turned-under portion with string at about 1¹⁄₂-inch intervals. Place in shallow roasting pan. Sprinkle with salt and cracked black pepper. Insert ovenproof meat thermometer so tip is in center of thickest part of beef.

2. For medium-rare, roast uncovered 30 to 40 minutes or until thermometer reads 135°F. Cover loosely with foil; let stand 15 to 20 minutes until thermometer reads 145°F. (Temperature will continue to rise about 10°F, and beef will be easier to carve.) For medium, roast uncovered 40 to 50 minutes or until thermometer reads 150°F. Cover loosely with foil; let stand 15 to 20 minutes until thermometer reads 160°F.

3. Meanwhile, in 8-inch skillet, melt 2 tablespoons of the butter over medium-high heat. Add shallots; cook about 1 minute, stirring frequently. Add wine; cook about 4 minutes until reduced slightly. Stir in broth. Heat to boiling. Reduce heat to medium-low; cook about 10 minutes longer, stirring occasionally, until reduced to about 1 cup. Beat in remaining 4 tablespoons butter, 1 tablespoon at a time, with wire whisk. Beat in ¹⁄₂ teaspoon pepper.

4. Remove string from beef before carving. Serve sauce with beef.

8 servings

1 Serving: Calories 350 (Calories from Fat 180); Total Fat 20g (Saturated 10g; Trans 1g); Cholesterol 95mg; Sodium 390mg; Total Carbohydrate 1g (Dietary Fiber 0g; Sugars 0g); Protein 40g
% Daily Value: Vitamin A 8%; Vitamin C 0%; Calcium 2%; Iron 20%
Exchanges: 6 Lean Meat, ¹⁄₂ Fat
Carbohydrate Choices: 0

KITCHEN TIPS

✿ Add ¹⁄₄ cup ruby port to the sauce for a more intense wine flavor.
✿ Tying the smaller end of the tenderloin under helps the meat cook evenly.

Kielbasa Kabobs

Prep Time: 15 min Start to Finish: 1 hour

2	rings (1 pound each) kielbasa sausage
12	wooden skewers (6 to 8 inch)
1/4	cup apricot preserves
2	tablespoons orange juice

1. If using bamboo skewers, soak in water at least 30 minutes before using to prevent burning. Heat oven to 350°F. Line 15 × 10 × 1-inch pan with foil; spray with cooking spray.

2. Cut kielbasa at an angle into 48 chunks, about 1 inch each. On each skewer, thread 4 chunks of sausage; place in pan.

3. In small bowl, mix preserves and orange juice with fork; brush glaze over kabobs. Turn kabobs over; brush other side.

4. Bake about 45 minutes or until kielbasa is browned.

12 kabobs
1 Kabob: Calories 250 (Calories from Fat 190); Total Fat 21g (Saturated 8g; Trans 0.5g); Cholesterol 45mg; Sodium 710mg; Total Carbohydrate 7g (Dietary Fiber 0g; Sugars 5g); Protein 8g
% Daily Value: Vitamin A 0%; Vitamin C 0%; Calcium 0%; Iron 2%
Exchanges: 1/2 Other Carbohydrate, 1 High-Fat Meat, 2 1/2 Fat
Carbohydrate Choices: 1/2

KITCHEN TIPS

✪ For a fun presentation, insert skewers into half of a fresh pineapple that's been sliced lengthwise.

Creole-Style Skillet Dinner

Prep Time: 30 min Start to Finish: 30 min

1	medium onion, chopped (3/4 cup)
1	clove garlic, finely chopped
1/2	cup chopped green bell pepper
1/2	pound fully cooked kielbasa sausage, cut lengthwise into fourths, sliced
3	large tomatoes, chopped (2 1/2 cups)
1	cup chicken broth
1/2	teaspoon salt
1/2	teaspoon Cajun seasoning
1 1/2	cups uncooked instant rice
	Red pepper sauce, if desired

1. Spray 12-inch skillet with cooking spray; heat over medium-high heat. Add onion, garlic and bell pepper to skillet. Cover; cook 3 to 5 minutes, stirring once, until vegetables are crisp-tender.

2. Stir in kielbasa, tomatoes, broth, salt and Cajun seasoning. Heat to boiling; stir in rice. Heat to boiling; reduce heat to low. Cook 8 to 10 minutes or until rice is tender. Fluff with fork before serving. Serve with pepper sauce.

4 servings
1 Serving: Calories 390 (Calories from Fat 150); Total Fat 17g (Saturated 6g; Trans 0g); Cholesterol 35mg; Sodium 1150 mg; Total Carbohydrate 47g (Dietary Fiber 3g; Sugars 7g); Protein 13g
% Daily Value: Vitamin A 25%; Vitamin C 30%; Calcium 4%; Iron 15%
Exchanges: 2 Starch, 1 Other Carbohydrate, 1 Vegetable, 1 High-Fat Meat, 1 Fat
Carbohydrate Choices: 3

KITCHEN TIPS

✪ Boost the fiber to 4 grams per serving by using instant brown rice instead of the white rice. Just increase the cooking time by 5 minutes.

Creole-Style Skillet Dinner

Kielbasa Kabobs

Grilled Veggie and Steak Appetizer

Prep Time: 20 min Start to Finish: 30 min

1 package (6 ounces) small fresh portabella mushrooms

½ pound boneless beef sirloin steak (about ¾ inch thick), trimmed of fat and cut into ¾-inch cubes

1 cup frozen small whole onions (from 1-pound bag), thawed

½ cup plus 2 tablespoons balsamic vinaigrette

½ cup halved grape or cherry tomatoes

1. Heat gas or charcoal grill. In large bowl, place mushrooms, beef, onions and ½ cup of the vinaigrette; toss to coat. Let stand 10 minutes; drain. Place mixture in grill basket (grill "wok").

2. Place basket on grill. Cover grill; cook over medium-high heat 7 to 9 minutes, shaking basket or stirring beef mixture twice, until vegetables are tender and beef is desired doneness. Stir in tomatoes.

3. Spoon beef mixture into serving dish. Stir in remaining 2 tablespoons vinaigrette. Serve with toothpicks.

8 servings
1 Serving: Calories 150 (Calories from Fat 100); Total Fat 11g (Saturated 2g; Trans 0g); Cholesterol 15mg; Sodium 140mg; Total Carbohydrate 5g (Dietary Fiber 1g; Sugars 2g); Protein 8g
% Daily Value: Vitamin A 0%; Vitamin C 2%; Calcium 0%; Iron 4%
Exchanges: 1 Vegetable, 1 Lean Meat, 1½ Fat
Carbohydrate Choices: ½

KITCHEN TIPS

❂ Portabella mushrooms provide a meaty flavor, but regular button mushrooms can be substituted in this recipe.

❂ A little chopped fresh parsley sprinkled over the top of the cooked food adds both flavor and color.

Hamburger Steaks with Grilled Onions

Prep Time: 25 min Start to Finish: 25 min

4 lean ground beef patties (4 to 6 ounces each)
2 tablespoons steak sauce
1 package (1 ounce) onion soup mix
2 large Bermuda onions, sliced, rings separated
2 tablespoons packed brown sugar
1 tablespoon balsamic vinegar
4 sandwich buns

1. Heat gas or charcoal grill. Cut 2 (18 × 2-inch) sheets of heavy-duty foil; spray with cooking spray.

2. Brush patties with steak sauce; sprinkle with half of soup mix (dry). Place half of the onions on center of each foil sheet. Sprinkle with remaining soup mix, the brown sugar and vinegar. Bring up 2 sides of foil so edges meet. Seal edges, making tight $^1/_2$-inch fold; fold again, allowing space for heat circulation and expansion. Fold other sides to seal.

3. Place packets and beef patties on grill. Cover grill; cook over medium heat 10 to 15 minutes, turning patties and rotating packets $^1/_2$ turn once or twice, until meat thermometer inserted in center of patties reads 160°F. Cut large X across top of packets; carefully fold back foil to allow steam to escape. Serve patties and onions in buns.

4 sandwiches
1 Sandwich: Calories 440 (Calories from Fat 130); Total Fat 15g (Saturated 5g; Trans 1g); Cholesterol 70mg; Sodium 990mg; Total Carbohydrate 51g (Dietary Fiber 5g; Sugars 20g); Protein 26g
% Daily Value: Vitamin A 0%; Vitamin C 15%; Calcium 15%; Iron 25%
Exchanges: $1^1/_2$ Starch, $1^1/_2$ Other Carbohydrate, 1 Vegetable, 3 Medium-Fat Meat
Carbohydrate Choices: $3^1/_2$

Parmesan Orzo and Meatballs

Old-Fashioned Oven Beef Stew

Quick

Parmesan Orzo and Meatballs

Prep Time: 30 min Start to Finish: 30 min

1½ cups frozen bell pepper and onion stir-fry (from 1-pound bag)
2 tablespoons Italian dressing
1 can (14 ounces) beef broth
1 cup uncooked orzo or rosamarina pasta (6 ounces)
16 frozen cooked Italian-style meatballs (from 16-ounce bag)
1 large tomato, chopped (1 cup)
2 tablespoons chopped fresh parsley
¼ cup shredded Parmesan cheese

1. In 12-inch nonstick skillet, cook stir-fry vegetables and dressing over medium-high heat 2 minutes. Stir in broth; heat to boiling. Stir in pasta and meatballs. Heat to boiling; reduce heat to low. Cover; cook 10 minutes, stirring occasionally.

2. Stir in tomato. Cover; cook 3 to 5 minutes or until most of the liquid has been absorbed and pasta is tender. Stir in parsley. Sprinkle with cheese.

4 servings
1 Serving: Calories 500 (Calories from Fat 190); Total Fat 21g (Saturated 7g; Trans 1g); Cholesterol 125mg; Sodium 1240mg; Total Carbohydrate 45g (Dietary Fiber 4g; Sugars 7g); Protein 32g
% Daily Value: Vitamin A 15%; Vitamin C 25%; Calcium 20%; Iron 25%
Exchanges: 2 Starch, ½ Other Carbohydrate, 1 Vegetable, 3½ Medium-Fat Meat, ½ Fat
Carbohydrate Choices: 3

KITCHEN TIPS

⚙ Orzo is a rice-shaped pasta that cooks fairly quickly. It's a great pasta to serve to kids because it is easier to eat than long spaghetti.

Old-Fashioned Oven Beef Stew

Prep Time: 15 min Start to Finish: 4 hr 15 min

1½ pounds beef stew meat
3 tablespoons Gold Medal all-purpose flour
2 bags (1 pound each) frozen vegetables for stew
1 can (14.5 ounces) diced tomatoes, undrained
2 cans (10 ounces each) condensed beef consommé
1 tablespoon sugar
⅛ teaspoon pepper
2 dried bay leaves

1. Heat oven to 325°F. In 5-quart Dutch oven or 13 × 9-inch (3-quart) glass baking dish, toss beef with flour. Add frozen vegetables.

2. In large bowl, mix remaining ingredients. Pour over beef and vegetables; gently stir until mixed.

3. Cover; bake 3 hours 30 minutes to 4 hours or until beef is tender. Remove bay leaves before serving.

6 servings (1½ cups each)
1 Serving: Calories 340 (Calories from Fat 130); Total Fat 14g (Saturated 5g; Trans 0.5g); Cholesterol 65mg; Sodium 600mg; Total Carbohydrate 29g (Dietary Fiber 4g; Sugars 7g); Protein 25g
% Daily Value: Vitamin A 90%; Vitamin C 15%; Calcium 6%; Iron 20%
Exchanges: 1½ Starch, 1 Vegetable, 2½ Medium-Fat Meat
Carbohydrate Choices: 2

KITCHEN TIPS

⚙ If you'd like to reduce the fat in this recipe, use sirloin steak cubes instead of stew meat.
⚙ Two 1-pound bags of Green Giant frozen mixed vegetables can also be used for this easy beef stew, but wait to add them until the last 30 minutes of cooking.

Meat Loaf, Potato and Carrot Packets

Prep Time: 1 hr 10 min Start to Finish: 1 hr 10 min

1½ pounds lean (at least 80%) ground beef
1 package (1 ounce) onion soup mix
1 egg
¾ cup milk
½ cup Progresso plain bread crumbs
⅓ cup ketchup
1 bag (20 ounces) refrigerated cooked new potato wedges
3 cups ready-to-eat baby-cut carrots

1. Heat gas or charcoal grill. Cut 6 (16 × 12-inch) sheets of heavy-duty foil; spray with cooking spray. In large bowl, mix beef, soup mix (dry), egg, milk and bread crumbs. Shape into 6 loaves, 4 × 2½ × 1 inch. Place 1 loaf on center of each foil sheet; top each with 1 tablespoon ketchup. Place about ½ cup potatoes and ½ cup carrots around each loaf.

2. Bring up 2 sides of foil so edges meet. Seal edges, making tight ½-inch fold; fold again, allowing space for heat circulation and expansion. Fold other sides to seal.

3. Place packets on grill. Cover grill; cook over low heat 25 to 30 minutes, rotating packets ½ turn after 15 minutes, until meat thermometer inserted in center of loaves reads 160°F and vegetables are tender. To serve, cut large X across top of each packet; carefully fold back foil to allow steam to escape.

6 servings
1 Serving: Calories 370 (Calories from Fat 130); Total Fat 15g (Saturated 6 g; Trans 1 g); Cholesterol 110 mg; Sodium 850mg; Total Carbohydrate 32g (Dietary Fiber 5 g; Sugars 12g); Protein 27g
% Daily Value: Vitamin A 150%; Vitamin C 8%; Calcium 10%; Iron 20%
Exchanges: 1 Starch, 1 Other Carbohydrate, 1 Vegetable, 3 Medium-Fat Meat
Carbohydrate Choices: 2

On the Side
On the Side

Vegetables, Potatoes and Stuffings

Roasted Autumn Vegetables (page 182)

Green Beans with Browned Butter (page 181)

Grilled Corn with Chili-Lime Spread

Prep Time: 25 min Start to Finish: 30 min

½ cup butter or margarine, softened
½ teaspoon grated lime peel
3 tablespoons lime juice
1 to 2 teaspoons ground red chiles or chili powder
8 ears corn (with husks)

8 servings

1 Serving: Calories 230 (Calories from Fat 120); Total Fat 13g (Saturated 8g; Trans 0.5g); Cholesterol 30mg; Sodium 105mg; Total Carbohydrate 26g (Dietary Fiber 4g; Sugars 3g); Protein 4g
% Daily Value: Vitamin A 15%; Vitamin C 6%; Calcium 0%; Iron 4%
Exchanges: 1½ Starch, 2½ Fat
Carbohydrate Choices: 2

KITCHEN TIPS

◉ For a less spicy version, substitute Old El Paso taco seasoning mix (from 1.25-ounce package) for the red chiles or chili powder.

1. Heat gas or charcoal grill. In small bowl, mix all ingredients except corn.

2. Remove larger outer husks from each ear of corn; gently pull back inner husks and remove silk. Spread each ear of corn with about 2 teaspoons butter mixture; reserve remaining butter mixture. Pull husks up over ears.

3. Place corn on grill. Cook uncovered over medium heat 10 to 15 minutes, turning frequently, until tender. Let stand 5 minutes. Serve corn with remaining butter mixture.

Quick & Low-Fat

Asparagus with Tomatoes

Prep Time: 20 min Start to Finish: 30 min

2	teaspoons vegetable oil
1	small onion, chopped (¼ cup)
3	roma (plum) tomatoes, chopped (1 cup)
1	tablespoon lemon juice
1	tablespoon honey
¼	teaspoon salt
1½	pounds asparagus

1. In 10-inch skillet, heat oil over medium heat. Cook onion in oil 2 to 3 minutes, stirring occasionally, until tender. Stir in tomatoes, lemon juice, honey and salt. Cook 1 minute, stirring occasionally. Remove mixture from skillet; keep warm.

2. Wipe out skillet. Heat 1 inch water to boiling in skillet. Break off tough ends of asparagus as far down as stalks snap easily. Add asparagus to boiling water. Heat to boiling; reduce heat to medium.

Cover and cook 7 to 10 minutes or until stalk ends are crisp-tender; drain. Place asparagus in serving dish. Top with tomato mixture.

4 servings

1 Serving: Calories 70 (Calories from Fat 25); Total Fat 2.5g (Saturated 0g; Trans 0g); Cholesterol 0mg; Sodium 150mg; Total Carbohydrate 9g (Dietary Fiber 2g; Sugars 7g); Protein 3g
% Daily Value: Vitamin A 20%; Vitamin C 25%; Calcium 2%; Iron 4%
Exchanges: 2 Vegetable, ½ Fat
Carbohydrate Choices: ½

KITCHEN TIPS

✿ This dish is also wonderful served as a cold salad. Prepare as directed, but refrigerate until chilled before serving.

Artichokes with Rosemary Sauce

Prep Time: 10 min Start to Finish: 45 min

4	medium artichokes
$^{1}/_{2}$	cup butter or margarine
1	teaspoon chopped fresh or $^{1}/_{4}$ teaspoon dried rosemary leaves, crushed
1	teaspoon lemon juice

1. Remove any discolored leaves and the small leaves at base of artichokes. Trim stems even with base of artichokes. Cutting straight across, slice 1 inch off tops and discard tops. Snip off points of remaining leaves with scissors. Rinse artichokes with cold water.

2. Place steamer basket in $^{1}/_{2}$ inch water in 4-quart Dutch oven (water should not touch bottom of basket). Place artichokes in basket. Cover tightly and heat to boiling; reduce heat. Steam 20 to 25 minutes or until bottoms are tender when pierced with knife.

3. Meanwhile, melt butter; stir in rosemary and lemon juice. Serve artichokes with rosemary mixture. Pluck out artichoke leaves one at time. Dip base of leaf into rosemary mixture.

4 servings
1 Serving: Calories 280 (Calories from Fat 210); Total Fat 23g (Saturated 15g; Trans 1.5g); Cholesterol 60mg; Sodium 280mg; Total Carbohydrate 14g (Dietary Fiber 7g; Sugars 1g); Protein 4g
% Daily Value: Vitamin A 20%; Vitamin C 10%; Calcium 6%; Iron 8%
Exchanges: 2 Vegetable, 5 Fat
Carbohydrate Choices: 1

KITCHEN TIPS

✿ Artichokes can also be prepared in the microwave. Place artichokes in glass pie plate; add $^{1}/_{2}$ cup of water. Cover with plastic wrap, turning back edge to vent steam. Microwave on High 10 to 15 minutes or until bottoms are tender when pierced with knife.

Vegetable Kabobs with Mustard Dip

Prep Time: 35 min   Start to Finish: 1 hr 35 min

Dip

- ½   cup sour cream
- ½   cup plain yogurt
- 1   tablespoon finely chopped fresh parsley
- 1   teaspoon onion powder
- 1   teaspoon garlic salt
- 1   tablespoon Dijon mustard

Kabobs

- 1   medium green bell pepper, cut into 6 strips, then cut into thirds (18 pieces)
- 1   medium zucchini, cut diagonally into ½-inch slices
- 8   ounces fresh whole mushrooms
- 9   large cherry tomatoes
- 2   tablespoons olive or vegetable oil

1. In small bowl, mix all dip ingredients. Cover; refrigerate at least 1 hour.

2. Heat gas or charcoal grill. On 5 (12-inch) metal skewers, thread vegetables so that one kind of vegetable is on the same skewer (use 2 skewers for mushrooms); leave space between each piece. Brush vegetables with oil.

3. Place skewers of bell pepper and zucchini on grill. Cover grill; cook over medium heat 2 minutes. Add skewers of mushrooms and tomatoes. Cover grill; cook 4 to 5 minutes, carefully turning every 2 minutes, until vegetables are tender. Remove vegetables from skewers to serving plate. Serve with dip.

9 servings (9 vegetable pieces and 2 tablespoons dip each)
1 Serving: Calories 80 (Calories from Fat 50); Total Fat 6g (Saturated 2g; Trans 0g); Cholesterol 10mg; Sodium 170mg; Total Carbohydrate 5g (Dietary Fiber 1g; Sugars 3g); Protein 2g
% Daily Value: Vitamin A 8%; Vitamin C 15%; Calcium 4%; Iron 2%
Exchanges: 1 Vegetable, 1 Fat
Carbohydrate Choices: ½

KITCHEN TIPS

- Choose red bell pepper for a beautiful color and a sweeter flavor than green bell pepper.
- Remove vegetables from the skewers and pile them on a platter garnished with fresh herbs. Serve with toothpicks for easy dipping.

Brie Mashed Potatoes

Prep Time: 30 min Start to Finish: 1 hr 15 min

12 medium baking potatoes (about 5 pounds), peeled, cut into large pieces
1 cup milk
1/4 cup butter or margarine
1 teaspoon salt
1/2 teaspoon freshly ground pepper
1 package (8 ounces) Brie cheese, rind removed, cubed
2 teaspoons chopped fresh thyme leaves

1. In 4-quart saucepan or 5-quart Dutch oven, place potatoes; add enough water just to cover potatoes. Heat to boiling. Reduce heat; cover and simmer 20 to 30 minutes or until potatoes are tender when pierced with a fork. Drain.

2. Heat oven to 350°F. Spray 2- to 3-quart casserole with cooking spray. In 1-quart saucepan, heat milk, butter, salt and pepper over medium heat, stirring occasionally, until butter is melted. Measure out 1/4 cup milk mixture; set aside.

3. To potatoes, gradually add remaining milk mixture, cubed cheese and thyme, mashing with potato masher or electric mixer on medium speed until light and fluffy. Spoon potatoes into casserole. (Potatoes can be covered and refrigerated up to 24 hours at this point.)

4. Pour reserved 1/4 cup milk mixture over potatoes. Bake uncovered 40 to 45 minutes or until potatoes are hot. Stir potatoes before serving.

12 servings (3/4 cup each)
1 Serving: Calories 260 (Calories from Fat 90); Total Fat 10g (Saturated 6g; Trans 0g); Cholesterol 30mg; Sodium 360mg; Total Carbohydrate 35g (Dietary Fiber 4g; Sugars 2g); Protein 8g
% Daily Value: Vitamin A 6%; Vitamin C 10%; Calcium 8%; Iron 4%
Exchanges: 2 Starch, 1/2 High-Fat Meat, 1 Fat
Carbohydrate Choices: 2

KITCHEN TIPS

✿ Brie cheese adds a smooth texture and flavor to mashed potatoes.
✿ Use fresh parsley if you can't find fresh thyme.

Two-Cheese Potato Gratin

Prep Time: 30 min Start to Finish: 1 hr 35 min

$\frac{1}{2}$ cup butter or margarine

$\frac{1}{2}$ cup Gold Medal all-purpose flour

3 cups milk

1 tablespoon Dijon mustard

$\frac{1}{2}$ teaspoon salt

10 cups thinly sliced (about $\frac{1}{8}$ inch) Yukon gold potatoes (about 3 pounds)

$1\frac{1}{2}$ cups shredded Gruyere cheese (6 ounces)

$1\frac{1}{2}$ cups shredded Cheddar cheese (6 ounces)

1. Heat oven to 350°F. Grease 13 × 9-inch (3-quart) glass baking dish with shortening or cooking spray.

2. In 2-quart saucepan, melt butter over medium heat. Stir in flour with wire whisk until smooth. Gradually stir in milk. Heat to boiling. Reduce heat to low; cook about 5 minutes, stirring frequently, until sauce is slightly thickened. Stir in mustard and salt.

3. Place half of the potatoes in baking dish; top with half of the sauce and half of each of the cheeses. Repeat layers.

4. Bake 50 to 55 minutes or until potatoes are tender and top is golden brown. Let stand 5 to 10 minutes before serving.

12 servings ($\frac{1}{2}$ cup each)
1 Serving: Calories 330 (Calories from Fat 170); Total Fat 18g (Saturated 11g; Trans 0.5g); Cholesterol 55mg; Sodium 350mg; Total Carbohydrate 29g (Dietary Fiber 3g; Sugars 5g); Protein 12g
% Daily Value: Vitamin A 15%; Vitamin C 15%; Calcium 30%; Iron 15%
Exchanges: $1\frac{1}{2}$ Starch, $\frac{1}{2}$ Other Carbohydrate, 1 High-Fat Meat, 2 Fat
Carbohydrate Choices: 2

KITCHEN TIPS

⚙ Gruyere cheese has a rich, sweet, nutty flavor and melts easily.

⚙ Yukon gold potatoes, with a yellow-gold color and creamy texture, hold their shape without being waxy.

Ricotta-Stuffed Potatoes

Prep Time: 25 min Start to Finish: 1 hr 45 min

- 6 medium baking potatoes
- 1½ cups ricotta cheese
- 1 cup grated Parmesan cheese
- ¼ cup chopped fresh parsley
- ¼ teaspoon pepper
- 1 egg, beaten
  Additional fresh parsley, if desired

1. Heat oven to 375°F. Bake potatoes about 1 hour or until tender.

2. Cut each potato in half crosswise; scoop out inside into large bowl, leaving a thin shell. Mash potatoes until no lumps remain. Stir in cheeses, ¼ cup parsley, the pepper and egg until well blended.

3. Increase oven temperature to 400°F. Cut thin slice from bottom of each potato half if needed to stand upright. Place shells in ungreased 15 × 10-inch pan with sides; fill shells with potato mixture.

4. Bake about 20 minutes or until hot. Garnish with additional parsley.

6 servings
1 Serving: Calories 340 (Calories from Fat 100); Total Fat 11g (Saturated 6g; Trans 0g); Cholesterol 70mg; Sodium 360mg; Total Carbohydrate 41g (Dietary Fiber 4g; Sugars 3g); Protein 19g
% Daily Value: Vitamin A 10%; Vitamin C 15%; Calcium 40%; Iron 15%
Exchanges: 2 Starch, ½ Other Carbohydrate, 2 Medium-Fat Meat
Carbohydrate Choices: 3

KITCHEN TIPS

❁ If doubling the recipe, you can easily bake 12 potatoes at once, but prepare the filling for 6 potatoes at a time so that you can thoroughly blend the ingredients.

❁ The stuffed potatoes can be covered and refrigerated before baking; increase the baking time to 30 minutes. Or wrap airtight and freeze; bake about 40 minutes.

Low Fat
Butternut Squash Sauté

Prep Time: 40 min Start to Finish: 40 min

- 4 slices bacon, cut into 1-inch pieces
- 1 medium onion, chopped (½ cup)
- 2 small butternut squash, peeled, cut into ½-inch pieces (6 cups)
- ½ teaspoon chopped fresh or ⅛ teaspoon dried thyme leaves
- ⅛ teaspoon pepper
- 3 cups firmly packed baby spinach leaves

1. In 12-inch skillet, cook bacon over medium-low heat, stirring occasionally, until crisp. Stir in onion. Cook about 2 minutes, stirring occasionally, until onion is crisp-tender.

2. Stir in squash, thyme and pepper. Cover; cook 8 to 10 minutes, stirring occasionally, until squash is tender. Stir in spinach just until wilted.

8 servings
1 Serving: Calories 70 (Calories from Fat 15); Total Fat 2g (Saturated 0.5g; Trans 0g); Cholesterol 0mg; Sodium 105mg; Total Carbohydrate 11g (Dietary Fiber 2g; Sugars 4g); Protein 3g
% Daily Value: Vitamin A 220%; Vitamin C 15%; Calcium 6%; Iron 6%
Exchanges: ½ Other Carbohydrate, 1 Vegetable, ½ Fat
Carbohydrate Choices: 1

KITCHEN TIPS

❁ To save time, instead of washing spinach, purchase a bag of triple-washed baby spinach leaves in the produce section of the supermarket.
❁ When selecting butternut squash, look for those that have hard, tough rinds and are heavy for their size.

Ricotta-Stuffed Potatoes

Butternut Squash Sauté

Mashed Maple Sweet Potatoes

Prep Time: 15 min Start to Finish: 1 hr 50 min

3 pounds red garnet or dark-orange sweet potatoes

2 tablespoons maple-flavored syrup

¼ cup butter or margarine, softened

½ teaspoon salt

⅛ teaspoon ground nutmeg

2 tablespoons chopped pecans, toasted, if desired

6 servings (½ cup each)
1 Serving: Calories 230 (Calories from Fat 90); Total Fat 10g (Saturated 5g; Trans 0g); Cholesterol 20mg; Sodium 310mg; Total Carbohydrate 34g (Dietary Fiber 5g; Sugars 14g); Protein 3g
% Daily Value: Vitamin A 540%; Vitamin C 25%; Calcium 6%; Iron 6%
Exchanges: 1 Starch, 1 Other Carbohydrate, 2 Fat
Carbohydrate Choices: 2

KITCHEN TIPS

❂ To make ahead of time, cover and refrigerate mashed sweet potatoes up to 24 hours, then reheat in the microwave oven or a slow cooker on Low heat setting until warm.

❂ To toast pecans, bake uncovered in ungreased shallow pan in 350°F oven 6 to 10 minutes, stirring occasionally, until light brown. Or cook in ungreased heavy skillet over medium heat 5 to 7 minutes, stirring frequently until nuts begin to brown, then stirring constantly until nuts are light brown.

1. Heat oven to 350°F. Pierce potatoes with fork. Place potatoes in 9-inch square pan. Cover; bake about 1 hour 25 minutes or until potatoes are tender when pierced with a fork.

2. Let potatoes stand about 10 minutes or until cool enough to handle; slip off skins and discard.

3. In 2-quart saucepan, heat maple syrup and butter to boiling. Reduce heat to low. Add potatoes to saucepan; mash potatoes with syrup mixture, using electric mixer on medium speed, until light and fluffy. Stir in salt and nutmeg. Sprinkle with pecans.

Broccoli with Roasted Red Peppers and Hazelnuts

Prep Time: 30 min Start to Finish: 30 min

5 cups fresh broccoli florets

1 tablespoon olive or vegetable oil

1 clove garlic, finely chopped

1/4 cup chopped hazelnuts (filberts)

1/2 cup chopped roasted red bell peppers (from 7-ounce jar), drained

1/4 teaspoon salt

1. In 2-quart saucepan, heat 1 cup water to boiling. Add broccoli. Cover; cook about 1 minute or just until crisp. Drain and immediately place in ice water.

2. In 12-inch skillet, heat oil over medium heat. Add garlic and hazelnuts; cook over medium heat 1 to 2 minutes, stirring frequently, until nuts are lightly toasted.

3. Drain broccoli. Stir broccoli, bell peppers and salt into nut mixture. Cook about 3 minutes, stirring occasionally, until broccoli is crisp-tender.

8 servings (1/2 cup each)
1 Serving: Calories 70 (Calories from Fat 35); Total Fat 4g (Saturated 0g; Trans 0g); Cholesterol 0mg; Sodium 90mg; Total Carbohydrate 5g (Dietary Fiber 2g; Sugars 2g); Protein 2g
% Daily Value: Vitamin A 20%; Vitamin C 60%; Calcium 4%; Iron 4%
Exchanges: 1 Vegetable, 1 Fat
Carbohydrate Choices: 1/2

KITCHEN TIPS

❂ Roasted red peppers come packed in brine in jars of various sizes. They have a soft texture and roasted flavor.

❂ Hazelnuts are sweet, rich, grape-sized nuts that pair well with fresh broccoli.

Honeyed Carrots

Green Beans with Browned Butter

Honeyed Carrots

Prep Time: 25 min Start to Finish: 25 min

- 6 medium carrots ($^3/_4$ pound), cut into julienne (matchstick-cut) strips
- 4 medium green onions, sliced ($^1/_4$ cup)
- $^1/_3$ cup honey
- 1 tablespoon butter
- 1 tablespoon lemon juice
- $^1/_2$ teaspoon salt

1. In 10-inch skillet, heat 1 inch water (salted if desired) to boiling. Add carrots. Heat to boiling. Reduce heat; cover and simmer about 5 minutes or until tender. Drain; remove from skillet. Set aside.

2. In same skillet, cook remaining ingredients over low heat, stirring frequently, until bubbly. Stir in carrots. Cook uncovered 2 to 3 minutes, stirring occasionally, until carrots are glazed.

4 servings ($^1/_2$ cup each)
1 Serving: Calories 160 (Calories from Fat 30); Total Fat 3g (Saturated 2g; Trans 0g); Cholesterol 10mg; Sodium 380mg; Total Carbohydrate 32g (Dietary Fiber 3g; Sugars 28g); Protein 1g
% Daily Value: Vitamin A 210%; Vitamin C 6%; Calcium 4%; Iron 2%
Exchanges: 1$^1/_2$ Other Carbohydrate, 1 Vegetable, $^1/_2$ Fat
Carbohydrate Choices: 2

KITCHEN TIPS

✺ Julienne strips are small matchstick-size strips that cook faster than slices.

✺ If you don't have lemon juice, you can substitute orange juice.

Green Beans with Browned Butter

Prep Time: 15 min Start to Finish: 25 min

- $^3/_4$ pound fresh green beans
- 2 tablespoons butter (do not use margarine)
- 2 tablespoons pine nuts
- 1 teaspoon grated lemon peel

1. In 2$^1/_2$-quart saucepan, place beans in 1 inch water. Heat to boiling. Reduce heat; simmer uncovered 8 to 10 minutes or until crisp-tender. Drain; place in serving bowl. Cover to keep warm.

2. Meanwhile, in 1-quart saucepan, melt butter over low heat. Stir in pine nuts. Heat, stirring constantly, until butter is golden brown. (Once the butter begins to brown, it browns very quickly and can burn, so use low heat and watch carefully.) Immediately remove from heat.

3. Pour butter mixture over beans; toss to coat. Sprinkle with lemon peel.

6 servings ($^1/_2$ cup each)
1 Serving: Calories 70 (Calories from Fat 50); Total Fat 6g (Saturated 2.5g; Trans 0g); Cholesterol 10mg; Sodium 35mg; Total Carbohydrate 4g (Dietary Fiber 2g; Sugars 1g); Protein 1g
% Daily Value: Vitamin A 8%; Vitamin C 2%; Calcium 2%; Iron 2%
Exchanges: 1 Vegetable, 1 Fat
Carbohydrate Choices: 0

KITCHEN TIPS

✺ Do not use margarine because it doesn't brown or have the flavor of browned butter.

✺ Sliced or slivered almonds or chopped pecans or walnuts are tasty substitutes for the pine nuts.

Roasted Autumn Vegetables

Prep Time: 20 min Start to Finish: 1 hr 20 min

¼ cup butter or margarine

1 tablespoon chopped fresh or 1 teaspoon dried sage leaves

2 cloves garlic, finely chopped

½ pound Brussels sprouts, cut in half (2 cups)

½ pound parsnips, peeled, cut lengthwise into quarters, then cut into 2-inch pieces (2 cups)

½ small butternut squash (about 1 pound), peeled, seeded and cut into 1-inch pieces (2 cups)

1 bag (8 ounces) ready-to-eat baby-cut carrots (2 cups)

1. Heat oven to 375°F. In 1-quart saucepan, melt butter. Stir in sage and garlic.

2. In ungreased 13 × 9-inch pan, place remaining ingredients. Pour butter mixture over vegetables; stir to coat.

3. Cover with foil; bake 45 minutes. Remove foil; bake uncovered about 15 minutes longer or until vegetables are tender.

6 servings (1 cup each)
1 Serving: Calories 160 (Calories from Fat 70); Total Fat 8g (Saturated 5g; Trans 0g); Cholesterol 20mg; Sodium 90mg; Total Carbohydrate 19g (Dietary Fiber 5g; Sugars 7g); Protein 3g
% Daily Value: Vitamin A 190%; Vitamin C 25%; Calcium 6%; Iron 4%
Exchanges: ½ Other Carbohydrate, 2 Vegetable, 1½ Fat
Carbohydrate Choices: 1

KITCHEN TIPS

❁ You can use 2 cups of 1-inch pieces of Yukon gold potatoes in place of the butternut squash. Garnish with fresh sage leaves.

❁ Butternut squash is pear shaped with a pale yellow shell and dark orange flesh. It has a mild, sweet flavor.

Dried Cherry-Apple Stuffing

Prep Time: 20 min Start to Finish: 1 hr 10 min

1/2 cup butter or margarine

1 large onion, finely chopped (1 cup)

1 package (16 ounces) herb-seasoned stuffing mix crumbs

2 medium red apples, chopped (2 cups)

1 1/2 cups dried cherries

1 cup chopped pecans

2 1/2 cups chicken broth

1. Heat oven to 325°F. Grease 13 × 9-inch (3-quart) glass baking dish with shortening or cooking spray. In 8-inch skillet, melt butter over medium heat. Add onion; cook 4 to 6 minutes, stirring occasionally, until tender.

2. In large bowl, thoroughly mix cooked onion and remaining ingredients. Use 4 cups of the stuffing to fill body cavities of 12-pound turkey (do not pack stuffing because it will expand during roasting). Place remaining stuffing in baking dish. Cover with foil; refrigerate until ready to bake.

3. Roast stuffed turkey as directed in recipe. Bake stuffing in covered baking dish with turkey for at least 40 to 50 minutes of baking time or until thoroughly heated (165°F).

24 servings (1/2 cup each)
1 Serving: Calories 180 (Calories from Fat 70); Total Fat 8g (Saturated 3g; Trans 0g); Cholesterol 10mg; Sodium 440mg; Total Carbohydrate 24g (Dietary Fiber 2g; Sugars 7g); Protein 3g
% Daily Value: Vitamin A 8%; Vitamin C 0%; Calcium 4%; Iron 6%
Exchanges: 1 Starch, 1/2 Other Carbohydrate, 1 1/2 Fat
Carbohydrate Choices: 1 1/2

KITCHEN TIPS

✿ Use crisp, sweet apples, such as Braeburn, Cortland or Gala, for this stuffing.
✿ For Dried Cranberry-Apple Stuffing, substitute sweetened dried cranberries for the cherries.

Betty Crocker
IN SEASON

Cranberries

A holiday fruit with sass, crimson red cranberries adorn holiday tables in a variety of ways. Although fresh cranberries are only available October through December, cranberries can be enjoyed year-round as juice, sauces and relishes.

Choose

Although cranberries are almost always pre-packed, look for firm, plump berries with a deep red color. Avoid shriveled or soft berries.

Store

Fresh cranberries can be stored in the refrigerator for several months or in the freezer for a year. Remove any shriveled, pitted or soft cran-berries before storing.

Prepare

Wash cranberries in cool water before using. When using frozen berries for recipes other than salads and relishes, thaw and drain before using. If the cranberries will be cooked, you can use them frozen.

CRANBERRY EQUIVALENTS

► Traditionally, fresh cranberries are sold in 12-ounce bags, the equivalent of about 3 cups of berries.

► Finely chopping 12 ounces of cranberries will yield about $2\frac{1}{4}$ cups of chopped berries.

► One serving of cranberries is $\frac{1}{2}$ cup fresh cranberries, $\frac{1}{4}$ cup dried cranberries or $\frac{3}{4}$ cup 100% cranberry juice.

CRANBERRY CUISINE

▶ Fresh cranberries have a pocket of air that allows them to bounce and float.

▶ To chop cranberries quickly and easily, use a mini-chopper or food processor. Be sure to pulse on and off to get evenly sized pieces. You can also use a meat grinder.

▶ If you're making cranberry sauce, cook the cranberries just until they "pop." Cooking them longer will make them mushy and quite bitter. Adding 1 teaspoon butter or oil will help prevent them from boiling over.

▶ You can rehydrate dried cranberries by covering with water, or another liquid, in a microwavable bowl. Cover and microwave on High for 30 to 60 seconds; let stand 5 minutes. Or, pour very hot liquid over dried cranberries and let stand 20 minutes.

▶ Go beyond cranberry relish and try rich red cranberries in other parts of the meal.

▶ Toss a few fresh cranberries into a salad.

▶ Combine with other sweeter fruits to create fruit desserts like crisps, cobblers and pies.

▶ Stir dried cranberries into cooked cereals, add to your favorite snack mix or add to quick breads.

▶ Mix cranberry juice with your favorite mineral water for a refreshing beverage.

Nutrition Highlights

▶ Vitamin C (fresh cranberries only)
▶ Dietary fiber

A kissin' cousin to blueberries, red cranberries are a very tart berry that provides an array of health and nutritional benefits. Fresh cranberries supply the most benefits cranberries have to offer.

Health Highlights

▶ Once thought of as folklore, studies have now confirmed that cranberries can indeed help prevent urinary tract infections. The action of proanthocyanidins, a compound found in cranberries, prevents bacteria from sticking to the lining of the urinary tract. This means the bacteria cannot stick around to reproduce and cause an infection, but instead are flushed out.

▶ Emerging science also suggests that the proanthocyanidins' "anti-stick" effect may help prevent gingivitis and peptic ulcers. The same theory applies: By making it hard for bacteria to stick to tissues, the bacteria responsible for gum disease and peptic ulcers can't hang around long enough to produce an infection.

▶ Cranberries are packed with antioxidants, which neutralize free radical damage to cells. Cranberries rank among the highest in levels of antioxidants for all fruits and vegetables. Antioxidant activity is linked to reducing the risk of a number of chronic diseases and the effects of aging.

Recipes to try using cranberries:

Cranberry Cornbread, page 18

Mixed Greens with Cranberry Vinaigrette, page 70

Sausage-Cranberry Strata, page 17

Cornbread Stuffing

Prep Time: 20 min Start to Finish: 20 min

- ½ cup butter or margarine
- 1½ cups chopped celery (3 medium stalks)
- ¾ cup chopped onion (1½ medium)
- 9 cups cubes (½ inch) cornbread or soft bread
- 1½ teaspoons chopped fresh or ½ teaspoon dried sage leaves, crushed
- 1½ teaspoons chopped fresh or ½ teaspoon dried thyme leaves
- 1 teaspoon salt
- ⅛ teaspoon pepper

1. In 10-inch skillet, melt butter over medium heat. Add celery and onion; cook about 2 minutes, stirring occasionally, until crisp-tender. Remove from heat.

2. In large bowl, stir together celery mixture and remaining ingredients. Use to stuff one 12-pound turkey, or spoon into greased 3-quart casserole. Cover; bake 30 minutes. Uncover and bake 15 minutes longer or until thoroughly heated.

10 servings (½ cup each)
1 Serving: Calories 340 (Calories from Fat 160); Total Fat 17g (Saturated 8g; Trans 1g); Cholesterol 75mg; Sodium 930mg; Total Carbohydrate 40g (Dietary Fiber 4g; Sugars 13g); Protein 6g
% Daily Value: Vitamin A 10%; Vitamin C 0%; Calcium 8%; Iron 8%
Exchanges: 1½ Starch, 1 Other Carbohydrate, 3½ Fat
Carbohydrate Choices: 2½

KITCHEN TIPS

- One 8-inch square pan of baked cornbread will yield about 9 cups of cornbread cubes.
- You can make stuffing up to 4 hours ahead. Cover and refrigerate until it's time to bake. Add 5 to 10 minutes to the bake time since the stuffing will be cold.

Cupcakes, Bars and Cookies

Cupcakes, Ba
and Cook

Sweet Little Treats

Toasted Almond Cupcakes with Caramel Frosting (page 193)

Chocolate-Caramel Bars (page 216)

Low Fat

Cherry Mini-Cakes

Prep Time: 1 hr 50 min Start to Finish: 1 hr 50 min

Mini-Cakes

1	box Betty Crocker SuperMoist white cake mix
1	package (0.14 ounce) cherry-flavored unsweetened soft drink mix
1¼	cups water
⅓	cup vegetable oil
1	teaspoon almond extract
3	egg whites

Glaze

1	bag (2 pounds) powdered sugar (8 cups)
½	cup water
½	cup corn syrup
2	teaspoons almond extract
2	to 3 teaspoons hot water

Decoration

Miniature red candy hearts

1. Heat oven to 350°F (325°F for dark or nonstick pans). Grease bottoms only of about 60 mini muffin cups with shortening or cooking spray. In large bowl, beat all mini-cakes ingredients with electric mixer on low speed 30 seconds. Beat on medium speed 2 minutes, scraping bowl occasionally.

2. Divide batter evenly among muffin cups (about ½ full). (If using one pan, refrigerate batter while baking other cakes; wash pan before filling with additional batter.)

3. Bake 10 to 13 minutes or until toothpick inserted in center comes out clean. Cool 5 minutes. Remove cakes from muffin cups to cooling rack. Cool completely, about 30 minutes.

4. Place cooling rack on cookie sheet or waxed paper to catch glaze drips. In 3-quart saucepan, mix all glaze ingredients except hot water. Heat over low heat, stirring frequently, until sugar is dissolved. Remove from heat. Stir in 2 teaspoons hot water. If necessary, stir in up to 1 teaspoon more water so glaze will just coat cakes.

5. Turn each cake so top side is down on cooling rack. Pour about 1 tablespoon glaze over each cake, letting glaze coat sides. Let stand until glaze is set, about 15 minutes.

6. Top each cake with candy hearts. Store loosely covered at room temperature.

60 mini-cakes

1 Mini-Cake: Calories 120 (Calories from Fat 20); Total Fat 2g (Saturated 0g; Trans 0g); Cholesterol 0mg; Sodium 65mg; Total Carbohydrate 25g (Dietary Fiber 0g; Sugars 20g); Protein 0g % Daily Value: Vitamin A 0%; Vitamin C 0%; Calcium 0%; Iron 0% Exchanges: 1½ Other Carbohydrate, ½ Fat Carbohydrate Choices: 1½

KITCHEN TIPS

❀ Mini-cakes are great for themed parties. Pipe letters on the cakes to spell out "Congratulations" or "Bon Voyage."

❀ Bake the mini-cakes up to 2 weeks ahead of time and freeze. Add the glaze when it's time for the party.

All-Star Cupcakes

Prep Time: 40 min Start to Finish: 1 hr 40 min

- 1 box Betty Crocker SuperMoist white cake mix
- 1¼ cups water
- ⅓ cup vegetable oil
- ½ teaspoon almond extract
- 3 egg whites
- 1 container (1 pound) Betty Crocker Rich & Creamy vanilla frosting
  Blue paste food color
- ¼ cup blue candy sprinkles
- 2 ounces vanilla-flavored candy coating (almond bark)

1. Heat oven to 375°F. Place paper baking cup in each of 24 regular-size muffin cups. In large bowl, beat cake mix, water, oil, almond extract and egg whites with electric mixer on low speed 30 seconds. Beat on medium speed 2 minutes, scraping bowl occasionally. Divide batter evenly among muffin cups (about ⅔ full).

2. Bake 15 to 20 minutes or until toothpick inserted in center comes out clean. Cool 10 minutes; remove from pan to wire rack. Cool completely, about 30 minutes. Meanwhile, on piece of paper, draw free-form 5-pointed star, about 2 inches wide, to use as pattern.

3. Place half of frosting in small bowl. Dip toothpick into paste food color; stir food color into frosting in bowl until color is evenly distributed and desired shade.

4. Frost 12 cupcakes with blue frosting. Frost remaining 12 cupcakes with white frosting; sprinkle blue candy sprinkles over white cupcakes.

5. Chop candy coating; place in small microwavable bowl. Microwave uncovered on High 30 seconds; stir until melted and smooth. If necessary, microwave an additional 10 seconds. Place in heavy-duty plastic food-storage bag; cut tiny hole in one corner of bag.

6. Place paper star pattern under large piece of waxed paper. Squeezing bag of candy coating, trace the star on waxed paper; move pattern under waxed paper to make 12 stars. Let stars cool about 5 minutes or until candy coating is set. Remove stars from waxed paper; insert 1 star in each of 12 cupcakes.

24 cupcakes
1 Cupcake: Calories 220 (Calories from Fat 90); Total Fat 10g (Saturated 3g; Trans 2g); Cholesterol 0mg; Sodium 200mg; Total Carbohydrate 32g (Dietary Fiber 0g; Sugars 23g); Protein 2g
% Daily Value: Vitamin A 0%; Vitamin C 0%; Calcium 2%; Iron 2%
Exchanges: ½ Starch, 1½ Other Carbohydrate, 2 Fat
Carbohydrate Choices: 2

KITCHEN TIPS

- ✪ Make the cupcakes up to 2 weeks ahead of time. Remove from the freezer the night before your party and frost.
- ✪ Paste food color can be found at craft and specialty food stores. It adds a more intense color than liquid color.

Strawberry-Cream Cheese Cupcakes

Prep Time: 20 min Start to Finish: 1 hr 25 min

- 1 box Betty Crocker SuperMoist yellow cake mix
- 1 container (8 ounces) sour cream
- ½ cup vegetable oil
- ½ cup water
- 2 eggs
- 3 tablespoons strawberry preserves
- 1 package (3 ounces) cream cheese, cut into 24 pieces
- 1 container (1 pound) Betty Crocker Rich & Creamy cream cheese frosting
  Sliced fresh small strawberries, if desired

1. Heat oven to 350°F. Place paper baking cup in each of 24 regular-size muffin cups. In large bowl, mix cake mix, sour cream, oil, water and eggs with spoon until well blended (batter will be thick). Divide batter evenly among muffin cups.

2. In small bowl, stir strawberry preserves until smooth. Place 1 piece of cream cheese on top of batter in each cupcake; press in slightly. Place ¼ measuring teaspoon of preserves over cream cheese.

3. Bake 18 to 23 minutes or until tops are golden brown and spring back when touched lightly in center (some preserves may show in tops of cupcakes). Cool 10 minutes; remove from pan to wire rack. Cool completely, about 30 minutes.

4. Frost with frosting. Just before serving, garnish each cupcake with strawberry slices. Store covered in refrigerator.

24 cupcakes
1 Cupcake: Calories 260 (Calories from Fat 130); Total Fat 14g (Saturated 5g; Trans 0g); Cholesterol 30mg; Sodium 200mg; Total Carbohydrate 31g (Dietary Fiber 0g; Sugars 22g); Protein 2g
% Daily Value: Vitamin A 2%; Vitamin C 0%; Calcium 6%; Iron 2%
Exchanges: 1 Starch, 1 Other Carbohydrate, 2½ Fat
Carbohydrate Choices: 2

KITCHEN TIPS

✿ Make Raspberry-Cream Cheese Cupcakes by substituting raspberry preserves for the strawberry preserves and garnishing with fresh raspberries.

✿ These cupcakes would be delightful for a ladies' tea, wedding shower or dessert buffet.

S'mores Cupcakes

Prep Time: 45 min Start to Finish: 2 hr

1 box Betty Crocker SuperMoist yellow cake mix

Water, oil and eggs called for on cake mix box

1 cup graham cracker crumbs

4 bars (1.55 ounces each) milk chocolate candy, finely chopped

1 jar (7 ounces) marshmallow creme

$\frac{1}{2}$ cup butter or margarine, softened

2 cups powdered sugar

1 to 2 teaspoons milk

1 bar (1.55 ounces) milk chocolate candy, if desired

24 bear-shaped graham crackers, if desired

1. Heat oven to 375°F. Place paper baking cup in each of 24 regular-size muffin cups.

2. In large bowl, beat cake mix, water, oil and eggs with electric mixer on low speed 30 seconds. Beat on medium speed 2 minutes, scraping bowl occasionally. Fold in graham cracker crumbs and chopped chocolate bars. Divide batter evenly among muffin cups.

3. Bake 20 to 24 minutes or until toothpick inserted in center comes out clean. Cool 10 minutes; remove from pan to wire rack. Cool completely, about 30 minutes.

4. Remove lid and foil seal from jar of marshmallow creme. Microwave on High 15 to 20 seconds. In large bowl, beat marshmallow creme, butter and powdered sugar on low speed until blended. Beat in enough milk, $\frac{1}{2}$ teaspoon at a time, to make frosting spreadable. Spread over tops of cupcakes. Divide chocolate bar into rectangles. Cut each rectangle diagonally in half and place on top of each cupcake. Top each cupcake with bear-shaped cracker. After frosting has set, store loosely covered at room temperature.

24 cupcakes
1 Cupcake: Calories 280 (Calories from Fat 110); Total Fat 12g (Saturated 4.5g; Trans 0.5g); Cholesterol 40mg; Sodium 200mg; Total Carbohydrate 41g (Dietary Fiber 0g; Sugars 31g); Protein 2g
% Daily Value: Vitamin A 4%; Vitamin C 0%; Calcium 6%; Iron 4%
Exchanges: $\frac{1}{2}$ Starch, 2 Other Carbohydrate, $2\frac{1}{2}$ Fat
Carbohydrate Choices: 3

KITCHEN TIPS

✱ To keep the chocolate from sinking into the cake batter, chop it finely.
✱ Try chocolate-flavored graham crackers instead of regular graham crackers for more chocolate taste.

Piña Colada Cupcakes

Prep Time: 15 min Start to Finish: 1 hr 20 min

1 box Betty Crocker SuperMoist yellow cake mix

⅓ cup vegetable oil

¼ cup water

1 teaspoon rum extract

1 can (8 ounces) crushed pineapple in juice, undrained

3 eggs

1 teaspoon coconut extract

1 teaspoon rum extract

1 container (12 ounces) Betty Crocker Whipped vanilla frosting

¾ cup shredded coconut

1. Heat oven to 375°F. Place paper baking cup in each of 24 regular-size muffin cups.

2. In large bowl, beat cake mix, oil, water, 1 teaspoon rum extract, the pineapple and eggs with electric mixer on low speed 30 seconds. Beat on medium speed 2 minutes, scraping bowl occasionally. Divide batter evenly among muffin cups.

3. Bake 18 to 24 minutes or until toothpick inserted in center comes out clean. Cool 10 minutes; remove from pan to wire rack. Cool completely, about 30 minutes.

4. Stir coconut extract and 1 teaspoon rum extract into frosting. Spread frosting on cupcakes. Dip tops of frosted cupcakes in coconut. Store loosely covered at room temperature.

24 cupcakes

1 Cupcake: Calories 210 (Calories from Fat 90); Total Fat 10g (Saturated 3g; Trans 0g); Cholesterol 25mg; Sodium 170mg; Total Carbohydrate 29g (Dietary Fiber 0g; Sugars 20g); Protein 2g
% Daily Value: Vitamin A 0%; Vitamin C 0%; Calcium 4%; Iron 4%
Exchanges: ½ Starch, 1½ Other Carbohydrate, 2 Fat
Carbohydrate Choices: 2

KITCHEN TIPS

✿ For very white-on-white cupcakes, use Betty Crocker Whipped whipped cream frosting instead of the vanilla frosting.

✿ Decorate cupcakes with paper umbrellas to evoke feelings of sitting on the beach.

Toasted Almond Cupcakes with Caramel Frosting

Prep Time: 25 min Start to Finish: 2 hr 15 min

¹/₂ cup slivered almonds

1 box Betty Crocker SuperMoist white cake mix

1¹/₄ cups water

¹/₃ cup vegetable oil

3 eggs

1 teaspoon almond extract

1 cup sliced almonds

¹/₂ cup butter or margarine

1 cup packed brown sugar

¹/₄ cup milk

2 cups powdered sugar

1. Heat oven to 375°F. Place paper baking cup in each of 24 regular-size muffin cups. In shallow pan, bake slivered almonds 6 to 10 minutes, stirring occasionally, until golden brown; cool 15 minutes. In food processor, grind almonds until finely ground.

2. In large bowl, beat cake mix, water, oil, eggs and almond extract with electric mixer on low speed 30 seconds. Beat on medium speed 2 minutes, scraping bowl occasionally. Fold in ground almonds. Divide batter evenly among muffin cups.

3. Bake 20 to 24 minutes or until toothpick inserted in center comes out clean. Cool 10 minutes; remove from pan to wire rack. Cool completely, about 30 minutes.

4. Meanwhile, in shallow pan, bake sliced almonds at 375°F for 5 to 8 minutes, stirring occasionally, until golden brown.

5. In 2-quart saucepan, melt butter over medium heat. Stir in brown sugar. Heat to boiling, stirring constantly; reduce heat to low. Boil and stir 2 minutes. Stir in milk. Heat to boiling; remove from heat. Cool to lukewarm, about 30 minutes.

6. Gradually stir powdered sugar into brown sugar mixture. Place saucepan of frosting in bowl of cold water. Beat with spoon until smooth and spreadable. If frosting becomes too stiff, stir in additional milk, 1 teaspoon at a time. Frost a few cupcakes at a time with 1 tablespoon frosting each; press sliced almonds lightly into frosting. Store loosely covered at room temperature.

24 cupcakes

1 Cupcake: Calories 280 (Calories from Fat 120); Total Fat 13g (Saturated 3.5g; Trans 0.5g); Cholesterol 35mg; Sodium 180mg; Total Carbohydrate 37g (Dietary Fiber 1g; Sugars 28g); Protein 3g
% Daily Value: Vitamin A 4%; Vitamin C 0%; Calcium 6%; Iron 6%
Exchanges: 1 Starch, 1¹/₂ Other Carbohydrate, 2¹/₂ Fat
Carbohydrate Choices: 2¹/₂

KITCHEN TIPS

⊛ Try this recipe with other favorite nuts, such as hazelnuts or pecans, instead of the almonds.

⊛ For the richest and most intense caramel flavor, use real butter and dark brown sugar.

Red Velvet Cupcakes with Cream Cheese Frosting

Prep Time: 20 min Start to Finish: 2 hr

1   teaspoon water
1   bottle (1 ounce) red food color
1   box Betty Crocker SuperMoist devil's food cake mix
1¼   cups water
½   cup vegetable oil
3   eggs
1   container (1 pound) Betty Crocker Rich & Creamy cream cheese frosting

1. Heat oven to 375°F. Place paper baking cup in each of 24 regular-size muffin cups.

2. In small bowl, mix 1 teaspoon water and 3 or 4 drops of food color; set aside.

3. In large bowl, beat cake mix, 1¼ cups water, the oil, eggs and remaining bottle of food color with electric mixer on low speed 30 seconds. Beat on medium speed 2 minutes, scraping bowl occasionally. Divide batter evenly among muffin cups.

4. Bake 18 to 23 minutes or until toothpick inserted in center comes out clean. Cool 10 minutes; remove from pan to wire rack. Cool completely, about 30 minutes.

5. Frost tops of cupcakes with frosting. Using a fine-tip brush, paint cupcakes with red food color paint, swirling paint to create design. Store loosely covered at room temperature.

24 cupcakes
1 Cupcake: Calories 220 (Calories from Fat 100); Total Fat 11g (Saturated 3g; Trans 0g); Cholesterol 25mg; Sodium 220mg; Total Carbohydrate 29g (Dietary Fiber 0g; Sugars 21g); Protein 2g
% Daily Value: Vitamin A 0%; Vitamin C 0%; Calcium 2%; Iron 6%
Exchanges: 1 Starch, 1 Other Carbohydrate, 2 Fat
Carbohydrate Choices: 2

KITCHEN TIPS

✿ No one knows where the recipe for red velvet cake originated. It has been popular in the Southern United States since the early 1900s.

✿ If you're serving ice cream, try vanilla ice cream with red candy sprinkles or a drizzle of grenadine syrup.

Cream-Filled Cupcakes

Prep Time: 30 min Start to Finish: 1 hr 20 min

Cupcakes

- 1 box Betty Crocker SuperMoist devil's food cake mix

 Water, vegetable oil and eggs called for on cake mix box

Filling

- 1 cup Betty Crocker Whipped vanilla frosting (from 12-ounce container)
- $\frac{1}{2}$ cup marshmallow creme

Frosting

- 1 cup Betty Crocker Whipped chocolate frosting (from 12-ounce container)
- $\frac{1}{2}$ cup semisweet chocolate chips
- 2 teaspoons corn syrup
- 3 tablespoons Betty Crocker Whipped vanilla frosting (from 12-ounce container)

1. Heat oven to 350°F (325°F for dark or nonstick pans). Place paper baking cup in each of 24 regular-size muffin cups. Make and bake cake mix as directed on box for 24 cupcakes, using water, oil and eggs. Cool in pan 10 minutes; remove from pan to cooling rack. Cool completely, about 30 minutes.

2. With end of round handle of wooden spoon, make deep $\frac{1}{2}$-inch-wide indentation in center of each cupcake, not quite to the bottom (wiggle end of spoon in cupcake to make opening large enough). In small bowl, mix 1 cup vanilla frosting and the marshmallow creme. Spoon into small resealable plastic food-storage bag. Cut $\frac{3}{8}$-inch tip off 1 bottom corner of bag. Insert tip of bag into each cupcake and squeeze bag to fill.

3. In small microwavable bowl, microwave chocolate frosting, chocolate chips and corn syrup uncovered on High 30 seconds; stir. Microwave 15 to 30 seconds longer; stir until smooth. Dip top of each cupcake in frosting. Let stand until frosting is set.

4. Spoon 3 tablespoons vanilla frosting in small resealable plastic food-storage bag. Cut tiny tip off 1 bottom corner of bag. Pipe a squiggle of frosting or initials across top of each cupcake.

24 cupcakes
1 Cupcake: Calories 240 (Calories from Fat 100); Total Fat 11g (Saturated 3.5g; Trans 1g); Cholesterol 25mg; Sodium 210mg; Total Carbohydrate 32g (Dietary Fiber 1g; Sugars 23g); Protein 2g
% Daily Value: Vitamin A 0%; Vitamin C 0%; Calcium 0%; Iron 6%
Exchanges: 1 Starch, 1 Other Carbohydrate, 2 Fat
Carbohydrate Choices: 2

KITCHEN TIPS

❀ If you have a melon baller, use it to make the indentation in the cupcake.

❀ Dipping the cupcakes in frosting is easiest if there's plenty of frosting, so you may have frosting left. Frost graham crackers with the rest of it for a later treat.

Happy Birthday Marshmallow Cupcakes

Prep Time: 25 min Start to Finish: 1 hr 25 min

1 box Betty Crocker SuperMoist white cake mix

Water, vegetable oil and egg whites called for on cake mix box

2 containers (1 pound each) Betty Crocker Rich & Creamy creamy white frosting

24 to 30 large marshmallows

Betty Crocker colored sugar or candy sprinkles

White or colored birthday candles

1. Heat oven to 350°F (325°F for dark or nonstick pans). Place paper baking cup in each of 24 regular-size muffin cups. Make and bake cake mix as directed on box for 24 cupcakes, using water, oil and egg whites. Cool in pan 10 minutes; remove from pan to cooling rack. Cool completely, about 30 minutes.

2. Frost cupcakes with frosting.

3. Cut marshmallow with dampened kitchen scissors into slices; sprinkle with colored sugar. Arrange on cupcakes in flower shape. Place candle in middle of each flower.

24 cupcakes
1 Cupcake: Calories 280 (Calories from Fat 120); Total Fat 14g (Saturated 4g; Trans 3g); Cholesterol 0mg; Sodium 240mg; Total Carbohydrate 38g (Dietary Fiber 0g; Sugars 30g); Protein 1g
% Daily Value: Vitamin A 0%; Vitamin C 0%; Calcium 2%; Iron 2%
Exchanges: 2½ Other Carbohydrate, 3 Fat
Carbohydrate Choices: 2½

KITCHEN TIPS

✿ Use edible glitter in place of the colored sugar or candy sprinkles. It adds sparkle to cake decorations.

✿ Check out party-supply or cake-decorating stores for fun birthday candles. Lots of new and unique shapes are available.

Surprise Cupcake Cones

Prep Time: 40 min Start to Finish: 1 hr 25 min

1   box Betty Crocker SuperMoist yellow cake mix

Water, vegetable oil and eggs called for on cake mix box

1   cup candy-coated chocolate candies

18   flat-bottom ice cream cones

3   containers (12 ounces each) Betty Crocker Whipped strawberry frosting

1/4   cup Betty Crocker candy decors

1. Heat oven to 350°F (325°F for dark or nonstick pans). Place paper baking cup in each of 18 regular-size muffin cups, place mini paper baking cup in each of 18 mini muffin cups. Make cake mix as directed on box, using water, oil and eggs. Spoon evenly into regular and mini muffin cups.

2. Bake mini-cupcakes 11 to 13 minutes, regular cupcakes 17 to 22 minutes, or until toothpick inserted in center comes out clean. Remove from pans to cooling rack. Cool completely, about 30 minutes.

3. Tightly cover the tops of 2 empty square or rectangular pans that are at least 2 to 2½ inches deep with heavy-duty foil. Cut 18 "stars" in foil, 3 inches apart, by making slits about 1 inch long with a sharp knife.

4. Remove paper cups from cupcakes. Place about 2 teaspoons candies in each cone. For each cone, frost top of 1 regular cupcake with frosting; turn upside down onto a cone. Frost bottom (now the top) and side of cupcakes. Place mini-cupcake upside down on frosted regular cupcake; frost completely (it's easiest to frost from the cone toward the top). Sprinkle with candy decors. Push cone through opening in foil; the foil will keep it upright.

18 cones
1 Cupcake Cone: Calories 490 (Calories from Fat 190); Total Fat 22g (Saturated 7g; Trans 4g); Cholesterol 35mg; Sodium 270mg; Total Carbohydrate 72g (Dietary Fiber 0g; Sugars 54g); Protein 3g
% Daily Value: Vitamin A 0%; Vitamin C 0%; Calcium 6%; Iron 4%
Exchanges: 1 Starch, 4 Other Carbohydrate, 4 Fat
Carbohydrate Choices: 5

KITCHEN TIPS

❀ If strawberry frosting is not available, tint vanilla frosting a light pink with red food color.

❀ For extra pizzazz, top each "cone" with a maraschino cherry.

Chocolate Cupcakes with White Truffle Frosting

Prep Time: 35 min Start to Finish: 1 hr 10 min

1   box Betty Crocker SuperMoist devil's food
    cake mix

    Water, vegetable oil and eggs called for on
    cake mix box

1   cup white vanilla baking chips

1   container (1 pound) Betty Crocker Rich &
    Creamy vanilla frosting

1. Heat oven to 350°F (325°F for dark or nonstick pans).
Place paper baking cup in each of 24 regular-size
muffin cups. Make and bake cake mix as directed on
box for 24 cupcakes, using water, oil and eggs. Cool
in pan 10 minutes; remove from pan to cooling rack.
Cool completely, about 30 minutes.

2. In medium microwavable bowl, microwave baking
chips uncovered on Medium (50%) 4 to 5 minutes,
stirring after 2 minutes. Stir until smooth; cool 5
minutes. Stir in frosting until well blended. Immediately frost cupcakes or pipe frosting on cupcakes.

3. If desired, tie ribbons around cupcakes for decoration. Store loosely covered.

24 cupcakes
1 Cupcake: Calories 270 (Calories from Fat 120); Total Fat 13g
(Saturated 5g; Trans 1.5g); Cholesterol 25mg; Sodium 240mg; Total
Carbohydrate 36g (Dietary Fiber 0g; Sugars 27g); Protein 2g
% Daily Value: Vitamin A 0%; Vitamin C 0%; Calcium 4%; Iron 4%
Exchanges: $\frac{1}{2}$ Starch, 2 Other Carbohydrate, 2$\frac{1}{2}$ Fat
Carbohydrate Choices: 2$\frac{1}{2}$

KITCHEN TIPS

❂ For Chocolate Truffle Frosting, substitute chocolate chips
and Betty Crocker Rich & Creamy chocolate frosting.

❂ You can decorate these basic cupcakes any way you like.
Use colored sugar, edible glitter or any purchased decoration.

Wedding Cupcakes

Prep Time: 1 hr Start to Finish: 1 hr 25 min

Cupcakes

1 box Betty Crocker SuperMoist white cake mix

White paper baking cups

Water, vegetable oil and egg whites called for on cake mix box

2 containers (1 pound each) Betty Crocker Rich & Creamy creamy white frosting

Decorating Options

White Chocolate Curls (below)

Pink rose petals

Handmade paper, cut into 8 × 1¼-inch strips

Decorator sugar crystals or edible glitter

Ribbon

1. Heat oven to 350°F (325°F for dark or nonstick pans). Place white paper baking cup in each of 24 regular-size muffin cups. Make and bake cake mix as directed on box for 24 cupcakes, using water, oil and egg whites. Cool in pan 10 minutes; remove from pan to cooling rack. Cool completely, about 30 minutes.

2. Frost cupcakes with frosting. Choose from these decorating options:

   • Top cupcakes with White Chocolate Curls (see below) or rose petals.

   • Wrap handmade paper around each cupcake; attach permanent double-stick tape.

   • Sprinkle decorator sugar crystals or edible glitter over frosting.

   • Wrap ribbon around each cupcake and tie in a bow.

3. White Chocolate Curls: Place bar of room-temperature white chocolate on waxed paper. Make curls by pulling a vegetable peeler toward you in long, thin strokes while pressing firmly against the chocolate. (If curls crumble or stay too straight, chocolate may be too cold; placing the heel of your hand on the chocolate will warm it enough to get good curls.) Transfer each curl carefully with a toothpick to a waxed paper-lined cookie sheet or directly onto frosted cupcake.

24 cupcakes

1 Cupcake: Calories 280 (Calories from Fat 120); Total Fat 14g (Saturated 4g; Trans 3g); Cholesterol 0mg; Sodium 240mg; Total Carbohydrate 38g (Dietary Fiber 0g; Sugars 30g); Protein 1g
% Daily Value: Vitamin A 0%; Vitamin C 0%; Calcium 2%; Iron 2%
Exchanges: 2½ Other Carbohydrate, 3 Fat
Carbohydrate Choices: 2½

KITCHEN TIPS

❂ Look for edible flowers and/or rose petals in the produce department of the grocery store. Edible flowers have not been treated with chemicals so they're safe to eat.

❂ Use the bride's wedding colors for the frosting and decorations for these cupcakes.

Pull-Apart Turtle Cupcakes

Prep Time: 30 min Start to Finish: 2 hr

1   box Betty Crocker SuperMoist yellow cake mix

Water, oil and eggs called for on cake mix box

1   container (1 pound) Betty Crocker Rich & Creamy vanilla frosting

Green food color

1   container (1 pound) Betty Crocker Rich & Creamy chocolate frosting

1   can (6.4 ounces) Betty Crocker Easy Flow green decorating icing

4   candy-coated chocolate candies

1   piece red string licorice

1   piece green peelable licorice

1   can (6.4 ounces) Betty Crocker Easy Flow black decorating icing

1. Heat oven to 375°F. Place paper baking cup in each of 24 regular-size muffin cups.

2. In large bowl, beat cake mix, water, oil and eggs with electric mixer on low speed 30 seconds. Beat on medium speed 2 minutes, scraping bowl occasionally. Divide batter evenly among muffin cups.

3. Bake 17 to 20 minutes or until toothpick inserted in center comes out clean. Cool 10 minutes; remove from pan to wire rack. Cool completely, about 30 minutes.

4. Tint vanilla frosting with green food color. Reserve 1/2 cup green frosting and 1/2 cup chocolate frosting.

5. On each of 2 large serving trays, arrange 12 cupcakes as shown in diagram. Frost shell of one turtle with remaining chocolate frosting. Frost head and feet with reserved 1/2 cup green frosting. (Push cupcakes together slightly to frost entire turtle, not just individual cupcakes.) Pipe canned green icing on chocolate shell to create turtle design. Add 2 candies for eyes, a piece of red string licorice for mouth and a piece of green peelable string licorice for tail.

6. Frost remaining cupcakes using remaining green frosting for the shell and reserved chocolate frosting for head and feet. Pipe canned black icing on green shell to create turtle design. Add 2 candies for eyes, a piece of red string licorice for mouth and a piece of green peelable string licorice for tail. Store loosely covered at room temperature.

24 cupcakes (2 turtles)
1 Cupcake: Calories 360 (Calories from Fat 150); Total Fat 17g (Saturated 6g; Trans 0g); Cholesterol 25mg; Sodium 270mg; Total Carbohydrate 50g (Dietary Fiber 0g; Sugars 39g); Protein 2g
% Daily Value: Vitamin A 0%; Vitamin C 0%; Calcium 4%; Iron 4%
Exchanges: 1 Starch, 2 1/2 Other Carbohydrate, 3 Fat
Carbohydrate Choices: 3

KITCHEN TIPS

⊕ You can vary the cake mix to suit your taste. Just follow the directions on the box for amounts of water, oil and eggs.
⊕ For each cake, push cupcakes together slightly and frost entire turtle.

For each cake, push cupcakes together slightly and frost entire turtle.

May Day Baskets

Prep Time: 20 min Start to Finish: 1 hr 30 min

1 box Betty Crocker SuperMoist yellow cake mix

Water, oil and eggs called for on cake mix box

1 container (1 pound) Betty Crocker Rich & Creamy frosting (any flavor)

Red and blue berry twist licorice

Assorted small candies or jelly beans

1. Heat oven to 350°F. Place paper baking cup in each of 24 regular-size muffin cups. Make cake mix as directed on box for cupcakes, using water, oil and eggs. Divide batter evenly among muffin cups.

2. Bake 21 to 26 minutes or until toothpick inserted in center comes out clean. Cool 10 minutes; remove from pan to wire rack. Cool completely, about 30 minutes.

3. Spread frosting over cupcakes. Make basket handles with licorice. Decorate with candies. Store loosely covered at room temperature.

24 cupcakes
1 Cupcake (Cake and Frosting): Calories 210 (Calories from Fat 90); Total Fat 10g (Saturated 3g; Trans 0g); Cholesterol 25mg; Sodium 190mg; Total Carbohydrate 29g (Dietary Fiber 0g; Sugars 20g); Protein 2g
% Daily Value: Vitamin A 0%; Vitamin C 0%; Calcium 4%; Iron 2%
Exchanges: 1/2 Starch, 1 1/2 Other Carbohydrate, 2 Fat
Carbohydrate Choices: 2

KITCHEN TIPS

✿ Tint white frosting with yellow, blue, pink or green food color for colorful May baskets.

✿ Rekindle the childhood tradition of giving May baskets. Make a batch of cupcakes and deliver them to your neighbors and friends.

Birthday Cupcakes

Prep Time: 10 min Start to Finish: 1 hr 20 min

1   box Betty Crocker SuperMoist yellow cake mix

  Water, oil and eggs called for on cake mix box

1   container (1 pound) Betty Crocker Rich & Creamy creamy white frosting

24   ring-shaped hard candies or jelly beans, if desired

  Assorted small colorful candies and sugars, if desired

1. Heat oven to 350°F. Place paper baking cup in each of 24 regular-size muffin cups. Make cake mix as directed on box, using water, oil and eggs. Divide batter evenly among muffin cups.

2. Bake 21 to 26 minutes or until toothpick inserted in center comes out clean. Cool 10 minutes; remove from pan to wire rack. Cool completely, about 30 minutes.

3. Frost cupcakes with frosting. Use ring candies as candleholders. Decorate with assorted candies. Store loosely covered at room temperature.

24 cupcakes
1 Cupcake: Calories 220 (Calories from Fat 90); Total Fat 10g (Saturated 3g; Trans 2g); Cholesterol 25mg; Sodium 200mg; Total Carbohydrate 31g (Dietary Fiber 0g; Sugars 23g); Protein 2g
% Daily Value: Vitamin A 0%; Vitamin C 0%; Calcium 4%; Iron 2%
Exchanges: 1 Starch, 1 Other Carbohydrate, 2 Fat
Carbohydrate Choices: 2

KITCHEN TIPS

✿ Save time the day of the party by baking and frosting cupcakes up to one month ahead of time. Freeze in a covered cake pan, and bring to room temperature several hours before serving. Add candies just before serving to keep color from bleeding into frosting.

Bug Cupcakes

Prep Time: 25 min Start to Finish: 1 hr 25 min

1   box Betty Crocker SuperMoist white cake mix

  Water, vegetable oil and egg whites called for on cake mix box

2   containers (1 pound each) Betty Crocker Rich & Creamy creamy white frosting

  Green and yellow paste or gel food color

  Assorted candies (such as round mints, jelly beans, Jordan almonds, wafer candies, pieces from candy necklaces)

  String licorice

  Betty Crocker white decorating icing (from 4.25-ounce tube)

1. Heat oven to 350°F (325°F for dark or nonstick pans). Place paper baking cup in each of 24 regular-size muffin cups. Make and bake cake mix as directed on box for 24 cupcakes, using water, oil and egg whites. Cool in pan 10 minutes; remove from pan to cooling rack. Cool completely, about 30 minutes.

2. Tint frosting with desired food color; frost cupcakes.

3. Arrange candies on cupcakes to make bug heads, bodies and wings. In addition to candies, you can use whole marshmallows or sliced marshmallows sprinkled with colored sugar. Use pieces of licorice for antennae. For eyes, add dots of decorating icing.

24 cupcakes
1 Cupcake: Calories 280 (Calories from Fat 120); Total Fat 14g (Saturated 4g; Trans 3g); Cholesterol 0mg; Sodium 240mg; Total Carbohydrate 38g (Dietary Fiber 0g; Sugars 30g); Protein 1g
% Daily Value: Vitamin A 0%; Vitamin C 0%; Calcium 2%; Iron 2%
Exchanges: 2½ Other Carbohydrate, 3 Fat
Carbohydrate Choices: 2½

KITCHEN TIPS

✿ For a kids' party, have the cupcakes baked and frosted. Set out dishes of decorating candies and tubes of decorating gel, and let the kids create their own bugs.

✿ If your birthday child prefers chocolate, make chocolate cupcakes instead.

Bug Cupcakes

Birthday Cupcakes

Goin' Fishin' Cupcakes

Prep Time: 35 min Start to Finish: 1 hr 35 min

Cupcakes

- 1 box Betty Crocker SuperMoist devil's food cake mix

  Water, oil and eggs called for on cake mix box

- 1 container (1 pound) Betty Crocker Rich & Creamy vanilla frosting

  Blue liquid or paste food color

Fishing Poles

- 24 cocktail straws
- 24 pieces thick craft thread, dental floss or fishing line, each 6½ inches long
- 24 Betty Crocker Shark Bites® chewy fruit snacks (2 to 3 packets)

1. Heat oven to 350°F. Place paper baking cup in each of 24 regular-size muffin cups. Make cake as directed on box, using water, oil and eggs. Divide batter evenly among muffin cups.

2. Bake 15 to 20 minutes or until toothpick inserted in center comes out clean. Cool 10 minutes; remove from pan to wire rack. Cool completely, about 30 minutes.

3. Mix frosting and a few drops of food color. Frost cupcakes with blue frosting. Pull up on frosting, using metal spatula, so frosting looks like waves.

4. Cut each straw to make one 3-inch piece. Insert piece of craft thread into end of each straw to look like fishing line. Attach 1 shark snack to end of each piece of craft thread. Decorate cakes with fishing poles. Store loosely covered at room temperature.

24 cupcakes
1 Cupcake: Calories 230 (Calories from Fat 100); Total Fat 11g (Saturated 3g; Trans 0g); Cholesterol 25mg; Sodium 230mg; Total Carbohydrate 31g (Dietary Fiber 0g; Sugars 22g); Protein 2g
% Daily Value: Vitamin A 0%; Vitamin C 0%; Calcium 2%; Iron 6%
Exchanges: 1 Starch, 1 Other Carbohydrate, 2 Fat
Carbohydrate Choices: 2

KITCHEN TIPS

- Add more fish to the pond by sprinkling the serving plate with fish-shaped pretzel crackers.
- Make the fishing poles up to three days ahead. Place in a resealable plastic bag to keep the shark snacks from drying out.

Picnic Pals

Prep Time: 1 hr Start to Finish: 2 hr 10 min

1 box Betty Crocker SuperMoist cake mix (any flavor)

Water, oil and eggs called for on cake mix box

1 container (12 ounces) Betty Crocker Whipped fluffy white or vanilla frosting

Assorted gumdrops or small candies

Betty Crocker Fruit by the Foot® chewy fruit snack, any flavor (from 4.5-ounce box)

1 tube (0.68 ounce) Betty Crocker black decorating gel

1. Heat oven to 350°F. Place paper baking cup in each of 24 regular-size muffin cups. Make cake mix as directed on box for cupcakes, using water, oil and eggs.

2. Bake as directed on box. Cool 10 minutes; remove from pan to wire rack. Cool completely, about 30 minutes.

3. Frost and decorate 1 cupcake at a time. Decorate with whole or cut-up gumdrops, small candies, cut-up or thinly rolled fruit snacks and decorating gel to look like ladybugs, bumblebees, butterflies, caterpillars and beetles. Store loosely covered at room temperature.

24 cupcakes
1 Cupcake (Cake and Frosting): Calories 190 (Calories from Fat 80); Total Fat 9g (Saturated 2g; Trans 0g); Cholesterol 25mg; Sodium 160mg; Total Carbohydrate 26g (Dietary Fiber 0g; Sugars 18g); Protein 2g
% Daily Value: Vitamin A 0%; Vitamin C 0%; Calcium 4%; Iron 2%
Exchanges: $\frac{1}{2}$ Starch, 1 Other Carbohydrate, 2 Fat
Carbohydrate Choices: 2

KITCHEN TIPS

✿ All the cupcake recipes recommend using paper baking cups so cupcakes bake more evenly. Plus, the pan is easier to wash and cupcakes are easier to serve.

✿ Create a grass-lined tray for these picnic pals. Place 1 cup shredded coconut in a jar, add a few drops of green food color and shake until coconut is green.

Bunny Cupcakes

Prep Time: 30 min Start to Finish: 1 hr 45 min

1 box Betty Crocker SuperMoist yellow or white cake mix

Water, vegetable oil and eggs called for on cake mix box

Pink food color

2 containers (12 ounces each) Betty Crocker Whipped fluffy white frosting

5 large marshmallows

Pink sugar

Candy decorations and sprinkles, as desired

1. Heat oven to 350°F (325°F for dark or nonstick pans). Place paper baking cup in each of 24 regular-size muffin cups. Make and bake cake mix as directed on box for 24 cupcakes, using water, oil and eggs. Cool in pan 10 minutes; remove from pan to cooling rack. Cool completely, about 30 minutes.

2. Stir a few drops pink food color into 1 container of frosting. Frost cupcakes with pink frosting.

3. Spoon 1 heaping teaspoonful white frosting on center of each cupcake. To make ears, cut each large marshmallow crosswise into 5 pieces with kitchen scissors. Using scissors, cut through center of each marshmallow piece to within 1/4 inch of edge. Separate to look like bunny ears; press 1 side of cut edges into pink sugar, flattening slightly. Arrange on each of the white frosting mounds. Use candy decorations and sprinkles to make eyes, nose and whiskers. Store loosely covered.

24 cupcakes

1 Cupcake (Cake and Frosting only): Calories 250 (Calories from Fat 100); Total Fat 11g (Saturated 3g; Trans 2.5g); Cholesterol 25mg; Sodium 180mg; Total Carbohydrate 35g (Dietary Fiber 0g; Sugars 25g); Protein 1g
% Daily Value: Vitamin A 0%; Vitamin C 0%; Calcium 4%; Iron 2%
Exchanges: 1/2 Starch, 2 Other Carbohydrate, 2 Fat
Carbohydrate Choices: 2

KITCHEN TIPS

❀ Cupcakes are a nice size for a kids' party. These would be great for an Easter party or a Peter Rabbit-themed birthday party.

❀ You can substitute Betty Crocker Whipped strawberry frosting for the pink-tinted white frosting.

Frog Cupcakes

Prep Time: 25 min   Start to Finish: 1 hr 25 min

1 box Betty Crocker SuperMoist white cake mix

Water, vegetable oil and egg whites called for on cake mix box

2 containers (1 pound each) Betty Crocker Rich & Creamy creamy white frosting

Green paste or gel food color

48 green miniature vanilla wafer cookies

48 red cinnamon candies

Betty Crocker red decorating icing (from 4.25-ounce tube)

Large red gumdrops

1. Heat oven to 350°F (325°F for dark or nonstick pans). Place paper baking cup in each of 24 regular-size muffin cups. Make and bake cake mix as directed on box for 24 cupcakes, using water, oil and egg whites. Cool in pan 10 minutes; remove from pan to cooling rack. Cool completely, about 30 minutes.

2. Reserve 2 tablespoons frosting. Tint remaining frosting with food color to make green; frost cupcakes.

3. For eyes, place 2 cookies near top edge of each cupcake, inserting on end so they stand up. Attach 1 cinnamon candy to each cookie with reserved white frosting. Add dots of white frosting for nostrils.

4. For mouth, pipe on red icing. Slice gumdrops; add slice to each cupcake for tongue.

24 cupcakes
1 Cupcake (Cake and Frosting only): Calories 280 (Calories from Fat 120); Total Fat 14g (Saturated 4g; Trans 3g); Cholesterol 0mg; Sodium 240mg; Total Carbohydrate 38g (Dietary Fiber 0g; Sugars 30g); Protein 1g
% Daily Value: Vitamin A 0%; Vitamin C 0%; Calcium 2%; Iron 2%
Exchanges: 2½ Other Carbohydrate, 3 Fat
Carbohydrate Choices: 2½

KITCHEN TIPS

✿ If your kids don't like the cinnamon taste of the red candies, use the red colored mini candy-coated chocolate baking bits from a 12-ounce bag.

✿ For a touch of whimsy, cut small pieces of black gumdrops and place one on each "tongue" to resemble a fly.

Key West Cupcakes

Prep Time: 25 min Start to Finish: 1 hr 30 min

Filling

1   box (4-serving size) vanilla instant pudding and pie filling mix

1¹⁄₂   cups whipping cream

¹⁄₄   cup fresh Key lime or regular lime juice

4   drops green food color

1¹⁄₂   cups powdered sugar

Cupcakes

1   box Betty Crocker SuperMoist yellow cake mix

Water, vegetable oil and eggs called for on cake mix box

Frosting

1   container (12 ounces) Betty Crocker Whipped fluffy white frosting

1   tablespoon fresh Key lime or regular lime juice

¹⁄₂   teaspoon grated Key lime or regular lime peel

1. In large bowl, beat pudding mix and whipping cream with wire whisk 2 minutes. Let stand 3 minutes. Beat in ¹⁄₄ cup lime juice and the food color; stir in powdered sugar until smooth. Cover; refrigerate.

2. Heat oven to 350°F (325°F for dark or nonstick pans). Place paper baking cup in each of 24 regular-size muffin cups. Make and bake cake mix as directed on box for 24 cupcakes, using water, oil and eggs. Cool in pan 10 minutes; remove from pan to cooling rack. Cool completely, about 30 minutes.

3. Spread 1 rounded tablespoonful filling on top of each cupcake. Stir frosting in container 20 times. Gently stir in 1 tablespoon lime juice and the lime peel. Spoon frosting into 1-quart resealable plastic food-storage bag. Cut ¹⁄₂-inch opening from bottom corner of bag. Squeeze 1 tablespoon frosting from bag onto filling on each cupcake. Garnish with fresh lime wedge if desired. Store covered in refrigerator.

24 cupcakes

1 Cupcake: Calories 280 (Calories from Fat 120); Total Fat 13g (Saturated 5g; Trans 1.5g); Cholesterol 45mg; Sodium 230mg; Total Carbohydrate 38g (Dietary Fiber 0g; Sugars 29g); Protein 2g
% Daily Value: Vitamin A 4%; Vitamin C 0%; Calcium 4%; Iron 2%
Exchanges: 1 Starch, ¹⁄₂ Other Carbohydrate, 2¹⁄₂ Fat
Carbohydrate Choices: 2¹⁄₂

KITCHEN TIPS

⚙ Key limes are tiny and green in color. You can purchase them in the produce department, or purchase a bottle of Key lime juice.

⚙ Cut tiny Key limes into wedges or thin slices for an ideal garnish.

Low Fat

Almond Petits Fours

Prep Time: 1 hr 50 min Start to Finish: 1 hr 50 min

Cake

1	package Betty Crocker SuperMoist white cake mix
1¼	cups water
⅓	cup vegetable oil
1	teaspoon almond extract
3	egg whites

Almond Glaze

1	bag (2 pounds) powdered sugar (8 cups)
½	cup water
½	cup corn syrup
2	teaspoons almond extract
1	to 3 teaspoons hot water

Decoration

Assorted color Betty Crocker decorating icing (in 4.25-ounce tubes), fresh edible flowers or purchased candy flowers

1. Heat oven to 350°F (325°F for dark or nonstick pan). Spray bottoms only of about 60 mini muffin cups with baking spray with flour.

2. In large bowl, beat cake mix, 1¼ cups water, the oil, 1 teaspoon almond extract and egg whites with electric mixer on low speed 30 seconds. Beat on medium speed 2 minutes, scraping bowl occasionally. Divide batter evenly among muffin cups (about ½ full). (If using one pan, refrigerate batter while baking other cakes; wash pan before filling with additional batter.)

3. Bake 10 to 15 minutes or until toothpick inserted in center comes out clean. Cool 5 minutes; remove from pan to cooling rack. Cool completely, about 30 minutes.

4. Place cooling rack on cookie sheet or waxed paper to catch glaze drips. In 3-quart saucepan, stir powdered sugar, ½ cup water, the corn syrup and 2 teaspoons almond extract. Heat over low heat, stirring frequently, until sugar is dissolved; remove from heat. Stir in hot water, 1 teaspoon at a time, until glaze is pourable. Turn each mini-cake on cooling rack so top side is down. Pour about 1 tablespoon glaze over each cake, letting glaze coat the sides. Let stand 15 minutes.

5. With decorating icing, pipe designs on cakes, or garnish cakes with flowers just before serving. Store loosely covered at room temperature.

60 petits fours
1 Petit Four: Calories 120 (Calories from Fat 20); Total Fat 2g (Saturated 0g; Trans 0g); Cholesterol 0mg; Sodium 65mg; Total Carbohydrate 24g (Dietary Fiber 0g; Sugars 19g); Protein 0g
% Daily Value: Vitamin A 0%; Vitamin C 0%; Calcium 0%; Iron 0%
Exchanges: 1 Other Carbohydrate, ½ Fat
Carbohydrate Choices: 1½

KITCHEN TIPS

❂ You can make the cakes up to 2 weeks earlier and freeze, but wait to add the glaze until shortly before you serve them.

❂ Miniature desserts are great choices for a dessert buffet. Guests can sample several of the desserts if they are only one or two bites each.

Cupcakes, Bars and Cookies   **209**

Molten Chocolate Cupcakes

Prep Time: 30 min Start to Finish: 2 hr

- $^1/_2$ cup whipping cream
- 1 cup semisweet chocolate chips (6 ounces)
- 1 box Betty Crocker SuperMoist devil's food cake mix
- 1 cup water
- $^1/_3$ cup vegetable oil
- 3 eggs
- 1 container (1 pound) Betty Crocker Rich & Creamy chocolate frosting

  Powdered sugar, if desired

  Sliced strawberries, if desired

1. In 1-quart saucepan, heat whipping cream over medium-high heat until hot but not boiling. Stir in chocolate chips until melted and mixture is smooth. Refrigerate about 1 hour, stirring occasionally, until thick.

2. Heat oven to 350°F (325°F for dark or nonstick pans). Spray 18 large muffin cups, $2^3/_4 \times 1^1/_4$ inches, with baking spray with flour. In large bowl, beat cake mix, water, oil and eggs with electric mixer on low speed 30 seconds; beat on medium speed 2 minutes, scraping bowl constantly. Place $^1/_4$ cup batter in each muffin cup. Spoon 1 tablespoon cold chocolate mixture on top of batter in center of each cup.

3. Bake 18 to 22 minutes or until top springs back when lightly touched. Cool 1 minute. Carefully remove from pan; place on cooking parchment paper. Cool 10 minutes. Frost with chocolate frosting. Just before serving, dust with powdered sugar; garnish with strawberry slices. Serve warm.

18 cupcakes
1 Cupcake: Calories 340 (Calories from Fat 150); Total Fat 17g (Saturated 6g; Trans 2.5g); Cholesterol 45mg; Sodium 320mg; Total Carbohydrate 43g (Dietary Fiber 1g; Sugars 31g); Protein 3g
% Daily Value: Vitamin A 2%; Vitamin C 0%; Calcium 4%; Iron 10%
Exchanges: $^1/_2$ Starch, $2^1/_2$ Other Carbohydrate, $3^1/_2$ Fat
Carbohydrate Choices: 3

KITCHEN TIPS

❀ If you have just one muffin pan, refrigerate remaining batter while baking the first cupcakes. Wash the pan before filling with additional batter.

❀ These warm, gooey cakes are delicious served with a small scoop of vanilla ice cream.

Creepy Crawler Cupcakes

Prep Time: 25 min Start to Finish: 1 hr 15 min

Cake

- ½ cup unsweetened baking cocoa
- 1 cup hot water
- 1⅔ cups Gold Medal all-purpose flour
- 1½ cups sugar
- ½ teaspoon baking powder
- 1 teaspoon baking soda
- ½ teaspoon salt
- ½ cup shortening
- 2 eggs

Frosting and Decorations

- 1 container (1 pound) Betty Crocker Rich & Creamy chocolate frosting
- Candy rocks, if desired
- 24 gummy worms

1. Heat oven to 400°F. Place paper baking cups in 24 regular-size muffin cups. In small bowl, mix cocoa and water with spoon until smooth; cool.

2. In large bowl, beat cooled cocoa mixture and re-maining cake ingredients with electric mixer on low speed 2 minutes, scraping bowl constantly. Beat on medium speed 2 minutes, scraping bowl frequently. Fill muffin cups half full.

3. Bake 15 to 20 minutes or until toothpick inserted in center comes out clean. Cool completely, about 30 minutes.

4. Spread frosting on cupcakes. Sprinkle with candy rocks. Add gummy worms, gently pushing one end into cupcake.

24 cupcakes

1 Cupcake: Calories 240 (Calories from Fat 80); Total Fat 9g (Saturated 2.5g; Trans 2g); Cholesterol 20mg; Sodium 180mg; Total Carbohydrate 38g (Dietary Fiber 0g; Sugars 26g); Protein 2g
% Daily Value: Vitamin A 0%; Vitamin C 0%; Calcium 0%; Iron 6%
Exchanges: ½ Starch, 2 Other Carbohydrate, 2 Fat
Carbohydrate Choices: 2½

KITCHEN TIPS

- Look for colorful Halloween-themed paper baking cups at your local craft store.
- Serve these rich chocolate cupcakes with a tall glass of cold milk.

Betty Crocker
IN SEASON

Strawberries

Strawberries are one of nature's sweetest treats. These crimson berries combine perfectly with desserts of all kinds, including cakes. Preparing cakes with strawberries or serving cakes with strawberries—either choice is truly divine. Check out the recipe for delectable Strawberry-Cream Cheese Cupcakes on page 190.

Choose

Strawberries are available year-round but are best during peak times, April through July. The best berries are fresh-picked. Often you can pick your own or get them from a local farmers' market. Berries should be bright red, shiny and fully ripe, not bruised or wrinkled. Green leaf-like caps, or hulls, should be attached to the berries. The size of the berries does not influence the taste or sweetness.

Store

Fresh strawberries are best used within two or three days of purchase or picking. Do not wash until ready to use. Store loosely covered in the refrigerator.

BERRY BASICS

▶ 1 pint strawberries = about 2 cups sliced

▶ 1 quart strawberries = about 4 cups sliced

Prepare

Remove the hull, or "cap," from the top of the strawberry with a paring knife or a strawberry huller. A strawberry huller is a small tweezer-like utensil with rounded ends. To use, grasp the green, leafy hull with the huller, then pull to remove the green hull and the white core without removing any of the strawberry. Look for hullers at kitchen stores, department stores or shops online that carry kitchen supplies.

Freeze

Gently wash strawberries and pat dry. Remove hulls from strawberries. Arrange in a single layer on a cookie sheet, and place in the freezer. Once the berries are frozen, transfer to a freezer-safe plastic bag or container, and freeze up to a year. Use them frozen, or thaw before using if desired. Thawed berries will be soft.

Puree

Place strawberries in a blender or food processor, and process until smooth. Use berry puree in lemonade or iced tea. Add sugar to taste, and serve over ice cream or cheesecake. Use in daiquiris or margaritas.

Health Highlights

▶ A bowl of strawberries rivals any orange any-where. One cup of berries contains a day's worth of vitamin C.

▶ Laboratory tests show some of the phytonu-trients in strawberries may help discourage the development and growth of cancer cells.

▶ The vitamin C and phytonutrients in strawber-ries have been shown, in laboratories, to affect plaque formation and blood clotting. Both these actions may help lower the risk for heart disease.

▶ Animal studies hint that extracts from berries, including strawberries, may help minimize some age-related changes in the brain, such as those that affect memory.

Nutrition Highlights

▶ Potassium   ▶ Vitamin C   ▶ Phytonutrients

Strawberries are something special. They are the first fruit to ripen in spring and, once picked, they offer one of the sweetest, most refreshing treats of the season. But there's more. Although the research is still evolving, the healthful substances these ber-ries contain may be just as wonderful as their great taste and good looks.

STRAWBERRIES TAKE THE CAKE

If you like strawberries on the top of a cake, it's time to try strawberries in the cake. Here are special recipes made with strawberries:

Strawberry-Cream Cheese Cupcakes, page 190

Chocolate-Covered Strawberry Cake, page 263

Strawberry-Rhubarb Angel Torte, page 277

Strawberry-Rhubarb Upside-Down Cake, page 249

Chocolate-Dipped Strawberries

Arrange these elegant berries around the base of a cake, or place on top to dress up any dessert.
Prep Time: 20 minutes Start to Finish: 50 minutes

1 pint (2 cups) medium-large strawberries (18 to 20 strawberries)
$\frac{1}{2}$ cup semisweet chocolate chips or white vanilla baking chips
1 teaspoon shortening or vegetable oil

1. Gently rinse strawberries and dry on paper towels (berries must be completely dry). Line cookie sheet with waxed paper.

2. In 1-quart saucepan, melt chocolate chips and shortening over low heat, stirring fre-quently. Remove from heat.

3. Dip lower half of each strawberry into chocolate mixture; allow excess to drip back into saucepan. Place on waxed paper–lined cookie sheet.

4. Refrigerate uncovered about 30 minutes or until chocolate is firm, or until ready to serve. Store covered in refrigerator so chocolate does not soften (if made with oil, chocolate will soften more quickly at room temperature).

18 to 20 strawberries

Halloween Brownies

Prep Time: 30 min Start to Finish: 3 hr 10 min

Brownies

1 box Betty Crocker Original Supreme® brownie mix (with chocolate syrup pouch)

Water, oil and eggs called for on brownie mix box

Decorations

1 container (1 pound) Betty Crocker Rich & Creamy creamy white frosting

Neon green, pink and blue food colors

24 large marshmallows

Gummy worms

Miniature candy-coated chocolate baking bits

Betty Crocker black decorating gel (from 0.68-ounce tube)

1 roll Betty Crocker Fruit Roll-Ups® chewy fruit snack (any red variety)

1. Heat oven to 350°F. Make and bake brownies in 13 × 9-inch pan as directed on box, using water, oil and eggs. Cool completely, about 2 hours. Cut into 6 rows by 4 rows, making 24 brownies.

2. Remove lid and foil cover from container of frosting. Microwave frosting uncovered on High about 20 seconds or until frosting can be stirred smooth. Divide warm frosting among 3 small bowls, 1 for each color. Decorate as directed below, using 8 brownies for each.

24 brownies
1 Brownie: Calories 280 (Calories from Fat 100); Total Fat 11g (Saturated 3g; Trans 2g); Cholesterol 20mg; Sodium 150mg; Total Carbohydrate 45g (Dietary Fiber 0g; Sugars 34g); Protein 2g
% Daily Value: Vitamin A 0%; Vitamin C 0%; Calcium 2%; Iron 6%
Exchanges: ½ Starch, 2½ Other Carbohydrate, 2 Fat
Carbohydrate Choices: 3

KITCHEN TIPS

⚙ Look for neon food colors next to the standard food colors in your supermarket.

⚙ To make cutting these brownies easier, cool them completely and use a plastic or table knife.

Spider Brownies

Add 5 drops pink food color and 3 drops blue food color to frosting in 1 bowl; mix well. Top each of 8 brownies with 1 large marshmallow. Tuck gummy worms candies under each marshmallow for legs. Spoon 1 tablespoon purple frosting over each marshmallow to coat. Use orange baking bits for eyes. Use black gel for mouths, centers of eyes and eyebrows.

Boo-Brownies

Top each of 8 brownies with 1 large marshmallow. Spoon 1 tablespoon white frosting over each marshmallow to coat. Use black gel for eyes and mouths.

Franken-Brownies

Add 5 drops green food color to frosting in 1 bowl; mix well. Top each of 8 brownies with 1 large marshmallow. Spoon 1 tablespoon green frosting over each marshmallow to coat. Decorate with green baking bits for eyes and ears. Use black gel for mouths and centers of eyes. Cut fruit snack to use for hair.

Tiramisu Cheesecake Dessert

Prep Time: 20 min Start to Finish: 2 hr 25 min

- 2 cups crushed vanilla wafer cookies (about 60 cookies)
- 1/3 cup butter or margarine, melted
- 2 tablespoons whipping cream
- 2 tablespoons instant espresso coffee granules
- 3 packages (8 ounces each) cream cheese, softened
- 3/4 cup sugar
- 3 eggs
- 1 ounce bittersweet baking chocolate, grated Chocolate-covered espresso beans, if desired

1. Heat oven to 350°F. Line 13 × 9-inch pan with foil; spray with cooking spray. In small bowl, mix crushed cookies and melted butter with fork. Press mixture in bottom of pan. Refrigerate while continuing with recipe.

2. In small bowl, mix whipping cream and coffee granules with fork until coffee is dissolved; set aside.

3. In large bowl, beat cream cheese with electric mixer on medium speed 2 to 3 minutes, scraping bowl occasionally, until smooth and creamy. On low speed, beat in sugar, eggs and coffee mixture, about 30 seconds. Beat on medium speed about 2 minutes longer or until ingredients are well blended. Using rubber spatula, spread cream cheese filling over crust. Bake 25 to 35 minutes or until center is set.

4. Cool 30 minutes. Sprinkle with grated chocolate or top with espresso beans. Refrigerate about 1 hour or until completely chilled. For servings, cut into 6 rows by 4 rows, using sharp knife dipped in water.

24 servings

1 Serving: Calories 200 (Calories from Fat 140); Total Fat 15g (Saturated 9g; Trans 0.5g); Cholesterol 65mg; Sodium 140mg; Total Carbohydrate 12g (Dietary Fiber 0g; Sugars 9g); Protein 4g
% Daily Value: Vitamin A 10%; Vitamin C 0%; Calcium 4%; Iron 4%
Exchanges: 1/2 Starch, 1/2 Other Carbohydrate, 1/2 High-Fat Meat, 2 Fat
Carbohydrate Choices: 1

KITCHEN TIPS

- ❂ Dress up these dessert bars by serving them in colorful paper baking cups.
- ❂ In a hurry? Sift unsweetened baking cocoa over the tiramisu bars instead of grating chocolate.

Chocolate-Caramel Bars

Prep Time: 25 min Start to Finish: 2 hr 30 min

1 box Betty Crocker SuperMoist devil's food cake mix

¾ cup butter or margarine, softened

1 egg

2 cups quick-cooking or old-fashioned oats

1 bag (14 ounces) vanilla caramels, unwrapped

¼ cup milk

½ cup semisweet chocolate chips

½ cup chopped pecans or walnuts, if desired

1. Heat oven to 350°F (325°F for dark or nonstick pan). Generously grease bottom and sides of 13 × 9-inch pan with shortening or cooking spray.

2. In large bowl, beat cake mix, butter and egg with electric mixer on low speed until well mixed. Stir in oats until crumbly (may need to use hands to mix dough). Reserve 1½ cups cake mixture. Press remaining mixture in pan (use plastic wrap or waxed paper to press mixture if it is too sticky).

3. In heavy 2-quart saucepan, heat caramels and milk over medium-low heat, stirring frequently, until melted. Pour over chocolate layer in pan. Sprinkle with chocolate chips and pecans. Sprinkle reserved cake mixture over top.

4. Bake 22 to 28 minutes or until caramel bubbles along edges and cake mixture on top appears crisp and dry. Run knife around sides of pan to loosen bars. Cool completely, about 1 hour 30 minutes. For bars, cut into 6 rows by 4 rows. Store covered at room temperature.

24 bars

1 Bar: Calories 250 (Calories from Fat 90); Total Fat 10g (Saturated 5g; Trans 0.5g); Cholesterol 25mg; Sodium 250mg; Total Carbohydrate 37g (Dietary Fiber 2g; Sugars 20g); Protein 3g
% Daily Value: Vitamin A 4%; Vitamin C 0%; Calcium 6%; Iron 8%
Exchanges: 1 Starch, 1½ Other Carbohydrate, 2 Fat
Carbohydrate Choices: 2½

KITCHEN TIPS

✿ Old-fashioned oats would be more visible in the bars than quick-cooking oats will be, but either works fine.

✿ Try milk chocolate or white vanilla baking chips instead of semisweet chocolate chips for a different flavor and appearance.

Honey-Apricot Bars

Prep Time: 40 min Start to Finish: 2 hr 15 min

Apricot Filling

2	cups dried apricots (10 ounces), chopped
1/2	cup honey
1/2	cup water
1/2	cup apple juice
2	tablespoons butter or margarine
1	tablespoon lemon juice
1/2	teaspoon salt
1	egg

Base

1 1/2	cups Gold Medal all-purpose flour
1 1/2	cups quick-cooking oats
1	cup packed brown sugar
3/4	cup butter or margarine, melted
1	teaspoon salt
1/2	teaspoon baking soda

1. Heat oven to 350°F (325°F for dark or nonstick pan). Grease bottom and sides of 13 × 9-inch pan with shortening or spray with cooking spray.

2. In 2-quart saucepan, cook all filling ingredients except egg over medium heat about 15 minutes, stirring frequently, until slightly thickened. Pour mixture into food processor. Cover and process 10 to 15 seconds, pulsing on and off, until finely chopped. Add egg; cover and process, pulsing on and off, until mixed.

3. In large bowl, mix all base ingredients with fork until crumbly. Pat half of the mixture in bottom of pan. Spread filling over base. Sprinkle with remaining oat mixture; press lightly.

4. Bake 25 to 35 minutes or until edges are golden brown. Cool completely, about 1 hour. For bars, cut into 6 rows by 4 rows.

24 bars

1 Bar: Calories 200 (Calories from Fat 60); Total Fat 7g (Saturated 3.5g; Trans 0g); Cholesterol 20mg; Sodium 220mg; Total Carbohydrate 32g (Dietary Fiber 2g; Sugars 21g); Protein 2g
% Daily Value: Vitamin A 15%; Vitamin C 0%; Calcium 2%; Iron 6%
Exchanges: 1 Starch, 1 Fruit, 1 1/2 Fat
Carbohydrate Choices: 2

KITCHEN TIPS

⊙ Pop the dried apricots in the freezer for an hour so chopping them will be easier.

⊙ To keep bars longer, wrap tightly, label and freeze up to 6 months.

Thanksgiving Turkey Cupcakes

Prep Time: 45 min Start to Finish: 2 hr

- 1 box Betty Crocker SuperMoist yellow cake mix
- 1¼ cups water
- ¼ cup vegetable oil
- 3 eggs
- ¾ cup creamy peanut butter
- 1 container (1 pound) Betty Crocker Rich & Creamy chocolate frosting
- 4 ounces vanilla-flavored candy coating (almond bark)
- 4 ounces semisweet baking chocolate
- 30 Hershey®'s Kisses® milk chocolates, unwrapped

1. Heat oven to 350°F. Place paper baking cup in each of 30 regular-size muffin cups. In large bowl, beat cake mix, water, oil, eggs and peanut butter with electric mixer on low speed 30 seconds. Beat on medium speed 2 minutes, scraping bowl occasionally. Fill cups two-thirds full with batter.

2. Bake 20 to 25 minutes or until toothpick inserted in center comes out clean. Remove cupcakes from pan to cooling rack. Cool completely, about 30 minutes. Frost cupcakes with frosting.

3. Line cookie sheet with waxed paper. In separate small microwavable bowls, microwave candy coating and baking chocolate uncovered on High 30 to 60 seconds, stirring every 15 seconds, until melted and smooth. Place coating and chocolate in separate resealable plastic food-storage bags; snip off tiny corner of each bag. Pipe coating and chocolate into feather shapes, about 3 inches long and 2½ inches wide (see photo, right). Refrigerate coating and chocolate about 5 minutes until set.

4. When set, peel feathers off waxed paper and insert into cupcakes. Place milk chocolate candy on each cupcake for head of turkey.

KITCHEN TIPS

✿ Cooking parchment paper can be used instead of the waxed paper when making the turkey tail feathers.
✿ To make the turkey feathers even more colorful, stir a small amount of red and yellow food color into the melted white candy coating to make it orange.

30 cupcakes

1 Cupcake: Calories 260 (Calories from Fat 130); Total Fat 14g (Saturated 4.5g; Trans 1.5g); Cholesterol 20mg; Sodium 200mg; Total Carbohydrate 31g (Dietary Fiber 0g; Sugars 23g); Protein 3g
% Daily Value: Vitamin A 0%; Vitamin C 0%; Calcium 4%; Iron 6%
Exchanges: 1 Starch, 1 Other Carbohydrate, 2½ Fat
Carbohydrate Choices: 2

Honey-Pumpkin Dessert Squares

Prep Time: 25 min Start to Finish: 2 hr 15 min

Crust

1	cup Gold Medal all-purpose flour
1	cup quick-cooking oats
1/2	cup butter or margarine, softened
1/4	cup packed brown sugar

Filling

2	cans (15 ounces each) pumpkin (not pumpkin pie mix)
4	eggs
1	cup half-and-half
1	cup honey
3/4	cup packed brown sugar
2	teaspoons pumpkin pie spice
1	teaspoon vanilla
1/2	teaspoon salt

Garnish

1/2	cup whipping cream
1	tablespoon powdered sugar
15	candy pumpkins

1. Heat oven to 350°F. In medium bowl, mix all crust ingredients with fork until crumbly. Press in bottom of ungreased 13 × 9-inch pan. Bake 10 minutes.

2. Meanwhile, in large bowl, beat all filling ingredients with wire whisk or electric mixer on medium speed until blended. Pour over partially baked crust.

3. Bake 55 to 60 minutes or until set and knife inserted in center comes out clean. Cool completely, about 40 minutes.

4. In chilled small bowl, beat whipping cream and powdered sugar with electric mixer on high speed until soft peaks form. Cut dessert into squares. Serve with whipped cream. Garnish each serving with candy pumpkin.

15 servings
1 Serving: Calories 310 (Calories from Fat 100); Total Fat 11g (Saturated 5g; Trans 0g); Cholesterol 80mg; Sodium 150mg; Total Carbohydrate 50g (Dietary Fiber 3g; Sugars 37g); Protein 4g
% Daily Value: Vitamin A 180%; Vitamin C 2%; Calcium 4%; Iron 10%
Exchanges: 1 Starch, 2 Other Carbohydrate, 1 Vegetable, 2 Fat
Carbohydrate Choices: 3

KITCHEN TIPS

✿ Canned pumpkin pie mix contains spices, sugar, water and salt, so it can't be substituted for canned plain pumpkin.
✿ If you don't have candy pumpkins for the garnish, sprinkle a little pumpkin pie spice over the whipped cream.

Pumpkin-Spice Bars with Cream Cheese Frosting

Prep Time: 20 min   Start to Finish: 2 hr 50 min

Bars

4	eggs
2	cups granulated sugar
1	cup vegetable oil
1	can (15 ounces) pumpkin (not pumpkin pie mix)
2	cups Gold Medal all-purpose flour
2	teaspoons baking powder
1	teaspoon baking soda
1/2	teaspoon salt
2	teaspoons ground cinnamon
1/2	teaspoon ground ginger
1/4	teaspoon ground cloves
1	cup raisins, if desired

Cream Cheese Frosting

1	package (8 ounces) cream cheese, softened
1/4	cup butter or margarine, softened
2	to 3 teaspoons milk
1	teaspoon vanilla
4	cups powdered sugar
1/2	cup chopped walnuts, if desired

1. Heat oven to 350°F. Spray 15 × 10 × 1-inch pan with cooking spray.

2. In large bowl, beat eggs, granulated sugar, oil and pumpkin with wire whisk until smooth. Stir in flour, baking powder, baking soda, salt, cinnamon, ginger and cloves. Stir in raisins. Spread in pan.

3. Bake 25 to 30 minutes or until toothpick inserted in center comes out clean and bars spring back when touched lightly in center. Cool completely, about 2 hours.

4. In medium bowl, beat cream cheese, butter, milk and vanilla with electric mixer on low speed until smooth. Gradually beat in powdered sugar, 1 cup at a time, on low speed until smooth and spreadable. Spread frosting over bars. Sprinkle with walnuts. For bars, cut into 7 rows by 7 rows. Store covered in refrigerator.

49 bars
1 Bar: Calories 160 (Calories from Fat 70); Total Fat 8g (Saturated 2.5g; Trans 0g); Cholesterol 25mg; Sodium 95mg; Total Carbohydrate 23g (Dietary Fiber 0g; Sugars 18g); Protein 1g
% Daily Value: Vitamin A 20%; Vitamin C 0%; Calcium 2%; Iron 2%
Exchanges: 1/2 Starch, 1 Other Carbohydrate, 1 1/2 Fat
Carbohydrate Choices: 1 1/2

KITCHEN TIPS

❁ In a pinch, use 2 1/2 teaspoons pumpkin pie spice instead of the cinnamon, ginger and cloves.

Chocolate-Glazed Pecan Pie Bars

Prep Time: 30 min Start to Finish: 3 hr 15 min

Crust

- ²/₃ cup granulated sugar
- ½ cup butter or margarine, softened
- 1 teaspoon vanilla
- 1 egg
- 1½ cups Gold Medal all-purpose flour

Filling

- ²/₃ cup packed brown sugar
- ½ cup corn syrup
- 1 teaspoon vanilla
- 3 eggs
- 1 cup broken pecans

Melted Chocolate

- 1 cup semisweet chocolate chips (6 ounces)
- 2 teaspoons shortening

1. Heat oven to 350°F. Spray 13 × 9-inch pan with cooking spray. In large bowl, mix granulated sugar, butter, 1 teaspoon vanilla and 1 egg. Stir in flour. Press dough in bottom and ½ inch up sides of pan (if necessary, use floured fingers).

2. Bake 10 to 15 minutes or until edges are light brown.

3. Meanwhile, in medium bowl, beat filling ingredients except pecans with spoon. Stir in pecans. Pour over crust.

4. Bake 25 to 30 minutes or until set. While warm, loosen edges from sides of pan. Cool completely, about 2 hours.

5. For triangular bars, cut into 6 rows by 3 rows. Cut each bar in half diagonally. In small microwavable bowl, microwave chocolate chips and shortening uncovered on High 1 minute to 1 minute 30 seconds or until melted; stir until smooth. Dip 1 side of each bar into melted chocolate; lay flat to dry.

36 bars

1 Bar: Calories 150 (Calories from Fat 60); Total Fat 7g (Saturated 3g; Trans 0g); Cholesterol 30mg; Sodium 35mg; Total Carbohydrate 19g (Dietary Fiber 0g; Sugars 12g); Protein 2g
% Daily Value: Vitamin A 2%; Vitamin C 0%; Calcium 0%; Iron 4%
Exchanges: ½ Starch, ½ Other Carbohydrate, 1½ Fat
Carbohydrate Choices: 1

KITCHEN TIPS

✿ You can purchase broken pecans or you can break them up yourself by putting them in a plastic bag and rolling over them with a rolling pin or can.

✿ Cut the bars into squares instead of triangles if you like.

White Chocolate-Macadamia-Caramel Bars

Fudgy Pecan Bars

White Chocolate-Macadamia-Caramel Bars

Prep Time: 15 min Start to Finish: 2 hours

- 1 box Betty Crocker SuperMoist yellow cake mix
- 1/2 cup vegetable oil
- 1/4 cup water
- 2 eggs
- 1/2 cup butterscotch caramel topping (from 17-ounce jar)
- 1 package (18 oz) Pillsbury Ready to Bake!™ Big Deluxe Classics® refrigerated white chunk macadamia nut cookies

1. Heat oven to 350°F (325°F for dark or nonstick pan). In large bowl, beat cake mix, oil, water and eggs with electric mixer on low speed until smooth. Spread in ungreased 13 × 9-inch pan.

2. Bake 18 to 22 minutes or until top is golden brown.

3. Remove partially baked crust from oven. In 1-cup microwavable measuring cup, microwave caramel topping on High about 15 seconds or until warm and pourable. Lightly drizzle over crust. Crumble cookies over crust.

4. Bake 18 to 23 minutes longer or until golden brown. Cool completely, about 1 hour. For bars, cut into 8 rows by 6 rows.

48 bars
1 Bar: Calories 130 (Calories from Fat 60); Total Fat 6g (Saturated 1.5g; Trans 1g); Cholesterol 10mg; Sodium 110mg; Total Carbohydrate 17g (Dietary Fiber 0g; Sugars 10g); Protein 1g
% Daily Value: Vitamin A 0%; Vitamin C 0%; Calcium 0%; Iron 2%
Exchanges: 1 Other Carbohydrate, 1 1/2 Fat
Carbohydrate Choices: 1

KITCHEN TIPS

❀ To prevent scratching the bottom of an aluminum cake pan, cut bars and cakes with a plastic knife instead of a sharp knife.

❀ These brownie-like bars are perfect for bag lunches or family picnics.

Fudgy Pecan Bars

Prep Time: 25 min Start to Finish: 1 hr 50 min

- 1 box Betty Crocker SuperMoist devil's food cake mix
- 1/3 cup butter or margarine, softened
- 2 tablespoons milk
- 1 teaspoon vanilla
- 1 egg
- 1 1/4 cups semisweet chocolate chips
- 1/4 cup butter or margarine, melted
- 2 eggs
- 1 cup chopped pecans
- 1 tablespoon powdered sugar

1. Heat oven to 350°F (325°F for dark or nonstick pan). Spray bottom only of 13 × 9-inch pan with baking spray with flour. Measure 1/2 cup of the cake mix into medium bowl; set aside.

2. In large bowl, beat remaining cake mix, 1/3 cup butter, the milk, vanilla and egg with electric mixer on low speed until crumbly. Press dough in pan. Sprinkle with chocolate chips; press into dough.

3. Add melted butter and 2 eggs to reserved cake mix. Beat on medium speed until smooth. Stir in pecans. Spread mixture over crust.

4. Bake 25 to 28 minutes or until center is set. Cool completely, about 1 hour. Sprinkle powdered sugar over top. For bars, cut into 8 rows by 4 rows.

32 bars
1 Bar: Calories 170 (Calories from Fat 80); Total Fat 9g (Saturated 4g; Trans 0g); Cholesterol 30mg; Sodium 160mg; Total Carbohydrate 18g (Dietary Fiber 1g; Sugars 12g); Protein 2g
% Daily Value: Vitamin A 2%; Vitamin C 0%; Calcium 2%; Iron 4%
Exchanges: 1/2 Starch, 1/2 Other Carbohydrate, 2 Fat
Carbohydrate Choices: 1

KITCHEN TIPS

❀ If your family prefers, you can substitute cashews for the pecans.

❀ Use a tea strainer to lightly sift the powdered sugar over the bars.

Rhubarb Squares

Tropical Fruit Bars

Tropical Fruit Bars

Prep Time: 20 min Start to Finish: 3 hr

1 box Betty Crocker SuperMoist yellow cake mix

½ cup butter or margarine, melted

1 egg

1½ cups white vanilla baking chips (from 12-ounce bag)

1 bag (7 ounces) dried tropical fruit mix

1 cup flaked coconut

1 cup cashew pieces

1 can (14 ounces) sweetened condensed milk (not evaporated)

1. Heat oven to 350°F (325°F for dark or nonstick pan). Spray bottom and sides of 13 × 9-inch pan with baking spray with flour.

2. In medium bowl, stir cake mix, butter and egg until mixed. Press in bottom of pan. Sprinkle evenly with baking chips, dried fruit, coconut and cashews. Pour milk evenly over top.

3. Bake 35 to 40 minutes or until edges and center are golden brown. Cool completely, about 2 hours. For bars, cut into 8 rows by 4 rows.

32 bars
1 Bar: Calories 240 (Calories from Fat 100); Total Fat 11g (Saturated 6g; Trans 0.5g); Cholesterol 20mg; Sodium 170mg; Total Carbohydrate 33g (Dietary Fiber 0g; Sugars 25g); Protein 3g
% Daily Value: Vitamin A 4%; Vitamin C 0%; Calcium 8%; Iron 4%
Exchanges: 1 Starch, 1 Other Carbohydrate, 2 Fat
Carbohydrate Choices: 2

KITCHEN TIPS

✿ The tropical fruit mix has dried mango, pineapple and papaya in it. You can use any dried fruit mixture.

✿ These bars are rich and chewy but not messy. They are perfect to tote to a family picnic.

Quick
Rhubarb Squares

Prep Time: 15 min Start to Finish: 1 hr 25 min

1 box Betty Crocker SuperMoist yellow cake mix

1 cup butter or margarine, cut into small pieces

1¾ cups sugar

3 eggs

4 cups sliced fresh rhubarb
Whipped cream, if desired

1. Heat oven to 350°F (325°F for dark or nonstick pan). Reserve 2 tablespoons of the cake mix. In large bowl, cut butter into remaining cake mix, using pastry blender (or pulling 2 table knives through ingredients in opposite directions), until crumbly. In bottom of ungreased 13 × 9-inch pan, pat 2¼ cups of the mixture (if mixture is sticky, lightly flour hands). Bake 15 minutes. Remove from oven.

2. In large bowl, beat reserved 2 tablespoons cake mix, the sugar and eggs with electric mixer on medium speed until creamy. Stir in rhubarb. Pour over partially baked crust. Sprinkle remaining crumbly mixture over top.

3. Bake 45 to 55 minutes or until golden brown and center is set. Cool slightly before serving. Serve warm or cold with whipped cream. Store in refrigerator.

16 servings
1 Serving: Calories 250 (Calories from Fat 140); Total Fat 15g (Saturated 9g; Trans 1.5g); Cholesterol 70mg; Sodium 300mg; Total Carbohydrate 27g (Dietary Fiber 0g; Sugars 16g); Protein 2g
% Daily Value: Vitamin A 8%; Vitamin C 0%; Calcium 10%; Iron 4%
Exchanges: 2 Other Carbohydrate, 3 Fat
Carbohydrate Choices: 2

KITCHEN TIPS

✿ If fresh rhubarb isn't available, use 4 cups frozen (slightly thawed) rhubarb (from two 16-ounce bags).

✿ If you have a food processor, you can cut the butter into the cake mix, using on-and-off pulses, until crumbly.

Quick

Carrot-Raisin Bars

Prep Time: 10 min Start to Finish: 1 hr 40 min

1   box Betty Crocker SuperMoist carrot cake
    mix
½   cup vegetable oil
¼   cup water
2   eggs
¾   cup raisins
½   cup chopped nuts
1   container (1 pound) Betty Crocker Rich &
    Creamy cream cheese frosting

1. Heat oven to 350°F (325°F for dark or nonstick pan).
Spray bottom and sides of 15 × 10 × 1-inch pan with
baking spray with flour.

2. In large bowl, mix cake mix, oil, water and eggs with
spoon. Stir in raisins and nuts. Spread evenly in pan.

3. Bake 18 to 24 minutes (25 to 29 minutes for dark or
nonstick pan) or until bars spring back when touched
lightly in center. Cool completely, about 1 hour.

4. Spread with frosting. For bars, cut into 8 rows by 6
rows. Store loosely covered at room temperature.

48 bars
1 Bar: Calories 120 (Calories from Fat 50); Total Fat 6g (Saturated 1.5g;
Trans 1g); Cholesterol 10mg; Sodium 90mg; Total Carbohydrate 16g
(Dietary Fiber 0g; Sugars 12g); Protein 0g
% Daily Value: Vitamin A 2%; Vitamin C 0%; Calcium 2%; Iron 0%
Exchanges: ½ Starch, ½ Other Carbohydrate, 1 Fat
Carbohydrate Choices: 1

KITCHEN TIPS

❂ For a hint of orange flavor, substitute orange juice for the
water. You can also stir a little grated orange peel into the
frosting.

❂ For a simple garnish, dip a small cookie cutter in cinnamon
and press into the frosting.

Rocky Road Bars

Prep Time: 15 min Start to Finish: 1 hr 50 min

1 box Betty Crocker SuperMoist chocolate fudge or devil's food cake mix

$1/2$ cup butter or margarine, melted

$1/3$ cup water

$1/4$ cup packed brown sugar

2 eggs

1 cup chopped nuts

3 cups miniature marshmallows

$1/2$ cup pastel colored candy-coated chocolate candies, if desired

$1/3$ cup Betty Crocker Rich & Creamy chocolate frosting (from 1-pound container)

1. Heat oven to 350°F (325°F for dark or nonstick pan). Spray bottom and sides of 13 × 9-inch pan with baking spray with flour.

2. In large bowl, mix half of the cake mix, the butter, water, brown sugar and eggs with spoon until smooth. Stir in remaining cake mix and the nuts. Spread in pan.

3. Bake 20 minutes (25 minutes for dark or nonstick pan); sprinkle with marshmallows. Bake 10 to 15 min-

utes longer (14 to 18 minutes for dark or nonstick pan) or until marshmallows are puffed and golden. Sprinkle with candies.

4. In small microwavable bowl, microwave frosting uncovered on High 15 seconds; drizzle over bars. Cool completely, about 1 hour. For easier cutting, use plastic knife dipped in hot water. For bars, cut into 6 rows by 4 rows. Store covered.

24 bars

1 Bar: Calories 210 (Calories from Fat 90); Total Fat 10g (Saturated 3.5g; Trans 1g); Cholesterol 30mg; Sodium 220mg; Total Carbohydrate 28g (Dietary Fiber 0g; Sugars 18g); Protein 2g
% Daily Value: Vitamin A 2%; Vitamin C 0%; Calcium 4%; Iron 4%
Exchanges: 2 Other Carbohydrate, 2 Fat
Carbohydrate Choices: 2

KITCHEN TIPS

❂ To easily remove and cut the bars, line the pan with foil before spraying, allowing foil to extend over sides. Just lift out of the pan after baking.

❂ You can use any kind of nuts, but peanuts are classic in Rocky Road recipes.

Citrus Shortbread Cookies

Prep Time: 15 min Start to Finish: 50 min

- ¾ cup butter or margarine, softened
- ¼ cup granulated sugar
- 2 cups Gold Medal all-purpose flour
- 1½ teaspoons grated lime peel
- 1½ teaspoons grated orange peel
- 1 cup powdered sugar
- 1 to 2 tablespoons lime juice

1. Heat oven to 350°F. In large bowl, beat butter and granulated sugar with electric mixer on medium speed 2 to 3 minutes or until light and creamy. Add flour, lime peel and orange peel. Beat on low speed until mixture is blended. Gather dough into a ball.

2. On lightly floured surface, roll dough into 8 × 6-inch rectangle, about ½ inch thick. (If dough cracks around edges, press edges to smooth.) Cut into 12 (2-inch) squares, then cut each square diagonally in half into triangles. On ungreased cookie sheet, place triangles ½ inch apart.

3. Bake 12 to 17 minutes or until edges just begin to brown. Cool 1 minute; remove from cookie sheet to wire rack. Cool completely, about 15 minutes.

4. In small bowl, mix powdered sugar and lime juice with spoon until smooth and thin enough to drizzle. Drizzle glaze over cookies.

24 cookies
1 Cookie: Calories 120 (Calories from Fat 50); Total Fat 6g (Saturated 3.5g; Trans 0g); Cholesterol 15mg; Sodium 40mg; Total Carbohydrate 15g (Dietary Fiber 0g; Sugars 7g); Protein 1g
% Daily Value: Vitamin A 4%; Vitamin C 0%; Calcium 0%; Iron 2%
Exchanges: ½ Starch, ½ Other Carbohydrate, 1 Fat
Carbohydrate Choices: 1

KITCHEN TIPS

❂ For easy glazing, put powdered sugar mixture into quart-size food-storage bag. Snip off a tip with kitchen scissors, and drizzle glaze over shortbread.

Chocolate-Peanut Butter Candy Cookies

Prep Time: 45 min Start to Finish: 1 hr 15 min

- ½ cup granulated sugar
- ½ cup packed brown sugar
- ½ cup butter or margarine, softened
- ½ cup chocolate-flavored or regular peanut butter (from 14-ounce jar)
- ½ teaspoon vanilla
- 1 egg
- 1¼ cups Gold Medal all-purpose flour
- ¼ cup unsweetened baking cocoa
- 1 teaspoon baking soda
- ¼ teaspoon salt
- 1¼ cups (about 12 ounces) orange, yellow and brown candy-coated peanut butter candies

1. Heat oven to 350°F. Lightly grease cookie sheet with shortening or spray with cooking spray.

2. In large bowl, beat sugars and butter with electric mixer on medium speed until creamy. Beat in peanut butter, vanilla and egg. Stir in flour, cocoa, baking soda and salt. Stir in candies. Drop dough by heaping teaspoonfuls onto cookie sheet.

3. Bake 8 to 12 minutes or until edges are set (centers will be soft). Cool 1 minute; remove from cookie sheet to cooling rack. Cool completely, about 30 minutes.

2½ dozen cookies
1 Cookie: Calories 140 (Calories from Fat 60); Total Fat 6g (Saturated 2g; Trans 0g); Cholesterol 15mg; Sodium 105mg; Total Carbohydrate 19g (Dietary Fiber 0g; Sugars 14g); Protein 3g
% Daily Value: Vitamin A 2%; Vitamin C 0%; Calcium 2%; Iron 4%
Exchanges: 1 Starch, 1 Fat
Carbohydrate Choices: 1

KITCHEN TIPS

❂ These yummy chocolate- and peanut butter-flavored cookies are great to take to after-school events, potlucks and scout meetings.

❂ Be sure the cookie sheets are cool before placing dough on them. A warm cookie sheet will cause the cookies to spread.

Citrus Shortbread Cookies

Chocolate-Peanut Butter Candy Cookies

Double Chocolate Cherry Cookies

Prep Time: 1 hr Start to Finish: 1 hr

1¼ cups sugar

1 cup butter or margarine, softened

¼ cup milk

¼ teaspoon almond extract

1 egg

1¾ cups Gold Medal all-purpose flour

⅓ cup unsweetened baking cocoa

½ teaspoon baking soda

1 cup quick-cooking oats

1 cup semisweet chocolate chips

1 cup dried cherries

1. Heat oven to 350°F. In large bowl, beat sugar, butter, milk, almond extract and egg with electric mixer on medium speed until smooth. Stir in remaining ingredients. Drop dough by rounded tablespoonfuls about 2 inches apart onto ungreased cookie sheets.

2. Bake 10 to 12 minutes or until almost no indentation remains when touched in center and surface is no longer shiny. Immediately remove from cookie sheet; place on cooling rack.

4 dozen cookies

1 Cookie: Calories 110 (Calories from Fat 45); Total Fat 5g (Saturated 3g; Trans 0g); Cholesterol 15mg; Sodium 45mg; Total Carbohydrate 15g (Dietary Fiber 0g; Sugars 9g); Protein 1g
% Daily Value: Vitamin A 4%; Vitamin C 0%; Calcium 0%; Iron 2%
Exchanges: ½ Starch, ½ Other Carbohydrate, 1 Fat
Carbohydrate Choices: 1

KITCHEN TIPS

✿ Try using 1 teaspoon vanilla instead of the almond extract.

✿ To make all the cookies similar in size, use a spring-handled ice-cream scoop to drop the dough onto the cookie sheet.

Orange-Flavored Cranberry Cookies

Prep Time: 1 hr 20 min Start to Finish: 1 hr 50 min

Cookies

1	cup granulated sugar
$1/2$	cup packed brown sugar
1	cup butter or margarine, softened
1	teaspoon grated orange peel
2	tablespoons orange juice
1	egg
$2^1/_2$	cups Gold Medal all-purpose flour
$1/2$	teaspoon baking soda
$1/2$	teaspoon salt
2	cups coarsely chopped fresh or frozen cranberries
$1/2$	cup chopped nuts, if desired

Orange Frosting

$1^1/_2$	cups powdered sugar
$1/2$	teaspoon grated orange peel
2	to 3 tablespoons orange juice

1. Heat oven to 375°F. Spray cookie sheet with cooking spray.

2. In large bowl, beat sugars, butter, orange peel, orange juice and egg with electric mixer on medium speed, or mix with spoon. Stir in flour, baking soda and salt. Stir in cranberries and nuts. Drop dough by rounded tablespoonfuls about 2 inches apart on cookie sheet.

3. Bake 12 to 14 minutes or until edges and bottoms of cookies are light golden brown. Remove from cookie sheet to cooling rack. Cool completely, about 30 minutes.

4. In small bowl, stir all frosting ingredients until smooth and spreadable. Frost cookies.

About 4 dozen cookies
1 Cookie: Calories 100 (Calories from Fat 35); Total Fat 4g (Saturated 2g; Trans 0g); Cholesterol 15mg; Sodium 65mg; Total Carbohydrate 16g (Dietary Fiber 0g; Sugars 10g); Protein 0g
% Daily Value: Vitamin A 4%; Vitamin C 0%; Calcium 0%; Iron 2%
Exchanges: 1 Starch, $1/2$ Fat
Carbohydrate Choices: 1

KITCHEN TIPS

❁ Cranberries, a Thanksgiving staple, are harvested in the autumn but can be found year-round in supermarkets.

❁ Save time and lower the calories! Skip the frosting, and dust cookies and serving plate with powdered sugar.

Scary Cat Cookies

Prep Time: 30 min Start to Finish: 1 hr 15 min

3 ounces semisweet baking chocolate

1 cup butter, softened (do not use margarine)

$\frac{1}{2}$ cup sugar

$2\frac{1}{4}$ cups Gold Medal all-purpose flour

1 teaspoon vanilla

1 egg

Yellow candy sprinkles

15 miniature candy-coated chocolate baking bits

1 package pull-apart yellow licorice twists, cut into 1-inch pieces

1 package pull-apart pink licorice twists, cut into bits

1. Heat oven to 350°F. Grease cookie sheets with shortening.

2. In small saucepan, melt chocolate over low heat, stirring constantly. In large bowl, beat butter and sugar with electric mixer on medium speed, or mix with spoon. Stir in melted chocolate, flour, vanilla and egg.

3. Shape dough into 30 (1-inch) balls. Pull a little bit of dough from each of 15 balls to make tails; set aside. Cut about $\frac{1}{4}$-inch slit in same balls, using scissors. Separate dough at slit for cat's ears. Place balls about 2 inches apart on cookie sheets.

4. Place remaining balls below each cat head on cookie sheets for body. Shape small pieces of dough into 15 ($2\frac{1}{2}$-inch-long) ropes. Place end of rope under each body.

5. Bake 12 to 14 minutes or until set. Remove from cookie sheets to cooling racks. Cool 30 minutes.

6. Use sprinkles to make eyes and baking bits to make noses. Add yellow licorice pieces for whiskers. Add pink licorice for tongues.

About 15 cookies
1 Cookie: Calories 250 (Calories from Fat 130); Total Fat 15g (Saturated 9g; Trans 0.5g); Cholesterol 45mg; Sodium 100mg; Total Carbohydrate 27g (Dietary Fiber 0g; Sugars 11g); Protein 3g
% Daily Value: Vitamin A 8%; Vitamin C 0%; Calcium 0%; Iron 6%
Exchanges: 1 Starch, 1 Other Carbohydrate, $2\frac{1}{2}$ Fat
Carbohydrate Choices: 2

KITCHEN TIPS

✿ Instead of greasing the cookie sheets, line them with parchment paper.
✿ You can melt the chocolate in the microwave instead of a saucepan, if you like. Follow directions on the box.

Giant Witch Cookies

Prep Time: 40 min Start to Finish: 2 hr 20 min

1 cup sugar

1 cup butter or margarine, softened

1 egg

1 teaspoon vanilla

3 cups Gold Medal all-purpose flour

$^{1}/_{2}$ teaspoon baking powder

$^{1}/_{2}$ teaspoon salt

1 container (1 pound) Betty Crocker Rich & Creamy vanilla frosting

3 to 4 drops green food color

3 to 4 drops yellow food color

1 container (1 pound) Betty Crocker Rich & Creamy chocolate frosting

Assorted candies for decorating

1. In large bowl, beat sugar and butter with electric mixer on medium speed until creamy. Beat in egg and vanilla. Stir in flour, baking powder and salt. Divide dough in half; wrap in plastic wrap. Refrigerate 1 hour for easier handling.

2. Heat oven to 375°F. Line cookie sheets with cooking parchment paper. Shape half of dough into 10 (1$^{1}/_{2}$-inch) balls. On parchment-lined cookie sheets, pat each ball of dough into 4-inch round, using floured fingers if necessary. Place 2 or 3 rounds on each cookie sheet, about 9 inches apart.

3. On floured surface, divide remaining half of dough into 2 portions. Roll each portion into 9 × 6-inch rectangle. Cut each rectangle into 4 whole triangles and 2 half triangles (see diagram). Press 2 half triangles together to form fifth whole triangle. Cut $^{1}/_{2}$-inch strip from top edge of each dough round on cookie sheet; set aside. Place triangle over each cut edge of round, covering $^{1}/_{4}$ inch of cut edge; press to seal, aligning edge of triangle with edge of round. Slightly bend point of "hat" if desired. Roll each $^{1}/_{2}$-inch strip into 2 (1-inch) ropes; attach to either side of "hat" for brim.

4. Bake 7 to 11 minutes or until edges of cookies are golden and surfaces look dry. With broad metal pancake turner, remove cookies from cookie sheets to cooling racks. Cool completely, about 30 minutes.

5. Tint vanilla frosting green with green and yellow food colors. Spread on rounds for witches' faces. Spread chocolate frosting on hats. Make faces using candies.

10 cookies

1 Cookie: Calories 780 (Calories from Fat 350); Total Fat 39g (Saturated 17g; Trans 8g); Cholesterol 70mg; Sodium 530mg; Total Carbohydrate 102g (Dietary Fiber 1g; Sugars 68g); Protein 5g
% Daily Value: Vitamin A 10%; Vitamin C 0%; Calcium 2%; Iron 15%
Exchanges: 1$^{1}/_{2}$ Starch, 5$^{1}/_{2}$ Other Carbohydrate, 7$^{1}/_{2}$ Fat
Carbohydrate Choices: 7

KITCHEN TIPS

◐ Lining the cookie sheets with parchment paper makes the cookies easier to remove, and cleanup is a snap.

◐ To color the frosting a more intense green, use electric green gel paste instead of food color.

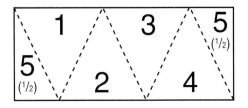

Maple-Nut Biscotti

Prep Time: 2 hr 10 min Start to Finish: 3 hr 30 min

½ cup packed brown sugar
¼ cup granulated sugar
½ cup butter or margarine, softened
1 teaspoon maple flavor
3 eggs
3 cups Gold Medal all-purpose flour
2 teaspoons baking powder
¾ cup chopped walnuts
1 teaspoon vegetable oil
4 ounces vanilla-flavored candy coating (almond bark), melted

1. Heat oven to 350°F. Lightly grease cookie sheet with shortening or spray with cooking spray.

2. In large bowl, beat sugars and butter with electric mixer on medium speed about 3 minutes or until creamy. Beat in maple flavor and eggs. Stir in flour and baking powder. Stir in walnuts. Divide dough in half. Shape each half into 10-inch roll. Place rolls 5 inches apart on cookie sheet; flatten to 3-inch width.

3. Bake 20 to 30 minutes or until set and edges begin to brown. Remove from cookie sheet to cooling rack. Cool 10 minutes. With serrated knife, cut rolls diagonally into ½-inch slices. Place slices cut side down on ungreased cookie sheet.

4. Bake 5 to 10 minutes or until lightly browned and dry. Turn cookies over; bake 5 to 8 minutes longer or until lightly browned and dry. Remove from cookie sheet to cooling rack. Cool completely, about 15 minutes.

5. Stir oil into melted candy coating; drizzle over biscotti. Let stand until coating is dry. Store in tightly covered container.

KITCHEN TIPS

⚙ These dunkable cookies are great with a cup of hot apple cider or cinnamon-spiced tea.

⚙ Instead of drizzling the biscotti, dip one end into the melted candy coating.

2½ dozen cookies
1 Cookie: Calories 150 (Calories from Fat 60); Total Fat 7g (Saturated 2.5g; Trans 0g); Cholesterol 30mg; Sodium 65mg; Total Carbohydrate 19g (Dietary Fiber 0g; Sugars 9g); Protein 3g
% Daily Value: Vitamin A 2%; Vitamin C 0%; Calcium 4%; Iron 4%
Exchanges: 1 Starch, 1½ Fat
Carbohydrate Choices: 1

Peppermint Shortbread Bites

Prep Time: 25 min Start to Finish: 2 hr

1 cup butter, softened (do not use margarine)
½ cup powdered sugar
2 cups Gold Medal all-purpose flour
1 teaspoon peppermint extract
3 tablespoons finely crushed hard peppermint candies (about 6 candies)
1 tablespoon granulated sugar
3 ounces vanilla-flavored candy coating (almond bark), melted

1. In large bowl, beat butter and powdered sugar with electric mixer on medium speed until fluffy. On low speed, beat in flour and peppermint extract.

2. On ungreased cookie sheet, pat dough into 6-inch square, about ³⁄₄ inch thick. Cover; refrigerate 30 minutes.

3. Heat oven to 325°F. On cookie sheet, cut dough into 8 rows by 8 rows, making 64 squares. With knife, separate rows by ¼ inch.

4. Bake 28 to 35 minutes or until set and edges are just starting to turn golden. Meanwhile, in small bowl, mix crushed candy and granulated sugar. In small resealable plastic food-storage bag, place melted candy coating. Seal bag; cut tiny hole in corner of bag.

5. Do not remove cookies from cookie sheet. Pipe candy coating over cookies. Before candy coating sets, sprinkle candy mixture over cookies. Place cookies on cooling racks. Cool completely, about 30 minutes.

64 cookies
1 Cookie: Calories 50 (Calories from Fat 30); Total Fat 3.5g (Saturated 2g; Trans 0g); Cholesterol 10mg; Sodium 20mg; Total Carbohydrate 5g (Dietary Fiber 0g; Sugars 3g); Protein 0g
% Daily Value: Vitamin A 0%; Vitamin C 0%; Calcium 0%; Iron 0%
Exchanges: ½ Other Carbohydrate, ½ Fat
Carbohydrate Choices: ½

KITCHEN TIPS

❉ To crush candy, place in a plastic freezer bag and seal, then pound with the flat side of a meat mallet or a rolling pin.
❉ These cookies will keep their shape better during baking if they're very cold when you put them in the oven.

Candy Bar Cookie Pops

Fudge Crinkles

Candy Bar Cookie Pops

Prep Time: 50 Start to Finish: 1 hr 20 min

- 1 bag (12.5 ounces) fun-size milk chocolate-covered candy bars with chewy caramel and crispy crunchies, cut in half (32 half-bars)
- 32 craft sticks (flat wooden sticks with round ends)
- 1 box Betty Crocker SuperMoist chocolate fudge cake mix
- 1/2 cup vegetable oil
- 2 eggs
- 1/2 cup powdered sugar or colored candy sprinkles

1. Heat oven to 350°F (325°F for dark or nonstick cookie sheet). Line cookie sheet with foil. Pierce side of each half candy bar with craft stick.

2. In large bowl, beat cake mix, oil and eggs with electric mixer on medium speed until smooth. For each cookie pop, form 1 rounded teaspoonful of dough into a ball; flatten in palm of hand and place candy on top. Form dough around candy, sealing well. Roll in powdered sugar or candy sprinkles to cover completely. Place 2 inches apart on cookie sheet.

3. Bake 11 to 13 minutes or until set. Cookie will appear moist in the cracks. Let cool on cookie sheet 2 minutes. Remove from cookie sheet to cooling rack. Cool completely, about 30 minutes.

32 pops
1 Cookie: Calories 170 (Calories from Fat 70); Total Fat 8g (Saturated 2.5g; Trans 1g); Cholesterol 15mg; Sodium 150mg; Total Carbohydrate 22g (Dietary Fiber 0g; Sugars 16g); Protein 2g
% Daily Value: Vitamin A 0%; Vitamin C 0%; Calcium 4%; Iron 2%
Exchanges: 1/2 Starch, 1 Other Carbohydrate, 1 1/2 Fat
Carbohydrate Choices: 1 1/2

KITCHEN TIPS

✿ For a bake sale, cover each cookie with plastic wrap and tie with colorful curly ribbon.
✿ Be sure the candy is sealed in the dough so it doesn't leak onto the cookie sheets.

Fudge Crinkles

Prep Time: 1 hr Start to Finish: 1 hr

- 1 box Betty Crocker SuperMoist devil's food cake mix
- 1/2 cup vegetable oil
- 2 eggs
- 1 teaspoon vanilla
- 1/3 cup powdered sugar

1. Heat oven to 350°F. In large bowl, mix cake mix, oil, eggs and vanilla with spoon until dough forms.

2. Shape dough into 1-inch balls. Roll balls in powdered sugar. On ungreased cookie sheet, place balls about 2 inches apart.

3. Bake 10 to 12 minutes or until set. Cool 1 minute; remove from cookie sheet to cooling rack. Cool completely, about 30 minutes. Store loosely covered.

30 cookies
1 Cookie: Calories 110 (Calories from Fat 45); Total Fat 5g (Saturated 1g; Trans 0g); Cholesterol 15mg; Sodium 140mg; Total Carbohydrate 15g (Dietary Fiber 0g; Sugars 10g); Protein 1g
% Daily Value: Vitamin A 0%; Vitamin C 0%; Calcium 0%; Iron 4%
Exchanges: 1 Other Carbohydrate, 1 Fat
Carbohydrate Choices: 1

KITCHEN TIPS

✿ Instead of rolling the cookies in powdered sugar, dip the tops into chocolate candy sprinkles before baking.
✿ For extra fun, stir 1 cup mini candy-coated chocolate baking bits into the dough.

Peanutty Granola Cookies

Prep Time: 1 hr Start to Finish: 1 hr 45 min

1 box Betty Crocker SuperMoist butter recipe yellow cake mix

$\frac{1}{2}$ cup butter or margarine, softened

2 eggs

4 Nature Valley® Sweet & Salty peanut granola bars (from 7.4-ounce box), coarsely chopped

$\frac{1}{2}$ cup peanut butter chips (from 10-ounce bag)

$1\frac{1}{2}$ teaspoons shortening

1. Heat oven to 350°F (325°F for dark or nonstick cookie sheet). In large bowl, beat cake mix, butter and eggs with electric mixer on medium speed until smooth. Stir in chopped granola bars. Onto ungreased cookie sheet, drop mixture by tablespoonfuls.

2. Bake 10 to 12 minutes or until set and light golden brown around edges. Let cool on cookie sheet 2 minutes. Remove from cookie sheet to cooling rack. Cool completely, about 30 minutes.

3. In microwavable plastic food-storage bag, place peanut butter chips and shortening; seal bag. Microwave on High 15 seconds; squeeze bag. Microwave 15 to 25 seconds longer or until melted; squeeze bag until mixture is smooth. Cut off tiny corner of bag; squeeze bag to drizzle mixture over cookies. Let stand about 10 minutes or until drizzle is set. Store in airtight container.

32 cookies

1 Cookie: Calories 120 (Calories from Fat 50); Total Fat 6g (Saturated 2.5g; Trans 0g); Cholesterol 20mg; Sodium 150mg; Total Carbohydrate 16g (Dietary Fiber 0g; Sugars 10g); Protein 1g
% Daily Value: Vitamin A 2%; Vitamin C 0%; Calcium 2%; Iron 2%
Exchanges: 1 Other Carbohydrate, $1\frac{1}{2}$ Fat
Carbohydrate Choices: 1

KITCHEN TIPS

❊ If you like the flavor combination of peanut butter and chocolate, substitute chocolate chips for the peanut butter chips.

❊ Use your favorite flavor of Nature Valley Sweet & Salty granola bars for these cookies.

Cakes Cakes Cakes

From Everyday to Elegant

Almond-Orange Cake (page 256)

Chocolate-Cherry Cola Cake (page 251)

Treasure Chest Cake

Prep Time: 35 min Start to Finish: 2 hr 50 min

1 box Betty Crocker SuperMoist chocolate fudge cake mix

Water, vegetable oil and eggs called for on cake mix box

Tray, 24 × 20 inches

Yellow and orange paste food colors

1 container (1 pound) Betty Crocker Rich & Creamy creamy white frosting

Red pull-and-peel licorice

Gold foil-covered chocolate coins

Candy necklaces

Round hard candies

Gummy ring, halved

1. Heat oven to 350°F (325°F for dark or nonstick pan). Spray bottom only of 13 × 9-inch pan with baking spray with flour. Make and bake cake mix as directed on box for 13 × 9-inch pan, using water, oil and eggs. Cool 10 minutes; remove from pan to cooling rack. Cool completely, about 30 minutes.

2. From center of cake, cut one 3-inch crosswise strip. Cut the strip diagonally in half to make two 9-inch triangular wedges. (Discard 1 cake wedge or reserve for another use.)

3. On tray, place a 9 × 5-inch cake piece. Stir food colors into frosting to make a golden yellow. Spread 1 tablespoon of frosting on 1 edge of triangular wedge of cake. Attach wedge, frosting side down, to 9 × 5-inch cake piece on tray, placing wedge along top edge of larger cake piece. Freeze all cake pieces 1 hour.

4. Spread 1 tablespoon of frosting on top edge of triangular wedge of cake. Attach remaining 9 × 5-inch cake piece to cake wedge to look like partially opened treasure chest. Spread remaining frosting over entire cake. Pull fork through frosting to look like wood grain.

5. Use pull-and-peel licorice to make handles and straps. Fill chest with chocolate coins, candy necklaces and other hard candies. Add gummy ring half for clasp.

15 servings
1 Serving (Cake and Frosting): Calories 350 (Calories from Fat 160); Total Fat 18g (Saturated 5g; Trans 2.5g); Cholesterol 40mg; Sodium 360mg; Total Carbohydrate 45g (Dietary Fiber 0g; Sugars 33g); Protein 3g
% Daily Value: Vitamin A 0%; Vitamin C 0%; Calcium 4%; Iron 6%
Exchanges: ½ Starch, 2½ Other Carbohydrate, 3½ Fat
Carbohydrate Choices: 3

KITCHEN TIPS

✪ This treasure chest can be turned into a jewelry box for a princess party. Tint the frosting pink, and use colorful hard candies for gems and strings of candy for necklaces.

✪ You can substitute a white cake mix for the chocolate.

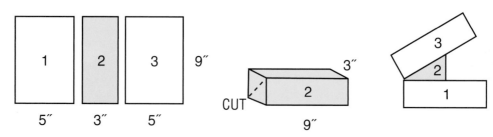

Groovy Jeans Cake

Prep Time: 35 min Start to Finish: 3 hr 15 min

1 box Betty Crocker SuperMoist cake mix (any flavor)

Water, oil and eggs called for on cake mix box

Tray or cardboard, 15 × 12 inches, covered

2½ cups Betty Crocker Rich & Creamy vanilla frosting (from two 1-pound containers)

Blue paste food color

1 roll Betty Crocker Fruit by the Foot Berry Tie-Dye® chewy fruit snack (from 4.5-ounce box)

Assorted decorations (licorice pieces, candy decors, yellow shot, candy-coated almonds)

1. Heat oven to 350°F. Grease bottom and sides of 13 × 9-inch pan with shortening (do not use cooking spray); lightly flour.

2. Make cake mix as directed on box, using water, oil and eggs. Pour into pan. Bake as directed on box. Cool 10 minutes; remove from pan to wire rack. Cool completely, about 1 hour.

3. Use toothpicks to mark sections of cake to be cut (see diagram). Use serrated knife to cut cake into sections.

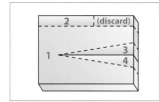 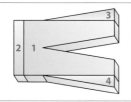

4. On tray, place largest piece. Place 1½-inch strip of cake along top edge of jeans; cut off excess. Place triangles along outer edges of legs. Cover; freeze 1 hour or until firm.

5. Tint frosting with blue food color. Remove cake from freezer; frost sides and top of cake. Use fork or decorating comb to create fabric texture.

6. To decorate cake, cut fruit snack into 8-inch length and 6-inch length. Place fruit snack on top edge of cake, overlapping in center, for belt. Decorate as desired with candies. Store loosely covered at room temperature.

12 servings
1 Serving (Cake and Frosting): Calories 500 (Calories from Fat 220); Total Fat 24g (Saturated 8g; Trans 0.5g); Cholesterol 55mg; Sodium 430mg; Total Carbohydrate 68g (Dietary Fiber 0g; Sugars 50g); Protein 3g
% Daily Value: Vitamin A 0%; Vitamin C 0%; Calcium 8%; Iron 6%
Exchanges: 1 Starch, 3½ Other Carbohydrate, 4½ Fat
Carbohydrate Choices: 4½

KITCHEN TIPS

✿ If the center of your cake is a lot higher than the sides, carefully level it off with a serrated knife so it is all the same height.
✿ Specialty candy stores may sell button-shaped candies that would look great on this cake.

Soccer Ball Cake

Prep Time: 40 min Start to Finish: 2 hr 55 min

1 box Betty Crocker SuperMoist yellow cake mix

Water, vegetable oil and eggs called for on cake mix box

Tray, 18 × 16 inches

3 drops green liquid food color

2 cups Betty Crocker Rich & Creamy creamy white frosting (from two 1-pound containers)

Betty Crocker black decorating icing (from 4.25-ounce tube)

Betty Crocker green decorating icing (from 4.25-ounce tube)

1. Heat oven to 350°F (325°F for dark or nonstick pan). Spray bottom only of 13 × 9-inch pan with baking spray with flour. Grease 1-quart ovenproof glass bowl with shortening; coat with flour (do not use baking spray). In large bowl, mix cake mix, water, oil and eggs as directed on box. Pour 1 1/2 cups batter into 1-quart bowl and remaining batter into 13 × 9-inch pan.

2. Bake 13 × 9-inch pan 25 to 30 minutes and 1-quart bowl 30 to 35 minutes or until toothpick inserted in center comes out clean. Cool 10 minutes; remove from pan and bowl to cooling racks (place cake from bowl with rounded side up). Cool completely, about 30 minutes.

3. Cut domed top off 13 × 9-inch cake so top is flat. Cut off uneven bottom of cake bowl so it will stand flat. Freeze cakes 1 hour.

4. On tray, place 13 × 9-inch cake. Stir food color into 1 1/2 cups of the white frosting. Spread over cake.

5. Spread remaining 1/2 cup white frosting over rounded side of other cake for soccer ball. Place ball on green field. Use black decorating icing to create soccer ball design. Use green decorating icing to make grass.

12 servings

1 Serving (Cake and Frosting): Calories 580 (Calories from Fat 250); Total Fat 28g (Saturated 9g; Trans 6g); Cholesterol 55mg; Sodium 480mg; Total Carbohydrate 78g (Dietary Fiber 0g; Sugars 61g); Protein 3g
% Daily Value: Vitamin A 0%; Vitamin C 0%; Calcium 6%; Iron 6%
Exchanges: 1 Starch, 4 Other Carbohydrate, 5 1/2 Fat
Carbohydrate Choices: 5

KITCHEN TIPS

❀ If you don't have a large enough tray, cut a piece of heavy cardboard box about 15 x 10 inches, and cover with foil.

❀ This is a fun cake for an end-of-season soccer party. You can also change the ball to a volleyball.

Happy Birthday Cell Phone Cake

Prep Time: 35 min Start to Finish: 1 hr 50 min

1 box Betty Crocker SuperMoist white cake mix

Water, vegetable oil and egg whites called for on cake mix box

Tray or cardboard, 18 × 16 inches, covered

1½ containers (1 pound each) Betty Crocker Rich & Creamy creamy white frosting

Pink paste or gel food color

Decorating bag with tips

12 white candy-coated chewing gum squares

1 package (3.2 ounces) marshmallow flowers

3 oval licorice candies

1 candy straw

1. Heat oven to 350°F (325°F for dark or nonstick pan). Spray bottom only of 13 × 9-inch pan with baking spray with flour. Make and bake cake mix as directed on box for 13 × 9-inch pan, using water, oil and egg whites. Cool 10 minutes; remove from pan to cooling rack. Cool completely, about 30 minutes.

2. Cut 1¼-inch strip from each long side of cake. Trim each corner of cake to round off, making cell phone shape. (Discard pieces trimmed from cake or reserve for another use.) On tray, place cake. Freeze 1 hour.

3. Divide 1 container of white frosting in half (about ¾ cup each). Stir food color into half of frosting to tint pink. Spread pink frosting over bottom half of cake. Spread white frosting over top half of cake.

4. From ½ container of frosting, reserve about 2 table-spoons white frosting. Tint about ¼ cup of the frosting pink. Onto center of white-frosted half of cake, spread some of the pink frosting in square shape for message screen. Place remaining pink frosting in decorating bag with writing tip. Pipe pink frosting along edge of white-frosted cake. Arrange gum on cake for number buttons; pipe on numbers with pink frosting.

5. With reserved white frosting, pipe desired message on message screen. Add marshmallow flowers and licorice candies. Add candy straw for antenna.

15 servings

1 Serving (Cake and Frosting): Calories 390 (Calories from Fat 170); Total Fat 18g (Saturated 5g; Trans 4g); Cholesterol 0mg; Sodium 350mg; Total Carbohydrate 52g (Dietary Fiber 0g; Sugars 39g); Protein 2g
% Daily Value: Vitamin A 0%; Vitamin C 0%; Calcium 4%; Iron 4%
Exchanges: ½ Starch, 3 Other Carbohydrate, 3½ Fat
Carbohydrate Choices: 3½

KITCHEN TIPS

❀ Look for paste or gel food color in cake decorating departments or craft stores.

❀ Instead of using a decorating bag and tip, place the frosting in a resealable plastic food-storage bag, cut a tiny hole in one corner and use to pipe the frosting. Use different bags for different colors.

Building Blocks Cakes

Prep Time: 35 min Start to Finish: 2 hr 55 min

1 box Betty Crocker SuperMoist cake mix (any flavor)

Water, oil and eggs called for on cake mix box

Tray or cardboard, 15 × 12 inches, covered

2 containers (1 pound each) Betty Crocker Rich & Creamy vanilla frosting

Red, yellow and blue paste food colors

12 large marshmallows, cut in half crosswise

1. Heat oven to 350°F. Grease bottom and sides of 13 × 9-inch pan with shortening (do not use cooking spray); lightly flour.

2. Make cake mix as directed on box, using water, oil and eggs. Pour into pan. Bake as directed on box. Cool 10 minutes; remove from pan to wire rack. Cool completely, about 1 hour.

3. Using serrated knife, cut cake crosswise into thirds. Cut one of the thirds in half crosswise to make 2 squares. On tray, place cake pieces. Cover; freeze 1 hour or until firm.

4. In small bowl for each color, tint 1 cup frosting red, 1 cup frosting yellow and $^2/_3$ cup frosting blue with food colors. Leave remaining frosting white.

5. Frost top and sides of 1 square cake with blue frosting. Frost 4 marshmallow halves with blue frosting; place in square design on cake. Frost remaining square cake and 4 marshmallow halves with white frosting; arrange marshmallows on top of cake. Frost 1 rectangle section of cake and 8 marshmallow halves with yellow frosting; arrange marshmallows on top of cake. Frost remaining section of cake and remaining marshmallows with red frosting; arrange marshmallows on top of cake. Store loosely covered at room temperature.

12 servings

1 Serving: Calories 620 (Calories from Fat 260); Total Fat 29g (Saturated 9g; Trans 0.5g); Cholesterol 55mg; Sodium 480mg; Total Carbohydrate 87g (Dietary Fiber 0g; Sugars 65g); Protein 3g
% Daily Value: Vitamin A 0%; Vitamin C 0%; Calcium 8%; Iron 6%
Exchanges: 1 Starch, 5 Other Carbohydrate, 5½ Fat
Carbohydrate Choices: 6

KITCHEN TIPS

✿ Work with one piece of cake at a time, keeping others in the freezer. As the cake defrosts, it is more likely to pick up crumbs as you frost.

✿ Place marshmallow halves on toothpicks to frost.

Piano Cake

Prep Time: 40 min Start to Finish: 3 hr 30 min

1 box Betty Crocker SuperMoist cake mix (any flavor)
  Water, oil and eggs called for on cake mix box
  Tray or cardboard, 15 × 12 inches, covered
2 bars (3.5 ounces each) white chocolate candy
1 bar (1.55 ounces) milk chocolate candy
1 container (1 pound) Betty Crocker Rich & Creamy chocolate frosting

1. Heat oven to 350°F. Grease bottom and sides of 13 × 9-inch pan with shortening (do not use cooking spray); lightly flour.

2. Make cake mix as directed on box, using water, oil and eggs. Pour into pan. Bake as directed on box. Cool 10 minutes; remove from pan to wire rack. Cool completely, about 1 hour.

3. Use serrated knife to cut cake as shown in diagram, below (for piano bench, cut $4\frac{1}{2} \times 1\frac{1}{2}$-inch piece; cut horizontally in half to make bench lower than piano, if desired). On tray, place cake. Cover; freeze 1 hour or until firm.

4. Cut one bar white chocolate into $1\frac{3}{4} \times \frac{1}{2}$-inch strips. From remaining bar, cut $2\frac{1}{2} \times 1\frac{1}{2}$-inch piece for music. Cut milk chocolate into $1 \times \frac{3}{8}$-inch pieces.

5. Place about 2 tablespoons frosting in small resealable plastic food-storage bag. Frost top and sides of cake with remaining frosting. Place white and milk chocolate pieces on cake for piano keys. Cut off tiny corner of bag with frosting; pipe frosting notes on white chocolate "music." Place above keys. Store loosely covered at room temperature.

12 servings
1 Serving: Calories 440 (Calories from Fat 200); Total Fat 22g (Saturated 8g; Trans 0.5g); Cholesterol 45mg; Sodium 370mg; Total Carbohydrate 58g (Dietary Fiber 0g; Sugars 42g); Protein 3g
% Daily Value: Vitamin A 0%; Vitamin C 0%; Calcium 10%; Iron 10%
Exchanges: 1 Starch, 3 Other Carbohydrate, 4 Fat
Carbohydrate Choices: 4

KITCHEN TIPS

- Pick up an extra white chocolate candy bar in case one breaks.
- To make it easier to cut chocolate bars, have chocolate at room temperature, and heat a sharp knife in hot water and dry before cutting chocolate.

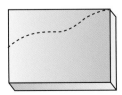

Cut cake to form piano.

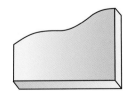
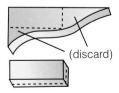

(discard)

Cut piano bench from remaining section.

Purse Cake

Prep Time: 35 min Start to Finish: 2 hr 45 min

1 box Betty Crocker SuperMoist cake mix (any flavor)

   Water, oil and eggs called for on cake mix box

1 container (1 pound) Betty Crocker Rich & Creamy vanilla frosting

   Desired food color

1 piece green peelable string licorice

1 jellied ring candy

   Assorted small multicolored hard candies

1. Heat oven to 350°F. Grease bottoms and sides of two 9-inch round cake pans with shortening or cooking spray.

2. Make cake mix as directed on box, using water, oil and eggs. Pour into pans. Bake as directed on box. Cool 10 minutes; remove from pans to wire rack. Cool completely, about 1 hour.

3. Use serrated knife to cut one-fourth off each cake to form a straight edge about 7 inches long as shown in diagram, right (discard small pieces of cake or save for another use). Spread about 2 tablespoons frosting on bottom side of cake. Place bottom side of other cake on frosting, matching cut edges. On serving plate or tray, stand cake, cut side down. Cover; freeze 1 hour or until firm.

4. Tint remaining frosting with food color. Frost cake.

5. Use peelable string licorice for handle and jellied ring candy for clasp. Decorate purse as desired with assorted candies. Store loosely covered at room temperature.

12 servings

1 Serving: Calories 400 (Calories from Fat 160); Total Fat 18g (Saturated 6g; Trans 0.5g); Cholesterol 45mg; Sodium 340mg; Total Carbohydrate 57g (Dietary Fiber 0g; Sugars 40g); Protein 2g
% Daily Value: Vitamin A 0%; Vitamin C 4%; Calcium 6%; Iron 4%
Exchanges: $1/2$ Starch, $3 1/2$ Other Carbohydrate, $3 1/2$ Fat
Carbohydrate Choices: 4

KITCHEN TIPS

❀ Bulk candy stores carry a wide variety of candies. You can see what you are purchasing and pick just the candies you want.

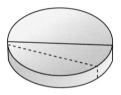

Cut one-fourth off each cake.

Stand cake, cut sides down, on tray.

Purse Cake

Pirate Cake

Prep Time: 30 min Start to Finish: 3 hr 10 min

1 box Betty Crocker SuperMoist cake mix (any flavor)
   Water, oil and eggs called for on cake mix box
   Tray or cardboard, 15 × 12 inches, covered
²⁄₃ cup Betty Crocker Rich & Creamy dark chocolate frosting (from 1-pound container)
1 cup Betty Crocker Rich & Creamy vanilla frosting (from 1-pound container)
1 chocolate-covered mint patty
1 slice marshmallow
1 gum ball
1 yellow ring-shaped hard candy
1 roll Betty Crocker Fruit by the Foot strawberry or other red chewy fruit snack (from 4.5-ounce box)
1 black licorice rope
   White candy-coated chewing gum squares
   Betty Crocker chocolate decors

1. Heat oven to 350°F. Grease bottoms and sides of one 8-inch and one 9-inch round cake pan with shortening or cooking spray.

2. Make cake as directed on box, using water, oil and eggs. Pour into pans. Bake as directed on box. Cool 10 minutes; remove from pans to wire rack. Cool completely, about 1 hour.

3. Use serrated knife to cut 9-inch cake in half and cut hat as shown in diagram. Remaining half of 9-inch cake will form body of pirate. Cut 8-inch cake as directed in diagram. On tray, place cake pieces. Cut ears and nose from small pieces of cake; attach to cake with small amount of frosting. Cover; freeze 1 hour or until firm.

4. Reserve 3 teaspoons dark chocolate frosting. Frost hat with remaining dark chocolate frosting. Frost body of pirate with vanilla frosting. Mix remaining vanilla frosting with reserved chocolate frosting. Frost head, ears and nose of pirate with tinted vanilla frosting. Add mint patty for eye patch, marshmallow slice and gum ball for eye, and ring-shaped candy for earring. Cut fruit snack into shapes for stripes, mouth and eye-patch holder; place on cake. Cut licorice to fit hat. Add gum for teeth and chocolate decors for whiskers. Store loosely covered at room temperature.

12 servings
1 Serving (Cake and Frosting): Calories 490 (Calories from Fat 210); Total Fat 23g (Saturated 7g; Trans 2g); Cholesterol 55mg; Sodium 430mg; Total Carbohydrate 66g (Dietary Fiber 0g; Sugars 55g); Protein 3g
% Daily Value: Vitamin A 0%; Vitamin C 0%; Calcium 8%; Iron 6%
Exchanges: 1 Starch, 3½ Other Carbohydrate, 4½ Fat
Carbohydrate Choices: 4½

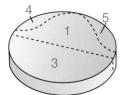

Cut 9-inch cake in half; cut hat.

Cut 8-inch cake as shown for face.

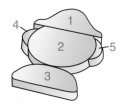

Arrange pieces on tray to form pirate.

Strawberry-Rhubarb Upside-Down Cake

Prep Time: 25 min Start to Finish: 1 hr 55 min

¼ cup butter or margarine

1 cup packed brown sugar

2 cups sliced fresh strawberries

2 cups chopped fresh rhubarb

1 box Betty Crocker SuperMoist French vanilla cake mix

1¼ cups water

⅓ cup vegetable oil

3 eggs

1. Heat oven to 350°F (325°F for dark or nonstick pan). In 13 × 9-inch pan, melt butter in oven. Sprinkle brown sugar evenly over butter. Arrange strawberries on brown sugar; sprinkle evenly with rhubarb. Press strawberries and rhubarb gently into brown sugar.

2. In large bowl, beat cake mix, water, oil and eggs with electric mixer on low speed 30 seconds. Beat on medium speed 2 minutes, scraping bowl occasionally. Pour batter over strawberries and rhubarb.

3. Bake 45 to 55 minutes or until toothpick inserted in center comes out clean. Immediately run knife around side of pan to loosen cake. Place heatproof serving plate upside down on pan; turn plate and pan over. Leave pan over cake 1 minute so brown sugar topping can drizzle over cake. Cool 30 minutes. Serve warm or cool. Store loosely covered at room temperature.

12 servings
1 Serving: Calories 370 (Calories from Fat 130); Total Fat 15g (Saturated 4g; Trans 1g); Cholesterol 65mg; Sodium 330mg; Total Carbohydrate 55g (Dietary Fiber 0g; Sugars 40g); Protein 3g % Daily Value: Vitamin A 4%; Vitamin C 15%; Calcium 15%; Iron 8% Exchanges: 1 Starch, 2½ Other Carbohydrate, 3 Fat Carbohydrate Choices: 3½

KITCHEN TIPS

❂ If fresh rhubarb is out of season, use frozen rhubarb. Just thaw and drain it before making the cake.

❂ Add a dollop of sweetened whipped cream or whipped topping to each piece of cake.

Banana Split Cake

Prep Time: 25 min Start to Finish: 2 hr 15 min

Cake

1	box Betty Crocker SuperMoist yellow cake mix
1	box (4-serving size) banana instant pudding and pie filling mix
³⁄₄	cup vegetable oil
³⁄₄	cup buttermilk
1	teaspoon vanilla
4	eggs
2	ripe bananas, mashed (about ³⁄₄ cup)

Toppings

1¹⁄₂	quarts (6 cups) vanilla ice cream
1	box (10 ounces) frozen sweetened sliced strawberries, thawed
³⁄₄	cup hot fudge sauce
³⁄₄	cup frozen (thawed) whipped topping
12	maraschino cherries with stems

1. Heat oven to 350°F (325°F for dark or nonstick pan). Spray bottom only of 13 × 9-inch pan with baking spray with flour. In large bowl, beat all cake ingredients with electric mixer on low speed 30 seconds. Beat on medium speed 2 minutes. Pour into pan.

2. Bake 50 to 55 minutes or until deep golden brown and toothpick inserted in center comes out clean. Cool completely, about 1 hour. Cut cake in half lengthwise, then cut crosswise 11 times to make a total of 24 slices.

3. Place 2 cake slices in each banana split dish or parfait glass. Top each serving with 2 small scoops of ice cream. Spoon strawberries over one scoop. Drizzle hot fudge sauce over other scoop. Top each with whipped topping and cherry.

12 servings
1 Serving: Calories 640 (Calories from Fat 270); Total Fat 30g (Saturated 11g; Trans 1.5g); Cholesterol 105mg; Sodium 560mg; Total Carbohydrate 85g (Dietary Fiber 2g; Sugars 58g); Protein 7g
% Daily Value: Vitamin A 8%; Vitamin C 10%; Calcium 20%; Iron 8%
Exchanges: 1 Starch, 4 Other Carbohydrate, ¹⁄₂ Low-Fat Milk, 5¹⁄₂ Fat
Carbohydrate Choices: 5¹⁄₂

KITCHEN TIPS

⚙ Banana splits usually have three toppings: strawberry, chocolate and pineapple. If your family likes pineapple, spoon a little pineapple topping over the ice cream.

⚙ If you don't have long banana split or parfait dishes, just cut the cake into squares and use round dessert bowls.

Chocolate-Cherry Cola Cake

Prep Time: 30 min Start to Finish: 2 hr 15 min

1 jar (10 ounces) maraschino cherries, drained, ¼ cup liquid reserved

1 box Betty Crocker SuperMoist devil's food cake mix

1 cup cherry cola carbonated beverage

½ cup vegetable oil

3 eggs

1 container (12 ounces) Betty Crocker Whipped vanilla frosting

1 cup marshmallow creme

24 maraschino cherries with stems, well drained, if desired

1. Heat oven to 350°F (325°F for dark or nonstick pan). Spray bottom only of 13 × 9-inch pan with baking spray with flour. Chop cherries; set aside.

2. In large bowl, beat cake mix, cola beverage, oil, eggs and ¼ cup reserved cherry liquid with electric mixer on low speed 30 seconds. Beat on medium speed 2 minutes. Stir in chopped cherries. Pour into pan.

3. Bake 35 to 43 minutes or until toothpick inserted in center comes out clean. Cool completely, about 1 hour.

4. In small bowl, mix frosting and marshmallow creme until smooth. Frost cake. Top each piece with 2 cherries.

12 servings

1 Serving: Calories 480 (Calories from Fat 170); Total Fat 19g (Saturated 5g; Trans 2.5g); Cholesterol 55mg; Sodium 390mg; Total Carbohydrate 72g (Dietary Fiber 2g; Sugars 53g); Protein 4g
% Daily Value: Vitamin A 0%; Vitamin C 0%; Calcium 4%; Iron 10%
Exchanges: 1 Starch, 4 Other Carbohydrate, 3½ Fat
Carbohydrate Choices: 5

KITCHEN TIPS

- Cola Cake is an old Southern recipe. This updated recipe uses a cake mix and cherry cola.

- For chocolate-dipped cherries, melt ¼ cup semisweet chocolate chips and 1 teaspoon shortening in microwave; stir. Dip well-drained cherries with stems into chocolate; refrigerate to set.

Pineapple-Carrot Cake

Prep Time: 35 min Start to Finish: 2 hr 50 min

Cake

- 1 box Betty Crocker SuperMoist butter recipe yellow cake mix
- $\frac{1}{2}$ cup water
- $\frac{1}{3}$ cup butter or margarine, softened
- 1 teaspoon grated orange peel
- 1 teaspoon vanilla
- 4 eggs
- 1 can (8 ounces) crushed pineapple, undrained
- $2\frac{1}{2}$ cups finely shredded carrots (3 to 4 large)

Frosting

- 3 cups powdered sugar
- 1 package (8 ounces) cream cheese, softened
- 2 tablespoons butter or margarine, softened
- 1 teaspoon vanilla
- 12 chocolate wafer cookies, finely crushed, if desired
- 15 sugared carrot decorations, if desired

1. Heat oven to 350°F (325°F for dark or nonstick pan). Spray bottom only of 13 × 9-inch pan with baking spray with flour. In large bowl, beat all cake ingredients except carrots with electric mixer on low speed 30 seconds. Beat on medium speed 2 minutes. Stir in carrots. Pour into pan.

2. Bake 35 to 45 minutes or until toothpick inserted in center comes out clean. Cool completely, about 1 hour.

3. In large bowl, beat powdered sugar, cream cheese, 2 tablespoons butter and the vanilla on low speed until blended. Beat on medium speed until smooth and creamy. Spread frosting over cake. With knife tip, score cake into 5 rows by 3 rows (15 squares).

4. Diagonally on each marked cake piece, sprinkle a small amount of crushed cookies for "dirt." Insert carrot decoration into each piece. Refrigerate 30 minutes before serving. Store in refrigerator.

15 servings
1 Serving: Calories 370 (Calories from Fat 130); Total Fat 14g (Saturated 8g; Trans 1g); Cholesterol 90mg; Sodium 340mg; Total Carbohydrate 57g (Dietary Fiber 0g; Sugars 43g); Protein 4g
% Daily Value: Vitamin A 50%; Vitamin C 2%; Calcium 8%; Iron 6%
Exchanges: 1 Starch, 3 Other Carbohydrate, $2\frac{1}{2}$ Fat
Carbohydrate Choices: 4

KITCHEN TIPS

- If desired, use a can (12 ounces) of Betty Crocker Whipped cream cheese frosting in place of the homemade frosting.
- A serving of this cake contains 50% of the recommended daily value for vitamin A.

Peachy Pineapple Upside-Down Cake

Prep Time: 15 min Start to Finish: 2 hr

1/4 cup butter or margarine

1 cup packed brown sugar

15 maraschino cherries (from 6-ounce jar)

15 peach halves in heavy syrup (from two 15 1/2-ounce cans), drained

1 can (8 ounces) crushed pineapple, drained, juice reserved

1 box Betty Crocker SuperMoist yellow cake mix

1/3 cup vegetable oil

3 eggs

1. Heat oven to 325°F (300°F for dark or nonstick pan). In 13 × 9-inch pan, melt butter in oven. Sprinkle brown sugar evenly over butter. Place maraschino cherry in center of peach half; place cut side down on brown sugar (cherries will be on bottom). Spoon pineapple around peaches.

2. Add enough water to reserved pineapple juice to measure 1 1/4 cups. In large bowl, beat cake mix, juice mixture, oil and eggs with electric mixer on low speed 30 seconds. Beat on medium speed 2 minutes, scraping bowl occasionally. Pour batter over peaches and pineapple.

3. Bake 1 hour 10 minutes to 1 hour 15 minutes or until toothpick inserted in center of cake comes out clean and top is very dark golden brown. Immediately run knife around side of pan to loosen cake. Place heatproof serving plate upside down on pan; turn pan and plate over. Leave pan over cake 1 minute so topping can drizzle over cake. Cool 30 minutes. Serve warm or cool.

15 servings
1 Serving: Calories 360 (Calories from Fat 110); Total Fat 12g (Saturated 4g; Trans 1g); Cholesterol 50mg; Sodium 270mg; Total Carbohydrate 61g (Dietary Fiber 2g; Sugars 46g); Protein 3g
% Daily Value: Vitamin A 15%; Vitamin C 2%; Calcium 8%; Iron 6%
Exchanges: 1/2 Starch, 3 1/2 Other Carbohydrate, 2 1/2 Fat
Carbohydrate Choices: 4

KITCHEN TIPS

◎ Serve this homey dessert warm with scoops of peach or vanilla ice cream.
◎ To serve leftover dessert warm, scoop servings into small microwavable bowls and microwave individual servings on High for 15 to 20 seconds.

Caramel Pudding Cake

Prep Time: 15 min Start to Finish: 1 hr 10 min

1¼ cups Gold Medal all-purpose flour
¾ cup granulated sugar
1½ teaspoons baking powder
½ teaspoon baking soda
¼ teaspoon salt
½ cup buttermilk
2 tablespoons butter or margarine, melted
½ cup chopped dates, if desired
¼ cup chopped nuts
¾ cup packed brown sugar
1½ cups very warm water (120°F to 130°F)
Ice cream, if desired

1. Heat oven to 350°F. In large bowl, mix flour, granulated sugar, baking powder, baking soda and salt with spoon. Stir in buttermilk and butter. Stir in dates and nuts (batter will be thick). Spread in ungreased 8- or 9-inch square pan.

2. In small bowl, mix brown sugar and very warm water with spoon. Pour over batter.

3. Bake 45 to 55 minutes or until cake is deep golden brown and toothpick inserted in center comes out clean. Serve warm with ice cream.

9 servings
1 Serving: Calories 250 (Calories from Fat 45); Total Fat 5g (Saturated 1.5g; Trans 0g); Cholesterol 10mg; Sodium 250mg; Total Carbohydrate 49g (Dietary Fiber 0g; Sugars 35g); Protein 3g
% Daily Value: Vitamin A 2%; Vitamin C 0%; Calcium 8%; Iron 8%
Exchanges: 1 Starch, 2 Other Carbohydrate, 1 Fat
Carbohydrate Choices: 3

KITCHEN TIPS

❁ Spoon the caramel sauce that forms at the bottom of this dessert over the warm cake and ice cream.
❁ Prepare this dessert just before you sit down to dinner so that it will still be warm when you serve it.

Premium Tres Leches Cake

Prep Time: 15 min Start to Finish: 1 hr 55 min

1 box Betty Crocker SuperMoist yellow cake mix

1¼ cups water

1 tablespoon vegetable oil

2 teaspoons vanilla

4 eggs

1 can (14 ounces) sweetened condensed milk (not evaporated)

1 cup whole milk or evaporated milk

1 cup whipping cream

1 container Betty Crocker Whipped fluffy white frosting

Cut-up fresh fruit, if desired

1. Heat oven to 350°F (325°F for dark or nonstick pan). Grease and flour or spray bottom and sides of 13 × 9-inch pan.

2. In large bowl, beat cake mix, water, oil, vanilla and eggs with electric mixer on low speed 30 seconds, then on medium speed 2 minutes, scraping bowl occasionally. Pour into pan.

3. Bake 29 to 35 minutes or until edges are golden brown and toothpick inserted in center comes out clean. Let stand 5 minutes. Poke top of hot cake every ½ inch with long-tined fork, wiping fork occasionally to reduce sticking.

4. In large bowl, stir together sweetened condensed milk, whole milk and whipping cream. Carefully pour evenly over top of cake. Cover; refrigerate about 1 hour or until mixture is absorbed into cake. Frost with frosting. Top with fresh fruit.

15 servings
1 Serving: Calories 410 (Calories from Fat 160); Total Fat 18g (Saturated 8g; Trans 2.5g); Cholesterol 85mg; Sodium 310mg; Total Carbohydrate 58g (Dietary Fiber 0g; Sugars 44g); Protein 5g
% Daily Value: Vitamin A 6%; Vitamin C 0%; Calcium 15%; Iron 4%
Exchanges: 1 Starch, 3 Other Carbohydrate, 3½ Fat
Carbohydrate Choices: 4

KITCHEN TIPS

❀ *Tres leches* is the Spanish term for three milks. The three types of milk create this cake's signature indulgence and moistness.

❀ Top this moist cake with cut-up fresh fruit such as mango, papaya and kiwifruit.

Almond-Orange Cake

Prep Time: 30 min Start to Finish: 2 hr 35 min

Cake

- 1 cup slivered almonds
- 2 cups Gold Medal all-purpose flour
- 1 cup granulated sugar
- 1/2 cup butter or margarine, softened
- 1 cup fresh orange juice
- 1 1/2 teaspoons almond extract
- 2 teaspoons baking powder
- 1 teaspoon salt
- 2 eggs
- 1/2 cup orange marmalade

Garnish

- 3/4 cup whipping cream
- 2 tablespoons powdered or granulated sugar
- 1/3 cup slivered almonds, toasted
- Orange twist, if desired

1. Heat oven to 350°F (325°F for dark or nonstick pan). Spray 9-inch springform pan with cooking spray. In food processor or blender, place 1 cup almonds; cover and process until almonds are finely ground. In large bowl, beat almonds and remaining cake ingredients except marmalade with electric mixer on low speed 30 seconds, scraping bowl constantly. Beat on high speed 3 minutes, scraping bowl occasionally. Pour batter into pan.

2. Bake 45 to 55 minutes or until top is evenly dark golden brown and cake springs back when touched lightly in center.

3. Cool in pan 10 minutes. Remove side of pan. Spread marmalade over top of cake. Cool completely, about 1 hour.

4. In chilled small bowl, beat whipping cream and 2 tablespoons sugar on high speed until soft peaks form. Spoon or pipe whipped cream around edge of cake; sprinkle 1/3 cup almonds over whipped cream. Refrigerate until serving. Garnish with orange twist.

12 servings
1 Serving: Calories 390 (Calories from Fat 180); Total Fat 19g (Saturated 9g; Trans 0.5g); Cholesterol 70mg; Sodium 350mg; Total Carbohydrate 48g (Dietary Fiber 2g; Sugars 28g); Protein 6g
% Daily Value: Vitamin A 10%; Vitamin C 8%; Calcium 10%; Iron 10%
Exchanges: 2 Starch, 1 Other Carbohydrate, 3 1/2 Fat
Carbohydrate Choices: 4

KITCHEN TIPS

✪ Use a knife dipped in warm water to cut the cake easily.
✪ Instead of beating whipping cream and powdered sugar, you can use whipped cream topping from an aerosol can.
✪ To toast nuts, bake uncovered in ungreased shallow pan in 350°F oven 6 to 10 minutes, stirring occasionally, until golden brown.

Apple-Walnut Cake with Caramel Glaze

Prep Time: 25 min Start to Finish: 2 hr 10 min

Cake

- 2 cups packed brown sugar
- 1½ cups vegetable oil
- 3 eggs
- 3 cups Gold Medal all-purpose flour
- 2 teaspoons baking soda
- ¼ teaspoon salt
- 1 teaspoon ground ginger
- 2 teaspoons ground cinnamon
- ¼ teaspoon ground cloves
- 1 cup chopped walnuts
- 2 large apples, peeled, shredded (about 2 cups)

Glaze

- 2 tablespoons butter or margarine, softened
- 1 cup powdered sugar
- 3 tablespoons butterscotch-caramel topping
- 1 tablespoon milk
  Additional ground cinnamon, if desired

1. Heat oven to 350°F. Grease 12-cup fluted tube cake pan with shortening; lightly flour.

2. In large bowl, beat brown sugar, oil and eggs with electric mixer on medium speed until light and fluffy. Add remaining ingredients except walnuts and apples; beat on low speed until smooth. With spoon, gently stir in walnuts and apples. Spoon batter into pan.

3. Bake 1 hour to 1 hour 10 minutes or until toothpick inserted near center comes out clean. Cool 10 minutes. Place heatproof plate upside down over pan; turn plate and pan over. Remove pan. Cool 30 minutes.

4. Meanwhile, in medium bowl, beat all glaze ingredients except cinnamon until smooth. Pour glaze over top of cake, allowing some to run down side. Sprinkle with cinnamon.

16 servings
1 Serving: Calories 500 (Calories from Fat 250); Total Fat 28g (Saturated 4.5g; Trans 0g); Cholesterol 45mg; Sodium 240mg; Total Carbohydrate 58g (Dietary Fiber 2g; Sugars 38g); Protein 5g
% Daily Value: Vitamin A 2%; Vitamin C 0%; Calcium 4%; Iron 10%
Exchanges: 1 Starch, 3 Other Carbohydrate, 5½ Fat
Carbohydrate Choices: 4

KITCHEN TIPS

❂ It's okay to use any variety or color of apple for this cake.
❂ Out of walnuts? Use pecans instead.

Lemon-Zucchini Pound Cake

Prep Time: 30 min Start to Finish: 3 hr 45 min

Cake

3	cups Gold Medal all-purpose flour
1	teaspoon baking powder
1/4	teaspoon baking soda
1/4	teaspoon salt
1	cup butter or margarine, softened
2	cups powdered sugar
4	eggs
2/3	cup milk
2	tablespoons lemon juice
2	teaspoons grated lemon peel
1	cup shredded zucchini (about 1 medium), squeezed to drain

Lemon Glaze

1	cup powdered sugar
1	tablespoon butter or margarine, softened
1	tablespoon half-and-half
2	tablespoons lemon juice
1	teaspoon grated lemon peel

1. Heat oven to 350°F. Grease 12-cup fluted tube cake pan with shortening; lightly flour.

2. In medium bowl, mix flour, baking powder, baking soda and salt with spoon; set aside.

3. In large bowl, beat 1 cup butter with electric mixer on medium speed about 2 minutes or until creamy. Beat in 2 cups powdered sugar. Add eggs, one at a time, beating well after each addition. Add flour mixture to butter mixture alternately with milk, beating well on low speed after each addition. Beat on low speed 1 minute. Stir in lemon juice, lemon peel and zucchini. Spoon into pan.

4. Bake 50 to 60 minutes or until toothpick inserted in center comes out clean. Cool 15 minutes in pan. Remove from pan onto serving plate. Cool completely, about 1 1/2 hours.

5. In 1-quart saucepan, heat all glaze ingredients just to boiling over medium heat, stirring constantly; remove from heat. Let stand 30 minutes until slightly thickened. Drizzle over cake.

16 servings
1 Serving: Calories 310 (Calories from Fat 130); Total Fat 14g (Saturated 7g; Trans 0.5g); Cholesterol 85mg; Sodium 190mg; Total Carbohydrate 42g (Dietary Fiber 0g; Sugars 23g); Protein 5g
% Daily Value: Vitamin A 10%; Vitamin C 0%; Calcium 4%; Iron 8%
Exchanges: 2 Starch, 1 Other Carbohydrate, 2 Fat
Carbohydrate Choices: 3

KITCHEN TIPS

- If you prefer an orange glaze, substitute orange juice for the lemon juice and orange peel for the lemon peel.
- Pound cakes get their name from the fact that they originally were made with 1 pound each of flour, sugar and eggs.

Rainbow Angel Birthday Cake

Prep Time: 20 min Start to Finish: 3 hr

1   box Betty Crocker white angel food cake mix

1¼ cups cold water

1   teaspoon grated lemon or orange peel
    Red, yellow and green liquid food colors

1   cup Betty Crocker Rich & Creamy vanilla frosting (from 1-pound container)

12 to 15 square candy fruit chews

1. Move oven rack to lowest position (remove other racks). Heat oven to 350°F. In extra-large glass or metal bowl, beat cake mix, water and lemon peel with electric mixer on low speed 30 seconds; beat on medium speed 1 minute.

2. Divide batter evenly among 3 bowls. Gently stir 6 to 8 drops of one food color into each of the batters. Pour red batter into ungreased 10-inch angel food (tube) cake pan. (Do not use fluted tube cake pan or 9-inch angel food pan or batter will overflow.) Spoon yellow batter over red batter. Spoon green batter over top.

3. Bake 37 to 47 minutes or until top is golden brown and cracks feel very dry and not sticky. Do not underbake. Immediately turn pan upside down onto glass bottle until cake is completely cool, about 2 hours. Run knife around edges of cake; remove from pan to serving plate.

4. Spoon ½ cup of the frosting into microwavable bowl. Microwave uncovered on High about 15 seconds or until frosting can be stirred smooth and is thin enough to drizzle. (Or spoon frosting into 1-quart saucepan and heat over low heat, stirring constantly, until thin enough to drizzle.) Drizzle over cake.

5. Place remaining frosting in decorating bag with writing tip. Pipe a ribbon and bow on each candy square to look like a wrapped package. Arrange packages on top of cake. Store loosely covered at room temperature.

12 servings
1 Serving (Cake and Frosting): Calories 240 (Calories from Fat 50); Total Fat 5g (Saturated 2g; Trans 0g); Cholesterol 0mg; Sodium 370mg; Total Carbohydrate 45g (Dietary Fiber 0g; Sugars 35g); Protein 3g
% Daily Value: Vitamin A 0%; Vitamin C 0%; Calcium 6%; Iron 0%
Exchanges: 1 Starch, 2 Other Carbohydrate, 1 Fat
Carbohydrate Choices: 3

KITCHEN TIPS

❀ Add a scoop of rainbow sherbet to each serving for more rainbow fun.

❀ Serrated knives work best when cutting a foam-type cake like angel food.

Peach Cake with Sour Peach Frosting

Prep Time: 15 min Start to Finish: 2 hr

Cake

- 1 box Betty Crocker SuperMoist white cake mix
- 1¼ cups water
- ⅓ cup vegetable oil
- 3 eggs
- 1 box (4-serving size) peach-flavored gelatin

Frosting

- 1 box (4-serving size) peach-flavored gelatin
- ¼ cup water
- 4½ cups powdered sugar
- ½ cup butter or margarine, softened
- 2 teaspoons lemon juice
- 2 to 3 teaspoons water
  Red and yellow liquid food colors

Garnish

- 1 teaspoon granulated sugar, if desired
- 12 sour peach gummy candy rings, if desired

1. Heat oven to 350°F (325°F for dark or nonstick pans). Grease bottoms and sides of two 8- or 9-inch round cake pans with shortening (do not use cooking spray); lightly flour.

2. In large bowl, beat cake mix, 1¼ cups water, the oil, eggs and 1 box gelatin (dry) with electric mixer on low speed 30 seconds. Beat on medium speed 2 minutes. Divide batter between pans.

3. Bake 8-inch rounds 38 to 40 minutes, 9-inch rounds 33 to 35 minutes, or until toothpick inserted in center comes out clean. Cool 10 minutes. Run knife around side of pans to loosen cakes; remove from pans to wire rack. Cool completely, about 1 hour.

4. In 2-cup microwavable bowl or measuring cup, stir 1 box gelatin (dry) into ¼ cup water. Microwave uncovered on High about 1 minute 30 seconds, stirring 2 or 3 times to dissolve gelatin, until mixture boils. In large bowl, beat gelatin mixture, powdered sugar, butter, lemon juice and 2 teaspoons water on low speed until frosting is thick but spreadable. (Add additional 1 teaspoon water if needed to make frosting spreadable.)

5. On serving plate, place 1 cake, rounded side down. Spread with ½ cup frosting. Drop 2 drops red food color and 1 drop yellow food color on frosting on cake; swirl with spatula to create deep orange. Top with second cake, rounded side up. Reserve ½ cup frosting. Frost side and top of cake with remaining frosting. Add 1 or 2 drops red and yellow food colors to reserved frosting. Swirl around cake. Sprinkle with granulated sugar. Decorate with peach candies. Cut cake gently with serrated knife. Store loosely covered at room temperature.

12 servings

1 Serving: Calories 560 (Calories from Fat 170); Total Fat 19g (Saturated 7g; Trans 1.5g); Cholesterol 75mg; Sodium 420mg; Total Carbohydrate 92g (Dietary Fiber 0g; Sugars 76g); Protein 5g
% Daily Value: Vitamin A 8%; Vitamin C 0%; Calcium 6%; Iron 6%
Exchanges: 2 Starch, 4 Other Carbohydrate, 3½ Fat
Carbohydrate Choices: 6

KITCHEN TIPS

✿ Get creative with the sour peach gummy candy rings—cut through one side of each to make long piece, then twist and arrange on the cake in a swirled pattern.

✿ Because this is a delicate cake, cool it completely before frosting and decorating, and use a serrated knife to cut it into pieces.

Butter Pecan Cake with Apricots

Prep Time: 15 min Start to Finish: 2 hr

1 box Betty Crocker SuperMoist butter pecan cake mix

1 cup water

¼ cup vegetable oil

3 eggs

1 can (15.25 ounces) apricot halves, drained, chopped (1 cup)

¾ cup apricot preserves

1 container (12 ounces) Betty Crocker Whipped cream frosting

15 pecan halves or pieces

1. Heat oven to 350°F (325°F for dark or nonstick pan). Grease bottom only of 13 × 9-inch pan with shortening or cooking spray.

2. In large bowl, beat cake mix, water, oil, eggs and apricots with electric mixer on low speed 30 seconds. Beat on medium speed 2 minutes, scraping bowl occasionally. Pour into pan.

3. Bake 40 to 45 minutes or until toothpick inserted in center comes out clean. Cool completely, about 1 hour.

4. Spread preserves evenly over top of cake. Spread frosting over preserves. Garnish with pecan halves. Store loosely covered at room temperature.

15 servings
1 Serving: Calories 350 (Calories from Fat 120); Total Fat 13g (Saturated 3.5g; Trans 1g); Cholesterol 40mg; Sodium 260mg; Total Carbohydrate 55g (Dietary Fiber 0g; Sugars 38g); Protein 2g
% Daily Value: Vitamin A 10%; Vitamin C 2%; Calcium 8%; Iron 6%
Exchanges: 1 Starch, 2½ Other Carbohydrate, 2½ Fat
Carbohydrate Choices: 3½

KITCHEN TIPS

✿ Make it peachy by using canned peaches and peach preserves instead of apricots.

✿ Stirring the preserves first will make it easier to spread them on the cake.

Coffee Cake with Caramel Frosting

Prep Time: 15 min Start to Finish: 2 hr

$\frac{1}{4}$ cup instant coffee granules

$\frac{1}{4}$ cup boiling water

1 box Betty Crocker SuperMoist white cake mix

1 cup water

$\frac{1}{3}$ cup vegetable oil

3 eggs

1 container (1 pound) Betty Crocker Rich & Creamy vanilla frosting

$\frac{1}{4}$ cup caramel topping

3 bars (1.4 ounces each) chocolate-covered English toffee candy, coarsely chopped

1. Heat oven to 350°F (325°F for dark or nonstick pan). Grease bottom only of 13 × 9-inch pan with shortening or cooking spray.

2. In small cup, dissolve coffee granules in boiling water.

3. In large bowl, beat cake mix, 1 cup water, the oil, eggs and coffee mixture with electric mixer on low speed 30 seconds. Beat on medium speed 2 minutes, scraping bowl occasionally. Pour into pan.

4. Bake 28 to 33 minutes or until toothpick inserted in center comes out clean. Cool completely, about 1 hour.

5. In medium bowl, mix frosting and caramel topping. Frost cake with frosting mixture. Sprinkle with toffee candy. Store loosely covered at room temperature.

15 servings
1 Serving: Calories 400 (Calories from Fat 170); Total Fat 19g (Saturated 6g; Trans 1g); Cholesterol 45mg; Sodium 360mg; Total Carbohydrate 54g (Dietary Fiber 0g; Sugars 39g); Protein 3g
% Daily Value: Vitamin A 2%; Vitamin C 0%; Calcium 6%; Iron 4%
Exchanges: 1 Starch, 2½ Other Carbohydrate, 3½ Fat
Carbohydrate Choices: 3½

KITCHEN TIPS

❂ For an Irish Cream Cake, substitute $\frac{1}{4}$ cup Irish cream liqueur for the caramel topping.

Chocolate-Covered Strawberry Cake

Prep Time: 15 min Start to Finish: 2 hr

- 1 box Betty CrockerSuperMoist white cake mix
- 1 box (4-serving size) strawberry-flavored gelatin
- 1¼ cups water
- ⅓ cup vegetable oil
- 3 eggs
- 1 cup seedless strawberry jam
- 1 container (1 pound) Betty Crocker Rich & Creamy milk chocolate frosting
- 6 Chocolate-Dipped Strawberries (page 213) or 1 pint (2 cups) fresh strawberries, cut in half

1. Heat oven to 350°F (325°F for dark or nonstick pans). Grease bottoms and sides of two 9-inch round cake pans with shortening (do not use cooking spray); lightly flour.

2. In large bowl, stir together cake mix (dry) and gelatin (dry). Add water, oil and eggs. Beat with electric mixer on low speed 30 seconds. Beat on medium speed 2 minutes, scraping bowl occasionally. Divide batter between pans.

3. Bake 23 to 28 minutes or until toothpick inserted in center comes out clean. Cool 10 minutes; remove from pans to wire rack. Cool completely, about 1 hour.

4. Split each cake horizontally into 2 layers. On serving plate, place top of 1 layer, cut side up; spread with ⅓ cup of the jam. Add bottom half of layer, cut side down; spread with ⅓ cup jam. Add top of second layer, cut side up; spread with remaining ⅓ cup jam. Add bottom of remaining layer. Frost side and top of cake with frosting. Arrange dipped strawberries around top of cake. Store loosely covered in refrigerator.

16 servings
1 Serving: Calories 380 (Calories from Fat 110); Total Fat 13g (Saturated 3.5g; Trans 2.5g); Cholesterol 40mg; Sodium 330mg; Total Carbohydrate 63g (Dietary Fiber 1g; Sugars 45g); Protein 3g
% Daily Value: Vitamin A 0%; Vitamin C 10%; Calcium 6%; Iron 8%
Exchanges: 1 Starch, 3 Other Carbohydrate, 2½ Fat
Carbohydrate Choices: 4

KITCHEN TIPS

✿ Split the layers by pulling a piece of dental floss or heavy thread horizontally through the middle of the layer, moving floss in a back-and-forth motion.

Betty Crocker
MAKES IT EASY

Make & Bake Cake Basics

Looking for a "recipe" to create a picture-perfect cake? Start with a generous amount of cake-baking tips, stir in easy directions and add a dash of love.

Pick the Pan

▶ Use the pan size called for in the recipe. For easy pan removal, make sure to follow recipe instructions for greasing and flouring pans, as well as special instructions for using waxed paper or parchment paper.

▶ Shiny metal aluminum pans are best because they reflect heat away from the cake and produce a tender, light brown crust.

▶ If you use dark, nonstick or glass baking pans, follow the manufacturer's directions, which may call for reducing the oven temperature by 25°F. These pans absorb heat so cakes will bake and brown faster.

▶ For the best volume when making cupcakes, use paper or foil baking cups.

The Great Bake

▶ Be sure to follow the recipe directions for each recipe rather than following the package directions. Many of the recipes call for additional ingredients, which can change how the cake bakes.

▶ Bake cakes on the rack in the center of the oven, unless the recipe tells you otherwise.

▶ Check for doneness as directed in each recipe. If a bake range is for 35 to 40 minutes, don't open the oven before 35 minutes or your cake could fall. Use a toothpick to test for doneness in the center of the cake. If it comes out clean, the cake is done.

▶ Cool cakes on a cooling rack away from drafts (see Removing Cake Layers, below) for the length of time the recipe recommends.

REMOVING CAKE LAYERS

1. After removing cakes from the oven, cool them in the pan on a cooling rack for 10 to 15 minutes.
2. Run a dinner knife around the side of the pan to loosen the cake. Cover a cooling rack with a towel. Place rack, towel side down, on top of one cake layer; turn rack and pan upside down together. Remove pan. Remove waxed or parchment paper.
3. Place a second cooling rack, top side down, on bottom of cake layer; turn over both racks so the layer is right side up. Remove towel and top cooling rack. Repeat with remaining layer(s). Let layers cool completely on racks.

FROSTING A LAYER CAKE

1. Place 4 strips of waxed paper around the edge of a large plate. Brush any loose crumbs from the cooled cake. Place one layer, rounded side down, on the plate (unless directed otherwise in the recipe).
2. Spread about $1/3$ cup creamy frosting (or $1/2$ cup fluffy frosting) over the top of the first layer to within $1/4$ inch of the edge.
3. Place second layer, rounded side up, on top of first layer so that the 2 flat sides are together with frosting in between. Coat side of cake with a very thin layer of frosting to seal in crumbs.
4. Frost the side of the cake in swirls, making a rim about $1/4$ inch high above the top of the cake.
5. Frost top of cake.

Lemon-Raspberry Cake

Prep Time: 10 min Start to Finish: 1 hr 40 min

Cake

1 box Betty Crocker SuperMoist lemon cake mix

$1\frac{1}{4}$ cups water

$\frac{1}{3}$ cup vegetable oil

3 eggs

6 tablespoons raspberry preserves

Lemon Buttercream Frosting

$1\frac{1}{4}$ cups butter or margarine, softened

2 teaspoons grated lemon peel

3 tablespoons lemon juice

3 cups powdered sugar

Garnish

Fresh raspberries, if desired

1. Heat oven to 350°F. Grease bottoms and sides of three 9-inch round pans with shortening or cooking spray; lightly flour. Make cake mix as directed on box, using water, oil and eggs. Pour into pans.

2. Bake 18 to 20 minutes or until toothpick inserted in center comes out clean. Cool 10 minutes; remove from pans to wire rack. Cool completely, about 1 hour.

3. In medium bowl, beat butter, lemon peel and lemon juice with electric mixer on medium speed 30 seconds. Gradually beat in powdered sugar. Beat 2 to 3 minutes longer or until light and fluffy.

4. On serving plate, place 1 cake layer, rounded side down. Spread with 3 tablespoons of the preserves. Add second layer, rounded side down. Spread with remaining 3 tablespoons preserves. Top with third layer, rounded side up. Frost side and top of cake with frosting. Sprinkle with raspberries. Store covered in refrigerator.

16 servings
1 Serving: Calories 430 (Calories from Fat 200); Total Fat 22g (Saturated 11g; Trans 1.5g); Cholesterol 80mg; Sodium 330mg; Total Carbohydrate 54g (Dietary Fiber 0g; Sugars 40g); Protein 2g
% Daily Value: Vitamin A 10%; Vitamin C 0%; Calcium 6%; Iron 4%
Exchanges: 1 Starch, $2\frac{1}{2}$ Other Carbohydrate, $4\frac{1}{2}$ Fat
Carbohydrate Choices: $3\frac{1}{2}$

KITCHEN TIPS

✿ Use blackberry preserves instead of the raspberry.
✿ Lightly sprinkle 1 tablespoon of rum over the surface of each layer before spreading the preserves.

Cream-Filled Butter Pecan Birthday Cake

Prep Time: 25 min Start to Finish: 2 hr 10 min

Cake

- ½ cup butter or margarine
- ¼ cup whipping cream
- 1 cup packed brown sugar
- 1 box Betty Crocker SuperMoist butter pecan cake mix
- 1¼ cups water
- ⅓ cup vegetable oil
- 3 eggs

Topping

- 1¾ cups whipping cream
- ¼ cup powdered sugar
- ¼ teaspoon vanilla
- ¼ cup chocolate-coated toffee bits

1. Heat oven to 325°F. In 1-quart saucepan, heat butter, ¼ cup whipping cream and the brown sugar over low heat, stirring occasionally, just until butter is melted. Pour into two 9-inch round pans (do not use dark or nonstick pans).

2. In large bowl, beat cake mix, water, oil and eggs with electric mixer on low speed 30 seconds. Beat on medium speed 2 minutes, scraping bowl occasionally. Carefully spoon half of cake batter into each pan, starting at outer edge and continuing toward the center so brown sugar mixture does not get moved out to the side of the pans.

3. Bake 35 to 45 minutes or until toothpick inserted in center comes out clean. Run knife around edge of cakes to loosen from pan. Turn upside down onto wire racks, placing waxed paper under racks to catch drips. Leave pans over cakes 1 minute before removing. Cool completely, about 1 hour.

4. In chilled medium bowl, beat whipping cream, powdered sugar and vanilla on high speed until stiff peaks form.

5. On serving tray, place 1 cake layer, brown sugar side up. Spread with half of the whipped cream. Top with second layer, brown sugar side up. Spread with remaining whipped cream. Sprinkle with toffee bits.

12 servings
1 Serving: Calories 530 (Calories from Fat 280); Total Fat 31g (Saturated 16g; Trans 2g); Cholesterol 120mg; Sodium 370mg; Total Carbohydrate 59g (Dietary Fiber 0g; Sugars 43g); Protein 4g
% Daily Value: Vitamin A 15%; Vitamin C 0%; Calcium 15%; Iron 8%
Exchanges: 1 Starch, 3 Other Carbohydrate, 6 Fat
Carbohydrate Choices: 4

KITCHEN TIPS

Use sparkler birthday candles for a festive effect.

Lemon Pudding Cake

Prep Time: 10 min Start to Finish: 1 hr 30 min

1 box Betty Crocker SuperMoist lemon cake mix

1¼ cups water

⅓ cup vegetable oil

1 tablespoon grated lemon peel

3 eggs

2 boxes (4-serving size each) lemon instant pudding and pie filling mix

2¾ cups milk

Whipped cream, if desired

1. Heat oven to 350°F. Spray 13 × 9-inch pan with cooking spray (do not use dark or nonstick pan).

2. In large bowl, beat cake mix, water, oil, lemon peel and eggs with electric mixer on low speed 30 seconds. Beat on medium speed 2 minutes, scraping bowl occasionally. Pour into pan; set aside.

3. In medium bowl, beat pudding mix and milk with wire whisk or spoon 1 to 2 minutes or until smooth. Drizzle pudding over batter to within ½ inch of edges of pan.

4. Bake 50 to 60 minutes or until top springs back when lightly touched in center and edges begin to pull away from sides of pan (center will be set but slightly jiggly). Cool 20 minutes. Top of cake will have irregular surface and appear sunken in center.

5. Spoon warm pudding cake, top side down, into bowls; top with whipped cream. Store covered in refrigerator.

15 servings
1 Serving: Calories 270 (Calories from Fat 80); Total Fat 9g (Saturated 2.5g; Trans 0.5g); Cholesterol 45mg; Sodium 450mg; Total Carbohydrate 42g (Dietary Fiber 0g; Sugars 28g); Protein 4g
% Daily Value: Vitamin A 2%; Vitamin C 0%; Calcium 10%; Iron 4%
Exchanges: 1 Starch, 2 Other Carbohydrate, 1½ Fat
Carbohydrate Choices: 3

KITCHEN TIPS

❂ Garnish each serving of cake with a candied lemon slice and mint leaf.
❂ When shopping for the pudding mix, be sure to buy the instant pudding mix, not the cook-and-serve variety.

Mango Margarita Cake

Prep Time: 20 min Start to Finish: 1 hr 50 min

Cake

1 box Betty Crocker SuperMoist yellow cake mix

1 cup nonalcoholic margarita mix

⅓ cup vegetable oil

2 teaspoons grated lime peel

4 eggs

1 jar (1 pound 8 ounces) sliced mango in extra-light syrup, well drained, diced

Frosting

Remaining diced mango

1½ cups frozen (thawed) whipped topping

2 containers (6 ounces each) Yoplait Original 99% Fat Free apricot-mango yogurt

1. Heat oven to 350°F. Spray bottom only of 13 × 9-inch pan with baking spray with flour (do not use dark or nonstick pan). In large bowl, beat cake mix, margarita mix, oil, lime peel, eggs and 1 cup of the diced mango with electric mixer on low speed 30 seconds. Beat on medium speed 2 minutes. Pour into pan.

2. Bake 30 to 35 minutes or until toothpick inserted in center comes out clean. Cool completely, about 1 hour.

3. In blender, place remaining ¼ cup diced mango. Cover; blend until smooth. In medium bowl, fold together whipped topping and yogurt; frost cake. Spoon small dollops of pureed mango over frosting, then swirl with back of spoon. Store in refrigerator.

15 servings
1 Serving: Calories 280 (Calories from Fat 90); Total Fat 10g (Saturated 3.5g; Trans 1g); Cholesterol 55mg; Sodium 260mg; Total Carbohydrate 43g (Dietary Fiber 0g; Sugars 30g); Protein 4g
% Daily Value: Vitamin A 10%; Vitamin C 20%; Calcium 10%; Iron 4%
Exchanges: ½ Starch, 2½ Other Carbohydrate, 2 Fat
Carbohydrate Choices: 3

KITCHEN TIPS

❂ If apricot-mango yogurt isn't available, you can substitute peach yogurt.
❂ Look for jars of sliced mango in the refrigerated section of the produce department.

Lemon Pudding Cake

Mango Margarita Cake

Mexican Chocolate Cake

Prep Time: 15 min Start to Finish: 1 hr 50 min

Cake

1 box Betty Crocker SuperMoist devil's food cake mix

1⅓ cups water

½ cup vegetable oil

1 teaspoon ground cinnamon

3 eggs

Caramelized-Sugar Frosting

¾ cup granulated sugar

⅓ cup butter

4 to 5 tablespoons milk

3 cups powdered sugar

1. Heat oven to 350°F. Grease bottom only of 13 × 9-inch pan with shortening or cooking spray.

2. In large bowl, beat all cake ingredients with electric mixer on low speed 30 seconds. Beat on medium speed 2 minutes, scraping bowl occasionally. Pour into pan. Bake 33 to 38 minutes or until toothpick inserted in center comes out clean. Cool completely, about 1 hour.

3. In 2-quart heavy saucepan, heat granulated sugar over medium-low heat 6 to 8 minutes, stirring occasionally with wooden spoon and watching carefully, until sugar begins to melt. As sugar begins to melt, stir with wooden spoon until sugar is melted and golden brown (sugar becomes very hot and could melt a plastic spoon). Remove from heat; carefully stir in butter and 1 tablespoon of the milk (mixture will be lumpy). Return to medium-low heat, stirring constantly, until mixture is smooth. Cool 5 minutes.

4. Add powdered sugar to caramel mixture and beat with electric mixer on low speed until well combined. Add 3 tablespoons milk, mixing until frosting is glossy and spreadable. If necessary, add up to 1 tablespoon more milk, 1 teaspoon at a time. Spread frosting over cake. Store loosely covered at room temperature.

15 servings
1 Serving: Calories 390 (Calories from Fat 130); Total Fat 15g (Saturated 4.5g; Trans 0.5g); Cholesterol 55mg; Sodium 310mg; Total Carbohydrate 62g (Dietary Fiber 1g; Sugars 50g); Protein 3g
% Daily Value: Vitamin A 4%; Vitamin C 0%; Calcium 4%; Iron 8%
Exchanges: 1 Starch, 3 Other Carbohydrate, 3 Fat
Carbohydrate Choices: 4

KITCHEN TIPS

❂ Try Betty Crocker Rich & Creamy dulce de leche frosting instead of the homemade frosting.
❂ Garnish cake with chocolate shavings.

Orange Flan Cakes

Prep Time: 20 min Start to Finish: 1 hr 50 min

Caramel

1 cup sugar

$^1\!/_2$ cup water

Flan

1 cup milk

2 tablespoons orange-flavored liqueur or orange juice

1 teaspoon grated orange peel

4 egg yolks

2 whole eggs

1 can (14 ounces) sweetened condensed milk

Cake

1 box Betty Crocker SuperMoist yellow cake mix

$1^1\!/_4$ cups water

$^1\!/_3$ cup vegetable oil

2 teaspoons grated orange peel

3 whole eggs

1. In 2-quart heavy saucepan, heat sugar and $^1\!/_2$ cup water to boiling. Reduce heat to medium. Cook without stirring 18 to 22 minutes or until sugar turns golden brown in color and is caramelized. Into 2 ungreased 9-inch round cake pans (do not use dark or nonstick pans), quickly pour caramelized sugar and immediately tilt pans so sugar covers bottoms; set aside.

2. Fill shallow pan half full with water; place on lowest oven rack. Heat oven to 325°F.

3. In medium bowl, beat 1 cup milk, the liqueur, 1 teaspoon orange peel, egg yolks, whole eggs and sweetened condensed milk with wire whisk or fork until blended. Pour milk mixture over caramelized sugar in each pan.

4. In large bowl, beat cake mix, $1^1\!/_4$ cups water, the oil, 2 teaspoons orange peel and 3 eggs with electric mixer on low speed 30 seconds. Beat on medium speed 2 minutes, scraping bowl occasionally. Spoon mixture evenly over milk mixture in pans.

5. Bake cakes on middle rack 45 to 55 minutes or until cakes spring back when touched lightly in center. Cool 30 minutes; run knife or spatula around edges of pans. Place serving plate upside down on each pan; turn plate and pan over. Leave pans over cakes 1 minute so caramel can drizzle over cakes. Serve warm or cold. Store covered in refrigerator.

16 servings
1 Serving: Calories 350 (Calories from Fat 110); Total Fat 12g (Saturated 4g; Trans 0.5g); Cholesterol 130mg; Sodium 270mg; Total Carbohydrate 54g (Dietary Fiber 0g; Sugars 42g); Protein 6g
% Daily Value: Vitamin A 6%; Vitamin C 0%; Calcium 15%; Iron 6%
Exchanges: 2 Starch, $1^1\!/_2$ Other Carbohydrate, 2 Fat
Carbohydrate Choices: $3^1\!/_2$

KITCHEN TIPS

⊙ Use only 9-inch, light-colored pans; 8-inch pans are too small to hold the caramel and flan mixtures, and dark pans may scorch the flan.

⊙ Don't be surprised if some of the caramel soaks into the flan and cake during cooling. This adds to the richness of the cake.

Springtime Sprinkles Cake

Prep Time: 25 min Start to Finish: 1 hr 20 min

1 box Betty Crocker SuperMoist butter recipe white cake mix

Water, butter and egg whites called for on cake mix box

1 container (15 ounces) Betty Crocker Pour & Frost® vanilla frosting

Betty Crocker Decorating Decors pink, blue and green sugars

1. Heat oven to 350°F. Grease bottom only of 13 × 9-inch pan with shortening or cooking spray.

2. In large bowl, beat cake mix, water, butter and egg whites with electric mixer on low speed 30 seconds. Beat on medium speed 2 minutes, scraping bowl occasionally. Pour into pan.

3. Bake 33 to 38 minutes or until toothpick inserted in center comes out clean. Cool 15 minutes. Microwave frosting uncovered on High 20 seconds. Stir thoroughly 20 times or until smooth. Pour over cake; spread evenly.

4. To decorate, gently press cookie cutter into frosting on cake where you want sugar design; remove cutter and dip bottom edge into one of the colored sugars, then gently press cutter back into same stamped image on cake. Continue with other sugars and different sizes of cookie cutters as desired. Store loosely covered at room temperature.

16 servings
1 Serving (Cake and Frosting): Calories 310 (Calories from Fat 130); Total Fat 14g (Saturated 6g; Trans 2.5g); Cholesterol 15mg; Sodium 330mg; Total Carbohydrate 42g (Dietary Fiber 0g; Sugars 29g); Protein 2g
% Daily Value: Vitamin A 4%; Vitamin C 0%; Calcium 4%; Iron 4% Exchanges: 1/2 Starch, 2 1/2 Other Carbohydrate, 3 Fat Carbohydrate Choices: 3

KITCHEN TIPS

✿ Kids love colored sugar, so let them pick their favorite colored sugars and cookie cutter shapes to make an original piece of cake.

✿ Sprinkle serving plates with different colored sugars before placing cake on plates.

Lemon Cheesecake

Prep Time: 15 min Start to Finish: 6 hr 50 min

Crust

- 1 box Betty Crocker SuperMoist yellow cake mix
- 1/2 cup butter or margarine, softened
- 1 teaspoon grated lemon peel

Filling

- 2 packages (8 ounces each) cream cheese, softened
- 3/4 cup sugar
- 3 containers (3.5 ounces each) lemon pudding (from 4-pack container)
- 1/2 cup sour cream
- 3 eggs
- 2 cups frozen (thawed) whipped topping

1. Heat oven to 300°F. Spray bottom and side of 10-inch springform pan with baking spray with flour. Wrap foil around outside of pan to catch drips. Reserve 1/4 cup of the cake mix; set aside. In large bowl, beat remaining cake mix, butter and lemon peel with electric mixer on low speed until crumbly. Press in bottom and 1 1/2 inches up side of pan.

2. In same large bowl, beat reserved cake mix, the cream cheese, sugar, pudding and sour cream on medium speed until smooth and creamy. Beat in eggs, one at a time, until mixed. Pour over crust.

3. Bake 1 hour 20 minutes to 1 hour 35 minutes or until edges are set but center of cheesecake jiggles slightly when moved. Turn oven off; open oven door at least 4 inches. Leave cheesecake in oven 30 minutes longer.

4. Remove cheesecake from oven; place on cooling rack. Without releasing side of pan, run knife around edge of pan to loosen cheesecake. Cool in pan on cooling rack 30 minutes. Cover loosely; refrigerate 4 hours or overnight. Remove side of pan before serving. Pipe or spoon whipped topping around outside edge of cheesecake. Store in refrigerator.

16 servings
1 Serving: Calories 400 (Calories from Fat 210); Total Fat 23g (Saturated 14g; Trans 1.5g); Cholesterol 90mg; Sodium 380mg; Total Carbohydrate 43g (Dietary Fiber 0g; Sugars 30g); Protein 5g
% Daily Value: Vitamin A 15%; Vitamin C 0%; Calcium 10%; Iron 6%
Exchanges: 1/2 Starch, 2 1/2 Other Carbohydrate, 1/2 High-Fat Meat, 3 1/2 Fat
Carbohydrate Choices: 3

KITCHEN TIPS

- If you don't have a fresh lemon to grate for the crust, just omit it. There is still plenty of lemon flavor in the cheesecake.
- For clean cuts when serving the cheesecake, dip a sharp knife in hot water and dry on a paper towel before each cut.

Caramel Cappuccino Cheesecake

Prep Time: 30 min Start to Finish: 8 hr 50 min

Crust

1¼ cups chocolate cookie crumbs (from 15-ounce box)

¼ cup butter or margarine, melted

Filling

2 tablespoons instant espresso coffee granules

2 teaspoons vanilla

4 packages (8 ounces each) cream cheese, softened

1½ cups granulated sugar

4 eggs

1 teaspoon ground cinnamon

¼ cup caramel topping

Topping

1 cup whipping cream

2 tablespoons powdered or granulated sugar

¼ cup caramel topping

1. Heat oven to 300°F. Wrap outside of 10-inch springform pan with foil. In small bowl, mix cookie crumbs and melted butter with fork. Press mixture evenly over bottom of pan. Refrigerate crust while preparing filling.

2. In small bowl, stir coffee granules and vanilla until coffee is dissolved; set aside.

3. In large bowl, beat cream cheese with electric mixer on medium speed until smooth. Gradually add 1½ cups sugar, beating until light and fluffy. Add eggs, one at a time, beating well after each addition. Add espresso mixture, cinnamon and ¼ cup caramel topping; beat about 30 seconds or until mixture is well blended. Pour over crust in pan.

4. Bake 1 hour 10 minutes to 1 hour 20 minutes or until cheesecake is set 1½ inches from edge and center is slightly jiggly. Turn oven off; open oven door at least 4 inches. Let cheesecake remain in oven 30 minutes. Remove cheesecake from oven. Run knife around edge of pan to loosen; cool 30 minutes at room temperature. Cover; refrigerate 6 hours or overnight.

5. Remove side of pan. In chilled medium bowl, beat whipping cream and 2 tablespoons sugar on high speed until soft peaks form. Spread whipped cream over top of cheesecake; drizzle ¼ cup caramel topping over whipped cream.

16 servings

1 Serving: Calories 440 (Calories from Fat 270); Total Fat 30g (Saturated 18g; Trans 1g); Cholesterol 140mg; Sodium 300mg; Total Carbohydrate 35g (Dietary Fiber 0g; Sugars 29g); Protein 7g
% Daily Value: Vitamin A 20%; Vitamin C 0%; Calcium 8%; Iron 8%
Exchanges: ½ Starch, 2 Other Carbohydrate, 1 High-Fat Meat, 4 Fat
Carbohydrate Choices: 2

KITCHEN TIPS

❀ For a party-perfect cheesecake without cracks, try baking in a water bath. Place filled, foil-wrapped springform pan in a large roasting pan and pour enough boiling water into roasting pan to come halfway up sides of springform pan. Bake as directed.

Butter Rum-Glazed Applesauce Cake

Prep Time: 20 min Start to Finish: 1 hr 25 min

Cake

- ⅓ cup butter (do not use margarine)
- ¾ cup granulated sugar
- 1 cup applesauce
- 1 teaspoon vanilla
- 1½ cups Gold Medal all-purpose flour
- 1 teaspoon baking soda
- 1 teaspoon ground cinnamon
- ½ teaspoon salt

Butter Rum Glaze

- 2 tablespoons butter (do not use margarine)
- 1 cup powdered sugar
- ½ teaspoon rum flavor
- 3 to 4 teaspoons half-and-half or milk

1. Heat oven to 350°F. Grease bottom and sides of 8-inch square pan with shortening or spray with cooking spray.

2. In 1½-quart saucepan, melt ⅓ cup butter over medium heat. Cook 2 to 2½ minutes, stirring occasionally, until butter just begins to brown. Immediately remove from heat. Stir in granulated sugar, applesauce and vanilla.

3. In large bowl, mix flour, baking soda, cinnamon and salt. Stir in applesauce mixture. Pour into pan.

4. Bake 30 to 35 minutes or until toothpick inserted in center comes out clean.

5. In 1½-quart saucepan, melt 2 tablespoons butter over medium heat; cook about 3 minutes or until butter just begins to brown. Immediately remove from heat. Stir in remaining glaze ingredients until smooth and spreadable. Pour over warm cake. Cool 30 minutes. Serve warm.

9 servings

1 Serving: Calories 300 (Calories from Fat 90); Total Fat 10g (Saturated 5g; Trans 0.5g); Cholesterol 25mg; Sodium 340mg; Total Carbohydrate 51g (Dietary Fiber 1g; Sugars 33g); Protein 2g
% Daily Value: Vitamin A 8%; Vitamin C 0%; Calcium 0%; Iron 6%
Exchanges: 1 Starch, ½ Fruit, 2 Other Carbohydrate, 1½ Fat
Carbohydrate Choices: 3½

KITCHEN TIPS

- After adding glaze, sprinkle the top of the warm cake with a bit of cinnamon.
- It's important to use real butter in this recipe. You won't get the toasty flavor that comes from browning if you use margarine.

Strawberry-Rhubarb Angel Torte

Strawberry-Rhubarb Angel Torte

Prep Time: 25 min Start to Finish: 3 hr 10 min

Cake

1	box Betty Crocker white angel food cake mix
1¼	cups cold water
2	teaspoons grated orange peel

Filling

2	cups sliced fresh rhubarb
½	cup granulated sugar
2	tablespoons orange juice
1½	cups sliced strawberries
	Red food color, if desired

Frosting

1½	cups whipping (heavy) cream
3	tablespoons granulated or powdered sugar
1	container (15 ounces) ricotta cheese
¼	cup powdered sugar

Garnish

½	cup sliced strawberries

1. Move oven rack to lowest position (remove other racks). Heat oven to 350°F. In extra-large glass or metal bowl, beat cake mix, water and orange peel with electric mixer on low speed 30 seconds; beat on medium speed 1 minute. Pour into ungreased 10-inch angel food (tube) cake pan. (Do not use fluted tube cake pan or 9-inch angel food pan or batter will overflow.)

2. Bake 37 to 47 minutes or until top is dark golden brown and cracks feel very dry and not sticky. Do not underbake. Immediately turn pan upside down onto glass bottle until cake is completely cool, about 2 hours.

3. Meanwhile, in 2-quart saucepan, mix rhubarb, ½ cup granulated sugar and the orange juice. Cook over medium heat 10 minutes, stirring occasionally. Cool 15 minutes. Stir in 1½ cups strawberries. Stir in 4 drops food color if deeper red color is desired. Refrigerate about 1 hour.

4. In chilled medium bowl, beat whipping cream and 3 tablespoons sugar on high speed until soft peaks form. In large bowl, beat ricotta cheese and ¼ cup powdered sugar on medium speed until fluffy. Fold in whipped cream.

5. Run knife around edges of cake; remove from pan. Cut cake horizontally to make 3 layers. Fill layers with filling. Frost side and top of cake with frosting. Arrange ½ cup strawberries over top of cake. Store covered in refrigerator.

12 servings
1 Serving: Calories 350 (Calories from Fat 110); Total Fat 12g (Saturated 8g; Trans 0g); Cholesterol 45mg; Sodium 380mg; Total Carbohydrate 51g (Dietary Fiber 0g; Sugars 40g); Protein 8g
% Daily Value: Vitamin A 10%; Vitamin C 15%; Calcium 20%; Iron 0%
Exchanges: 2½ Starch, 1 Other Carbohydrate, 2 Fat
Carbohydrate Choices: 3½

KITCHEN TIPS

❀ For Blueberry-Rhubarb Angel Torte, substitute 1½ cups fresh or frozen (thawed) blueberries for the strawberries in the filling. Omit food color and garnish.

❀ Use 2 containers (12 ounces each) Betty Crocker Whipped cream or vanilla frosting instead of the ricotta frosting.

Spiderweb Applesauce Cake

Prep Time: 30 min Start to Finish: 2 hr 5 min

2   cups Gold Medal all-purpose flour
1   cup granulated sugar
1   cup packed brown sugar
2   teaspoons baking powder
1   teaspoon baking soda
1   teaspoon ground cinnamon
1   cup vegetable oil
1   cup applesauce
1   teaspoon vanilla
4   eggs
1   container (1 pound) Betty Crocker Rich & Creamy dulce de leche or cream cheese frosting
¼   cup Betty Crocker Rich & Creamy vanilla frosting (from 1-pound container)
24 brown candy-coated peanut butter candies (from 12.7-ounce bag of multicolored candies)
24 brown miniature candy-coated chocolate baking bits (from 12-ounce bag of multicolored baking bits)
2   tablespoons Betty Crocker Rich & Creamy chocolate frosting (from 1-pound container)

1. Heat oven to 350°F. Grease bottom and sides of 15 × 10 × 1-inch pan with shortening or cooking spray.

2. In large bowl, mix flour, sugars, baking powder, baking soda and cinnamon. Add oil, applesauce, vanilla and eggs; beat with electric mixer on low speed until smooth. Spread in pan.

3. Bake 28 to 32 minutes or until toothpick inserted in center comes out clean and surface is deep golden brown. Cool completely, about 1 hour.

4. Frost with dulce de leche frosting. Cut into 6 rows by 4 rows, but leave in pan.

5. To decorate, spoon vanilla frosting into resealable plastic food-storage bag; seal bag and cut off 1 tiny corner. Pipe vanilla frosting in a spiral in corner where 4 squares meet (see dia-

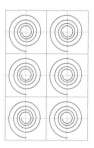

gram). Pull a toothpick from corner of each square through lines of frosting 4 to 5 times to create spiderweb. Repeat to make 6 webs.

6. Place 1 peanut butter candy and 1 baking bit next to spider web on each square. Spoon chocolate frosting into another resealable plastic food-storage bag; seal bag and cut off 1 tiny corner. Pipe chocolate frosting to make 6 legs for each spider.

24 servings
1 Serving: Calories 320 (Calories from Fat 140); Total Fat 15g (Saturated 3g; Trans 1.5g); Cholesterol 35mg; Sodium 170mg; Total Carbohydrate 43g (Dietary Fiber 0g; Sugars 33g); Protein 2g
% Daily Value: Vitamin A 0%; Vitamin C 0%; Calcium 4%; Iron 6%
Exchanges: 3 Other Carbohydrate, 3 Fat
Carbohydrate Choices: 3

KITCHEN TIPS

❂ Skip the spider decorations to make a tasty everyday bar. Drizzle the vanilla frosting randomly over the caramel (dulce de leche) frosting.
❂ Dulce de leche refers to a rich, sweet, caramelized milk that's popular in Latin America.

Streusel In-Between Pumpkin Cake

Prep Time: 20 min Start to Finish: 3 hr 55 min

Streusel

- ½ cup packed brown sugar
- 2 tablespoons Gold Medal all-purpose flour
- 1 teaspoon ground cinnamon
- ¼ teaspoon pumpkin pie spice
- 1 tablespoon butter or margarine, softened

Cake

- 3 cups Gold Medal all-purpose flour
- 2 teaspoons baking soda
- 1 tablespoon ground cinnamon
- 1 teaspoon salt
- 1 cup butter or margarine, softened
- 2 cups granulated sugar
- 4 eggs
- 1 cup canned pumpkin (not pumpkin pie mix)
- 1 cup sour cream
- 1 teaspoon vanilla
  Powdered sugar, if desired

1. Heat oven to 350°F. Grease 12-cup fluted tube cake pan with shortening; lightly flour. In small bowl, stir in streusel ingredients until crumbly; set aside.

2. In medium bowl, mix flour, baking soda, cinnamon and salt; set aside. In large bowl, beat butter and granulated sugar with electric mixer on medium speed, scraping bowl occasionally, until creamy. Add eggs, two at a time, beating well after each addition. Beat in pumpkin, sour cream and vanilla. Gradually beat in flour mixture on low speed until blended.

3. Spread half of the batter in pan. Sprinkle streusel over batter, making sure streusel does not touch side of pan. Top with remaining batter, making sure batter layer touches side of pan.

4. Bake 58 to 62 minutes or until toothpick inserted in cake comes out clean. Cool 30 minutes; remove from pan to cooling rack. Cool completely, about 2 hours. Sprinkle with powdered sugar.

16 servings
1 Serving: Calories 380 (Calories from Fat 150); Total Fat 17g (Saturated 10g; Trans 1g); Cholesterol 95mg; Sodium 420mg; Total Carbohydrate 53g (Dietary Fiber 2g; Sugars 33g); Protein 5g
% Daily Value: Vitamin A 60%; Vitamin C 0%; Calcium 4%; Iron 10%
Exchanges: 1 Starch, 2½ Other Carbohydrate, 3½ Fat
Carbohydrate Choices: 3½

KITCHEN TIPS

- Serve with vanilla frozen yogurt or ice cream, or for a super-spice hit, cinnamon ice cream.
- Put the remaining pumpkin in a resealable plastic food-storage bag and freeze to use later in another recipe.

Apricot-Filled Pumpkin Cake with Browned Butter Frosting

Apricot-Filled Pumpkin Cake
with Browned Butter Frosting

Prep Time: 20 min Start to Finish: 3 hr 25 min

Filling

- 1/2 cup packed brown sugar
- 2 tablespoons Gold Medal all-purpose flour
- 3 tablespoons firm butter or margarine
- 1/2 cup finely chopped dried apricots (about 14)

Cake

- 3 cups Gold Medal all-purpose flour
- 3 teaspoons baking powder
- 2 teaspoons ground cinnamon
- 1 teaspoon ground ginger
- 1/2 teaspoon salt
- 1 cup butter or margarine, softened
- 2 cups granulated sugar
- 5 eggs
- 1 cup canned pumpkin (not pumpkin pie mix)

Browned Butter Frosting

- 1/3 cup butter (do not use margarine)
- 2 cups powdered sugar
- 3 to 4 tablespoons milk
- 1/4 cup finely chopped dried apricots (about 7)

1. Heat oven to 325°F. Grease 12-cup fluted tube cake pan with shortening or cooking spray; lightly flour. (Do not use dark or nonstick pan.)

2. In small bowl, mix all filling ingredients except apricots with fork until mixture resembles fine crumbs. Stir in 1/2 cup chopped apricots; set aside.

3. In medium bowl, mix flour, baking powder, cinnamon, ginger and salt; set aside.

4. In large bowl, beat 1 cup butter and granulated sugar with electric mixer on medium speed, scraping bowl occasionally, until creamy. Add eggs, one at a time, beating well after each addition. Beat in pumpkin. Gradually beat in flour mixture on low speed until blended.

5. Spread 3 cups of the batter in pan. With back of spoon, make 1/2-inch-deep tunnel in middle of batter. Spoon filling into tunnel, making sure filling does not touch side of pan. Top with remaining batter, making sure batter layer touches side of pan.

6. Bake 1 hour to 1 hour 15 minutes or until toothpick inserted in cake comes out clean and top is golden brown. Cool 15 minutes. Remove cake from pan to cooling rack. Cool completely, about 1 hour.

7. In 2-quart saucepan, heat 1/3 cup butter over medium heat, stirring constantly, until light golden brown; cool slightly. Stir in powdered sugar. Stir in 3 tablespoons of the milk until smooth. Add additional milk, 1 teaspoon at a time, until desired consistency. Spoon frosting over cake, letting some run down sides of cake. Garnish with 1/4 cup chopped apricots.

16 servings
1 Serving: Calories 470 (Calories from Fat 180); Total Fat 20g (Saturated 12g; Trans 1g); Cholesterol 115mg; Sodium 310mg; Total Carbohydrate 69g (Dietary Fiber 2g; Sugars 49g); Protein 5g
% Daily Value: Vitamin A 60%; Vitamin C 0%; Calcium 8%; Iron 10%
Exchanges: 1 Starch, 3 1/2 Other Carbohydrate, 4 Fat
Carbohydrate Choices: 4 1/2

KITCHEN TIPS

- If the apricots are too dry, cover them with boiling water and let stand about 3 minutes. Drain and chop.
- To garnish cake, roll dried apricot halves between sheets of waxed paper to flatten slightly, then cut into desired shapes with small cookie cutters.

Ginger-Orange Pound Cake

Prep Time: 25 min Start to Finish: 3 hr

Cake

3	cups Gold Medal all-purpose flour
1	teaspoon baking powder
1/4	teaspoon salt
2	tablespoons grated gingerroot
1	tablespoon grated orange peel
2	cups sugar
1 1/2	cups butter or margarine, softened
5	eggs
1	cup orange juice

Topping

1/2	cup orange marmalade
1/4	cup chopped candied ginger

1. Heat oven to 350°F. Grease 12-cup fluted tube cake pan with shortening or cooking spray; lightly flour. (Do not use dark or nonstick pan.)

2. In large bowl, mix flour, baking powder, salt, gingerroot and orange peel; set aside.

3. In another large bowl, beat sugar and butter with electric mixer on low speed 30 seconds, scraping bowl constantly, until creamy. Add eggs; beat on low speed until well blended. Beat on high speed 5 minutes, scraping bowl occasionally. Beat in flour mixture alternately with orange juice on low speed until smooth. Pour into pan.

4. Bake 1 hour 5 minutes to 1 hour 15 minutes or until toothpick inserted in center comes out clean and top is dark golden brown. Cool 30 minutes; remove from pan to cooling rack. Cool completely, about 1 hour.

5. Spoon marmalade over cake; top with candied ginger.

16 servings
1 Serving: Calories 400 (Calories from Fat 170); Total Fat 19g (Saturated 11g; Trans 1g); Cholesterol 110mg; Sodium 210mg; Total Carbohydrate 53g (Dietary Fiber 0g; Sugars 32g); Protein 5g
% Daily Value: Vitamin A 15%; Vitamin C 6%; Calcium 4%; Iron 8%
Exchanges: 1 Starch, 2 1/2 Other Carbohydrate, 3 1/2 Fat
Carbohydrate Choices: 3 1/2

KITCHEN TIPS

- Use a sharp, fine mesh grater to grate fresh gingerroot; discard the fibers that are left on the grater.
- Garnish with sugared kumquats. To sugar the kumquats, brush with corn syrup and roll in granulated sugar.

Apple Pudding Cake with Cinnamon-Butter Sauce

Prep Time: 15 min Start to Finish: 50 min

Cake

- 1 cup packed brown sugar
- 1/4 cup butter or margarine, softened
- 1 egg
- 1 cup Gold Medal all-purpose flour
- 1 teaspoon baking soda
- 1 teaspoon ground cinnamon
- 1/2 teaspoon ground nutmeg
- 1/4 teaspoon salt
- 2 cups chopped peeled or unpeeled cooking apples (2 medium)

Sauce

- 1/3 cup butter or margarine
- 2/3 cup granulated sugar
- 1/3 cup half-and-half
- 1/2 teaspoon ground cinnamon

1. Heat oven to 350°F. Grease bottom and sides of 8-inch square pan with shortening.

2. In large bowl, mix brown sugar and softened butter with spoon until light and fluffy. Beat in egg. Stir in flour, baking soda, 1 teaspoon cinnamon, the nutmeg and salt. Stir in apples. Spread batter in pan.

3. Bake 25 to 35 minutes or until toothpick inserted in center comes out clean.

4. Meanwhile, in 1-quart saucepan, heat sauce ingredients over medium heat, stirring frequently, until butter is melted and sauce is hot. Serve warm sauce over warm cake.

9 servings

1 Serving: Calories 350 (Calories from Fat 120); Total Fat 14g (Saturated 8g; Trans 0.5g); Cholesterol 60mg; Sodium 310mg; Total Carbohydrate 54g (Dietary Fiber 1g; Sugars 42g); Protein 3g % Daily Value: Vitamin A 8%; Vitamin C 0%; Calcium 4%; Iron 8% Exchanges: 1 Starch, 2 1/2 Other Carbohydrate, 2 1/2 Fat Carbohydrate Choices: 3 1/2

KITCHEN TIPS

- Braeburn, Cortland, Granny Smith or Rome apples are all good choices for this pudding cake.
- You can bake the cake and make the sauce a day ahead and store them separately (refrigerate sauce). Warm the sauce in a saucepan over low heat, and heat individual pieces of cake uncovered in the microwave on High for 25 to 30 seconds or until warm.

Banana Nut Cake with Peanut Butter Frosting

Prep Time: 25 min Start to Finish: 2 hr 25 min

Cake

2⅓	cups Gold Medal all-purpose flour
1⅔	cups granulated sugar
1¼	cups mashed ripe bananas (2½ medium)
⅔	cup butter or margarine, softened
⅔	cup finely chopped nuts
⅔	cup buttermilk
1¼	teaspoons baking powder
1¼	teaspoons baking soda
¾	teaspoon salt
3	eggs

Frosting

⅓	cup peanut butter
3	cups powdered sugar
1½	teaspoons vanilla
¼	to ⅓ cup milk

1. Heat oven to 350°F. Grease bottom and sides of 1 (13 × 9-inch) pan or 2 (9-inch) round cake pans with shortening; lightly flour. In large bowl, beat cake ingredients with electric mixer on low speed 30 seconds, scraping bowl constantly. Beat on medium speed 3 minutes, scraping bowl occasionally. Pour into pan(s).

2. Bake 13 × 9-inch pan 45 to 50 minutes, round cake pans 35 to 40 minutes, or until toothpick inserted in center comes out clean. Cool round cakes 10 minutes before removing from pans to cooling racks. Cool completely, about 1 hour.

3. In medium bowl, beat peanut butter and powdered sugar with spoon or electric mixer on low speed until blended. Add vanilla and ¼ cup milk; beat until smooth and spreadable. If necessary, beat in more milk, a few drops at a time. Frost 13 × 9-inch cake, or fill and frost round cake layers with frosting.

24 servings
1 Serving: Calories 280 (Calories from Fat 90); Total Fat 10g (Saturated 4g; Trans 0g); Cholesterol 40mg; Sodium 230mg; Total Carbohydrate 43g (Dietary Fiber 1g; Sugars 31g); Protein 4g
% Daily Value: Vitamin A 4%; Vitamin C 0%; Calcium 4%; Iron 4%
Exchanges: ½ Starch, 2½ Other Carbohydrate, 2 Fat
Carbohydrate Choices: 3

KITCHEN TIPS

- To make your own buttermilk, pour 2 teaspoons lemon juice or white vinegar into a liquid measuring cup and add enough milk to equal ⅔ cup. Let the mixture stand for 5 minutes before using.
- The flavors of buttermilk and peanut butter combine to make this a very kid-friendly cake.

Chocolate Cake à l'Orange

Prep Time: 40 min Start to Finish: 2 hr 35 min

Cake

- 2 ounces unsweetened baking chocolate
- 1 cup butter or margarine
- 1 cup granulated sugar
- 1 cup sour cream
- 2 tablespoons grated orange peel
- 2 teaspoons vanilla
- 3 eggs
- 1½ cups Gold Medal all-purpose flour
- 1 teaspoon baking powder
- 1 teaspoon baking soda
- ¼ teaspoon salt

Glaze and Garnish

- 1 ounce unsweetened baking chocolate
- 2 tablespoons butter or margarine
- ⅓ cup powdered sugar
- 1 to 2 tablespoons fresh orange juice
  Orange peel strips

1. Heat oven to 350°F. Grease 12-cup fluted tube (bundt cake) pan with shortening; lightly flour. In small microwavable bowl, microwave 2 ounces chocolate uncovered on High 1 minute. Stir; microwave in 30-second increments, stirring after each, until melted. Set aside to cool slightly.

2. In large bowl, beat 1 cup butter and the granulated sugar with electric mixer on medium speed until blended. Beat in melted chocolate. Add sour cream, orange peel, vanilla and eggs; beat until well blended. On low speed, beat in remaining cake ingredients. Spread batter in pan.

3. Bake 30 to 40 minutes or until toothpick inserted in center comes out clean. Cool 15 minutes. Remove from pan to cooling rack. Cool completely, about 1 hour.

4. In 1-quart saucepan, heat 1 ounce chocolate and 2 tablespoons butter over low heat 2 to 3 minutes, stirring occasionally, until melted. Remove from heat. With wire whisk, beat in powdered sugar and 1 tablespoon of the orange juice. Beat in additional orange juice, 1 teaspoon at a time, until glaze is smooth and consistency of thick syrup. Drizzle glaze over cake, allowing some to run down side. Garnish with orange peel strips.

12 servings
1 Serving: Calories 400 (Calories from Fat 240); Total Fat 26g (Saturated 16g; Trans 1g); Cholesterol 110mg; Sodium 340mg; Total Carbohydrate 36g (Dietary Fiber 2g; Sugars 21g); Protein 5g
% Daily Value: Vitamin A 15%; Vitamin C 2%; Calcium 6%; Iron 10%
Exchanges: 1 Starch, 1½ Other Carbohydrate, ½ High-Fat Meat, 4 Fat
Carbohydrate Choices: 2½

KITCHEN TIPS

☼ All you need to create your own invitations are some blank cards, a rubber stamp and your imagination. Stamp "You're Invited" at the top of each card and handwrite the date, time, place and RSVP information. For added "wow," punch holes in the card and weave a pretty ribbon through the holes.

Chocolate Cake with Raspberry Sauce

Chocolate Cake with Raspberry Sauce

Prep Time: 25 min Start to Finish: 2 hr 5 min

1 cup semisweet chocolate chips (6 ounces)
1/2 cup butter or margarine
1/2 cup Gold Medal all-purpose flour
4 eggs, separated
1/2 cup sugar

Sauce

1 box (10 ounces) frozen raspberries, thawed, drained and juice reserved
1/4 cup sugar
2 tablespoons cornstarch
1 to 2 tablespoons orange- or raspberry-flavored liqueur, if desired

Glaze

1/2 cup semisweet chocolate chips
2 tablespoons butter or margarine
2 tablespoons light corn syrup

Garnish

1/2 cup whipped cream
Fresh raspberries, if desired

1. Heat oven to 325°F. Grease bottom and side of 8-inch springform pan or 9-inch round cake pan with shortening. In 2-quart heavy saucepan, melt 1 cup chocolate chips and 1/2 cup butter over medium heat, stirring occasionally. Cool 5 minutes. Stir in flour until smooth. Stir in egg yolks until well blended; set aside.

2. In large bowl, beat egg whites with electric mixer on high speed until foamy. Beat in 1/2 cup sugar, 1 tablespoon at a time, until soft peaks form. Using rubber spatula, fold chocolate mixture into egg whites. Spread in pan.

3. Bake springform pan 35 to 40 minutes, round cake pan 30 to 35 minutes, or until toothpick inserted in center comes out clean (top will appear dry and cracked). Cool 10 minutes. Run knife along side of cake to loosen; remove side of springform pan. Place cooling rack upside down over cake; turn rack and

cake over. Remove bottom of springform pan or round cake pan. Cool completely, about 1 hour.

4. Meanwhile, add enough water to reserved raspberry juice to measure 1 cup. In 1-quart saucepan, mix 1/4 cup sugar and the cornstarch. Stir in juice and thawed raspberries. Heat to boiling over medium heat. Boil and stir 1 minute. Place small strainer over small bowl. Pour mixture through strainer to remove seeds; discard seeds. Stir liqueur into mixture; set aside.

5. Place cake on serving plate. In 1-quart saucepan, heat glaze ingredients over medium heat, stirring occasionally, until chips are melted. Spread over top of cake, allowing some to drizzle down side. Place whipped cream in decorating bag fitted with star tip. Pipe a rosette on each serving. Serve cake with sauce. Garnish with fresh raspberries.

12 servings
1 Serving: Calories 360 (Calories from Fat 190); Total Fat 21g (Saturated 12g; Trans 0.5g); Cholesterol 105mg; Sodium 100mg; Total Carbohydrate 40g (Dietary Fiber 2g; Sugars 31g); Protein 4g
% Daily Value: Vitamin A 10%; Vitamin C 4%; Calcium 2%; Iron 8%
Exchanges: 2 1/2 Other Carbohydrate, 1/2 High-Fat Meat, 3 1/2 Fat
Carbohydrate Choices: 2 1/2

KITCHEN TIPS

❁ Be as creative as you like with the chocolate glaze! Drizzle it over the cake using a fork, or place it in a plastic food-storage bag and squeeze it through a snipped-off corner.

❁ Make your own whipped cream by beating 1/4 cup whipping cream and 1 1/2 teaspoons granulated or powdered sugar in a small chilled bowl until soft peaks form.

Gingerbread with Lemon Sauce and Whipped Cream

Prep Time: 20 min Start to Finish: 1 hr 5 min

Gingerbread

2⅓	cups Gold Medal all-purpose flour
½	cup shortening
⅓	cup granulated sugar
1	cup molasses
¾	cup hot water
1	teaspoon baking soda
1	teaspoon ground ginger
1	teaspoon ground cinnamon
¾	teaspoon salt
1	egg

Lemon Sauce

½	cup granulated sugar
2	tablespoons cornstarch
¾	cup water
1	tablespoon grated lemon peel
¼	cup lemon juice
2	tablespoons butter or margarine

Sweetened Whipped Cream

1	cup whipping cream
2	tablespoons granulated or powdered sugar

1. Heat oven to 325°F. Grease bottom and sides of 9-inch square pan with shortening; lightly flour. In large bowl, beat gingerbread ingredients with electric mixer on low speed 30 seconds, scraping bowl constantly. Beat on medium speed 3 minutes, scraping bowl occasionally. Pour into pan.

2. Bake 50 to 55 minutes or until toothpick inserted in center comes out clean.

3. Meanwhile, in 1-quart saucepan, mix ½ cup granulated sugar and the cornstarch. Gradually stir in ¾ cup water. Cook over medium heat, stirring constantly, until mixture thickens and boils. Boil and stir 1 minute. Remove from heat. Stir in remaining lemon sauce ingredients. Serve warm or cool.

4. In chilled medium bowl, beat sweetened whipped cream ingredients on high speed until soft peaks form. Serve lemon sauce and sweetened whipped cream with warm gingerbread.

9 servings
1 Serving: Calories 540 (Calories from Fat 210); Total Fat 23g (Saturated 10g; Trans 2.5g); Cholesterol 60mg; Sodium 390mg; Total Carbohydrate 77g (Dietary Fiber 1g; Sugars 43g); Protein 5g
% Daily Value: Vitamin A 8%; Vitamin C 2%; Calcium 10%; Iron 20%
Exchanges: 1½ Starch, 3½ Other Carbohydrate, 4½ Fat
Carbohydrate Choices: 5

KITCHEN TIPS

- Instead of making the whipped cream yourself, use purchased whipped cream topping from an aerosol can.
- The Lemon Sauce can be made up to a week ahead of time. Store covered in the refrigerator.

Raspberry-Laced Vanilla Cake

Prep Time: 25 min Start to Finish: 2 hr 5 min

Cake

2²/₃ cups Gold Medal all-purpose flour

3 teaspoons baking powder

¹/₂ teaspoon salt

¹/₄ teaspoon baking soda

1¹/₂ cups butter or margarine, softened

1¹/₄ cups granulated sugar

²/₃ cup milk

1¹/₂ teaspoons vanilla

4 eggs

1 cup seedless raspberry jam

Frosting

1 cup butter or margarine, softened

3 cups powdered sugar

¹/₂ cup raspberry-flavored liqueur or raspberry syrup for pancakes

¹/₂ teaspoon vanilla

Fresh raspberries, if desired

1. Heat oven to 350°F. Grease bottoms and sides of 3 (9-inch) round cake pans with shortening; lightly flour. In small bowl, mix flour, baking powder, salt and baking soda; set aside.

2. In large bowl, beat 1¹/₂ cups butter and the granulated sugar with electric mixer on high speed, scraping bowl occasionally, until fluffy. On medium speed, beat in flour mixture, milk, 1¹/₂ teaspoons vanilla and the eggs until blended. Beat 2 minutes longer. Pour evenly into pans.

3. Bake 25 to 30 minutes or until toothpick inserted in center comes out clean. Cool 10 minutes; remove from pans to cooling racks. Cool completely, about 1 hour.

4. In medium bowl, beat 1 cup butter and the powdered sugar on medium speed until smooth. Gradually add in liqueur and ¹/₂ teaspoon vanilla until smooth and spreadable.

5. Cut each cake horizontally to make 2 layers. (Mark side of cake with toothpicks and cut with long, thin serrated knife.) Place 1 layer, cut side up, on serving plate; spread with ¹/₃ cup raspberry jam to within

¹/₄ inch of edge. Top with another layer, cut side down; spread with ¹/₃ cup frosting. Repeat with remaining layers.

6. Frost side and top of cake with remaining frosting. Garnish with raspberries. Store loosely covered.

12 servings
1 Serving: Calories 760 (Calories from Fat 370); Total Fat 41g (Saturated 25g; Trans 2.5g); Cholesterol 175mg; Sodium 550mg; Total Carbohydrate 92g (Dietary Fiber 1g; Sugars 64g); Protein 6g
% Daily Value: Vitamin A 25%; Vitamin C 0%; Calcium 10%; Iron 10%
Exchanges: 2 Starch, 4 Other Carbohydrate, 8 Fat
Carbohydrate Choices: 6

KITCHEN TIPS

❁ Fresh edible flowers make a beautiful decoration for this cake when raspberries aren't available.

❁ If you own only 2 round cake pans, cover and refrigerate ¹/₂ of the batter while the other two layers bake. Remove the baked cakes from the pans and wash the pan before you bake the last layer.

Red Velvet Torte

Prep Time: 20 min Start to Finish: 2 hr

Cake

1   box Betty Crocker SuperMoist German chocolate cake mix

1¼   cups water

½   cup vegetable oil

1   tablespoon unsweetened baking cocoa

3   eggs

1   bottle (1 ounce) red food color

Frosting

1½   cups white vanilla baking chips

2¼   cups Betty Crocker Rich & Creamy vanilla frosting (from two 1-pound containers)

1. Heat oven to 350°F (325°F for dark or nonstick pans). Spray bottoms only of 2 (8-inch) round cake pans with baking spray with flour. In large bowl, beat all cake ingredients with electric mixer on low speed 30 seconds; beat on medium speed 2 minutes. Pour into pans.

2. Bake as directed on box for two 8-inch rounds. Cool in pans 10 minutes. Remove from pans to cooling racks. Cool completely, about 1 hour. Cut each cake layer horizontally to make 2 layers. (To cut, mark side of cake with toothpicks and cut with long, thin knife.)

3. In medium microwavable bowl, microwave baking chips uncovered on Medium (50%) 4 to 5 minutes, stirring after 2 minutes. Stir until smooth; cool 5 minutes. Stir in frosting until well blended. On serving plate, place 1 cake layer, cut side up; spread with 1 cup of the frosting. Repeat with second and third cake layers. Top with remaining cake layer, cut side down; frost top with remaining frosting.

12 servings

1 Serving: Calories 640 (Calories from Fat 280); Total Fat 32g (Saturated 12g; Trans 4.5g); Cholesterol 55mg; Sodium 520mg; Total Carbohydrate 84g (Dietary Fiber 1g; Sugars 67g); Protein 6g
% Daily Value: Vitamin A 0%; Vitamin C 0%; Calcium 8%; Iron 6%
Exchanges: ½ Starch, 5 Other Carbohydrate, ½ Medium-Fat Meat, 6 Fat
Carbohydrate Choices: 5½

KITCHEN TIPS

✿ Although white frosting is classic for a red velvet cake, you can substitute chocolate chips and chocolate frosting if you prefer. It still tastes wonderful!

✿ Red velvet cake was originally a scratch cake with a cooked butter frosting. This cake has the same great flavor in a fraction of the time.

Chocolate Mousse Raspberry Cake

Prep Time: 25 min Start to Finish: 3 hr 15 min

1 box Betty Crocker SuperMoist devil's food cake mix

Water, vegetable oil and eggs called for on cake mix box

1 cup semisweet chocolate chips (6 ounces)

1½ cups whipping cream

⅓ cup powdered sugar

2 tablespoons seedless raspberry jam

1 container (6 ounces) fresh raspberries

White chocolate truffle candies, if desired

Cocoa, if desired

1. Heat oven to 350°F (325°F for dark or nonstick pan). Spray bottoms and sides of 2 (9- or 8-inch) round cake pans with baking spray with flour. Make cake mix as directed on box, using water, oil and eggs. Pour into pans.

2. Bake 9-inch pans 24 to 29 minutes, 8-inch pans 29 to 34 minutes, or until toothpick inserted in center comes out clean. Cool in pans 10 minutes. Remove from pans to cooling racks. Cool completely, about 1 hour.

3. Meanwhile, in medium microwavable bowl, microwave chocolate chips and ½ cup of the whipping cream uncovered on High 45 to 60 seconds; stir until smooth and melted. Refrigerate 15 to 30 minutes or until cool.

4. In large bowl, beat remaining 1 cup whipping cream and the powdered sugar with electric mixer on high speed until mixture starts to thicken. Add melted chocolate. Beat until stiff peaks form (do not overbeat or mixture will begin to look curdled).

5. On serving plate, place 1 cake layer, rounded side down. Spread raspberry jam over cake layer. Spread ½-inch-thick layer of chocolate mixture over jam. Cut ½ cup of the raspberries in half; press into chocolate mixture. Add other cake layer, rounded side up; press lightly. Frost side and top of cake with remaining chocolate mixture. Refrigerate about 1 hour or until firm. Let stand at room temperature about 10 minutes before serving. Garnish with remaining raspberries and candies. Lightly dust with cocoa. Store in refrigerator.

16 servings

1 Serving: Calories 350 (Calories from Fat 180); Total Fat 20g (Saturated 9g; Trans 0.5g); Cholesterol 65mg; Sodium 280mg; Total Carbohydrate 39g (Dietary Fiber 2g; Sugars 26g); Protein 4g
% Daily Value: Vitamin A 6%; Vitamin C 2%; Calcium 4%; Iron 10%
Exchanges: 1 Starch, 1½ Other Carbohydrate, 4 Fat
Carbohydrate Choices: 2½

KITCHEN TIPS

⊚ Cover the cake with a layer cake storage container so refrigerator odors aren't transferred to the cake.

⊚ Add tall thin candles to transform this special cake into a birthday cake.

Deep Dark Mocha Torte

Prep Time: 50 min Start to Finish: 2 hr 40 min

Torte

1 box Betty Crocker SuperMoist chocolate fudge cake mix

Water, oil and eggs called for on cake mix box

1/3 cup granulated sugar

1/3 cup rum or water

1 1/4 teaspoons instant espresso coffee (dry)

Filling

2 packages (8 ounces each) cream cheese, softened

2 to 3 teaspoons milk

1 cup powdered sugar

1 teaspoon vanilla

Ganache

1 1/2 cups semisweet chocolate chips

6 tablespoons butter (do not use margarine)

1/3 cup whipping (heavy) cream

1. Heat oven to 350°F. Grease bottoms only of two 8- or 9-inch round pans with shortening (do not use cooking spray); lightly flour.

2. In large bowl, beat cake mix, water, oil and eggs with electric mixer on low speed 1 minute, scraping bowl constantly. Pour into pans.

3. Bake 8-inch rounds 33 to 38 minutes, 9-inch rounds 28 to 33 minutes, or until toothpick inserted in center comes out clean. Cool 10 minutes. Run knife around sides of pans to loosen cakes; remove from pans to wire rack. Cool completely, about 1 hour.

4. Meanwhile, in 1-quart saucepan, stir granulated sugar, rum and coffee (dry) until coffee is dissolved. Heat to boiling, stirring occasionally; remove from heat. Cool completely. Continue with next step.

5. In medium bowl, beat all filling ingredients on low speed just until blended, adding enough milk for spreading consistency; set aside. In 1-quart saucepan, heat all ganache ingredients over low heat, stirring frequently, until chips are melted and mixture is smooth. Refrigerate about 30 minutes, stirring occasionally, until slightly thickened.

6. Cut each cake layer horizontally to make 2 layers. (To cut, mark side of cake with toothpicks and cut with long, thin knife.) Brush about 1 tablespoon of the rum mixture over cut side of each layer; let stand 1 minute to soak into cake. Fill each layer with about 2/3 cup filling. Frost side and top of cake with ganache. Store loosely covered in refrigerator.

12 to 16 servings

1 Serving: Calories 650 (Calories from Fat 350); Total Fat 39g (Saturated 18g; Trans 1g); Cholesterol 105mg; Sodium 410mg; Total Carbohydrate 69g (Dietary Fiber 2g; Sugars 47g); Protein 6g % Daily Value: Vitamin A 15%; Vitamin C 0%; Calcium 8%; Iron 10% Exchanges: 2 Starch, 2 1/2 Other Carbohydrate, 7 1/2 Fat Carbohydrate Choices: 4 1/2

KITCHEN TIPS

☻ Garnish cake by piping on sweetened whipped cream and adding chocolate-covered coffee beans.

☻ If ganache becomes too thick to spread, let it stand at room temperature a few minutes and stir to soften.

Deep Dark Mocha Torte

Toffee Butter Torte with Chocolate Ganache Frosting

Prep Time: 25 min Start to Finish: 2 hr 50 min

Cake

1 box Betty Crocker SuperMoist butter recipe yellow cake mix

Water, butter and eggs called for on cake mix box

Frosting

3 cups semisweet chocolate chips

1½ cups whipping cream

1 bag (8 ounces) toffee bits (1½ cups)

Pirouette cookies, if desired

1. Heat oven to 350°F (325°F for dark or nonstick pan). Spray bottoms and sides of 2 (9- or 8-inch) round cake pans with baking spray with flour. Make cake mix as directed on box, using water, butter and eggs. Pour into pans.

2. Bake 9-inch pans 27 to 32 minutes, 8-inch pans 32 to 37 minutes, or until toothpick inserted in center comes out clean. Cool in pans 10 minutes. Remove from pans to cooling racks. Cool completely, about 1 hour.

3. In medium microwavable bowl, microwave chocolate chips and whipping cream uncovered on High 1 minute 30 seconds to 2 minutes 30 seconds, stirring every 30 seconds, until cream is hot. Stir until chocolate is melted and smooth. Refrigerate 30 to 40 minutes or until cool. Stir just until mixture is thick enough to spread but is still glossy.

4. Cut each cake layer horizontally to make 2 layers. (To cut, mark side of cake with toothpicks and cut with long, thin knife.) On serving plate, place 1 layer, rounded side down. Spread with thin layer of frosting; sprinkle with ⅓ cup of the toffee bits. Repeat with 2 more layers. Place remaining layer on top, rounded side up. Frost side and top of cake with remaining frosting. Sprinkle remaining toffee bits on top of cake. Garnish with pirouette cookies.

16 servings

1 Serving: Calories 540 (Calories from Fat 290); Total Fat 32g (Saturated 18g; Trans 1g); Cholesterol 95mg; Sodium 360mg; Total Carbohydrate 59g (Dietary Fiber 2g; Sugars 44g); Protein 4g
% Daily Value: Vitamin A 10%; Vitamin C 0%; Calcium 8%; Iron 10%
Exchanges: 1 Starch, 3 Other Carbohydrate, 6 Fat
Carbohydrate Choices: 4

KITCHEN TIPS

⊛ Use a serrated knife to cut this cake. Wiping the knife clean after each cut helps make neat slices.

⊛ You'll find toffee bits near the chocolate chips in the supermarket.

Pies and Other Desserts

Pies and
Other De

Show-Stopping Confections

Decadent Chocolate Tart (page 319)

Frosted Maple-Apple Pie Dessert (page 325)

Almond Streusel Apple Pie

Prep Time: 30 min Start to Finish: 2 hr 25 min

Pastry

One-Crust Flaky Pastry (page 297)

Filling

1/2	cup granulated sugar
2	tablespoons Gold Medal all-purpose flour
1/2	teaspoon ground cinnamon
1/8	teaspoon salt
1/4	teaspoon almond extract
7	cups thinly sliced peeled apples (about 7 medium)

Streusel

1/2	cup Gold Medal all-purpose flour
1/2	cup packed brown sugar
1/4	cup firm butter or margarine, cut into pieces
1/2	cup sliced almonds

1. Place sheet of foil on oven rack below the rack pie will be baked on to catch any drips. Heat oven to 425°F. Make One-Crust Flaky Pastry. Bake 4 to 5 minutes or until pastry is dry.

2. In large bowl, mix all filling ingredients except apples. Stir in apples until coated. Spoon into partially baked crust.

3. In small bowl, mix all streusel ingredients except almonds with pastry blender or fork until crumbly. Sprinkle over apples.

4. Bake 35 to 45 minutes, covering entire surface of pie with sheet of foil for last 15 to 20 minutes of baking to prevent excessive browning. Bake until apples are tender and juice is bubbly. Sprinkle with almonds. Bake uncovered 2 to 3 minutes longer or until almonds are toasted. Cool completely, about 1 hour.

8 servings
1 Serving: Calories 430 (Calories from Fat 170); Total Fat 19g (Saturated 6g; Trans 2g); Cholesterol 15mg; Sodium 230mg; Total Carbohydrate 61g (Dietary Fiber 3g; Sugars 37g); Protein 4g
% Daily Value: Vitamin A 6%; Vitamin C 4%; Calcium 4%; Iron 10%
Exchanges: 1 Starch, 2 Fruit, 1 Other Carbohydrate, 4 Fat
Carbohydrate Choices: 4

KITCHEN TIPS

✿ The word *streusel* is German for "sprinkle."
✿ A scoop of ice cream goes well with this delicious pie.

One-Crust Flaky Pastry

Prep Time: 20 min Start to Finish: 1 hr 5 min

1 cup Gold Medal all-purpose flour
$\frac{1}{2}$ teaspoon salt
$\frac{1}{3}$ cup plus 1 tablespoon shortening
2 to 3 tablespoons cold water

1. In medium bowl, mix flour and salt. Cut in short-ening, using pastry blender (or pulling 2 table knives through ingredients in opposite directions), until particles are size of small peas. Sprinkle with cold water, 1 tablespoon at a time, tossing with fork until all flour is moistened and pastry almost leaves side of bowl (1 to 2 teaspoons more water can be added if necessary).

2. Gather pastry into a ball. Shape into flattened round on lightly floured surface. Wrap flattened round of pastry in plastic wrap and refrigerate about 45 min-utes or until dough is firm and cold, yet pliable. This allows the shortening to become slightly firm, which helps make the baked pastry flakier. If refrigerated longer, let pastry soften slightly before rolling.

3. Roll pastry on lightly floured surface, using floured rolling pin, into circle 2 inches larger than upside-down 9-inch glass pie plate. Fold pastry into quar-ters; place in pie plate. Unfold and ease into plate, pressing firmly against bottom and side. Trim over-hanging edge of pastry 1 inch from rim of pie plate. Fold and roll pastry under, even with plate; flute as desired.

8 servings
1 Serving: Calories 150 (Calories from Fat 90); Total Fat 10g (Saturated 2.5g; Trans 1.5g); Cholesterol 0mg; Sodium 150mg; Total Carbohydrate 12g (Dietary Fiber 0g; Sugars 0g); Protein 2g
% Daily Value: Vitamin A 0%; Vitamin C 0%; Calcium 0%; Iron 4%
Exchanges: 1 Other Carbohydrate, 2 Fat
Carbohydrate Choices: 1

KITCHEN TIPS

✿ For the best results, roll pastry from the center to the outside edge in all directions.
✿ Easy does it. If you overwork pastry, it'll get tough.

Apple, Pear and Cranberry Pie

Prep Time: 30 min Start to Finish: 1 hr 40 min

Crust

 1 refrigerated pie crust (from 15-ounce box), softened as directed on box

Filling

 ³⁄₄ cup sugar
 2 tablespoons cornstarch
 1 teaspoon ground cinnamon
 ¹⁄₂ teaspoon ground nutmeg
 3 cups thinly sliced peeled tart apples
 3 cups thinly sliced peeled ripe pears
 ¹⁄₂ cup sweetened dried cranberries

Topping

 ¹⁄₂ cup Gold Medal all-purpose flour
 ¹⁄₄ cup packed brown sugar
 ¹⁄₄ cup cold butter
 ¹⁄₂ cup coarsely chopped walnuts

1. Heat oven to 400°F. Place pie crust in 9-inch glass pie plate as directed on box for One-Crust Filled Pie.

2. In large bowl, mix sugar, cornstarch, cinnamon and nutmeg. Gently stir in apples, pears and dried cran-berries. Pour filling into crust-lined pie plate.

3. In small bowl, mix topping ingredients until crumbly; sprinkle over filling.

4. Line 15 × 10-inch pan with foil; place on oven rack below the rack pie will be baked on to catch any spillover. Loosely cover pie with sheet of foil; bake 1 hour. Uncover; bake 10 minutes longer or until apples are tender and topping is golden brown.

8 servings
1 Serving: Calories 440 (Calories from Fat 160); Total Fat 18g (Saturated 7g; Trans 0g); Cholesterol 20mg; Sodium 150mg; Total Carbohydrate 69g (Dietary Fiber 4g; Sugars 41g); Protein 2g
% Daily Value: Vitamin A 4%; Vitamin C 4%; Calcium 2%; Iron 6%
Exchanges: 1 Starch, ¹⁄₂ Fruit, 3 Other Carbohydrate, 3¹⁄₂ Fat
Carbohydrate Choices: 4¹⁄₂

KITCHEN TIPS

❂ Ripe Anjou or Bosc pears work well for pies; choose fruit that is fragrant and slightly soft to the touch.
❂ Serve this pie warm with a scoop of vanilla bean ice cream drizzled with caramel sauce.

Apple-Cherry Cobbler Pie

Prep Time: 30 min Start to Finish: 2 hr 30 min

Pastry

One-Crust Flaky Pastry (page 297)

Filling

$^1/_2$ cup sugar

$^1/_4$ cup cornstarch

$^1/_2$ teaspoon ground cinnamon

$^1/_4$ teaspoon almond extract

5 cups thinly sliced peeled tart apples

1 can (14.5 ounces) tart red cherries, well drained

Topping

1 cup Gold Medal all-purpose flour

$^3/_4$ cup sugar

$^1/_3$ cup butter or margarine

$^1/_2$ teaspoon almond extract

1 egg

1. Place sheet of foil on oven rack below the rack pie will be baked on to catch any drips. Heat oven to 375°F. Make One-Crust Flaky Pastry.

2. In large bowl, mix all filling ingredients until fruit is coated. Spoon into pastry-lined pie plate.

3. In medium bowl, mix flour and $^3/_4$ cup sugar. Using pastry blender or fork, cut butter into flour mixture until coarse crumbs form. Stir in almond extract and egg. Spoon topping over filling.

4. Bake pie uncovered 20 minutes or until topping and crust begin to brown. Cover entire surface of pie with another sheet of foil to prevent overbrowning; bake 30 to 40 minutes longer or until topping is golden brown. Cool completely, about 1 hour.

8 servings

1 Serving: Calories 480 (Calories from Fat 170); Total Fat 19g (Saturated 8g; Trans 2g); Cholesterol 45mg; Sodium 210mg; Total Carbohydrate 74g (Dietary Fiber 3g; Sugars 43g); Protein 5g
% Daily Value: Vitamin A 6%; Vitamin C 4%; Calcium 2%; Iron 10%
Exchanges: $1^1/_2$ Starch, $^1/_2$ Fruit, 3 Other Carbohydrate, $3^1/_2$ Fat
Carbohydrate Choices: 5

KITCHEN TIPS

❀ The almond extract in the pie filling and topping complements the tart cherries.

❀ Tart apples, such as Granny Smith, McIntosh and Pippin, make the most flavorful pies.

Sour Cream–Pear Fold-Over Pie

Prep Time: 30 min Start to Finish: 1 hr 35 min

Filling

- ²⁄₃ cup sugar
- ½ cup sour cream
- ½ cup golden or dark raisins
- ⅓ cup Gold Medal all-purpose flour
- 1 teaspoon ground cinnamon
- 3 large pears, peeled, cut into ½-inch-thick slices (about 4 cups)

Pastry

One-Crust Flaky Pastry (page 297)

Topping

- ¼ cup coarsely chopped walnuts
- 1 to 2 tablespoons milk, if desired
- 1 tablespoon sugar, if desired

1. Heat oven to 425°F. In large bowl, mix all filling ingredients except pears. Fold in pears; set aside.

2. Make One-Crust Flaky Pastry—except roll into 13-inch circle. Place on ungreased large cookie sheet.

3. Mound filling on center of pastry to within 3 inches of edge. Sprinkle walnuts over filling. Fold edge of pastry over filling, overlapping to make about 12 pleats and leaving 6-inch circle of filling showing in center. Brush milk over pastry; sprinkle with 1 tablespoon sugar.

4. Bake 30 to 35 minutes or until crust is golden brown, covering crust with foil for the last 10 to 15 minutes of baking to prevent excessive browning. Cool 30 minutes. Cut pie into wedges. Serve warm.

8 servings
1 Serving: Calories 370 (Calories from Fat 140); Total Fat 16g (Saturated 4.5g; Trans 2g); Cholesterol 10mg; Sodium 160mg; Total Carbohydrate 54g (Dietary Fiber 4g; Sugars 31g); Protein 4g % Daily Value: Vitamin A 2%; Vitamin C 4%; Calcium 4%; Iron 8% Exchanges: 1 Starch, ½ Fruit, 2 Other Carbohydrate, 3 Fat Carbohydrate Choices: 3½

KITCHEN TIPS

✪ Because this recipe calls for ripe pears, it requires a bit of planning. Store-bought pears may take up to 1 week to ripen.

✪ For a holiday twist, use sweetened dried cranberries instead of raisins in this recipe.

Maple-Pecan Pie

Prep Time: 15 min Start to Finish: 1 hr 30 min

1 Pillsbury refrigerated pie crust (from 15-ounce box), softened as directed on box

⅔ cup sugar

⅓ cup butter or margarine, melted

1 cup real maple or maple-flavored syrup

½ teaspoon salt

3 eggs

1 cup pecan halves

¼ cup semisweet chocolate chips

1 teaspoon shortening

1. Heat oven to 375°F. Place pie crust in 9-inch glass pie plate as directed on box for One-Crust Filled Pie.

2. In medium bowl, beat sugar, butter, syrup, salt and eggs with hand beater or wire whisk until smooth. Stir in pecans. Pour into crust-lined pie plate.

3. Bake 15 minutes. Cover crust edge with 2- to 3-inch-wide strips of foil to prevent excessive browning. Bake 25 to 35 minutes longer or until filling is set. Cool 15 minutes.

4. In small microwavable bowl, microwave chocolate chips and shortening uncovered on High 1 minute. Stir until smooth; drizzle over top of pie. Serve pie warm or cool. Store pie covered in refrigerator.

8 servings
1 Serving: Calories 510 (Calories from Fat 250); Total Fat 28g (Saturated 10g; Trans 0.5g); Cholesterol 105mg; Sodium 340mg; Total Carbohydrate 62g (Dietary Fiber 2g; Sugars 44g); Protein 4g
% Daily Value: Vitamin A 8%; Vitamin C 0%; Calcium 4%; Iron 6%
Exchanges: 4 Other Carbohydrate, ½ High-Fat Meat, 5 Fat
Carbohydrate Choices: 4

KITCHEN TIPS

✿ Use dark-colored real maple syrup to get the most maple flavor.

✿ Serve pie with whipped cream.

Toffee Apple Turnover Pie

Prep Time: 40 min Start to Finish: 1 hr 50 min

Pastry

1	cup Gold Medal all-purpose flour
1/4	teaspoon salt
1/3	cup plus 1 tablespoon shortening
2	to 3 tablespoons cold water

Filling

1 1/2	cups sliced peeled apples (2 small)
1	tablespoon Gold Medal all-purpose flour
1/2	cup toffee bits (from 10-ounce bag)
1	egg, beaten
1	tablespoon coarse white sparkling sugar

1. Heat oven to 375°F. Line cookie sheet with sides or 15 × 10 × 1-inch pan with cooking parchment paper or foil. In medium bowl, mix 1 cup flour and the salt. Using pastry blender (or pulling 2 table knives through ingredients in opposite directions), cut in shortening until particles are size of small peas. Sprinkle with cold water, 1 tablespoon at a time, tossing with fork until all flour is moistened and pastry almost leaves side of bowl (if necessary, 1 to 2 teaspoons more water can be added).

2. Gather pastry into a ball. On lightly floured surface, shape pastry into flattened round. Using rolling pin, roll into 12-inch round, about 1/8 inch thick. Place on cookie sheet.

3. In medium bowl, toss apples and 1 tablespoon flour. Mound apple mixture on half of pastry to within 3/4 inch of edge. Sprinkle with toffee bits. Fold pastry in half over apple mixture. Fold 1/2 inch of sealed edge of pastry over; firmly press tines of fork around edge to seal. Brush top of turnover with egg. Cut 3 slits, 1 inch long, in top to vent steam. Sprinkle top with sugar.

4. Bake 30 to 40 minutes or until golden brown. Immediately remove from cookie sheet to serving plate. Cool 30 minutes before cutting.

4 servings

1. Food Processor Directions for Making Pastry: Into small bowl, measure 2 tablespoons water. In food processor, place shortening, flour and salt. Cover; process with on-and-off pulses until mixture is crumbly. With food processor running, pour water all at once through feed tube, processing just until dough leaves side of bowl (dough should not form a ball).

1 Serving: Calories 500 (Calories from Fat 280); Total Fat 31g (Saturated 11g; Trans 3.5g); Cholesterol 75mg; Sodium 280mg; Total Carbohydrate 50g (Dietary Fiber 2g; Sugars 24g); Protein 5g % Daily Value: Vitamin A 0%; Vitamin C 0%; Calcium 0%; Iron 10% Exchanges: 1 Starch, 2 1/2 Other Carbohydrate, 6 Fat Carbohydrate Choices: 3

KITCHEN TIPS

❁ To ramp up the indulgence factor, drizzle the turnover pie with caramel topping and serve the wedges with a scoop of vanilla ice cream.

❁ For a richer-tasting crust, use 3 tablespoons each butter and shortening instead of just shortening.

Toffee Apple Turnover Pie

Brown Sugar-Pumpkin Pie with Caramel Whipped Cream

Prep Time: 25 min Start to Finish: 5 hr 55 min

Pastry

One-Crust Flaky Pastry (page 297)

Filling

3	eggs
¾	cup packed dark brown sugar
¾	cup whipping cream
1	teaspoon ground cinnamon
½	teaspoon ground ginger
¼	teaspoon ground allspice
1	can (15 ounces) pumpkin (not pumpkin pie mix)

Topping

½	cup whipping cream, whipped
¼	cup caramel topping

1. Heat oven to 425°F. Make One-Crust Flaky Pastry.

2. In large bowl, beat eggs slightly with wire whisk or hand beater. Beat in remaining filling ingredients until smooth.

3. Cover edge of pie crust with 2- to 3-inch strips of foil to prevent excessive browning; remove foil for last 15 minutes of baking. To prevent spilling filling, place pastry-lined pie plate on oven rack. Pour filling into pie plate. Bake pie 15 minutes.

4. Reduce oven temperature to 350°F. Bake about 45 minutes longer or until knife inserted in center comes out clean. Cool on cooling rack 30 minutes. Refrigerate until chilled, about 4 hours. Serve pie topped with whipped cream and drizzle with caramel topping.

8 servings
1 Serving: Calories 420 (Calories from Fat 220); Total Fat 24g (Saturated 10g; Trans 2g); Cholesterol 120mg; Sodium 230mg; Total Carbohydrate 45g (Dietary Fiber 2g; Sugars 28g); Protein 6g
% Daily Value: Vitamin A 180%; Vitamin C 2%; Calcium 8%; Iron 10%
Exchanges: 2 Starch, 1 Other Carbohydrate, 4½ Fat
Carbohydrate Choices: 3

KITCHEN TIPS

✿ To get a head start on this recipe, beat the whipping cream up to 2 hours ahead and store in the refrigerator until serving.

✿ After refrigerating the pastry, make sure to give it time to become soft and pliable. Pastry that is too cold will crack, making it difficult to flute the crust.

Streusel-Topped Pumpkin Pie

Prep Time: 20 min Start to Finish: 5 hr 50 min

Crust

1 Pillsbury refrigerated pie crust (from 15-ounce box), softened as directed on box

Filling

2 eggs, beaten

$1/2$ cup granulated sugar

1 can (15 ounces) pumpkin (not pumpkin pie mix)

1 can (12 ounces) evaporated milk

1 teaspoon ground cinnamon

$1/2$ teaspoon salt

$1/2$ teaspoon ground ginger

$1/8$ teaspoon ground cloves

Topping

$1/2$ cup quick-cooking oats

$1/2$ cup packed brown sugar

$1/4$ cup butter or margarine, softened

1. Heat oven to 425°F. Place pie crust in 9-inch glass pie plate as directed on box for One-Crust Filled Pie.

2. In large bowl, beat all filling ingredients with hand beater or wire whisk until blended. Pour filling into pie crust-lined pie plate.

3. Bake 15 minutes. Remove pie from oven; reduce oven temperature to 350°F. Cover crust edge with 2- to 3-inch-wide strips of foil to prevent excessive browning. Bake 35 minutes. Meanwhile, in small bowl, mix topping ingredients with fork until crumbly; set aside.

4. Sprinkle topping over pie. Bake about 10 minutes longer or until knife inserted in center comes out clean. Cool on cooling rack 30 minutes. Refrigerate about 4 hours or until chilled before serving. Store pie covered in refrigerator.

8 servings
1 Serving: Calories 380 (Calories from Fat 150); Total Fat 16g (Saturated 8g; Trans 0g); Cholesterol 80mg; Sodium 370mg; Total Carbohydrate 52g (Dietary Fiber 2g; Sugars 32g); Protein 6g
% Daily Value: Vitamin A 180%; Vitamin C 2%; Calcium 15%; Iron 10%
Exchanges: $1^{1}/2$ Starch, 2 Other Carbohydrate, 3 Fat
Carbohydrate Choices: $3^{1}/2$

KITCHEN TIPS

● Serve with whipped cream or vanilla ice cream.
● This traditional pumpkin pie is made easy with a refrigerated pie crust, but it now has a delicious brown sugar and oats topping.

Macadamia Nut-Banana Cream Pie

Prep Time: 40 min Start to Finish: 3 hr 15 min

Crust

1¼	cups Gold Medal all-purpose flour
½	cup macadamia nuts, finely chopped
⅓	cup butter or margarine, softened
2	tablespoons granulated sugar
½	teaspoon vanilla
1	egg, beaten

Filling

⅔	cup granulated sugar
¼	cup cornstarch
½	teaspoon salt
3	cups whole milk
4	egg yolks
2	tablespoons butter or margarine
1	tablespoon vanilla
2	large bananas, sliced

Topping

1	cup whipping cream
2	tablespoons powdered or granulated sugar
½	cup macadamia nuts, coarsely chopped, toasted

1. In medium bowl, beat all crust ingredients with electric mixer on low speed about 1 minute or just until blended. Press mixture on bottom and up side of ungreased 9-inch glass pie plate; prick mixture with fork. Refrigerate 30 minutes while preparing filling.

2. In 2-quart saucepan, mix ⅔ cup sugar, the cornstarch and salt. In large bowl, beat milk and egg yolks with wire whisk until blended; gradually stir into sugar mixture. Cook over medium-low heat about 15 minutes, stirring constantly, until mixture thickens and boils. Boil 2 minutes, beating constantly with wire whisk; remove from heat. Beat in 2 tablespoons butter and 1 tablespoon vanilla. Press plastic wrap on filling to prevent a tough layer from forming. Cool at room temperature while baking crust.

3. Heat oven to 400°F. Bake crust 16 to 18 minutes or until edge is golden brown. Cool at room temperature 15 minutes. Place banana slices on pie crust. Stir filling well; pour filling over bananas. Press plastic wrap on filling; refrigerate at least 2 hours until thoroughly chilled.

4. In chilled small bowl, beat whipping cream and 2 tablespoons sugar on high speed until soft peaks form; spread over top of pie. Sprinkle with toasted nuts.

8 servings

1 Serving: Calories 590 (Calories from Fat 330); Total Fat 36g (Saturated 17g; Trans 1g); Cholesterol 200mg; Sodium 320mg; Total Carbohydrate 55g (Dietary Fiber 3g; Sugars 32g); Protein 9g
% Daily Value: Vitamin A 20%; Vitamin C 2%; Calcium 15%; Iron 10%
Exchanges: 1½ Starch, 2 Other Carbohydrate, ½ High-Fat Meat, 6½ Fat
Carbohydrate Choices: 3½

KITCHEN TIPS

❀ Pecans or walnuts can be substituted for the macadamia nuts.

❀ For a chocolate version of this pie, add 2 ounces unsweetened baking chocolate to the filling with the milk and egg yolks.

❀ To toast nuts, bake uncovered in ungreased shallow pan in 350°F oven 6 to 10 minutes, stirring occasionally, until golden brown.

Quick

Pecan Pie

Prep Time: 20 min Start to Finish: 3 hr 10 min

One-Crust Flaky Pastry (page 297)

$^2/_3$ cup sugar

$^1/_3$ cup butter or margarine, melted

1 cup corn syrup

$^1/_2$ teaspoon salt

3 eggs

1 cup pecan halves or broken pecans

1. Heat oven to 375°F. Make One-Crust Flaky Pastry.

2. In medium bowl, beat all remaining ingredients except pecans with wire whisk or hand beater until well blended. Stir in pecans. Pour into pastry-lined pie plate.

3. Cover edge of pastry with 2- to 3-inch strips of foil to prevent excessive browning; remove foil for last 15 minutes of baking. Bake 40 to 50 minutes or until center is set. Cool completely on cooling rack, about 2 hours.

8 servings

1 Serving: Calories 530 (Calories from Fat 260); Total Fat 29g (Saturated 8g; Trans 2g); Cholesterol 100mg; Sodium 420mg; Total Carbohydrate 62g (Dietary Fiber 2g; Sugars 33g); Protein 5g
% Daily Value: Vitamin A 8%; Vitamin C 0%; Calcium 2%; Iron 8%
Exchanges: 2 Starch, 2 Other Carbohydrate, 5$^1/_2$ Fat
Carbohydrate Choices: 4

KITCHEN TIPS

❀ For Kentucky Pecan Pie, add 2 tablespoons bourbon with the corn syrup. Stir in 1 cup (6 ounces) semisweet chocolate chips with the pecans.

❀ To make ahead, cool pie completely after baking. Freeze uncovered at least 3 hours. Wrap tightly and freeze up to 1 month. Before serving, unwrap pie and thaw in refrigerator 20 minutes.

Chocolate Truffle Pie

Prep Time: 25 min Start to Finish: 3 hr 25 min

Crust

1¼ cups chocolate cookie crumbs

¼ cup butter or margarine, melted

Filling

1 bag (12 ounces) semisweet chocolate chips (2 cups)

½ pint (1 cup) whipping cream

1 teaspoon vanilla

2 egg yolks

Topping

½ cup whipping cream

1 tablespoon powdered sugar

Unsweetened baking cocoa, if desired

1. In small bowl, mix cookie crumbs and butter. In ungreased 9-inch glass pie plate, press crumb mixture in bottom and 1 inch up side.

2. In double boiler set over hot simmering water, heat chocolate chips 2 to 3 minutes, stirring frequently, until melted and smooth. Gradually add 1 cup whipping cream, stirring constantly, until combined. Stir in vanilla and egg yolks until well blended. Cook over medium-low heat 5 to 6 minutes, stirring frequently, until thickened and hot. Pour filling into crust. Refrigerate at least 3 hours or until firm.

3. In medium bowl, beat ½ cup whipping cream and the powdered sugar with electric mixer on high speed 1 to 2 minutes or until soft peaks form. Top individual servings with whipped cream. Dust with cocoa.

12 servings

1 Serving: Calories 350 (Calories from Fat 220); Total Fat 24g (Saturated 14g; Trans 1g); Cholesterol 80mg; Sodium 125mg; Total Carbohydrate 30g (Dietary Fiber 2g; Sugars 21g); Protein 3g
% Daily Value: Vitamin A 10%; Vitamin C 0%; Calcium 4%; Iron 8%
Exchanges: 2 Other Carbohydrate, ½ High-Fat Meat, 4 Fat
Carbohydrate Choices: 2

KITCHEN TIPS

⚙ Don't own a double boiler? Place a small saucepan in a larger skillet or saucepan filled with 1 to 2 inches of simmering water.

⚙ To evenly press the crumb mixture into the pie plate, use the bottom of a dry measuring cup.

Tart Red-Fruit Crisp

Prep Time: 20 min Start to Finish: 55 min

Fruit Mixture

- 1 can (14.5 ounces) tart red cherries, drained, reserving juice
- $2/3$ cup granulated sugar
- $1/4$ cup cornstarch
- $1/2$ teaspoon ground cinnamon
- 2 cups fresh or frozen raspberries
- 1 cup fresh cranberries

Topping

- $1/2$ cup Gold Medal all-purpose flour
- $1/2$ cup old-fashioned oats
- $1/2$ cup packed brown sugar
- $1/4$ teaspoon ground cinnamon
- $1/4$ cup butter or margarine, cut into pieces

1. Heat oven to 375°F. Grease bottom and sides of 8-inch square (2-quart) glass baking dish with shortening.

2. In 3-quart saucepan, mix reserved juice from cherries, the granulated sugar, cornstarch and $1/2$ teaspoon cinnamon. Cook over medium heat, stirring con-stantly, until mixture is bubbly and thickened. Gently stir in cherries, raspberries and cranberries. Spoon into baking dish.

3. In medium bowl, mix all topping ingredients until crumbly; sprinkle over fruit mixture.

4. Bake 30 to 35 minutes or until topping is golden brown and fruit mixture is bubbly.

8 servings ($1/2$ cup each)
1 Serving: Calories 280 (Calories from Fat 60); Total Fat 6g (Saturated 3.5g; Trans 0g); Cholesterol 15mg; Sodium 50mg; Total Carbohydrate 54g (Dietary Fiber 4g; Sugars 37g); Protein 3g
% Daily Value: Vitamin A 4%; Vitamin C 10%; Calcium 4%; Iron 8%
Exchanges: 1 Starch, $1/2$ Fruit, 2 Other Carbohydrate, 1 Fat
Carbohydrate Choices: $3^1/2$

KITCHEN TIPS

✿ You can use a 2-quart heatproof glass or ceramic casserole dish to make this crisp.

✿ Crisps and cobblers are best served the same day you make them. The topping can be made a day ahead; just store it in the refrigerator.

Strawberry-Topped Orange Cream Pie

Prep Time: 10 min Start to Finish: 1 hr 10 min

- 1 box (4-serving size) white chocolate instant pudding and pie filling mix
- ¾ cup fat-free (skim) milk
- 1 teaspoon grated orange peel
- 1½ cups frozen (thawed) fat-free whipped topping
- 1 graham cracker crumb crust (6 ounces)
- 1½ cups quartered fresh strawberries

1. In medium bowl, beat pudding mix, milk and orange peel with wire whisk or electric mixer 1 minute. With rubber spatula, fold in whipped topping. Pour into crust.

2. Arrange strawberries on filling. Refrigerate at least 1 hour or until set before serving.

8 servings
1 Serving: Calories 200 (Calories from Fat 70); Total Fat 8g (Saturated 2g; Trans 2g); Cholesterol 0mg; Sodium 260mg; Total Carbohydrate 31g (Dietary Fiber 1g; Sugars 21g); Protein 2g
% Daily Value: Vitamin A 0%; Vitamin C 30%; Calcium 4%; Iron 4%
Exchanges: ½ Starch, 1½ Other Carbohydrate, 1½ Fat
Carbohydrate Choices: 2

KITCHEN TIPS

✪ To garnish, sprinkle grated orange peel around the edges of dessert plates and place small strawberry halves, cut sides down, around each plate.

✪ Mix things up by topping the pie with any fresh fruit. Try 1½ cups blueberries or raspberries or a mixture of both.

No-Bake Lime Chiffon Pie

Prep Time: 20 min Start to Finish: 2 hr 20 min

- ⅓ cup lime juice
- 1 envelope unflavored gelatin (2 teaspoons)
- 1 teaspoon grated lime peel
- ½ cup fat-free sweetened condensed milk (from 14-ounce can)
- 2 drops green food color, if desired
- 1 drop yellow food color, if desired
- 4 cups frozen (thawed) fat-free whipped topping (from 12-ounce container)
- 1 graham cracker crumb crust (6 ounces)
- 2 thin lime slices, cut into quarters, if desired

1. In 1-quart saucepan, place lime juice; sprinkle with gelatin. Let stand 1 minute to soften. Heat over medium heat about 2 minutes, stirring occasionally, until gelatin is dissolved. Remove from heat; cool slightly. Stir in lime peel.

2. In medium bowl, mix condensed milk and food colors. Stir in lime juice mixture. Using rubber spatula, fold in all but ¼ cup of the whipped topping. Spread in pie crust, smoothing top. Cover; refrigerate at least 2 hours or until firm.

3. Before serving, garnish pie with remaining ¼ cup whipped topping and lime slices.

8 servings
1 Serving: Calories 230 (Calories from Fat 70); Total Fat 8g (Saturated 2.5g; Trans 2g); Cholesterol 0mg; Sodium 105mg; Total Carbohydrate 37g (Dietary Fiber 0g; Sugars 27g); Protein 3g
% Daily Value: Vitamin A 0%; Vitamin C 4%; Calcium 6%; Iron 0%
Exchanges: ½ Starch, 2 Other Carbohydrate, 1½ Fat
Carbohydrate Choices: 2½

KITCHEN TIPS

✪ To keep this pie picture-perfect, use the plastic cover that came with the crust as a protective cover; just turn it upside down over the pie.

✪ You can store this creamy pie for up to a week in the refrigerator.

Strawberry-Topped Orange Cream Pie

No-Bake Lime Chiffon Pie

Raspberry-Pear-Granola Crisp

Prep Time: 25 min Start to Finish: 1 hr 30 min

- 5 cups sliced peeled pears (5 to 6 pears)
- 1 bag (12 ounces) frozen raspberries, thawed
- 1 cup granulated sugar
- ¼ cup Gold Medal all-purpose flour
- 6 Nature Valley roasted almond crunchy granola bars (3 pouches from 8.9-ounce box), finely crushed
- ½ cup Gold Medal all-purpose flour
- ¼ cup packed brown sugar
- ¼ cup butter or margarine, melted

1. Heat oven to 350°F. Spray 8-inch square (2-quart) glass baking dish with cooking spray. In large bowl, mix pears, raspberries, granulated sugar and ¼ cup flour. Spoon evenly into baking dish.

2. In medium bowl, mix crushed granola bars, ½ cup flour, the brown sugar and butter until crumbly. Sprinkle over pear mixture.

3. Bake 55 to 65 minutes or until top is golden brown and fruit is tender (mixture will be bubbly). Cool slightly. Serve warm or cool.

9 servings
1 Serving: Calories 340 (Calories from Fat 70); Total Fat 8g (Saturated 3.5g; Trans 0g); Cholesterol 15mg; Sodium 95mg; Total Carbohydrate 64g (Dietary Fiber 6g; Sugars 43g); Protein 3g
% Daily Value: Vitamin A 4%; Vitamin C 10%; Calcium 4%; Iron 8%
Exchanges: 1 Starch, ½ Fruit, 2½ Other Carbohydrate, 1½ Fat
Carbohydrate Choices: 4

KITCHEN TIPS

❁ Serve with whipped cream or vanilla ice cream.
❁ If your pears are not quite ripe, let them stand at room temperature for 1 to 2 days.
❁ Use the flat side of a meat mallet to crush the granola bars right in their pouches.

Peachy Pear-Coconut Crumble

Prep Time: 20 min Start to Finish: 1 hr 5 min

1 cup Gold Medal all-purpose flour

¾ cup sugar

¼ cup butter or margarine, softened

1 egg, beaten

1 can (29 ounces) sliced peaches in heavy syrup, drained and ½ cup syrup reserved

1 can (29 ounces) sliced pears in syrup, drained and ½ cup syrup reserved

3 tablespoons cornstarch

½ teaspoon almond extract

½ cup maraschino cherries, cut in half and drained

¼ cup flaked coconut

1. Heat oven to 400°F. In medium bowl, mix flour and sugar. Cut in butter, using pastry blender or fork, until crumbly. Stir in egg; set aside.

2. In 1-quart saucepan, mix reserved peach and pear syrups and the cornstarch. Cook over medium heat, stirring constantly, until mixture boils and thickens. Stir in almond extract.

3. In ungreased 12 × 8- or 11 × 7-inch glass baking dish, mix peaches, pears and cherries. Stir in syrup mixture. Crumble and spoon flour mixture over fruit mixture.

4. Bake 40 to 45 minutes, sprinkling with coconut for last 10 minutes of baking, until topping is deep golden brown and fruit is bubbly.

10 servings
1 Serving: Calories 360 (Calories from Fat 60); Total Fat 6g (Saturated 3g; Trans 0g); Cholesterol 35mg; Sodium 50mg; Total Carbohydrate 74g (Dietary Fiber 3g; Sugars 56g); Protein 3g
% Daily Value: Vitamin A 10%; Vitamin C 2%; Calcium 0%; Iron 6%
Exchanges: 1 Starch, 2 Fruit, 2 Other Carbohydrate, 1 Fat
Carbohydrate Choices: 5

KITCHEN TIPS

❂ A crumble is a British dessert in which fruit is topped with a crumbly pastry mixture and baked.

❂ Spoon into stemmed dessert cups for a beautiful presentation.

Quick Peach Cobbler

www.bettycrocker.com

Quick Peach Cobbler

Prep Time: 10 min Start to Finish: 35 min

1 can (21 ounces) peach pie filling
2 cups frozen peach slices, thawed
1 cup Original Bisquick mix
1 tablespoon sugar
¼ cup milk
1 tablespoon butter or margarine, softened
   Additional sugar, if desired
   Ground nutmeg, if desired

6 servings
1 Serving: Calories 250 (Calories from Fat 45); Total Fat 5g (Saturated 2g; Trans 0.5g); Cholesterol 5mg; Sodium 270mg; Total Carbohydrate 47g (Dietary Fiber 2g; Sugars 31g); Protein 2g
% Daily Value: Vitamin A 10%; Vitamin C 70%; Calcium 4%; Iron 6%
Exchanges: ½ Starch, ½ Fruit, 2 Other Carbohydrate, 1 Fat
Carbohydrate Choices: 3

KITCHEN TIPS

✿ Heating the pie filling before adding the biscuit topping ensures that the dough bakes through completely.
✿ Multitask—heat the pie filling while the oven heats to the right temperature.

1. In ungreased 8-inch square pan, spread pie filling and peach slices; place in cold oven. Heat oven to 400°F; let pie filling heat 10 minutes.

2. Meanwhile, mix Bisquick, 1 tablespoon sugar, the milk and butter with fork until soft dough forms.

3. Remove pan from oven. Drop dough onto warm peach mixture. Sprinkle with additional sugar and nutmeg.

4. Bake 18 to 20 minutes or until topping is light brown.

Chocolate Mousse Brownie Dessert

Prep Time: 15 min Start to Finish: 2 hr 20 min

1 box Betty Crocker Original Supreme brownie mix (with chocolate syrup pouch)

⅓ cup water

⅓ cup vegetable oil

2 eggs

¾ cup whipping cream

1 cup semisweet chocolate chips (6 ounces)

3 eggs

⅓ cup sugar

1. Heat oven to 350°F. Grease bottom only of 10-inch springform pan with shortening. Make brownie mix as directed on box, using water, oil and 2 eggs. Spread in pan.

2. In 2-quart saucepan, heat whipping cream and chocolate chips over medium heat, stirring constantly, until chocolate is melted and mixture is smooth; cool slightly.

3. In small bowl, beat 3 eggs and sugar with electric mixer on medium speed until foamy; stir into chocolate mixture. Pour evenly over batter.

4. Bake about 1 hour 5 minutes or until topping is set. Cool completely, about 1 hour. Run metal spatula around side of dessert to loosen; remove side of pan. Serve at room temperature, or cover tightly and refrigerate until chilled.

12 to 16 servings

1 Serving: Calories 440 (Calories from Fat 180); Total Fat 20g (Saturated 8g; Trans 1g); Cholesterol 105mg; Sodium 210mg; Total Carbohydrate 60g (Dietary Fiber 2g; Sugars 45g); Protein 5g % Daily Value: Vitamin A 6%; Vitamin C 0%; Calcium 6%; Iron 15% Exchanges: 1 Starch, 3 Other Carbohydrate, 4 Fat Carbohydrate Choices: 4

KITCHEN TIPS

✿ Top with whipped cream and, if desired, chocolate decorations or shavings.

Frozen Cinnamon Chocolate Dessert

Prep Time: 15 min Start to Finish: 2 hr 40 min

Dessert

- 1 cup chocolate wafer cookie crumbs (about 20 cookies)
- 1/4 cup butter or margarine, melted
- 1 quart (4 cups) cinnamon, vanilla or chocolate ice cream, slightly softened

Sauce

- 1/2 cup whipping cream
- 1/4 cup sugar
- 1 ounce unsweetened baking chocolate, chopped
- 1/2 teaspoon ground cinnamon

1. In small bowl, mix cookie crumbs and butter. Press in bottom of ungreased 8-inch springform pan. Freeze 10 minutes.

2. Spoon ice cream onto crumb crust; smooth top. Cover and freeze about 2 hours or until firm.

3. In 1-quart saucepan, heat whipping cream, sugar and chocolate to boiling over medium heat, stirring constantly. Boil and stir about 30 seconds or until chocolate is melted; remove from heat. Stir in cinnamon. Continue stirring 3 to 4 minutes or until thoroughly mixed, glossy and slightly thickened.

4. Remove dessert from freezer 15 minutes before serving. Run metal spatula around side of dessert to loosen; remove side of pan. Serve dessert with warm or cool sauce. Store dessert covered in freezer.

8 servings
1 Serving: Calories 360 (Calories from Fat 200); Total Fat 22g (Saturated 13g; Trans 1g); Cholesterol 65mg; Sodium 190mg; Total Carbohydrate 35g (Dietary Fiber 2g; Sugars 23g); Protein 4g
% Daily Value: Vitamin A 15%; Vitamin C 0%; Calcium 10%; Iron 8%
Exchanges: 1 Starch, 1 1/2 Other Carbohydrate, 4 Fat
Carbohydrate Choices: 2

KITCHEN TIPS

- For an alternative to the chocolate sauce, heat 1 cup caramel topping and 1/2 teaspoon ground cinnamon until warm.
- Save a bit of time by purchasing a premade chocolate cookie crumb crust and omitting step 1.

Lemon Crème Brûlée

Prep Time: 30 min Start to Finish: 6 hr

6 egg yolks
2 cups whipping cream
$1/3$ cup sugar
1 teaspoon vanilla
1 tablespoon grated lemon peel
Boiling water
8 teaspoons sugar
$1/2$ cup fresh raspberries

1. Heat oven to 350°F. In small bowl, slightly beat egg yolks with wire whisk. In large bowl, stir whipping cream, $1/3$ cup sugar, the vanilla and lemon peel until well mixed. Add egg yolks to cream mixture; beat with wire whisk until evenly colored and well blended.

2. In 13 × 9-inch pan, place four 6-ounce ceramic ramekins. Pour cream mixture evenly into ramekins.

3. Carefully place pan with ramekins in oven. Pour enough boiling water into pan, being careful not to splash water into ramekins, until water covers two-thirds of the height of the ramekins.

4. Bake 30 to 40 minutes or until top is light golden brown and sides are set (centers will be jiggly).

5. Carefully transfer ramekins to wire rack, grasping tops of ramekins with pot holder. Cool no longer than 1 hour or until room temperature. Cover tightly with plastic wrap; refrigerate until chilled, at least 4 hours but no longer than 2 days.

6. Uncover ramekins; gently blot any condensation on custards with paper towel. Sprinkle 2 teaspoons sugar over each custard. Holding kitchen torch 3 to 4 inches from custard, caramelize sugar on each custard by heating with torch about 2 minutes, moving flame continuously over sugar in circular motion, until sugar is melted and light golden brown. (To caramelize sugar in the broiler, see Kitchen Tip.) Place 2 tablespoons raspberries over each custard. Serve immediately, or refrigerate up to 8 hours before serving.

4 servings

1 Serving: Calories 550 (Calories from Fat 390); Total Fat 44g (Saturated 25g; Trans 1g); Cholesterol 440mg; Sodium 55mg; Total Carbohydrate 32g (Dietary Fiber 1g; Sugars 29g); Protein 7g
% Daily Value: Vitamin A 30%; Vitamin C 6%; Calcium 10%; Iron 4%
Exchanges: 2 Other Carbohydrate, 1 High-Fat Meat, 7 Fat
Carbohydrate Choices: 2

KITCHEN TIPS

✿ Do not use glass custard cups or glass pie plates; they cannot withstand the heat from the kitchen torch or broiler and may break.

✿ The sugar topping can be caramelized in the broiler. Sprinkle 2 teaspoons brown sugar over each chilled custard. Place ramekins on cookie sheet with sides. Broil with tops 4 to 6 inches from heat 5 to 6 minutes or until sugar is melted and forms a glaze.

Decadent Chocolate Tart

Prep Time: 40 min Start to Finish: 2 hr 50 min

Crust

- 1/3 cup butter or margarine, softened
- 1/4 cup powdered sugar
- 1/2 cup Gold Medal all-purpose flour
- 2 tablespoons unsweetened baking cocoa

Filling

- 1/4 cup butter or margarine
- 4 ounces semisweet baking chocolate
- 1/4 cup granulated sugar
- 2 eggs
- 1/4 cup sour cream
- 2 tablespoons Gold Medal all-purpose flour

Topping

- 2 ounces semisweet baking chocolate
- 1 tablespoon butter or margarine
- 1 tablespoon honey
- 2 kiwifruit, cut up
- 1 can (11 ounces) mandarin orange segments, drained

1. Heat oven to 350°F. Grease 9-inch tart pan with removable bottom with shortening or cooking spray. In medium bowl, beat 1/3 cup butter and the powdered sugar with electric mixer on medium speed until blended. Beat in 1/2 cup flour and the cocoa until coarse crumbs form. With floured fingers, press in bottom of tart pan.

2. Bake 5 to 7 minutes or until set. Meanwhile, in 1-quart saucepan, heat 1/4 cup butter and 4 ounces chocolate over low heat 2 to 3 minutes, stirring constantly, until melted and smooth. Set aside to cool.

3. In large bowl, beat granulated sugar and eggs with electric mixer on high speed 3 to 4 minutes, scraping bowl frequently, or until foamy and light in color. Add sour cream, 2 tablespoons flour and the chocolate mixture; continue beating 1 to 2 minutes, scraping bowl frequently, until well blended. Spread filling over crust.

4. Bake 20 to 25 minutes or until firm to the touch. Cool 15 minutes. Remove side of pan. Cool completely, about 30 minutes.

5. In 1-quart saucepan, heat 2 ounces chocolate, 1 tablespoon butter and the honey over low heat 2 to 3 minutes, stirring constantly, until melted and smooth. Spread chocolate mixture over tart. Lightly press fruit around outer edge of tart. Refrigerate until firm, about 1 hour. Let stand at room temperature about 20 minutes before serving.

12 servings
1 Serving: Calories 260 (Calories from Fat 150); Total Fat 16g (Saturated 10g; Trans 0.5g); Cholesterol 65mg; Sodium 85mg; Total Carbohydrate 26g (Dietary Fiber 2g; Sugars 19g); Protein 3g
% Daily Value: Vitamin A 15%; Vitamin C 30%; Calcium 2%; Iron 6%
Exchanges: 1 1/2 Other Carbohydrate, 1/2 High-Fat Meat, 2 1/2 Fat
Carbohydrate Choices: 2

KITCHEN TIPS

- Use 2 cups fresh raspberries instead of the kiwifruit and orange.
- The tart filling might bubble up during baking, but it will settle during cooling.

Cinnamon-Almond-Chocolate Tart

Prep Time: 15 min   Start to Finish: 1 hr 35 min

Almond Crust
- 1 cup Gold Medal all-purpose flour
- 2 tablespoons sugar
- 1 cup slivered almonds
- $\frac{1}{2}$ cup butter or margarine, softened
- 1 egg

Filling
- $\frac{1}{2}$ cup sugar
- 1 teaspoon ground cinnamon
- 1 tablespoon corn syrup
- $\frac{1}{8}$ teaspoon almond extract
- 3 eggs
- 3 ounces semisweet baking chocolate, melted, cooled
- 6 tablespoons butter or margarine, melted
  Whipped cream
  Additional ground cinnamon

1. Heat oven to 350°F. In food processor or blender, place flour, 2 tablespoons sugar and the almonds. Cover; process until almonds are finely chopped. Add $\frac{1}{2}$ cup butter and egg. Cover; process until well blended. Press mixture in bottom and $\frac{1}{2}$ inch up side of ungreased 9-inch tart pan with removable bottom.

2. Bake 20 to 25 minutes or until light brown. If crust puffs while baking, poke with fork.

3. Meanwhile, in medium bowl, beat $\frac{1}{2}$ cup sugar, 1 teaspoon cinnamon, the corn syrup, almond extract and 3 eggs with wire whisk until smooth. Stir in chocolate and 6 tablespoons butter.

4. Pour filling into hot crust. Bake 18 to 24 minutes or until almost set in center. Cool on cooling rack at least 30 minutes before serving.

5. Remove side of pan. Serve tart topped with whipped cream; sprinkle with additional cinnamon. Store covered in refrigerator.

8 servings
1 Serving: Calories 490 (Calories from Fat 300); Total Fat 33g (Saturated 16g; Trans 1g); Cholesterol 160mg; Sodium 180mg; Total Carbohydrate 39g (Dietary Fiber 3g; Sugars 23g); Protein 8g
% Daily Value: Vitamin A 15%; Vitamin C 0%; Calcium 6%; Iron 10%
Exchanges: $\frac{1}{2}$ Starch, 2 Other Carbohydrate, 1 Medium-Fat Meat, 5$\frac{1}{2}$ Fat
Carbohydrate Choices: 2$\frac{1}{2}$

KITCHEN TIPS

✿ Serve this cinnamon- and almond-flavored tart with a scoop of cinnamon ice cream.

French Silk Tarts

Prep Time: 20 min Start to Finish: 2 hr 50 min

1 box (15 ounces) Pillsbury refrigerated pie crusts, softened as directed on box

3 ounces unsweetened baking chocolate, cut into pieces

1 cup butter, softened (do not use margarine)

1 cup sugar

1/2 teaspoon vanilla

4 pasteurized eggs* or 1 cup fat-free egg product

1. Heat oven to 425°F. Remove crusts from pouches; unroll on work surface. Pat or roll each crust into 11 1/2-inch circle. With 3 1/2-inch round cutter, cut 8 rounds from each crust; discard scraps. Fit rounds into 16 ungreased regular-size muffin cups, pressing in gently; prick sides and bottom with fork.

2. Bake 7 to 9 minutes or until edges are golden brown. Cool 1 minute; remove from muffin cups to wire rack. Cool completely, about 15 minutes.

3. Meanwhile, in 1-quart saucepan, melt chocolate over low heat; cool. In small bowl, beat butter with electric mixer on medium speed until fluffy. Gradually beat in sugar until light and fluffy. Beat in cooled chocolate and vanilla until well blended. Add eggs, one at a time, beating on high speed 2 minutes after each addition; beat until mixture is smooth and fluffy.

4. Fill tart shells with chocolate mixture. Refrigerate at least 2 hours before serving. Store in refrigerator.

KITCHEN TIPS

❀ Place a chocolate-dipped strawberry on top of each tart for a beautiful presentation.

❀ Skip the pie crust and make 8 quick dessert parfaits by layering the chocolate filling, whipped cream and chocolate-covered toffee bits in clear 6-ounce plastic cups.

16 tarts

Because the eggs in this recipe are not cooked, pasteurized eggs must be used. Pasteurization eliminates Salmonella and other bacteria; using regular eggs in this recipe would not be food safe.

1 Tart: Calories 280 (Calories from Fat 180); Total Fat 20g (Saturated 11g; Trans 0.5g); Cholesterol 85mg; Sodium 170mg; Total Carbohydrate 22g (Dietary Fiber 0g; Sugars 13g); Protein 2g
% Daily Value: Vitamin A 8%; Vitamin C 0%; Calcium 0%; Iron 6%
Exchanges: 1/2 Starch, 1 Other Carbohydrate, 4 Fat
Carbohydrate Choices: 1 1/2

Chocolate-Hazelnut-Pumpkin Tart

Prep Time: 25 min Start to Finish: 3 hr 15 min

Crust

- ¼ cup chopped hazelnuts (filberts)
- 1 tablespoon sugar
- 1¼ cups Gold Medal all-purpose flour
- ½ teaspoon salt
- ¼ cup firm butter or margarine, cut into pieces
- 2½ to 3 tablespoons cold water

Filling

- ¾ cup hazelnut spread with cocoa (from 13-ounce jar)
- 2 eggs
- 1 can (15 ounces) pumpkin (not pumpkin pie mix)
- ¾ cup sugar
- ½ teaspoon ground cinnamon
- ½ teaspoon salt
- 1 teaspoon vanilla
- 1 cup evaporated milk

Garnish

- ½ cup whipped cream or whipped topping
- ½ ounce semisweet baking chocolate, grated
- 2 tablespoons chopped hazelnuts (filberts)

1. Heat oven to 400°F (375°F for dark or nonstick pan). In food processor, place ¼ cup hazelnuts and 1 tablespoon sugar; cover and process 45 seconds or until finely ground. Add flour and ½ teaspoon salt; cover and process 5 seconds or until mixed. Add butter; cover and process, pulsing on and off 5 to 10 times, until mixture looks like coarse crumbs. Add water, 1 tablespoon at a time, pulsing on and off, until mixture starts to hold together.

2. Press dough in bottom and 1½ inches up side of 10-inch springform pan. Spread hazelnut spread over dough on bottom of pan.

3. In large bowl, beat eggs with wire whisk. Add pumpkin, ¾ cup sugar, the cinnamon, salt and vanilla. Beat until well mixed. Stir in evaporated milk. Pour over hazelnut spread.

4. Bake 40 to 50 minutes or until knife inserted in center comes out clean. Cool completely, about 2 hours. If necessary, use tip of knife to loosen tart from pan. Remove side of pan. Pipe or spoon whipped cream around edge of tart. Sprinkle with grated chocolate and 2 tablespoons hazelnuts.

10 servings

1 Serving: Calories 410 (Calories from Fat 180); Total Fat 20g (Saturated 7g; Trans 0g); Cholesterol 70mg; Sodium 330mg; Total Carbohydrate 50g (Dietary Fiber 3g; Sugars 35g); Protein 8g
% Daily Value: Vitamin A 140%; Vitamin C 2%; Calcium 15%; Iron 10%
Exchanges: 3 Starch, 4 Fat
Carbohydrate Choices: 3

KITCHEN TIPS

- ✿ It's okay if the top of the crust isn't perfectly straight. A slightly rough edge adds a rustic touch to this tempting tart.
- ✿ Look for hazelnut spread near the peanut butter at your local grocery store.

Brown Sugar-Sweet Potato Tarts

Prep Time: 30 min Start to Finish: 1 hr 45 min

Pastry

2²/₃ cups Gold Medal all-purpose flour

1 teaspoon salt

1 cup shortening

7 to 8 tablespoons cold water

Filling

1 can (23 ounces) sweet potatoes, drained and 2 tablespoons syrup reserved

³/₄ cup packed brown sugar

3 eggs, beaten

1¹/₂ teaspoons pumpkin pie spice

¹/₂ teaspoon salt

1 cup evaporated milk

Whipped topping or whipped cream, if desired

1. Heat oven to 425°F. In large bowl, mix flour and 1 teaspoon salt. Cut in shortening, using pastry blender (or pulling 2 table knives through ingredients in opposite directions), until particles are size of small peas. Sprinkle with cold water, 1 tablespoon at a time, tossing with fork until all flour is moistened and pastry almost cleans side of bowl (1 to 2 teaspoons more water can be added if necessary).

2. Divide pastry in half. Roll each half into 13-inch rounds. Using individual 4¹/₂-inch foil tart pan as a guide and cutting ¹/₂ inch wider all the way around, cut each pastry round into 4 (5-inch) rounds. Fit pastry rounds in bottom and just up to top edge of 8 individual 4¹/₂-inch foil tart pans. Place tart pans on large cookie sheet. Bake tart shells 3 to 4 minutes or until dry; cool.

3. Cut pastry scraps into small leaf shapes or other fall shapes. Place cutouts on another cookie sheet; sprinkle with small amount of granulated sugar if desired. Bake 6 to 7 minutes or until golden brown; cool.

4. In food processor, place sweet potatoes and 2 tablespoons reserved syrup. Cover and process until smooth. Spoon into large bowl. Add brown sugar, eggs, pumpkin pie spice and ¹/₂ teaspoon salt. Beat with wire whisk until smooth. Stir in evaporated milk. Pour into partially baked tart shells.

5. Reduce oven temperature to 375°F. Bake 25 to 35 minutes or until knife inserted in center comes out clean. Cool completely, about 30 minutes. Remove from pans. Place on individual dessert plates. Garnish with pastry leaves and whipped topping.

8 tarts

1 Tart: Calories 620 (Calories from Fat 270); Total Fat 30g (Saturated 8g; Trans 4.5g); Cholesterol 85mg; Sodium 540mg; Total Carbohydrate 78g (Dietary Fiber 4g; Sugars 40g); Protein 10g
% Daily Value: Vitamin A 230%; Vitamin C 8%; Calcium 15%; Iron 20%
Exchanges: 3 Starch, 2 Other Carbohydrate, 6 Fat
Carbohydrate Choices: 5

KITCHEN TIPS

✿ Add a little glitz by sprinkling pastry leaves with coarse white sparkling sugar instead of granulated sugar.

✿ Try not to stretch the pastry when you fit it into the tart pans. It will shrink during baking if it's stretched.

Almond-Amaretto Tarts

Prep Time: 40 min Start to Finish: 2 hr 40 min

Pastry

1	cup butter or margarine, softened
$\frac{1}{2}$	cup granulated sugar
1	egg
1	teaspoon almond extract
$2\frac{1}{2}$	cups Gold Medal all-purpose flour

Filling

$2\frac{1}{4}$	cups blanched whole almonds
3	eggs
$\frac{3}{4}$	cup granulated sugar
3	tablespoons amaretto (or 2 teaspoons almond extract plus 2 tablespoons water)
2	tablespoons whipping cream

Garnish, if desired

$\frac{1}{2}$	cup whipping cream
1	tablespoon powdered or granulated sugar
48	fresh raspberries (about 1 cup)

1. In large bowl, beat butter, $\frac{1}{2}$ cup sugar, 1 egg and 1 teaspoon almond extract with electric mixer on medium speed 1 minute. Gradually add flour, beating 1 to 2 minutes just until blended. Cover and refrigerate at least 1 hour until thoroughly chilled.

2. Heat oven to 350°F. Divide pastry into 48 pieces. Gently press pastry onto bottoms and sides of 48 ungreased mini muffin cups.

3. Place almonds in food processor or blender; cover and process until almonds are finely ground. In medium bowl, mix almonds and remaining filling ingredients with spoon. Spoon about 2 heaping teaspoons filling into each tart crust. Bake 20 to 25 minutes or until golden brown and centers spring back when touched lightly. Cool 5 minutes; gently remove tarts from pan to wire rack. Cool 30 minutes.

4. In chilled small bowl, beat $\frac{1}{2}$ cup whipping cream and 1 tablespoon sugar with electric mixer on high speed until soft peaks form.

5. Place 1 teaspoon whipped cream and 1 raspberry on each tart.

48 mini-tarts

1 Mini-Tart: Calories 130 (Calories from Fat 70); Total Fat 8g (Saturated 3g; Trans 0g); Cholesterol 35mg; Sodium 30mg; Total Carbohydrate 12g (Dietary Fiber 1g; Sugars 6g); Protein 3g
% Daily Value: Vitamin A 4%; Vitamin C 0%; Calcium 2%; Iron 4%
Exchanges: 1 Starch, 1$\frac{1}{2}$ Fat
Carbohydrate Choices: 1

KITCHEN TIPS

✿ These tarts freeze well and can be stored in the freezer up to one month. Thaw at room temperature before serving.

Frosted Maple-Apple Pie Dessert

Prep Time: 45 min Start to Finish: 2 hr 30 min

Pastry

2⅔ cups Gold Medal all-purpose flour

1 teaspoon salt

1 cup shortening

7 to 8 tablespoons cold water

Filling

12 cups thinly sliced peeled apples (about 12 medium)

½ cup granulated sugar

½ cup packed brown sugar

2 tablespoons Gold Medal all-purpose flour

1 teaspoon ground cinnamon

1 teaspoon maple flavor

Maple Frosting

1 cup powdered sugar

¼ teaspoon maple flavor

1½ to 2 tablespoons milk

1. Heat oven to 450°F. In large bowl, mix 2⅔ cups flour and the salt. Cut in shortening, using pastry blender (or pulling 2 table knives through ingredients in opposite directions), until particles are size of small peas. Sprinkle with cold water, 1 tablespoon at a time, tossing with fork until all flour is moistened and pastry almost cleans side of bowl (1 to 2 teaspoons more water can be added if necessary).

2. Divide pastry in half. On lightly floured surface, roll 1 part into 17 × 12-inch rectangle, adding flour as necessary. Fold into fourths. Unfold and fit into bottom and up sides of ungreased 15 × 10 × 1-inch pan.

3. In large bowl, stir all filling ingredients until mixed. Spoon evenly over pastry.

4. Roll remaining half of pastry into 15½ × 10½-inch rectangle, adding flour as necessary. Cut several small leaf shapes out of pastry at regular intervals; carefully remove and set aside. Fold pastry into fourths; place over apples and unfold. Tuck under edges of pastry and press to seal. Lightly brush backs of leaf cutouts with water; place moistened side down on top crust between cutouts.

5. Bake 15 minutes. Reduce oven temperature to 400°F; bake 20 to 30 minutes longer or until juices are

bubbly and clear in center, apples are tender and crust is deep golden brown. Cover loosely with foil if necessary during last 10 minutes of baking to prevent overbrowning.

6. In small bowl, stir powdered sugar, ¼ teaspoon maple flavor and enough milk until glaze is thin enough to drizzle. Drizzle over top crust. Cool 1 hour before cutting. Serve warm or cool.

18 servings

1 Serving: Calories 290 (Calories from Fat 110); Total Fat 12g (Saturated 3g; Trans 2g); Cholesterol 0mg; Sodium 135mg; Total Carbohydrate 44g (Dietary Fiber 2g; Sugars 26g); Protein 2g
% Daily Value: Vitamin A 0%; Vitamin C 2%; Calcium 0%; Iron 6%
Exchanges: 1 Starch, 1 Fruit, 1 Other Carbohydrate, 2 Fat
Carbohydrate Choices: 3

KITCHEN TIPS

⊘ Rolling this pastry is easy if you have a pastry cloth. If you don't own one, lift the edges of the pastry and add flour as necessary.

⊘ This delicious dessert is a great option if you want to serve apple pie to a crowd.

Frozen Angel Toffee Dessert

Prep Time: 20 min Start to Finish: 4 hr 40 min

1 box Betty Crocker white angel food cake mix

1¼ cups cold water

6 bars (1.4 ounces each) chocolate-covered English toffee candy

1 container (8 ounces) frozen whipped topping, thawed

Unsweetened cocoa powder, if desired

1. Move oven rack to lowest position (remove other racks). Heat oven to 350°F.

2. In extra-large glass or metal bowl, beat cake mix and water with electric mixer on low speed 30 seconds; beat on medium speed 1 minute. Pour into ungreased 10-inch angel food (tube) cake pan. (Do not use fluted tube cake pan or 9-inch angel food pan or batter will overflow.)

3. Bake 37 to 47 minutes or until top is dark golden brown and cracks feel very dry and not sticky. Do not underbake. Immediately turn pan upside down onto glass bottle until cake is completely cool, about 2 hours. Run knife around edges of cake; remove from pan.

4. Crush or finely chop candy bars; reserve ⅓ cup. Fold remaining crushed candy into whipped topping.

5. Tear cake into about 1-inch pieces. In large bowl, mix cake pieces and whipped topping mixture. In ungreased 13 × 9-inch pan, lightly press cake mixture. Sprinkle with reserved crushed candy. Freeze dessert about 1 hour 30 minutes or until firm. Cut into squares or spoon into dessert dishes. Dust plates with cocoa powder. Store covered in freezer.

15 servings

1 Serving: Calories 240 (Calories from Fat 70); Total Fat 8g (Saturated 5g; Trans 0g); Cholesterol 10mg; Sodium 310mg; Total Carbohydrate 39g (Dietary Fiber 0g; Sugars 30g); Protein 3g
% Daily Value: Vitamin A 2%; Vitamin C 0%; Calcium 6%; Iron 0%
Exchanges: 1 Starch, 1½ Other Carbohydrate, 1½ Fat
Carbohydrate Choices: 2½

KITCHEN TIPS

❁ For a Frozen Chocolate Angel Toffee Dessert, stir 2 tablespoons unsweetened baking cocoa into dry cake mix before making cake.

❁ Dust plates with unsweetened baking cocoa before adding squares of dessert.

Orange-Cream Cheese Tart

Prep Time: 25 min Start to Finish: 3 hr 15 min

One-Crust Flaky Pastry (page 297)
1 package (8 ounces) cream cheese, softened
1½ cups milk
1 package (4-serving size) vanilla instant pudding and pie filling mix
1 can (15 ounces) mandarin orange segments, well drained and patted dry
¾ cup orange marmalade
½ ounce semisweet baking chocolate

1. Heat oven to 450°F. Make One-Crust Flaky Pastry—except roll pastry into 13-inch circle. Fold pastry into fourths; place in 10-inch tart pan with removable bottom. Unfold pastry and press against bottom and side of pan. Trim overhanging pastry edge even with top of pan. Prick bottom and side of pastry with fork.

2. Bake 9 to 11 minutes or until light golden brown. Cool crust completely, about 30 minutes.

3. In small bowl, beat cream cheese with electric mixer on medium speed until creamy. Gradually beat in milk. Beat in pudding mix. Spoon into baked crust; spread evenly. Top with orange segments.

4. In small microwavable bowl, microwave marmalade uncovered on High 20 to 30 seconds or until warm. Brush or spoon marmalade over orange segments. Refrigerate about 2 hours or until firm. Before serving, shave chocolate with a swivel-bladed vegetable peeler by slicing across block of chocolate in long, thin strokes. (If you let the chocolate come to room temperature, it will be easier to shave.) Garnish tart with shaved chocolate.

10 servings
1 Serving: Calories 340 (Calories from Fat 160); Total Fat 17g (Saturated 8g; Trans 1.5g); Cholesterol 30mg; Sodium 360mg; Total Carbohydrate 43g (Dietary Fiber 1g; Sugars 26g); Protein 5g
% Daily Value: Vitamin A 15%; Vitamin C 15%; Calcium 8%; Iron 6%
Exchanges: 2 Starch, 1 Other Carbohydrate, 3 Fat
Carbohydrate Choices: 3

KITCHEN TIPS

✺ To boost the orange flavor in this tart, add a little grated orange peel to the pastry ingredients.
✺ For a fancy presentation, drizzle a little chocolate topping over the serving plates before topping with slices of the tart.

Tiny Lemon Gem Tarts

Prep Time: 1 hr 30 min Start to Finish: 2 hr 15 min

1/2 cup butter or margarine, softened
3 tablespoons granulated sugar
1 cup Gold Medal all-purpose flour
1/2 cup granulated sugar
1 tablespoon Gold Medal all-purpose flour
3 tablespoons fresh lemon juice
2 teaspoons grated lemon peel
1/4 teaspoon baking powder
1/8 teaspoon salt
2 eggs
2 tablespoons powdered sugar

1. Heat oven to 350°F (325°F for dark or nonstick pan). Spray 24 mini muffin cups with cooking spray. In medium bowl, beat butter and 3 tablespoons granulated sugar with electric mixer on medium speed until well mixed. Beat in 1 cup flour until dough forms.

2. Shape dough into 3/4-inch balls. Press 1 ball in bottom and up side of each muffin cup for crust. Bake 14 to 16 minutes or until edges begin to turn golden brown.

3. Meanwhile, in same bowl, beat remaining ingredients except powdered sugar on medium speed until well mixed.

4. Spoon 1 heaping tablespoon mixture evenly into each baked crust. Bake 10 to 12 minutes or until filling is light golden. Cool in pan 15 minutes. Remove from muffin cups to cooling racks. Cool completely, about 30 minutes.

5. Sift powdered sugar over tops of tarts. Store covered in refrigerator. If desired, sift additional powdered sugar over tarts just before serving.

2 dozen
1 Tart: Calories 90 (Calories from Fat 40); Total Fat 4.5g (Saturated 2.5g; Trans 0g); Cholesterol 30mg; Sodium 50mg; Total Carbohydrate 11g (Dietary Fiber 0g; Sugars 6g); Protein 1g
% Daily Value: Vitamin A 2%; Vitamin C 0%; Calcium 0%; Iron 0%
Exchanges: 1/2 Starch, 1 Fat
Carbohydrate Choices: 1

KITCHEN TIPS

- A microplane makes quick work of grating the lemon peel. Look for this handy gadget at cookware stores.
- To freeze, arrange in a single layer on cookie sheets and freeze until firm. Then pop them in an airtight container and store in the freezer. To thaw, let stand at room temperature for 30 minutes.

Piña Colada Tart

Prep Time: 15 min Start to Finish: 1 hr 45 min

- 1 Pillsbury refrigerated pie crust (from 15-ounce box), softened as directed on box
- ¼ cup sugar
- ¼ cup cornstarch
- 1 cup canned cream of coconut (not coconut milk)
- 1 cup whole milk
- 2 egg yolks
- 1 tablespoon butter or margarine
- 2 tablespoons dark rum or 1½ teaspoons rum extract
- 1 can (20 ounces) sliced pineapple, drained, slices cut in half
- ¼ cup apricot jam
- 1 tablespoon dark rum or orange juice
- 2 tablespoons coconut, toasted

1. Heat oven to 425°F. Place pie crust in 10-inch tart pan with removable bottom. Press in bottom and up side of pan. Trim edge if necessary. Prick with fork. Bake 9 to 11 minutes or until lightly browned. Cool on wire rack.

2. Meanwhile, in 2-quart saucepan, mix sugar and cornstarch. In small bowl, mix cream of coconut, milk and egg yolks; gradually stir into sugar mixture. Cook over medium heat, stirring constantly, until mixture thickens and boils. Boil and stir 1 minute; remove from heat. Beat in butter and 2 tablespoons rum with wire whisk. Cool at room temperature 1 hour.

3. Pour cooled pie filling into baked tart shell. Arrange pineapple slices in decorative pattern over filling. In small microwavable bowl, microwave jam uncovered on High 20 seconds. Stir in 1 tablespoon rum; mix well with fork. Brush glaze over pineapple. Sprinkle with toasted coconut. Refrigerate until serving.

12 servings
1 Serving: Calories 250 (Calories from Fat 130); Total Fat 14g (Saturated 9g; Trans 0g); Cholesterol 40mg; Sodium 95mg; Total Carbohydrate 29g (Dietary Fiber 1g; Sugars 16g); Protein 2g
% Daily Value: Vitamin A 2%; Vitamin C 4%; Calcium 4%; Iron 4%
Exchanges: 1 Starch, 1 Other Carbohydrate, 2½ Fat
Carbohydrate Choices: 2

KITCHEN TIPS

- To toast coconut, bake uncovered in ungreased shallow pan in 350°F oven 5 to 7 minutes, stirring occasionally, until golden brown.
- Piña colada refers to a tropical drink made with cream of coconut, pineapple juice and rum.
- Cream of coconut is a canned mixture of coconut paste, water and sugar. It is available in supermarkets, near the soft drinks, and in liquor stores.

Banana-Chocolate Mousse Tart

Prep Time: 20 min Start to Finish: 3 hr 10 min

Pastry

- 1⅓ cups Gold Medal all-purpose flour
- ½ teaspoon salt
- ½ cup shortening
- 3 to 4 tablespoons cold water

Filling

- 1 package (4-serving size) chocolate pudding and pie filling mix (not instant)
- 1½ cups milk
- 2 ounces semisweet baking chocolate, chopped
- 1½ cups frozen (thawed) whipped topping
- 3 bananas, sliced

1. Heat oven to 400°F. In medium bowl, mix flour and salt. Cut in shortening, using pastry blender (or pulling 2 table knives through ingredients in opposite directions), until particles are size of small peas. Sprinkle with cold water, 1 tablespoon at a time, tossing with fork until all flour is moistened and pastry almost cleans side of bowl (1 to 2 teaspoons more water can be added if necessary).

2. On lightly floured surface, roll pastry into 13-inch circle, about ⅛ inch thick. Press in bottom and up side of 10-inch tart pan with removable bottom. Trim pastry even with top of pan. Prick bottom and side of pastry with fork.

3. Bake 15 to 20 minutes or until golden brown. Cool completely, about 30 minutes.

4. Meanwhile, in 2-quart saucepan, heat pudding mix and milk over medium heat, stirring occasionally, until mixture boils. Stir in chopped chocolate until melted. Pour into medium bowl; place plastic wrap directly on surface of pudding mixture. Refrigerate about 1 hour or until completely cool.

5. Fold ½ cup of the whipped topping into cooled chocolate mixture. Arrange banana slices in single layer in bottom of baked crust. Spoon chocolate mixture over bananas. Refrigerate about 1 hour or until thoroughly chilled. Garnish with remaining 1 cup whipped topping and, if desired, additional banana slices.

10 servings
1 Serving: Calories 310 (Calories from Fat 140); Total Fat 16g (Saturated 6g; Trans 2g); Cholesterol 0mg; Sodium 190mg; Total Carbohydrate 38g (Dietary Fiber 2g; Sugars 17g); Protein 4g
% Daily Value: Vitamin A 0%; Vitamin C 6%; Calcium 6%; Iron 8%
Exchanges: 1 Starch, ½ Fruit, 1 Other Carbohydrate, 3 Fat
Carbohydrate Choices: 2½

KITCHEN TIPS

- ❂ This delicious combo of banana cream and chocolate cream pies takes an elegant turn when made in a tart pan.
- ❂ Short on time? Use a refrigerated pie crust instead of making the crust from scratch.

Chocolate-Almond Cheesecake Bites

Prep Time: 50 min Start to Finish: 3 hr 30 min

Crust

1 cup chocolate cookie crumbs (from 15-ounce box)

$\frac{1}{4}$ cup butter or margarine, melted

Filling

1 package (8 ounces) cream cheese, softened

$\frac{1}{4}$ cup sour cream

$\frac{1}{4}$ cup sugar

1 egg

$\frac{1}{4}$ teaspoon almond extract

Coating

$2\frac{1}{3}$ cups semisweet chocolate chips

3 tablespoons shortening

2 ounces vanilla-flavored candy coating (almond bark), chopped

1 teaspoon vegetable oil

1. Heat oven to 300°F. Cut 14 × 12-inch sheet of heavy-duty foil; line 8-inch square pan with foil so foil extends over sides of pan. Spray foil with cooking spray. In small bowl, mix cookie crumbs and butter. Press in bottom of pan.

2. In large bowl, beat cream cheese, sour cream and sugar with electric mixer on medium speed until fluffy. Beat in egg and almond extract, scraping bowl if necessary. Pour over crust.

3. Bake 30 to 40 minutes or until edges are set (center will be soft but will set when cool). Cool on cooling rack 1 hour. Cover; refrigerate 1 hour. Meanwhile, cover 2 cookie sheets with waxed paper.

4. Remove cheesecake from pan by lifting foil. Cut into 8 rows by 6 rows, making 48 oblong cheesecake bites. In 1-quart microwavable bowl, microwave chocolate chips and shortening uncovered on Medium (50%) 3 minutes. Stir; microwave in 15-second increments, stirring after each, until melted and smooth.

5. Work with half of bites at a time (24 bites); refrigerate other half until needed. Place 1 bite on fork and dip fork into chocolate to coat. Lift fork from chocolate and allow excess chocolate to drain off. Place on 1 waxed paper–lined cookie sheet. Repeat

with second half of bites and second waxed paper–lined cookie sheet.

6. In small microwavable bowl, microwave candy coating and oil uncovered on High 1 minute. Stir; microwave in 15-second increments, stirring after each, until melted. Spoon into small, resealable plastic food-storage bag. Seal bag; cut tiny hole in corner of bag. Pipe melted coating over dipped bites. Store covered in refrigerator.

4 dozen

1 Cheesecake Bite: Calories 100 (Calories from Fat 60); Total Fat 7g (Saturated 4g; Trans 0g); Cholesterol 15mg; Sodium 40mg; Total Carbohydrate 9g (Dietary Fiber 0g; Sugars 7g); Protein 1g
% Daily Value: Vitamin A 2%; Vitamin C 0%; Calcium 0%; Iron 2%
Exchanges: $\frac{1}{2}$ Other Carbohydrate, $1\frac{1}{2}$ Fat
Carbohydrate Choices: $\frac{1}{2}$

KITCHEN TIPS

- Use any leftover chocolate to make a decadent fudge sauce. Just stir about $\frac{1}{4}$ cup of half-and-half into the melted chocolate.
- If the chocolate coating cools and starts to get thick, microwave it on High for 10 to 15 seconds to soften it.

Mango-Strawberry Sorbet Torte

Prep Time: 35 min Start to Finish: 4 hr 55 min

Cake

- 1 box Betty Crocker SuperMoist white cake mix
  Water, vegetable oil and egg whites called for on cake mix box
- 1 pint (2 cups) mango sorbet, softened
- 1 pint (2 cups) strawberry sorbet, softened

Frosting

- 1½ cups whipping cream
- ½ cup powdered sugar
- 1 teaspoon grated lime peel
- 2 tablespoons lime juice

Garnish, if desired

- Lime peel twists
- Fresh strawberries

1. Heat oven to 350°F (325°F for dark or nonstick pan). Spray bottom only of 15 × 10 × 1-inch pan with baking spray with flour. Line with waxed paper; spray waxed paper.

2. In large bowl, make cake mix as directed on box, using water, oil and egg whites. Pour into pan. Bake 20 to 30 minutes or until toothpick inserted in center comes out clean. Cool in pan 10 minutes. Remove from pan to cooling rack; remove waxed paper. Cool completely, about 1 hour.

3. Cut cake crosswise into 3 equal sections. On long serving platter, place 1 section, rounded side down. Spread mango sorbet evenly over top. Place another cake section onto the sorbet; press down. Spread with strawberry sorbet. Top with remaining cake section; press down. Cover lightly; freeze about 2 hours or until firm.

4. In large bowl, beat all frosting ingredients with electric mixer on high speed until stiff peaks form. Frost sides and top of torte. Freeze about 1 hour or until firm. Just before serving, garnish top with lime peel and strawberries. To serve, let stand at room temperature 10 minutes. Cut torte in half lengthwise, then cut crosswise 7 times to make a total of 16 slices.

16 servings
1 Serving: Calories 330 (Calories from Fat 130); Total Fat 15g (Saturated 6g; Trans 1g); Cholesterol 25mg; Sodium 240mg; Total Carbohydrate 47g (Dietary Fiber 0g; Sugars 32g); Protein 3g
% Daily Value: Vitamin A 4%; Vitamin C 0%; Calcium 4%; Iron 4%
Exchanges: 1 Starch, 2 Other Carbohydrate, 3 Fat
Carbohydrate Choices: 3

KITCHEN TIPS

- This is a great make-ahead dessert. Once it's frozen, cover tightly and freeze for up to 3 weeks.
- Serve this torte as a beautiful dessert for Easter or for a shower.
- Dip the strawberries in melted white vanilla baking chips for a lovely accent (page 213).

Cherry-Chocolate Ice Cream Pie

Prep Time: 30 min Start to Finish: 2 hr 40 min

15 cream-filled chocolate sandwich cookies, crumbled

¼ cup butter or margarine, melted

¾ cup hot fudge topping (room temperature)

1 quart (4 cups) vanilla ice cream, softened

¼ cup sugar

1 tablespoon cornstarch

½ cup water

2 tablespoons frozen cranberry juice cocktail concentrate

2 cups fresh or frozen dark sweet cherries, halved, pitted

1 tablespoon cherry-flavored liqueur, if desired

1. Heat oven to 375°F. In food processor, place crumbled cookies. Cover; process 10 to 15 seconds or until finely crushed. Add melted butter. Cover; process 5 to 10 seconds or until mixed. Press in bottom and up side of ungreased 9-inch pie plate. Bake 8 to 10 minutes or until set. Cool completely, about 30 minutes.

2. Stir hot fudge topping until smooth. Carefully spread over bottom of crust. Freeze 30 minutes. Spread ice cream over hot fudge topping. Cover; freeze at least 1 hour until firm.

3. Meanwhile, in 2-quart saucepan, mix sugar, cornstarch, water and frozen juice concentrate. Heat to boiling over medium heat, stirring occasionally. Stir in cherries; reduce heat. Simmer 5 minutes. Stir in liqueur. Cool completely, about 30 minutes. Let pie stand 10 minutes before cutting. Serve sauce over slices of frozen pie.

8 servings
1 Serving: Calories 460 (Calories from Fat 180); Total Fat 20g (Saturated 11g; Trans 1.5g); Cholesterol 50mg; Sodium 320mg; Total Carbohydrate 63g (Dietary Fiber 3g; Sugars 46g); Protein 5g
% Daily Value: Vitamin A 10%; Vitamin C 4%; Calcium 15%; Iron 8%
Exchanges: 1 Starch, 3 Other Carbohydrate, 4 Fat
Carbohydrate Choices: 4

Mud Slide Ice Cream Cake

Prep Time: 30 min Start to Finish: 6 hr

1 box Betty Crocker SuperMoist chocolate fudge cake mix

½ cup butter or margarine, melted

2 eggs

2 tablespoons coffee-flavored liqueur or strong coffee

4 cups vanilla ice cream

1 container (12 ounces) Betty Crocker Whipped chocolate frosting

2 tablespoons coffee-flavored liqueur, if desired

1. Heat oven to 350°F (325°F for dark or nonstick pan). Grease bottom only of 13 × 9-inch pan with shortening or cooking spray.

2. In large bowl, mix cake mix, butter and eggs with spoon. Spread in pan. Bake 20 to 25 minutes or until center is set (top will appear dry and cracked). Cool completely, about 1 hour.

3. Brush 2 tablespoons liqueur over cake. Let ice cream stand about 15 minutes at room temperature to soften. Spread ice cream over cake. Freeze 3 hours or until firm.

4. In medium bowl, mix frosting and 2 tablespoons liqueur; spread over ice cream. Freeze at least 1 hour.

15 servings
1 Serving: Calories 380 (Calories from Fat 160); Total Fat 18g (Saturated 8g; Trans 1g); Cholesterol 60mg; Sodium 400mg; Total Carbohydrate 51g (Dietary Fiber 2g; Sugars 36g); Protein 4g
% Daily Value: Vitamin A 8%; Vitamin C 0%; Calcium 8%; Iron 10%
Exchanges: 1 Starch, 2½ Other Carbohydrate, 3½ Fat
Carbohydrate Choices: 3½

KITCHEN TIPS

✿ Coffee lovers can substitute coffee-flavored ice cream for the vanilla.

✿ Mud slide drinks are popular on menus across the country. Here the concoction is made into a frozen dessert with a brownie-like base.

Mint Chocolate Ice Cream Cake

Prep Time: 25 min Start to Finish: 5 hr 50 min

Cake

1 box Betty Crocker SuperMoist butter recipe chocolate cake mix

Water, butter and eggs called for on cake mix

Filling

6 cups green mint-flavored ice cream with chocolate chips or chocolate swirl, slightly softened

Frosting

1¹/₂ cups whipping cream

2 tablespoons powdered sugar

4 drops green food color

1. Heat oven to 350°F (325°F for dark or nonstick pans). Grease bottoms only of 2 (9-inch) round cake pans; line bottoms with waxed paper. Make cake mix as directed on box, using water, butter and eggs. Spoon evenly into pans.

2. Bake as directed on box for 9-inch pans or until toothpick inserted in center comes out clean. Cool in pans 10 minutes. Remove from pans to cooling racks. Remove waxed paper. Cool completely, about 30 minutes.

3. Line 9-inch round cake pan with foil. Spoon and spread ice cream evenly in pan. Cover with foil; freeze until completely frozen, about 2 hours.

4. On serving plate, place 1 cake layer with rounded side down. Remove ice cream from pan; peel off foil. Place on top of cake. Top with remaining cake layer, rounded side up.

5. In medium bowl, beat whipping cream, powdered sugar and food color on high speed until stiff peaks form. Frost side and top of cake with whipped cream. Freeze about 2 hours or until firm. Let stand at room temperature 10 minutes before serving.

16 servings
1 Serving: Calories 380 (Calories from Fat 200); Total Fat 22g (Saturated 13g; Trans 1g); Cholesterol 105mg; Sodium 360mg; Total Carbohydrate 41g (Dietary Fiber 1g; Sugars 27g); Protein 5g
% Daily Value: Vitamin A 15%; Vitamin C 0%; Calcium 10%; Iron 6%
Exchanges: 1 Starch, 1¹/₂ Other Carbohydrate, 4¹/₂ Fat
Carbohydrate Choices: 3

KITCHEN TIPS

✿ This dessert, wrapped with foil, will keep up to a month in the freezer. You can also make the ice cream layer ahead of time and freeze it.

✿ For a restaurant-fancy finish, heat hot fudge topping as directed on the label and pipe onto individual serving plates.

Chocolate Malt Ice Cream Cake

Prep Time: 30 min Start to Finish: 7 hr 5 min

1½ cups Gold Medal all-purpose flour
1 cup sugar
¼ cup unsweetened baking cocoa
1 teaspoon baking soda
½ teaspoon salt
⅓ cup vegetable oil
1 teaspoon white vinegar
1 teaspoon vanilla
1 cup water
1 cup chocolate fudge topping
1½ quarts (6 cups) vanilla ice cream, slightly softened
2 cups malted milk ball candies, coarsely chopped
1 cup whipping cream
¼ cup chocolate fudge topping
Additional malted milk ball candies, if desired

1. Heat oven to 350°F. Grease bottom and side of 9- or 10-inch springform pan with shortening; lightly flour. In large bowl, mix flour, sugar, cocoa, baking soda and salt with spoon. Add oil, vinegar, vanilla and water; stir vigorously about 1 minute or until well blended. Immediately pour into pan.

2. Bake 30 to 35 minutes or until toothpick inserted in center comes out clean. Cool completely, about 1 hour.

3. Spread 1 cup fudge topping over cake. Freeze about 1 hour or until topping is firm.

4. In 3-quart bowl, mix ice cream and coarsely chopped candies; spread over cake. Freeze about 4 hours or until ice cream is firm.

5. In chilled medium bowl, beat whipping cream with electric mixer on high speed until stiff peaks form. Remove side of pan; place cake on serving plate. Top with whipped cream.

6. In small microwavable bowl, microwave fudge topping uncovered on High 30 seconds or until thin enough to drizzle. Drizzle over whipped cream. Garnish with additional candies.

16 servings
1 Serving: Calories 430 (Calories from Fat 180); Total Fat 20g (Saturated 10g; Trans 0g); Cholesterol 40mg; Sodium 310mg; Total Carbohydrate 58g (Dietary Fiber 2g; Sugars 41g); Protein 5g
% Daily Value: Vitamin A 8%; Vitamin C 0%; Calcium 15%; Iron 8%
Exchanges: 1 Starch, 3 Other Carbohydrate, 4 Fat
Carbohydrate Choices: 4

KITCHEN TIPS

⊛ Make this cake up to a month ahead of time and store it in the freezer. Before serving, top with whipped cream and fudge topping.

⊛ Love chocolate? Use chocolate ice cream instead of vanilla.

Profiteroles

Prep Time: 50 min Start to Finish: 2 hr

Puffs

1 cup water
$\frac{1}{2}$ cup butter or stick margarine
1 cup Gold Medal all-purpose flour
4 whole eggs

Filling

$\frac{1}{3}$ cup granulated sugar
2 tablespoons cornstarch
$\frac{1}{8}$ teaspoon salt
2 cups half-and-half
2 egg yolks, slightly beaten
2 tablespoons butter or margarine, softened
2 teaspoons vanilla

Garnish

1 tablespoon powdered sugar
$\frac{1}{4}$ cup chocolate topping

1. Heat oven to 400°F. In 2$\frac{1}{2}$-quart saucepan, heat water and $\frac{1}{2}$ cup butter to rolling boil. Stir in flour. Reduce heat to low; stir vigorously over low heat about 1 minute or until mixture forms a ball. Remove from heat.

2. Beat in eggs, all at once, with spoon. Continue beating until smooth. Drop dough by level table-spoonfuls about 1$\frac{1}{2}$ inches apart on ungreased cookie sheets to make 36 profiteroles.

3. Bake 20 to 25 minutes or until puffed and golden. Cool away from draft, about 30 minutes.

4. Meanwhile, in 2-quart saucepan, mix granulated sugar, cornstarch and salt. Gradually stir in half-and-half. Cook over medium heat, stirring constantly, until mixture thickens and boils. Boil and stir 1 minute. Gradually stir at least half of the hot mixture into egg yolks, then stir back into hot mixture in saucepan. Boil and stir 1 minute. Remove from heat. Stir in 2 tablespoons butter and the vanilla.

5. Pour filling into bowl. Press plastic wrap on filling to prevent a tough layer from forming on top. Refrigerate at least 1 hour or until cool.

6. Cut puffs horizontally in half. Fill puffs with filling; replace tops. Sift powdered sugar over tops. Cover; refrigerate until serving. Serve drizzled with chocolate topping. Store remaining profiteroles covered in refrigerator.

12 servings
1 Serving: Calories 260 (Calories from Fat 150); Total Fat 17g (Saturated 10g; Trans 0.5g); Cholesterol 145mg; Sodium 135mg; Total Carbohydrate 22g (Dietary Fiber 0g; Sugars 11g); Protein 5g
% Daily Value: Vitamin A 10%; Vitamin C 0%; Calcium 6%; Iron 6%
Exchanges: 1 Starch, $\frac{1}{2}$ Other Carbohydrate, 3$\frac{1}{2}$ Fat
Carbohydrate Choices: 1$\frac{1}{2}$

KITCHEN TIPS

⚬ For a change of pace, fill the puffs with vanilla or chocolate ice cream instead of the custard filling.
⚬ When making the puffs, add the flour all at once and stir vigorously with a wooden spoon.

Crème Brûlée

Prep Time: 20 min Start to Finish: 7 hr

  6 egg yolks
  2 cups whipping cream
  ⅓ cup granulated sugar
  1 teaspoon vanilla
     Boiling water
  8 teaspoons granulated sugar

1. Heat oven to 350°F. In 13 × 9-inch pan, place 4 (6-ounce) ceramic ramekins. In small bowl, slightly beat egg yolks with wire whisk. In large bowl, stir whipping cream, ⅓ cup granulated sugar and the vanilla until well mixed. Add egg yolks; beat with wire whisk until evenly colored and well blended. Pour cream mixture evenly into ramekins.

2. Carefully place pan with ramekins in oven. Pour enough boiling water into pan, being careful not to splash water into ramekins, until water covers two-thirds of the height of the ramekins.

3. Bake 30 to 40 minutes or until top is light golden brown and sides are set (centers will be jiggly).

4. Using tongs or grasping tops of ramekins with pot holder, carefully transfer ramekins to cooling rack. Cool to room temperature, about 2 hours. Cover tightly with plastic wrap; refrigerate until chilled, at least 4 hours but no longer than 48 hours.

5. Uncover ramekins; gently blot any liquid from tops of custards with paper towel. Sprinkle 2 teaspoons granulated sugar over each chilled custard. Holding kitchen torch 3 to 4 inches from custard, caramelize sugar on each custard by heating with torch about 2 minutes, moving flame continuously over sugar in circular motion, until sugar is melted and light golden brown. (To caramelize sugar in the broiler, see Broiler Directions right.) Serve immediately, or refrigerate up to 8 hours before serving.

4 servings
1 Serving: Calories 540 (Calories from Fat 390); Total Fat 44g (Saturated 25g; Trans 1g); Cholesterol 440mg; Sodium 55mg; Total Carbohydrate 30g (Dietary Fiber 0g; Sugars 29g); Protein 7g
% Daily Value: Vitamin A 30%; Vitamin C 0%; Calcium 10%; Iron 4%
Exchanges: 2 Other Carbohydrate, 1 High-Fat Meat, 7 Fat
Carbohydrate Choices: 2

KITCHEN TIPS

❀ Do not use glass custard cups or glass pie plates; they cannot withstand the heat from the kitchen torch or broiler and may break.

❀ If kitchen torch is unavailable, set oven control to broil. Sprinkle 2 teaspoons brown sugar over each chilled custard. Place ramekins in 15 × 10 × 1-inch pan or on cookie sheet with sides. Broil with tops 4 to 6 inches from heat 5 to 6 minutes or until brown sugar is melted and forms a glaze.

❀ After extensive testing, we've found that granulated sugar melts best when using a kitchen torch and brown sugar melts best under the broiler.

❀ Some cookware stores sell crème brûlée kits which include a rack that makes it easy to put the ramekins in and take them out of the pan.

Cappuccino Crème Brûlée

Prep Time: 15 min Start to Finish: 2 hr 20 min

1½ cups sugar

2 cups half-and-half

1 tablespoon instant espresso coffee granules

1 teaspoon vanilla

2 whole eggs

6 egg yolks

3 ounces bittersweet baking chocolate

1. Heat oven to 350°F. In large bowl, beat all ingredients except chocolate with wire whisk until smooth.

2. Pour mixture into 8 ungreased 6-ounce ramekins. Place ramekins in shallow roasting pan. Fill pan with hot water to halfway up sides of ramekins.

3. Bake 30 to 35 minutes or just until set. Remove ramekins to cooling rack. Cool 30 minutes. Meanwhile, in small microwavable bowl, microwave chocolate uncovered on High 30 to 40 seconds, stirring every 15 seconds, until melted and smooth.

4. Spoon about 2 teaspoons melted chocolate over top of each custard, spreading evenly to form a thin layer. Cover; refrigerate at least 1 hour or until well chilled.

8 servings

1 Serving: Calories 360 (Calories from Fat 150); Total Fat 17g (Saturated 9g; Trans 0g); Cholesterol 230mg; Sodium 50mg; Total Carbohydrate 44g (Dietary Fiber 2g; Sugars 40g); Protein 7g
% Daily Value: Vitamin A 10%; Vitamin C 0%; Calcium 10%; Iron 15%
Exchanges: 3 Other Carbohydrate, 1 Medium-Fat Meat, 2 Fat
Carbohydrate Choices: 3

KITCHEN TIPS

❂ Use 6-ounce custard cups if you don't have ramekins.

❂ For more intense coffee flavor, add an additional 2 teaspoons coffee granules.

Bananas Foster with Ice Cream

Prep Time: 10 min Start to Finish: 10 min

- ¹/₂ cup fat-free caramel topping
- 2 teaspoons dark rum or 1 teaspoon rum extract
- 2 bananas, cut into chunks
- 2 cups vanilla low-fat ice cream

1. In small microwavable bowl, mix caramel topping and rum. Microwave uncovered on High 30 seconds or until very warm. Stir in bananas.

2. Scoop ice cream into dessert dishes; top with banana mixture.

4 servings
1 Serving: Calories 290 (Calories from Fat 30); Total Fat 3g (Saturated 2g; Trans 0g); Cholesterol 20mg; Sodium 200mg; Total Carbohydrate 60g (Dietary Fiber 2g; Sugars 44g); Protein 5g
% Daily Value: Vitamin A 8%; Vitamin C 10%; Calcium 10%; Iron 0%
Exchanges: 1 Fruit, 2¹/₂ Other Carbohydrate, ¹/₂ Low-Fat Milk, ¹/₂ Fat
Carbohydrate Choices: 4

Blueberry- and Peach-Topped Ginger Pudding

Prep Time: 15 min Start to Finish: 55 min

- 2 cups fat-free (skim) milk
- 1 box (4-serving size) vanilla pudding and pie filling mix (not instant)
- 1 teaspoon finely grated gingerroot
- 2 ripe medium peaches, peeled, sliced (1¹/₂ cups)
- 1 cup fresh blueberries
- 2 tablespoons packed brown sugar

1. In 2-quart saucepan, beat milk and pudding mix with wire whisk until well blended. Cook over medium heat, stirring constantly, until mixture comes to a full boil. Stir in gingerroot.

2. Into 4 dessert cups or small bowls, pour pudding mixture. Cool completely, about 30 minutes.

3. Meanwhile, in small bowl, mix peaches, blueberries and brown sugar. Let stand 15 minutes or refrigerate until serving.

4. To serve, top pudding with fruit mixture.

4 servings
1 Serving: Calories 200 (Calories from Fat 0); Total Fat 0.5g (Saturated 0g; Trans 0g); Cholesterol 0mg; Sodium 190mg; Total Carbohydrate 45g (Dietary Fiber 2g; Sugars 39g); Protein 5g
% Daily Value: Vitamin A 10%; Vitamin C 6%; Calcium 15%; Iron 2%
Exchanges: ¹/₂ Fruit, 2 Other Carbohydrate, ¹/₂ Skim Milk
Carbohydrate Choices: 3

KITCHEN TIPS

✿ Blueberries are one of the best food sources of antioxidants, which may help reduce the risk of some cancers.

✿ Add a final touch to this fresh-tasting dessert with a dollop of whipped topping.

Blueberry- and Peach-Topped Ginger Pudding

Bananas Foster with Ice Cream

Coeur à la Crème

Prep Time: 15 min Start to Finish: 4 hr 15 min

$\frac{1}{4}$ cup water

1 envelope unflavored gelatin (2 teaspoons)

2 cups fat-free cottage cheese

4 ounces (half 8-ounce package) reduced-fat cream cheese (Neufchâtel)

4 ounces (half 8-ounce package) fat-free cream cheese

$\frac{1}{2}$ cup sugar

1 teaspoon vanilla

2 cups fresh raspberries, blackberries, blueberries or combination

1. In 1-quart saucepan, place water; sprinkle with gelatin. Let stand 1 minute to soften. Heat over medium heat about 2 minutes, stirring occasionally, until gelatin is dissolved. Remove from heat; cool slightly.

2. In food processor, place remaining ingredients except berries. Cover; process 1 to 2 minutes, stopping processor to scrape down sides as needed, until very smooth. Stir in cooled gelatin mixture.

3. Line 3-cup shallow heart-shaped mold or bowl with cheesecloth, leaving cloth hanging over side of mold. Pour in cheese mixture; fold cloth loosely over top. Refrigerate at least 4 hours until just firm or overnight.

4. Place serving plate upside down over mold; turn plate and mold over. Remove mold. Garnish with berries.

8 servings
1 Serving: Calories 160 (Calories from Fat 35); Total Fat 4g (Saturated 2.5g; Trans 0g); Cholesterol 15mg; Sodium 350mg; Total Carbohydrate 20g (Dietary Fiber 2g; Sugars 17g); Protein 11g
% Daily Value: Vitamin A 8%; Vitamin C 15%; Calcium 15%; Iron 0%
Exchanges: 1$\frac{1}{2}$ Other Carbohydrate, 1$\frac{1}{2}$ Very Lean Meat, $\frac{1}{2}$ Fat
Carbohydrate Choices: 2

KITCHEN TIPS

✿ This classic French dessert will remind you of a very creamy no-bake cheesecake minus the crust. It can be made up to 2 days ahead.

✿ Coeur à la crème molds can be found in gourmet shops. They are heart-shaped with holes in the bottom so liquid can drip off as the mold chills.

Coeur à la Crème

Dark Chocolate Hazelnut Truffles

Prep Time: 30 min Start to Finish: 2 hr 40 min

4 ounces bittersweet baking chocolate, chopped

4 ounces semisweet baking chocolate, chopped

¼ cup whipping cream

5 tablespoons cold butter, cut into pieces

2 tablespoons hazelnut liqueur

4 ounces (about 1 cup) hazelnuts (filberts)

1. In 1-quart heavy saucepan, heat both chocolates and whipping cream over low heat, stirring constantly, until chocolate is melted and smooth. Remove from heat. Stir in butter, a few pieces at a time. Stir in liqueur. Place plastic wrap over surface of chocolate. Refrigerate about 2 hours, stirring once, until firm enough to hold its shape.

2. Meanwhile, heat oven to 350°F. Place hazelnuts in ungreased shallow pan. Bake 6 to 10 minutes, stirring occasionally, until light brown. Rub with towel to remove skins. Cool 10 minutes. Place nuts in food processor. Cover; process with on-and-off pulses 20 to 30 seconds or until finely ground. Place on sheet of waxed paper.

3. Scoop rounded teaspoonfuls of chocolate mixture onto nuts. Roll lightly to coat and shape into 1-inch balls (truffles do not need to be smooth; they should be a little rough). Place on plate; cover loosely. Store in refrigerator. Let stand at room temperature 15 minutes before serving.

3 dozen

1 Truffle: Calories 80 (Calories from Fat 60); Total Fat 7g (Saturated 3g; Trans 0g); Cholesterol 5mg; Sodium 15mg; Total Carbohydrate 4g (Dietary Fiber 1g; Sugars 2g); Protein 1g
% Daily Value: Vitamin A 0%; Vitamin C 0%; Calcium 0%; Iron 4%
Exchanges: 1½ Fat
Carbohydrate Choices: 0

KITCHEN TIPS

❀ A 1-inch cookie or ice cream scoop (#100 size) comes in handy for scooping the truffles.

❀ For added "ahhh," place each truffle in a small paper candy cup.

Raspberry Bread Pudding

Prep Time: 25 min Start to Finish: 55 min

Bread Pudding

6	cups cubed (1 inch) day-old French bread
1	cup fresh raspberries
2	tablespoons miniature semisweet chocolate chips
2	cups fat-free (skim) milk
1/2	cup fat-free egg product
1/4	cup packed brown sugar
1	teaspoon vanilla

Sauce

1/2	cup granulated sugar
2	tablespoons cornstarch
3/4	cup water
1	bag (12 ounces) frozen unsweetened raspberries, thawed, undrained

1. Heat oven to 350°F. Spray bottom and sides of 8-inch square (2-quart) glass baking dish with cooking spray. In large bowl, place bread, 1 cup raspberries and chocolate chips.

2. In medium bowl, mix milk, egg product, brown sugar and vanilla with wire whisk or fork until blended. Pour egg mixture over bread mixture; stir gently until bread is coated. Spread in baking dish.

3. Bake 40 to 50 minutes or until golden brown and set.

4. Meanwhile, in 2-quart saucepan, mix granulated sugar and cornstarch. Stir in water and thawed raspberries. Heat to boiling over medium heat, stirring constantly and pressing raspberries to release juice. Boil about 1 minute or until thick. Place small strainer over small bowl. Pour mixture through strainer to remove seeds; discard seeds. Serve sauce with warm bread pudding.

8 servings

1 Serving: Calories 230 (Calories from Fat 20); Total Fat 2g (Saturated 1g; Trans 0g); Cholesterol 0mg; Sodium 210mg; Total Carbohydrate 46g (Dietary Fiber 5g; Sugars 26g); Protein 7g
% Daily Value: Vitamin A 4%; Vitamin C 15%; Calcium 10%; Iron 10%
Exchanges: 1 1/2 Starch, 1 1/2 Other Carbohydrate, 1/2 Fat
Carbohydrate Choices: 3

KITCHEN TIPS

✿ Crust or no crust? Some people prefer cutting off crusts for bread pudding, and others don't want to waste the bread. Nutritionally, it's the same.

✿ Instead of making the sauce from scratch, use raspberry pancake syrup.

Ultimate Frozen Mud Pie Dessert

Prep Time: 15 min Start to Finish: 1 hr 25 min

1   pint (2 cups) coffee-flavored frozen yogurt
¾   cup chocolate cookie crumbs
2   tablespoons sugar
2   tablespoons butter or margarine, melted
½   cup caramel topping
2   tablespoons finely chopped pecans
1¼ cups frozen (thawed) fat-free whipped
    topping

1. Remove frozen yogurt from freezer to soften. Spray 8-inch square pan with cooking spray. In small bowl, mix cookie crumbs and sugar. Stir in butter until crumbly and well blended. Press in pan. Freeze about 10 minutes or until set.

2. Spread slightly softened yogurt evenly over crust. Freeze about 1 hour or until firm.

3. In small bowl, mix caramel topping and pecans. To serve, top each serving with generous 2 tablespoons whipped topping. Carefully pour 1 tablespoon caramel mixture over top.

9 servings
1 Serving: Calories 220 (Calories from Fat 60); Total Fat 6g (Saturated 3g; Trans 0g); Cholesterol 10mg; Sodium 180mg; Total Carbohydrate 38g (Dietary Fiber 0g; Sugars 26g); Protein 3g
% Daily Value: Vitamin A 2%; Vitamin C 0%; Calcium 10%; Iron 4%
Exchanges: 1 Starch, 1½ Other Carbohydrate, 1 Fat
Carbohydrate Choices: 2½

KITCHEN TIPS

✪ Chocolate cookie crumbs can be purchased in a 15-ounce box in the baking aisle of your grocery store.
✪ Any flavor of frozen yogurt can be used in this dessert.

Helpful Nutritional and Cooking Information

Nutrition Guidelines

We provide nutrition information for each recipe, which includes calories, fat, cholesterol, sodium, carbohydrate, fiber and protein. Individual food choices can be based on this information.

Recommended intake for a daily diet of 2,000 calories as set by the Food and Drug Administration

Total Fat	Less than 65g
Saturated Fat	Less than 20g
Cholesterol	Less than 300mg
Sodium	Less than 2,400mg
Total Carbohydrate	300g
Dietary Fiber	25g

criteria used for calculating nutrition information

- The first ingredient was used wherever a choice is given (such as $1/3$ cup sour cream or plain yogurt).

- The first ingredient amount was used wherever a range is given (such as 3- to $3^1/_2$-pound cut-up broiler-fryer chicken).

- The first serving number was used wherever a range is given (such as 4 to 6 servings).

- "If desired" ingredients and recipe variations were not included (such as, sprinkle with brown sugar, if desired).

- Only the amount of a marinade or frying oil that is estimated to be absorbed by the food during preparation or cooking was calculated.

ingredients used in recipe testing and nutrition calculations

- Ingredients used for testing represent those that the majority of consumers use in their homes: large eggs, 2% milk, 80% lean ground beef, canned ready-to-use chicken broth and vegetable oil spread containing not less than 65 percent fat.

- Fat-free, low-fat or low-sodium products were not used, unless otherwise indicated.

- Solid vegetable shortening (not butter, margarine, nonstick cooking sprays or vegetable oil spread because they can cause sticking problems) was used to grease pans, unless otherwise indicated.

equipment used in recipe testing

We use equipment for testing that the majority of consumers use in their homes. If a specific piece of equipment (such as a wire whisk) is necessary for recipe success, it is listed in the recipe.

- Cookware and bakeware without nonstick coatings were used, unless otherwise indicated.

- No dark-colored, black or insulated bakeware was used.

- When a pan is specified in a recipe, a metal pan was used; a baking dish or pie plate means ovenproof glass was used.

- An electric hand mixer was used for mixing only when mixer speeds are specified in the recipe directions. When a mixer speed is not given, a spoon or fork was used.

cooking terms glossary

Beat: Mix ingredients vigorously with spoon, fork, wire whisk, hand beater or electric mixer until smooth and uniform.

Boil: Heat liquid until bubbles rise continuously and break on the surface and steam is given off. For a rolling boil, the bubbles form rapidly.

Chop: Cut into coarse or fine irregular pieces with a knife, food chopper, blender or food processor.

Cube: Cut into squares $\frac{1}{2}$ inch or larger.

Dice: Cut into squares smaller than $\frac{1}{2}$ inch.

Grate: Cut into tiny particles using small rough holes of grater (citrus peel or chocolate).

Grease: Rub the inside surface of a pan with shortening, using pastry brush, piece of waxed paper or paper towel, to prevent food from sticking during baking (as for some casseroles).

Julienne: Cut into thin, matchlike strips, using knife or food processor (vegetables, fruits, meats).

Mix: Combine ingredients in any way that distributes them evenly.

Sauté: Cook foods in hot oil or margarine over medium-high heat with frequent tossing and turning motion.

Shred: Cut into long, thin pieces by rubbing food across the holes of a shredder, as for cheese, or by using a knife to slice very thinly, as for cabbage.

Simmer: Cook in liquid just below the boiling point on top of the stove, usually after reducing heat from a boil. Bubbles will rise slowly and break just below the surface.

Stir: Mix ingredients until consistency is uniform. Stir once in a while for stirring occasionally, often for stirring frequently and continuously for stirring constantly.

Toss: Tumble ingredients (such as green salad) lightly with a lifting motion, usually to coat evenly or mix with another food.

metric conversion chart

Volume

U.S. Units	Canadian Metric	Australian Metric
¼ teaspoon	1 mL	1 ml
½ teaspoon	2 mL	2 ml
1 teaspoon	5 mL	5 ml
1 tablespoon	15 mL	20 ml
¼ cup	50 mL	60 ml
⅓ cup	75 mL	80 ml
½ cup	125 mL	125 ml
⅔ cup	150 mL	170 ml
¾ cup	175 mL	190 ml
1 cup	250 mL	250 ml
1 quart	1 liter	1 liter
1½ quarts	1.5 liters	1.5 liters
2 quarts	2 liters	2 liters
2½ quarts	2.5 liters	2.5 liters
3 quarts	3 liters	3 liters
4 quarts	4 liters	4 liters

Weight

U.S. Units	Canadian Metric	Australian Metric
1 ounce	30 grams	30 grams
2 ounces	55 grams	60 grams
3 ounces	85 grams	90 grams
4 ounces (¼ pound)	115 grams	125 grams
8 ounces (½ pound)	225 grams	225 grams
16 ounces (1 pound)	455 grams	500 grams
1 pound	455 grams	½ kilogram

Measurements

Inches	Centimeters
1	2.5
2	5.0
3	7.5
4	10.0
5	12.5
6	15.0
7	17.5
8	20.5
9	23.0
10	25.5
11	28.0
12	30.5
13	33.0

Temperatures

Fahrenheit	Celsius
32°	0°
212°	100°
250°	120°
275°	140°
300°	150°
325°	160°
350°	180°
375°	190°
400°	200°
425°	220°
450°	230°
475°	240°
500°	260°

Note: The recipes in this cookbook have not been developed or tested using metric measures. When converting recipes to metric, some variations in quality may be noted.

Index

Underscored page references indicate sidebar text or kitchen tips. **Boldfaced** page references indicate photographs.